The

UNOFFICIAL
SAT
WORD
DICTIONARY

Sam, Max and Bryan Burchers

New Monic Books

Manufactured in the United States of America.
Library of Congress Catalog Card Number: 96-96399
ISBN: 0-9652422-5-0
Cover Design: Bryan Burchers
Setup & Typography: Sam Burchers III, Bryan Burchers

New Monic Books
314-C Tamiami Trail
Punta Gorda, FL 33950
(941) 575-6669 $9.95

A special thanks to our writing staff:

> Samuel Burchers, Jr.
> Samuel Burchers III
> Bryan Burchers
> Sue Propert
> Kathy Himes
> Doni Weber

INTRODUCTION

Test-prep students! This is what you have been looking for! The Unofficial SAT Word Dictionary has the 3,000 words you need to know to score well on standardized tests. Unlike the average dictionary which may contain as many as 90,000 words, our staff of writers have crossed referenced popular SAT prep study guides as well as past SAT tests and compiled the most comprehensive collection of words likely to be found on verbal tests.

Most "aptitude" and "intelligence" tests are tests of vocabulary. Verbal sections of standardized tests, like those found in the verbal SAT, consist largely of analogy and sentence-completion questions. The vocabulary word you need to know is usually presented in the context of a sentence. The Unofficial SAT Word Dictionary provides not only one, but two sample sentences for each word. Well-crafted definitions written by our staff of experienced educators clarify meaning, illustrate current use, and aid in memorization.

The best technique for using this book is to read through the words covering the definition with your finger. If you know the definition cross it out and move on. Don't waste your time on words your already know. If you don't know the word read the definition and the samples sentences then move on. Once you have gone through the whole book repeat this process until you have crossed out all the words in the book. Now you are ready to take on any verbal standardized test with confidence.

Your vocabulary determines your ability to share your thoughts with other people. By improving your vocabulary, you broaden your ability to bring your intelligence to bear on the world around you. Whether you are preparing for a school test, or you just want to improve your command of the English language, this book will quickly help you reach your goal. Communication is an art and words are the medium. Possessing a rich vocabulary brings many rewards, confidence, material gains, and recognition from those around you.

abacus (AB uh kuss) *n.* a Chinese device used to perform arithmetic equations by moving beads along rods

Betty used her *abacus* to count her piggybank's change.

The boys entertained the class using their *abacus* to answer problems.

abase (uh BAYS) *v.* to degrade; to humiliate

The president is not willing to admit his mistake and *abase* himself before the nation.

The fire chief *abased* himself by drinking and driving a fire truck.

abash (ah BASH) *v.* to make ashamed or uneasy

Being caught listening to her sister's conversation *abashed* Jen, and she quickly put down the receiver.

Pete was not at all *abashed* when he opened a valentine from Linda.

abate (ah BAYT) *v.* to reduce

Marta's defeat in the tennis tournament did not *abate* her zeal for the game.

Tom went to a financial consultant to seek advice on how he might *abate* his burdensome debts.

abbess (AB iss) *n.* a woman, commonly called Mother Superior in charge of a convent of nuns

The *abbess* was very strict, but she was loved by the sisters.

The elderly *abbess* could be counted on to comfort those in need.

abbreviate (uh BREE vee ate) *v.* to reduce to a shorter form

Bathing suits today are greatly *abbreviated* compared to the those in the 1890s.

School was *abbreviated* today because of the false fire alarm.

abdicate (AB duh kayt) *v.* to step down from a powerful position

Jason *abdicated* his position as class president so he could spend more time on his studies.

Edward VIII of England *abdicated* his throne in order to marry a commoner.

abduct (ub DUCT) *v.* to carry off a person, usually by force; to kidnap

Charles Lindbergh's son was *abducted* from his home.

Abduction is a serious crime punishable by death if the person *abducted* is killed. (*n.*)

aberrant (AB uh runt) *adj.* straying from the correct or normal way

Sharon's *aberrant* way of spelling words cost her the spelling contest.

Joe's method of painting his car with his fingers was totally *aberrant*.

abet (uh BET) *v.* to help someone do something illegal or wrong; to incite, encourage, or aid, especially in wrongdoing

Three tax inspectors were accused of aiding and *abetting* men charged with cheating on their income taxes.

When he ran from the scene of a crime, Jonathan was charged with *abetting* Charlie.

abeyance (uh BAY uns) *n.* a state of not being presently used; temporary suspension or cessation

The road repair project is being held in *abeyance* until agreement is reached on project funding.

Hostilities between the two countries have been in *abeyance* since the peace agreement last June.

abhor (ab HOR) *v.* to hate deeply; detest

While most people *abhor* liver and beets, Zachary loves both.

It is generally believed that most women have an *abhorrence* of mice. (*n.*)

abide (ah BYDE) *v.* to remain; continue; stay; endure

Josh's father always told him if he made a promise, he must *abide* by it.

To survive, soldiers in battle need to have an *abiding* faith in their fellow soldiers. (*adj.*)

abut (UH but) *v.* border upon; to adjoin

Texas *abuts* Mexico on its southern border.

The *abutting* rocks formed a perfect wall for riflemen to defend the castle. (*adj.*)

abject (AB jekt) *adj.* extremely sad; hopeless; defeated

6

Many large cities are homes to *abject* people who live in cardboard boxes.

It is sad to see examples of *abject* poverty in a wealthy country.

abjure (ab JOOR) *v.* to repudiate or renounce; to give up

He *abjured* his life of luxury once he saw how the poor people of underdeveloped countries live.

Once Jane learned the risks of smoking, she *abjured* cigarettes for the sake of her health.

ablution (ah BLOO shun) *n.* a cleansing with water or other liquid, especially as a religious ritual; the liquid used in such an act

The witch doctor used *ablutions* of clear water to cleanse the stricken man of his illness.

The *ablutionary* water appeared to help the suffering woman. (*adj.*)

abnegate (AB nuh gayt) *v.* to deny oneself; to reject

People on diet programs are expected to *abnegate* fattening foods.

Monks often practice some form of *abnegation* in hopes of purifying themselves of sins. (*n.*)

abominate (uh BOM ih nate) *v.* to hate or loathe intensely

The world *abominates* the use of child labor in third world countries.

Fox hunting is an *abomination* because it involves torture and death of an animal for sport. (*n.*)

aboriginal (ab uh RIJ uh nul) *adj.* native to an area

The American Indian is the *aboriginal* inhabitant of the USA.

In Australia, there are groups of *aboriginal* residents who are called "Aborigines."

abortive (uh BOR tiv) *adj.* unsuccessful

Although they meant well, the children made an *abortive* effort to clean the kitchen floor with dirty mops.

The launching of the Atlantis was *aborted* because of cold weather. (*v.*)

abound (uh BOWND) *v.* to exist in large numbers; to be full; teem

Many theories *abound* about how the earth began.

Rabbits *abound* behind every tree in these woods.

abridge (uh BRIJ) *v.* to shorten; to condense; to diminish; to curtail

For people who don't want to read an entire newspaper, there are clipping services that *abridge* news stories to specification.

A TV *abridgement* of the movie *Gone With the Wind* lasts two hours, whereas the original lasts four. (*n.*)

abrogate (AB ruh gayt) *v.* to abolish, repeal, or nullify by authority; to do away with; to end formally

Congress *abrogated* the treaty, saying that it no longer applied.

Our town *abrogated* the old law regarding how many horses a person can have pulling his carriage.

abscond (ab SKAHND) *v.* take flight, escape, to leave quickly and secretly

The thief *absconded* from the country with the stolen jewels.

Millie's husband *absconded* from their home and was never heard of again.

absolute (AB suh loot) *adj.* total; complete

In the 1960s Castro declared himself the *absolute* ruler of Cuba.

The cat was *absolutely* soaked after falling into the pool. (*adv.*)

absolve (ab ZOLV) *v.* to make free of blame, obligation, or sin

After viewing the evidence, the jury *absolved* Joe of criminal intent in the auto accident.

Catholics attend confession with the purpose of being *absolved* of sins.

abstain (ub STAYN) *v.* to refrain from; denying oneself any action or practice

Jean *abstained* from eating chocolate cake in order to win a bet.

Jeff *abstained* from watching the television for a week after his eye operation.

abstract (AB strakt) *adj.* difficult to understand; impersonal; theoretical

Dad's paintings are all *abstracts*, and we can't tell what they are supposed to represent.

Christopher's directions to his house were so *abstract* we were lost for two hours.

abstruse (ab STROOS) *adj.* hard to understand

Chemistry is an *abstruse* subject of study for many students.

Elizabeth's directions for assembling the furniture were incomplete and very *abstruse*.

absurd (ub SIRD) *adj.* ridiculously unreasonable, laughable

When Jessie's parents asked why she had been out so late, her response was so *absurd* that they both laughed at her tall tale.

In the year 2000, the election process continued for an *absurd* amount of time.

abysmal (uh BIZ mul) *adj.* bottomless; hopeless

Because of the *abysmal* clutter in Gary's room, his mother decided to keep the door closed.

Our country's national deficit is so high as to be *abysmal*.

abyss (uh BISS) *n.* bottomless pit; a profound depth or void

The lost spaceship wandered endlessly in the vast *abyss* of space.

After digging for three days through the snow of the avalanche without finding the missing skier, the rescuers faced an emotional *abyss* of despair.

accede (uh SEED) *v.* to yield; give in to a request

Bill graciously *acceded* to our request to have the party at his house.

The police *acceded* to the terrorist's demands for a hamburger from the local drive-thru.

accentuate (ak SEN choo wayt) *v.* to emphasize; to make more noticeable; to accent

Her dress was tightly belted and *accentuated* the slimness of her waist.

Many women use eye-liner to *accentuate* their eyes.

access (AK sess) *n.* authorization or capacity to enter, look at, or use something

The only *access* to the island restaurant is by boat.

Our company accountant has *access* to all of our offices and records at any time.

acclaim (uh KLAYM) *v.* to give public approval and praise; to approve enthusiastically

Critics have *acclaimed* Peter's new novel, *The Hill of Ants*, as the best written in this decade.

Dr. Smith was universally *acclaimed* for his contribution to the discovery of a new common cold vaccine.

acclimate (AK lih mayt) *v.* to become suitable to a certain situation or use; adapt

The football team finally *acclimated* to the new formations and systems given them by the new coach.

Terry and her friends enthusiastically *acclimated* to the new shorter school day.

accolade (AK uh layd) *n.* an award, an honor; approval, praise

You cannot imagine the *accolades* received by the chemistry teacher from her students when she accidentally blew up the lab and class was canceled for the remainder of the term.

The *accolades* Rachel received for making the Olympic Swim Team were well deserved; she practices four hours a day.

accommodate (ah KAM ah DATE) *v.* to provide for; help; adapt; oblige

The young gentleman tried to *accommodate* the older woman by assisting her with her shopping cart.

Many immigrants in America try to *accommodate* themselves to the customs of their new home.

accomplice (ah KAM plis) *n.* a person who knowingly aids or abets another in an unlawful act or crime

Jerry was charged as an *accomplice* because he had been in on the murder plan from the start.

The teacher realized that the child must have had an *accomplice* to enable him to get back into the school after dark.

accord (uh KOWRD) *v.* agree; conform; to grant; bestow upon

The time I spent in the Army Reserve away from home *accorded* me the opportunity to realize how much I miss my wife and children.

Mrs. Larson was not in *accord* with her daughter's wishes to begin dating at the age of twelve. (*n.*)

accost (uh KAWST) *v.* to approach and speak to someone

Jessica was terrified she would be *accosted* by the dean for her choice of attire.

Mel *accosted* a taxi driver and accused him of taking the long way to the hotel to earn a higher fare.

accountable (ah KOWNT uh bul) *adj.* expected to answer for one's actions; responsible; liable

Timothy was *accountable* for counting the votes after the election.

You can't hold the cat *accountable* for the mess because the dog chased it through the kitchen.

accouterments (uh KOO tur munts) *n.* the equipment needed for a particular activity or way of life; one's outfit or equipment

She has all the *accouterments* of the successful businesswoman: a luxury car, designer clothes, and a beautiful house.

After completing his scuba diving course, Mike needed to purchase the appropriate *accouterments* to dive on his own.

accrete (uh KREET) *v.* to increase by growth, or addition; adhere

The Australian coral reef was built up by *accretion* over thousands of years. (*n.*)

We watched the sand *accrete* during the days of strong wind.

accrue (ah CROO) *v.* to accumulate over time

Bryan's unpaid parking tickets *accrued* to the point that they would have paid for his college tuition.

By the time he was eighteen, he had *accrued* a good knowledge of computer skills.

acerbic (uh SUR bik) *adj.* sour; bitter; severe

Mr. Russell's *acerbic* wit makes students afraid to respond to his questions.

Because the oranges were not quite ripe, the juice was *acerbic*.

acme (AK mee) *n.* the highest point

When he thought the stock market had reached its *acme,* Mr. Johnson sold his stock.

It had been a hot morning, but the sun had not yet reached its *acme.*

acquiesce (A kwye ess) *v.* to agree passively; comply; consent

Thankfully, the bank *acquiesced* to an extension of my loan.

She *acquiesced* to the thief's demands and handed over her wallet.

acquisitive (uh KWIZ uh tiv) *adj.* eager to possess and collect things; greedy

We live in an *acquisitive* society which views success primarily in terms of material possessions.

Mary Ann's children are so *acquisitive* she can't walk into a store before they start begging for something.

acquit (uh KWIT) *v.* to decide officially someone is not guilty of a particular crime; to free from an obligation

Tanya was *acquitted* of all criminal charges against her.

June *acquitted* herself well in front of the panel because she had planned her answers beforehand.

acrid (AK rid) *adj.* harsh; acidic

The *acrid* smell of smoke coming in through the open window woke us in the middle of the night.

The soup of the day was so *acrid* they should have called it the soup of last week.

acrimonious (ak ruh MOH nee us) *adj.* bitter; nasty; spiteful

Alex and Lisa's divorce was beset with *acrimonious* accusations from each side.

Football players make *acrimonious* comments at their opponents as a means of intimidation, hoping to get the other side upset and throw off their game.

acronym (AK ruh nim) *n.* a word created from the initials of other words

AIDS is an *acronym* for Acquired Immune Deficiency Syndrome.

SCUBA is an *acronym* for Self Contained Underwater Breathing Apparatus.

acuity (uh KUE uh tee) *n.* sharpness, keenness of perception, deftness

The student showed great *acuity* in his scientific study of comets.

John's *acuity* at knowing when to hold and when to fold in poker was unsurpassed.

acumen (AK yoo mun) *n.* mental keenness or sharpness

Bill's business *acumen* was evident even when he was a young boy with a paper route.

Mathematical *acumen* is an asset in the financial world.

acute (uh kyoot) *adj.* shrewd; sharp

Santiago's *acute* sense of sight was what made him a great fisherman.

Cindy thought she had only a stomach ache, but it turned out to be *cute* appendicitis.

ad lib (ad lib) *v.* to act, speak, and perform spontaneously or off the cuff

Unprepared for her monthly budget presentation, Barbara *ad libbed* her report.

Jack forgot his lines in the middle of the second act and had to *ad lib* his dialogue with the other actors.

adage (AD ij) *n.* a wise saying or proverb; an old familiar saying that expresses folk wisdom

He remembered the old *adage*, "Look before you leap," as he stepped back from the diving board above the pool that contained no water.

The old woman had an appropriate *adage* for every situation.

adamant (AD uh munt) *adj.* resolute; stubborn; inflexible

Nancy's mother was *adamant* about the curfew; her daughter had to be home by midnight.

Marco was *adamant* in maintaining his innocence, but the jury found him guilty based on circumstantial evidence.

addicted (ah DIKT ed) *adj.* devoting (oneself) habitually or compulsively

My mother regrets she allowed herself to become *addicted* to nicotine.

Betty became so *addicted* to soap operas that she found a night job in order to stay home during the day.

address (uh DRES) *v.* to speak to

The president made his annual *address* to congress. (*n.*)

When James picked up his date, he was careful to *address* her parents courteously.

adduce (uh DYOOS) *v.* to give as proof; to cite

She *adduced* several significant facts to support her thesis about the nutritional value of peanuts.

The defendant was directed to *adduce* his whereabouts on the night of the crime.

adherent (ad HEER unt) *n.* a follower of a leader; supporter

The political candidate praised his *adherents* for their support.

People who believe in a particular religion are said to be *adherents* of that faith.

adjourn (uh JURN) *v.* to make a pause or rest; suspend until later

Because of the hurricane, the city council meeting was *adjourned* until Tuesday.

The judge *adjourned* the court for a lunch break.

adjunct (AJ unkt) *n.* something connected or added in a subordinate position; an assistant

The library was an *adjunct* to the Blakemore's original home.

The general's adjutant is not an *adjunct*, but a permanent part of his staff command.

admonish (ad MAWN ish) *v.* to caution or warn; to criticize or scold mildly but firmly

His mother *admonished* him for eating his birthday cake with his fingers.

Jane's parents *admonished* her for spending all her allowance on shoes.

adrenaline (uh DREN uh lin) *n.* a hormone produced by the adrenal gland, stimulation of energy and strength

She won the race as one last surge of *adrenaline* propelled her forward

adjoin

to the finish line.

When he was frightened by the noises emanating from the cemetery, a surge of *adrenaline* enabled Roscoe to jump a six-foot fence and race down the street.

adroit (ah DROIT) *adj.* skillful; deft

Many fourth graders are more *adroit* on the computer than their parents are.

Mr. Smith *adroitly* removed Eric from the class before he could cause a problem. (*adv.*)

adulation (ad you LAY shun) *n.* extreme flattery or admiration

When George met his favorite musician, *adulation* was clearly written all over George's face.

All through her life, Melissa lived in *adulation* of her older sister.

adumbrate (a DUM brayt) *v.* to sketch, to outline, to give a hint of things to come

Betty *adumbrated* the plans for her wedding in June.

The president of the Alumni Association *adumbrated* his scheme to bring in more good athletes.

advent (AD vent) *n.* the arrival or beginning; coming

Quills made of bird feathers were the chief writing implement until the *advent* of steel fountain pens in the mid-19th century.

The *advent* of winter was apparent to Luke the morning he arose and discovered all the fallen leaves on the ground outside his bedroom window.

adventitious (ad vent TISH us) *adj.* accidental or incidental; not expected or planned; irrelevant

Dr. Edward's appointment to Chief of Staff was *adventitious* to his experience because his brother-in-law was the administrator.

Buying new shoes was *adventitious* to Ethel's shopping trip, considering she went out for groceries.

adverse (ad VURS) *adj.* unfavorable; antagonistic

The stormy weather was so *adverse* they called off the Super Bowl.

The doctor was surprised to learn his patient had an *adverse* reaction to aspirin.

advocate (AD vuh kut) *n.* one who supports a cause; one who defends or pleads on behalf of another

He is a strong *advocate* of capital punishment because he feels it will be a deterrent to criminals.

Joslyn *advocates* equal rights between the sexes, including the right for girls to play on boys sports teams.

aegis (E jis) *n.* a shield or protection

The dentist used a numbing agent as an *aegis* against the pain that would result when he performed the root canal.

The young actress's nasty attitude was her *aegis* against being hurt.

aesthetic (es THET ik) *adj.* having to do with artistic beauty

Japanese rock gardens demonstrate *aesthetic* values typical to a Far Eastern culture.

Jeannie molded the ugly lump of clay into an *aesthetically* pleasing masterpiece. (*adv.*)

affable (AF uh bul) *adj.* friendly; easy-going

Mrs. Propert has a wonderful personality and is the most *affable* teacher in the school.

No matter what the situation, Zachary's *affable* attitude toward life made him popular with his friends.

affect (uh FEKT) *v.* to influence, to impress the mind or move the feelings as emotion

The overall joyousness at the birthday party *affected* the attitude of everyone in a positive way.

The author was greatly *affected* by the uncomplimentary, disastrous reviews of his novel.

affectation (af ek TAY shun) *n.* false behavior intended to impress

Bonnie's *affectation* was that she personally knew every actor in Hollywood, which was an untruth.

When Ray came home from a vacation in England with a British accent, it was obviously an *affectation*.

affidavit (af uh DAY vit) *n.* a sworn written statement

16

The defense lawyer had a sworn *affidavit* claiming his client was playing bridge at a neighbor's home the night of the crime.

Roseanne had an *affidavit* from her neighbor giving her permission to cut down the tree on their mutual property line.

affiliate (uh FIL ee ayt) *v.* to cause to become part of or to form a close relationship with; to associate or connect with

The "Dive and Duck" driving school is *affiliated* with the United States National Association of driving schools.

Our local TV news station is an *affiliate* of NBC News. (*n.*)

affinity (uh FIN uh tee) *n.* a natural attraction; kinship; similarity

Max had an *affinity* for sports and excelled at football, basketball, and tennis.

Monkeys have an *affinity* for climbing, birds for flying, and fish for swimming.

affirm (uh FURM) *v.* to declare something to be true, to confirm or ratify

The committee *affirmed* the statements, so they were entered into the minutes.

In a radio address to the nation, President Roosevelt *affirmed* the attack on Pearl Harbor on December 7, 1941.

affliction (uh FLIK shun) *n.* a condition of pain or suffering; the cause of misery, illness, or suffering

Due to the lack of resources and food, malnutrition is one of the common *afflictions* in Third World countries like Nigeria and Borneo.

Osteoporosis is a degenerative bone disease which usually *afflicts* the elderly. (*v.*)

afflict (ah FLIKT) *v.* to cause suffering or pain

It was clear from the boxer's eyes that his main intention was to *afflict* his opponent.

After traveling to Africa, the missionary was *afflicted* with a rare disease.

affluent (AF loo unt) *adj.* wealthy, rich

The *affluent* couple sat in the first class section of the airplane.

In our town, all the *affluent* families live on the river.

17

afford (uh FOWRD) *v.* to allow to have; to provide; to have enough money to buy; to confer upon

On my salary, I can barely *afford* a Honda, much less a Cadillac.

The safari tent leaked in numerous places and *afforded* little protection from the jungle downpour.

affront (uh FRUNT) *n.* an action intended to insult or offend someone; an injury to one's dignity

She saw her fellow lawyers' rejection of her as a personal *affront.*

Littering public grounds such as parks and highways is an *affront* to the community and to the ecology.

aftermath (AF tur math) *n.* events following some occurrence; a consequence of

Poverty and economic depression are often the horrendous *aftermath* of wars.

The logical *aftermath* of Christmas shopping is a deluge of gifts returned to the stores where they were first purchased as gifts.

agenda (uh JEN duh) *n.* schedule; program

While touring Europe, we followed a strict *agenda* in order to see as much as possible in the time we had.

The politician seemed to have no hidden *agenda*, but after he was elected governor, the voters learned he was a pawn of wealthy industrial interests.

aggrandizement (uh GRAN dyze mint) *n.* an exaggeration, an apearance of greater power or influence

The greatest *aggrandizement* of the entire evening was when the Russian delegate claimed Russia had won World War II single-handedly.

Hitler feigned concern for other countries, but territorial *aggrandizement* was his true motive.

aggregate (AG ruh gut) *n.* total; collection of different things

The so-called "Soup de Jour" was actually an *aggregate* of the restaurant's leftovers.

In order to win the election, the Governor knew he must find an *aggregate* of voters to support his political platform.

aggrieve (uh GREEV) *v.* to distress or bring grief to; cause to suffer; to treat unfairly

The unsafe conditions at the nuclear plant *aggrieved* the employees because of the obvious dangers.

Her son's raucous behavior that caused him to be kicked off the school bus, *aggrieved* Mrs. Williams.

aghast (uh GAST) *adj.* filled with terror; shocked; feelings of anxiety or fear

Jimmy was *aghast* with shock and surprise when he saw a ghost enter his bedroom through a mouse hole.

He looked at her *aghast* when she unveiled her purple hair.

agnostic (ag NAHS tik) *n.* one who believes it is impossible to know whether God exists

Although Helen calls herself an atheist, she is really an *agnostic* because she says she really doesn't know.

Some scientists are *agnostic* because they say there is no proof that God exists, yet they admit there is no scientific proof that he does not.

agog (ah gog) *adj.* highly excited by eagerness

When they first see their presents under the Christmas tree, the children are always *agog* with joy.

Jim was *agog* and fell from his chair when his name was announced as the winner of the Pulitzer Prize.

agrarian (uh GRAR ee un) *adj.* related to farming and land

In its early years, America was an *agrarian* society.

Because New Jersey is a successful *agrarian* state, it became known as the "Garden State."

ague (AG yoo) *n.* a malarial fever characterized by drastic changes of hot and cold body temperature

The hunters returning from South America were struck with an attack of *ague*.

The physician diagnosed the patient as having *ague*.

ajar (uh JAR) *adj.* partially open

When the police carefully examined the crime scene, they found a second-story window adjacent to the large oak tree had been left *ajar*.

The rattlesnake escaped from the bottle because the lid had been left partially *ajar*.

alacrity (uh LAK ri tee) *n.* cheerful expectancy; eagerness

Mary Ellen packed with great *alacrity,* thinking of all the adventures she might encounter at summer camp.

In a moment of *alacrity*, Ben realized the gathering was a surprise party in his honor.

alchemy (AL kuh mee) *n.* a magical power or process of transmutation; a medieval study and practice of chemistry

The *alchemy* of medieval times may seem primitive to us, but it was the foundation of our present research to find cures for many illnesses.

The *alchemy* of cosmetics transforms ugly ducklings into beautiful swans.

alcove (AL kov) *n.* nook, corner, any recessed space

The living room had a dining *alcove* by the rear windows.

Henry turned the *alcove* off the kitchen into a recreation room.

allegory (AL uh gawr ee) *n.* a symbolic story

Saint Augustine's "City of God" is an *allegory* of the triumph of Good over Evil.

Alice in Wonderland can be interpreted as an *allegory*.

alibi (AL uh bye) *n.* an excuse to avoid blame, a credible excuse or explanation of innocence

John always had a credible *alibi* for not doing his homework on time.

In most murder movies the hero is the chief suspect who is innocent but who has no *alibi* for the time the murder was committed.

alienate (AY lee uh nayt) *v.* to make hostile; to cause to feel unwelcome or estranged

Mary's boss had an ugly habit of *alienating* his employees by shouting at them.

Barb was *alienated* from her group when they learned that she was the town gossip.

allay (au LAY) *v.* to relieve, calm or pacify

The mother sang a lullaby to *allay* the baby's fear.

The doctor hoped to *allay* the problem with medication.

allege (uh LEJ) *v.* to state without proof

Because Roger had not been proven guilty in court, the newspapers could only refer to him as the "*alleged* thief." (*adj.*)

Jack *alleges* that Jake ate all the cookies in the cookie jar but is blaming him.

allegiance (uh LEE junts) *n.* devotion or loyalty to a person, country, or cause

In many American schools, students pledge *allegiance* to the flag of the United States at the beginning of each school day.

Harry says he has no *allegiance* to any team and will play for the one that pays the best.

alleviate (uh LEE vee ayt) *v.* to make less severe; to relieve, to lessen

Peter's arrival with sacks of ice for the party *alleviated* the need to wait for the ice-maker to produce more.

Aspirin will *alleviate* headaches much of the time.

alliterative (uh LIT er ah tive) *adj.* the repeating of initial consonant sounds in language

"She sells seashells down by the seashore" is an *alliterative* tongue-twister.

"Round and round the rugged rock the rascal ran," is a sentence which *alliterates* the letter R. (*v.*)

allocate (AL uk kayt) *v.* to assign; allot

Each soldier was *allocated* three pairs of green socks.

The department head was told to *allocate* the remaining funds for the annual Christmas party.

allot (uh LAHT) *v.* to give a share of something; allocate; apportion

Due to the emergency, the boss *allotted* only two days for a job that would normally take an entire week.

The museum is planning to increase the amount of space *allotted* to modern art.

alloy (AL oy) *n.* combination of two or more metals

Bronze is an *alloy* consisting of copper and tin.

The wiring used in computers is mostly made up of *alloys* that are excellent conductors of electricity.

allude (uh LOOD) *v.* to refer to indirectly

All Jim's poems *allude* to the love of man for nature.

In her letter, Jane *alludes* to the reason she left our city ten years ago.

allure (uh LUHR) *v.* to entice with something desirable; tempt

The ship-wrecked sailors had been *allured* into believing the calm, balmy seas would last until they reached a safe port.

Psychologists agree that all movie stars have some *alluring* quality film audiences find irresistible. (*adj.*)

ally (AL LIE) *v./n.* to unite formally by treaty or league; a friend or close associate in a common cause

Little dogs find it a good idea to *ally* themselves with big dogs when for protection from even bigger dogs.

United States and England were *allies* during World War II.

alms (almz) n. money or goods given as charity to the poor

Goodwill collected *alms* from the community during its spring donation drive.

The *alms* were distributed to the poor.

aloof (uh LOOF) *adj.* distant, reserved in manner; uninvolved

Most everyone thought Theodore *aloof* when actually he was only very shy.

My cat acts *aloof* with strangers, but she really craves attention.

also-ran (AWL so ran) *n.* one who is defeated in a race, election, or other competition; a loser

Even though Al Gore received millions of votes in the presidential election, he was an *also-ran* to George W. Bush.

With twenty thousand runners in the New York Marathon, even if you defeat nineteen thousand nine hundred and ninety eight, you will be an *also-ran*.

altar (ALL tur) *n.* an elevated structure, as a mound or platform where religious rites are performed

The wedding was performed in front of the congregation at the church *altar*.

Gerry was a ham actor who devoted his life to the *altar* of fame and glory.

altercation (awl tur KAY shun) *n.* a vehement argument, a heated quarrel

The shoplifter had an *altercation* with the policeman.

When Professor Pitt said the South started the Civil War, an *altercation* broke out among the southern students in his class.

alternative (all TUR na tive) *n.* the choice between two possibilities; a situation presenting such a choice

"I've had two by-pass operations," said Harry. "It's no fun, but better than the *alternative*."

The hikers decided there was no *alternative* but to wade across the stream.

altruism (AL troo iz um) *n.* devotion to helping others; selflessness

The Salvation Army is an organization devoted to *altruism*.

The college depended on the *altruism* of its graduates to provide scholarships for deserving students.

amalgam (uh MAL gum) *n.* fusion; compound; a blend of different things

Julie's character is a curious *amalgam* of charm and aloofness.

Dr. Harvey, the dentist, filled the large cavity with an *amalgam* of gold and silver.

amass (uh MAS) *v.* to gather or accumulate

She *amassed* an impressive library, thanks to her membership in the book club.

The hiking group was *amassed* at the foot of the mountain ready to begin the climb.

ambiance (AM bee uns) *n.* mood, feeling; general atmosphere

The *ambiance* in the locker room was depressing after the team lost the championship.

For their daughter's birthday party, the Jeffersons created an *ambiance* of gaiety with balloons and party favors.

ambiguous (am BIG yoo us) *adj.* confusing; unclear as to meaning

Some of the questions on the verbal SAT appear *ambiguous* upon first reading.

Because the road map was *ambiguous*, we stopped at a gas station to get directions.

ambivalence (am BIV ah lents) *n.* indecision; experiencing contradictory emotions

Jim's *ambivalent* feelings of both respect and disgust for his boss made him unsure about accepting the promotion. (*adj.*)

Ric's *ambivalence* about whether to attend college or to take a job instead caused him many sleepless nights.

ambulatory (AM byu lah tor ee) *adj.* capable of walking

Although Robin's foot was in a cast, she was still *ambulatory* with the aid of a crutch.

Most *ambulatory* patients do not stay overnight at the hospital.

ameliorate (uh MEEL yuh rayt) *v.* to make better

On the first day of school, the kindergarten teacher *ameliorated* the children's anxieties by telling them a story.

Lou knew that winning the lottery would *ameliorate* his financial woes.

amenable (ah MEH nuh bul) *adj.* agreeable, pleasant, willing to give in to the wishes of another

The Seminole Indians were *amenable* to sharing revenue from the bingo hall games.

Jane was *amenable* to returning the call the next day when the main office would be open.

amend (uh MEND) *v.* to alter, modify, improve; change for the better

Congress failed to obtain the necessary votes to *amend* the U.S. Constitution.

The club *amended* the membership rules to allow younger

people to join.

amenity (ah MEN ih tee) *n.* a comfortable, pleasant feature

The hotels at Disney World offer all the athletic *amenities* one could hope for: swimming, golf, tennis, and a gymnasium for exercising.

The log cabin had no *amenities* such as electricity or running water.

amiable (AY mee uh bul) *adj.* friendly; agreeable

Teachers or coaches without *amiable* personalities have two strikes against them.

Princess Diana was well loved by the English because she was *amiable* with each person regardless of his or her station in life.

amicable (AM ik ahbull) *adj.* possessing or showing friendliness or good will; peaceable

The two countries came to an *amicable* understanding following the war.

When we moved into the neighborhood, the neighbors came to meet us and were most *amicable*.

amid (uh MID) *prep.* in the middle of or surrounded by

Hortensia wrote from Brazil that she was living *amid* savages in the jungle.

On the floor, *amid* mounds of books, we found two small envelopes full of money.

amity (AM uh tee) *n.* friendship, good will, harmony

The *amity* of the ship's crew made our cruise very enjoyable.

Because of their friendship, James and Mary decided *"Amity"* would be a good name for their new boat.

amnesty (AM nuh stee) *n.* political pardon

The new president granted full *amnesty* to all political prisoners. (*Amnesty* refers to a group of people, while "pardon" refers to one person.)

After the Vietnam War, many draft dodgers who had gone to Canada were granted *amnesty* and later returned home.

amoral (ay MOR ul) *adj.* lacking a sense of right and wrong; without moral feelings

The retarded man was completely *amoral* and could not judge good from bad.

Many animals are not *amoral*; they have standards of conduct in their relationships with each other.

amorous (AM ur us) *adj.* full of love; relating to love

Romeo and Juliet is a tragic and *amorous* love story about two people who commit suicide.

We don't double date with them anymore because their *amorous* behavior in public is embarrassing.

amplify (AM pluh fi) *v.* to make larger, louder, or more powerful

Their children had *amplified* the music to the point that the parents couldn't carry on a conversation.

General Rommel was unable to *amplify* the role of his tank corps in the Battle of El Alamein because he didn't have ample fuel to run the armored vehicles.

anachronism (uh NAK ruh niz um) *n.* incongruity; something out of time or place in history

In his play, *Romeo and Juliet*, Shakespeare makes mention of a clock. This is an *anachronism* because at the time of the play clocks had not yet been invented.

A caveman depicted watching television in his cave would be an *anachronism*.

analogous (uh NAL uh jee) *adj.* comparable; similar or equivalent

Forcing some men to retire is *analogous* to condemning them to an early death.

Driving and traffic laws are fairly *analogous* from state to state.

analogy (uh NAL uh jee) *n.* a comparison of two things; similarity

Our teacher drew an *analogy* between professional wrestlers and Roman gladiators.

The *analogy* section of the SAT asks students to find the relationship that is similar among pairs of words. (Words not similar are said to be not *analogous*.)

anarchy (AN ur kee) *n.* disorder; lawlessness; without government

After the military coup, the South American country was in a state of *anarchy*.

The day the substitute teacher arrived, *anarchy* broke out in the class-room.

anathema (uh NATH uh muh) *n.* something or someone greatly disliked or disapproved of

Fur coats are *anathema* for people who believe animals should not be killed to clothe humans.

Meat is *anathema* to vegetarians.

ancillary (AN sih ler ee) *adj.* helping; providing assistance; subordinate

Christopher worked as an auto mechanic but at night earned an *ancillary* income as a waiter.

Jack was an *ancillary* employee at the plant and was able only to work part time.

androgynous (an DROJ ih nuss) *adj.* having the characteristics and nature of both male and female, neither specific

Customers of both genders consider the tee shirt an *androgynous* item of clothing.

Pat, a character on *Saturday Night Live,* is *androgynous*, no one knows if Pat is a man or a woman.

anecdote (AN ik doht) *n.* a short, humorous story

The seminar was interesting because the speaker included many personal *anecdotes*.

Mr. Alkek told a humorous *anecdote* about the time he applied for his first job and was so nervous he couldn't remember his own name.

anemic (uh NEE mik) *adj.* lacking power, vitality

Jill's *anemic* condition was caused primarily by her starvation diet.

Phil finds most romance novels *anemic* fare and not worthy of being called literature.

angst (ahnkst) *n.* strong anxiety and unhappiness; a feeling of dread

Ken believes the world is coming to an end, so he is filled with *angst*, troubled by constant worries about the catastrophe ahead.

Bonnie chewed her nails and waited with *angst* for her lab results.

27

anguish (ANG wish) *n.* agonizing pain, mental or physical

George's remembrances of the war and his dead comrades filled him with *anguish*.

It was *anguishing* for Jill to see her husband after cancer had reduced him to a shadow of his former self. (*adj.*)

angular (AN gu lur) *adj.* having an angle or angles; crooked; gaunt

The mountain trail is *angular* and difficult to travel.

Jeb had an *angular* face with stark facial bones and a hooked nose.

animated (AN eh mate ed) *adj.* filled with activity; vigor; movement

Bill became *animated* on those topics that interested him, like hunting and fishing.

Tina became highly *animated* when she heard she was voted the "most likely to succeed."

animosity (an ih MAHS uh tee) *n.* a feeling of ill-will; bitter hostility

After fighting over the same boyfriend, the two sisters had a strong *animosity* toward each other.

The *animosity* between the opposing teams was evident in their vicious play.

annals (AN ulz) *n.* descriptive record; history

The championship team of 1963 went down in the school's *annals* as the best ever.

The *annals* of history are rife with endless wars between tribes, kingdoms, and nations.

annex (AN neks) *n.* an addition or attachment

The wedding reception was held in the *annex* of the church.

Bill built an *annex* adjacent to his office for storage purposes.

annotation (an oh TAY shun) *n.* an explanatory note added to a text

The *annotations* that explained in detail what was written on each page were printed in italics at the bottom of each page.

Carl read the explanatory *annotations* in his chemistry book before taking the test.

annuity (uh NOO uh tee) *n.* any income paid at fixed intervals

Each year Muriel receives a small *annuity* from her late husband's retirement account.

The farmer sold his farm with payments over twenty years, an *annuity* he and his wife now live on comfortably.

anomaly (uh NAHM uh lee) *n.* an irregularity; a deviation from the norm

A cold day in July is an *anomaly* in South Florida.

Its was an *anomaly* for Karen to fail her math test because she is usually a straight "A" student.

anomie (an uh MEE) *n.* condition of an individual or of society resulting from a breakdown in standards and values

Bill's general feeling of *anomie* caused him to lose interest in his career.

Anomie in the cities that summer was the basis for widespread labor riots.

anonymity (an uh NIM ih tee) *n.* the condition of being unknown or nameless

Although Emily Dickinson allowed several of her poems to be published, she did not use her name because she preferred to remain in *anonymity*.

It was difficult to trace the origin of the painting because of the *anonymity* of the artist.

antagonism (an TAG uh niz um) *n.* active hostility or opposition

Neighborhood gangs in large cities are encountering increasing *antagonism* from their communities.

Julie's aspirations as an actress met with *antagonism* from her father, who wanted her to be a test pilot.

antecedent (an tuh SEED unt) *n.* something going before; an occurrence or event preceding another

The steam engine was the *antecedent* to the gasoline engine.

The atomic bomb was the *antecedent* to the hydrogen bomb.

antedate (AN ti dayt) *v.* to be earlier than; precede in time; predate

The cold weather *antedated* their return from the city.

Rosie's birthday *antedates* her daughter's birthday by one week.

anterior (an TIR ee ur) *adj.* situated in front

The *anterior* is up front, the interior inside, the exterior outside, and the posterior bringing up the rear.

The *anterior* of a ship is called the "bow."

anthology (an THAHL uh jee) *n.* a collection of artistic works which usually have a similar form or subject

This Bob Dylan *anthology* includes some rare recordings of his best songs.

New Monic Books is planning an *anthology* of books of teaching techniques using easy-memory techniques.

anthropomorphic (an thruh puh MAWR fik) *adj.* ascribing human characteristics to something that is not human, i.e., animals, gods

Alice in Wonderland and *Winnie-the-Pooh* are classic examples of *anthropomorphic* works.

Young girls are almost always *anthropomorphic* toward their dolls.

anticlimactic (an tee klie MAK tik) *adj.* having an end that is less important than what precedes it

Ralph had been counting on celebrating his raise for so long that when it finally came, the moment was *anticlimactic*.

Green Bay was so far ahead, their final touchdown was *anticlimactic*.

antipathy (an TIP uh Thee) *n.* a natural basic dislike; aversion

Mary Ellen loves to cook but has always felt a certain *antipathy* toward housework.

Dr. Howell's *antipathy* toward students who cheat on tests is well known.

antipodal (an TIP ud ul) *adj.* situated on the opposite side of the globe; exactly opposite

The north and south poles are *antipodal*.

Their personalities are *antipodal*; he likes to party, and she likes to sit at home and read.

antiquity (an TIK wuh tee) *n.* the quality of ancientness; ancient times

The greater the rarity and *antiquity* of art objects, the more valuable they usually become.

Our doctor said the greater the *antiquity* of one's bones, the more brittle they become.

antiseptic (an ti SEP tik) *adj.* free from germs; exceptionally clean

Something *antiseptic* is free from germs and other microorganisms.

It is a prerequisite for hospital rooms to be *antiseptically* clean before surgery. (*adv.*)

antithesis (an TITH uh sis) *n.* the direct opposite

Although Jane and June are twins, in temperament the unflappable Jane is the *antithesis* of the expectable June.

North is the *antithesis* of South.

antonym (AN tuh nim) *n.* a word of opposite meaning; the opposite of "synonym"

"Hot" and "cold" are examples of *antonyms*.

"Short" and "tall," "ugly" and "pretty," "fast" and "slow," are opposites and therefore *antonyms*.

anxiety (ang ZI uh tee) *n.* apprehension; uneasiness; nervousness; disquiet

Seth felt pangs of *anxiety* because he knew he was going to be late for his daughter's wedding.

The rescue workers' *anxiety* deepened when the mountain climbers hadn't returned by nightfall.

apathy (AP uh thee) *n.* absence or suppression of emotion or excitement

The *apathy* of the senior class was apparent when so few came to the senior prom.

After a serious illness, it is common for a person to feel *apathetic* until he regains his strength.

aperture (AP ur chur) *n.* a narrow opening; usually a hole; esp. one that controls the amount of light reaching an optical instrument

All cameras have an *aperture* control that regulates the amount of light striking the undeveloped film.

The little *aperture* in the fence allowed the children to spy on our neighbors party.

apex (AY peks) *n.* the highest point; peak

Shadows are the shortest when the sun reaches its *apex*.

When the swing reached its *apex*, we feared the little girl might fall and be injured.

aphorism (AF uh riz um) *n.* a brief, witty saying

Benjamin Franklin was famous for his many *aphorisms*.

"A penny saved is a penny earned" is an example of a common *aphorism* almost everyone has heard.

apocalypse (uh PAHK uh lips) *n.* a prophetic prediction, esp. one concerning the end of the world

The *apocalyptic* visions of soothsayers predicting the end of the world have fortunately always been wrong. (*adj.*)

Many scientists have a theory that the *apocalypse* could occur when a huge meteor collides with Earth.

apogee (AP uh jee) *n.* the most important; the highest or most distant point, especially in space

At their *apogee*, the novels of Mickey Spillane claimed worldwide sales of over 180 million books.

The young model felt she had reached the *apogee* of her career when her face was on the cover of *Vogue* magazine.

apoplexy (AP uh plek see) *n.* the sudden loss of bodily functions caused by the rupture of a blood vessel

Suddenly paralyzed with *apoplexy*, which later turned out to be a brain hemorrhage, my grandfather was taken to the hospital by ambulance.

Molly was seized by *apoplexy* when she saw a giant man peering into her bedroom window.

apostasy (uh PAHS tuh see) *n.* the absolute rejection of one's religion, principles, or loyalties

The *apostasy* from communism in the Soviet Union during the 1980s has helped make peace efforts easier between Russia and democratic countries.

Coach Burrel was an *apostate*; he thought his team should never throw a forward pass. (A person who commits apostasy is called an apostate.)

apotheosis (uh pahth ee OH sis) *n.* the perfect example; divine

Einstein is often referred to as the *apotheosis* of intellect.

Many disagree as to whether Coke or Pepsi is the *apotheosis* of soft drinks.

appalling (uh PAWL ing) *adj.* causing dismay or horror

It was absolutely *appalling* the way the members of the band taunted the cheerleaders with accusations that their legs looked like twigs.

We were *appalled* at the way Nancy scolded her children for minor offenses. (*v.*)

apparel (uh PAIR ul) *n.* clothing, personal attire, something worn

The boutique is known for its designer *apparel*.

Uniforms are considered proper *apparel* at some schools.

apparition (ap uh RISH un) *n.* a ghostly image; phantom; specter

Josh claimed strange *apparitions* were entering his room at night.

An American Indian in war paint is a strange *apparition* to see in downtown Manhattan.

appease (ah PEEZ) *v.* to soothe; to pacify or relieve by giving in to

To *appease* his mother, Zachary always walked the dog before dinner.

The trainer *appeases* his performing monkeys when they are stressed; he gives them extra bananas.

appellation (ap uh LAY shun) *n.* a name, title, or other designation

Mussolini, the Italian dictator, was known by the more familiar *appellation* "El Duce."

My children create *appellations* like "Blue Bear" and "Frog Face" for their stuffed animals.

appendage (uh PEN dij) *n.* something which exists as a smaller and less important part of something larger

Arms and legs are *appendages* of the human body.

At parties John Paul hates being made to feel like an *appendage* to the company instead of an important part if it.

apportion (uh POHR shun) *v.* to assign, adjust or distribute parts so as to maintain the proper proportion

33

He *apportioned* the bread equally among the starving children.

When we know how much money is left after expenses, we will *apportion* that money equally among us.

apposite (AP uh zut) *adj.* suitable and right for the occasion; fitting; appropriate

The film starts in a graveyard, an *apposite* image for the decaying society, the theme of the film.

The husband's arguments about money spent on medicine are not *apposite* to the health of his wife.

appraise (uh PRAYZ) *v.* to examine something to determine the value

The diamond necklace was *appraised* at over two thousand dollars.

Some hotels leave cards in the rooms for guests to fill out so that the management may *appraise* the service rendered.

appreciate (uh PREE shee ayt) *v.* to increase in value

The cost of a car does not *appreciate*; it depreciates from the moment the car leaves the showroom.

Many people collect baseball cards in hopes that they will *appreciate* in value over time.

apprehensive (ap ruh HEN siv) *adj.* dreading or fearing coming adversity

The soldier's mother had great *apprehension* about her son's welfare as she opened a telegram from the Department of Defense. (*n.*)

Peter entered the classroom in an *apprehensive* state because he hadn't studied for the exam.

apprentice (uh PREN tiss) *n.* one who is learning a vocation

Jack was an *apprentice* electrician two years before he received his electrician's license.

A horse-racing jockey must serve a one year *apprenticeship* unless he first wins forty races.

apprise (uh PRYZE) *v.* to inform; to tell; to make aware of

Please *apprise* the harbormaster of the arrival of the King's yacht in the marina.

The General has been *apprised* that his army now refuses to fight anyone, anytime, anywhere.

approbation (ap ruh BAY shun) *n.* praise; approval

The Olympic team was met with parades and cheering *approbation* when they returned home.

The third graders all wanted to be liked and sought the *approbation* of their teachers.

appropriate (uh PROH pree ayt) *v.* to set aside; take without permission

Our cat *appropriated* the leftovers from the kitchen counter.

Congress voted to *appropriate* funds for three new national parks.

appurtenance (uh PURT nuns) *n.* an additional feature; something that supplements a more important thing; an accessory

The swimming pool was only an *appurtenance*, but it made the Handleys decide the house was the one they would purchase.

Military careers do not pay well, but the *appurtenances* are good: free room and board and a good retirement plan.

apropos (ap ruh POH) *adj.* appropriate; relevant; opportune; suitable

It was really *apropos* for the school principal to give credit to the coaches for their contribution to the team's victory.

Jack's comic remarks about his father's auto accident were not *apropos*; they were *malapropos*. (*Malapropos* is the opposite of *apropos* and means "inappropriate.")

apt (apt) *adj.* likely; having a tendency to; suitable

Considering his past history, Mr. Simmons is *apt* to continue being late for work at the factory.

The kitchen roof is *apt* to leak in a heavy rain until it is fixed.

aptitude (AP tuh tood) *n.* capacity for learning; natural ability

Jess is all thumbs and has no *aptitude* for fixing things around the house.

The special *aptitude* of flora and fauna to adapt to changing environmental conditions is what allows them to continue their existence.

arable (AR uh buhl) *adj.* tillable, productive, able to be farmed

Along the coast of Ireland the land is frequently too rocky to be *arable.*

The reason there are many exotic tree farms in Homestead, Florida, is that the climate is mild and the land is so *arable.*

arbiter (AHR buh tur) *n.* judge; one who makes decisions

To settle the problem between the two parties, an *arbiter* was called in to assess the disagreement.

The baseball plate umpire serves as *arbiter* for all pitched balls that cross home plate.

arbitrary (AHR buh trer ee) *adj.* decided by judgment rather than law or statute

The grading system of the young teacher was *arbitrary*, without rhyme or reason, depending on her mood that day.

Joseph Stalin was a cruel dictator, having millions of his fellow Russians *arbitrarily* put to death at his slightest whim. (*adv.*)

arcade (ahr KAYD) *n.* a covered area or passageway in which there are shops; archways connected by pillars or columns

They are building a new shopping *arcade,* and Jim's wife can't wait to see the new stores.

The kids love to visit the *arcade* to play video games.

arcane (ahr KAYN) *adj.* unknown to the masses; mysterious

Many of the symbols inside the pyramids are *arcane* to everyone except Egyptologists.

The Chinese secret society had *arcane* hand signals to be used only by members.

archaic (ahr KAY ik) *adj.* ancient; outdated

With the advent of personal computers, typewriters have become *archaic.*

Former social customs such as men opening car doors for women became *archaic* with the emergence of the women's rights movement.

archetype (AHR kuh type) *n.* the original model or pattern

The Wright Brothers' first airplane was an *archetype* of more advanced airplanes that were to follow.

Hercules is the *archetypal* strong man. (An *archetype* is similar to a prototype, both *archetypes* and prototypes usually preceded something else.)

archipelago (ahr kuh PEL uh goh) *n.* a large body of water containing many islands; a group of islands

The islands in the Hawaiian *archipelago* make up the fiftieth state in the United States.

The Florida Keys is an over a hundred mile long *archipelago* of islands connected by thirty-four bridges.

archival (are KIE vul) *adj.* pertaining to historical or public records, documents or archives

David's search for his family's *archival* genealogy sent him to Norway, the country from which his family had emigrated.

The official government *archival* vaults in Washington, D.C., were closed for the holidays. (The *archives* are a place where the *archival* documents are kept.)

ardent (AHR dunt) *adj.* passionate, full of desire or emotion

Christina has been Zach's *ardent* admirer since the first grade.

Millie is an *ardent* exerciser, riding her bike ten miles every day.

arduous (AHR joo us) *adj.* hard, difficult, tiresome

Swimming three miles was the most *arduous* exercise Jeannie ever had.

The long, *arduous* boat trip was made even worse by stormy seas and much seasickness.

arid (AR id) *adj.* having little rain; very dry; lacking imagination or feeling; uninteresting

The desert is so *arid* that nothing grows there.

Hillary found the book so *arid* that it put her to sleep.

aristocratic (uh ris tuh KRAT ik) *adj.* noble; snobbish

Fox hunts are an *aristocratic* pastime.

Kelly's phony English accent and pretense of an *aristocratic* background wins her few friends.

armada (ar MA duh) *n.* a fleet of warships

An *armada* entered the harbor ready for battle.

The Spanish *Armada* of 1733, eighteen ships in all, sank in the Florida Keys during a hurricane.

armament (ARM ah ment) *n.* military supplies and weapons; the process of arming for war

The United States government believes its nuclear *armament* is a deterrent to the possibility of a third world war.

Major Randolph is the *armaments* officer for the 36th Division.

armistice (AHR muh stus) *n.* an agreement between two countries or factions to stop fighting; a truce

A two-week *armistice* was declared between the rival gangs.

North and South Korea declared a temporary *armistice* so they could discuss a peace solution.

arraign (uh RAYN) *v.* to bring before a court of law; to respond to a charge; to accuse

He was *arraigned* on charges of aiding and abetting terrorists.

The district attorney wanted to *arraign* the felony suspect, but the police could not find him.

arrant (AR unt) *adj.* complete; unmitigated; downright; total

He dismissed the rumors as *arrant* nonsense, saying they were absolute falsehoods.

In the story of *"Pinnochio,"* the boy's nose kept growing longer because of his *arrant* dishonesty.

array (ah RAY) *v.* to place in an orderly arrangement for display

Combining flowers and candles, the florist *arrayed* the wedding cake.

The general *arrayed* his troops for inspection.

arrears (uh RIRZ) *n.* a debt that is late in being paid

The occupants learned if they didn't pay their rent in *arrears* by the first of the month they would be evicted.

Jose's charge account is badly in *arrears.*

arrogant (AHR uh gunt) *adj.* feeling superior to others, overbearing

The *arrogant* attitude of the French aristocracy was the chief cause of the French Revolution.

Harvey was an *arrogant* public official who lost the election because of his poor public relations with his constituents.

arsenal (AHRS nul) *n.* a building where weapons and military equipment are stored; a collection of weapons; armory; any supply or store

The army planned to attack enemy *arsenals* in order to cripple their armament supply.

The comedian had an *arsenal* of hilarious jokes that kept us laughing for hours.

arson (AR son) *n.* the malicious burning of a property

When the McDougall office building burned, the owners were arrested on suspicion of *arson*.

Arson is generally assumed to be an attempt to illegally collect fire insurance by the owners, or someone hired by them.

artful (AHRT ful) *adj.* sly; crafty

The Miami con men were *artful* at bilking senior citizens of their savings.

A good conversationalist, Jerome was *artful* at entertaining the museum visitors who came to see his paintings.

articulate (ahr TIK yuh layt) *v.* to speak or pronounce clearly and distinctly; to express effectively

When children first learn to talk, they do not *articulate* well.

Surveys show that women are more apt at *articulating* their feelings than are men.

artifact (ART ah fakt) *n.* an object made by human work of archaeological or historical interest

Even as a child, the museum curator had a penchant for collecting *artifacts*.

The children found several arrowheads and thought they were merely rocks rather than Indian *artifacts*.

artifice (AHRT uh fus) *n.* cunning; trickery

Mary's helpless demeanor was really an *artifice* she used around men to get what she wanted.

Mary Poppins resorted to an *artifice* when she told the children their medication was really a spoonful of sugar.

artisan (AHRT uh sun) *n.* a worker skilled in a craft

The *artisans* of Pueblo, Mexico are known for their beautiful pottery.

The Italian painter and sculptor Michaelangelo was both an artist and an *artisan*.

artless (ART lis) *adj.* having no skill or art; crude

Sarah was afraid to take her boyfriend home to meet her family because he tended to be *artless* when discussing politics and religion.

The boy claimed to be a juggler, but after he threw the balls in the air it was apparent that he was *artless*.

ascend (uh SEND) *v.* to go up; to rise or move upward, succeed

Drake quickly *ascended* to the new judgeship after he left his law practice.

The climbers *ascended* the northern face of the mountain.

ascent (uh SENT) *n.* the act of ascending, rising or going up

I could feel the air pressure in my ears during the plane's *ascent*.

The divers began their *ascent* from a depth of 75 feet.

ascertain (as ur TAYN) *v.* to discover; to make certain; to learn unquestionably

The medical examiner quickly *ascertained* that the cause of death was heart failure.

Herbert said he *ascertained* there would be twenty-eight people attending the party.

ascetic (uh SET ik) *adj.* monk-like; practicing self-denial

The American author Thoreau led an *ascetic* existence at Walden Pond for over two years, but he had each Sunday lunch with his Mom.

The priest had few basic comforts; he lived the life of an *ascetic* in a monastery. (*n.*)

ascribe (ah SKRYBE) *v.* to attribute to a specific cause, source, or origin

The physics professor *ascribes* to the theory that what goes up must come down.

Samantha *ascribed* her weight loss to a diet of fruit and vegetables.

asinine (AS ih nine) *adj.* silly; stupid

Adam is usually a nice guy, but sometimes he is so *asinine* no one can stand him.

The phone solicitor asked so many *asinine* questions that Ralph finally hung up.

askance (uh SKANS) *adv.* with suspicion, disapproval or a lack of trust

With riots in the city, tourists will be looking *askance* at vacationing here this summer.

The horse looked *askance* at the rattlesnake slithering up the hill toward him.

askew (uh SKEW) *adj.* to one side; crooked; awry

After the flood receded, the bridge was found to be *askew* of the road which connected to it.

After his pratfall, the clown's hat was *askew.*

asperity (ah SPER ah tee) *n.* roughness or harshness, as of surface, weather, sound, or manner

Although he seemed like a mild-mannered man, his *asperity* became clear when his children asked too often for money.

When the fishing boat was twenty miles offshore, the crew was amazed by the *asperity* of the sea.

aspersion (uh SPUR zhun) *n.* an insulting or malicious remark about someone

Sally's feelings were hurt when she overheard the *aspersions* her tennis coach cast on her intelligence.

Jill said she didn't wish to cast *aspersions* on her boss, but he was a jerk.

aspirant (ASS pah rant) *n.* someone who aspires, as to high honors or position

Prince Charles is the *aspirant* to the throne of England.

Although many people are *aspirants* to doctoral degrees, far fewer actually earn them.

aspiration (ass puh RAY shun) *n.* strong desire to achieve a goal

Her *aspiration* was to become first a beauty queen and then a movie star.

Father Flanagan had *aspirations* to start an orphanage for boys and call it "Boys' Town."

aspire (a SPIRE) *v.* to long for, aim, or seek ambitiously

Tim studied hard because he *aspired* to be the valedictorian of his class at graduation.

As a young child, General Custer *aspired* to become a musician, but he later decided to make the Army his career.

assail (ah SAIL) *v.* to attack violently

Henry claimed he did not *assail* his friend Norman, but Norman had bruises to prove otherwise.

Loud pop music *assailed* our ears as we entered the concert hall.

assay (AH say) *v.* to try or test; examine or analyze

George took a bag of ore to the *assay* company to determine the amount of gold he had found.

John entered the school debating contest to *assay* his debating strengths.

assent (uh SENT) *v.* agree to a situation, opinion, or proposal; to concur

The Moore Building Company *assented* to monthly building inspections for the new office complex it was building for the city.

A bill in Congress can only be passed with the *assent* of the majority. (*n.*)

asset (ASS et) *n.* an object of value; a useful or valuable person or resource

A student who is hard working in high school is usually an *asset* to his/her college.

Peter's greatest *asset* is his salesmanship.

assert (uh SURT) *v.* to state with force or confidence

King George *asserted* his view that there would be war if the French did not withdraw from the Crimea.

Randolph most often lost arguments with his friends because he was too timid to *assert* himself forcefully.

assess (uh SES) *v.* to judge or decide the amount, value, quality or importance of

One can be assured that the insurance company will want to *assess* the flood damage before paying the claim.

After *assessing* the superior competition in the state high jump, Clarence decided to withdraw from the meet.

assiduous (uh SIJ oo us) *adj.* hardworking; diligent, busy

Roger earned the job as foreman at the plant because he is the most *assiduous* worker they have.

Only the more *assiduous* students were invited to join the honor society.

assimilate (uh SIM uh layt) *v.* to learn completely; to take in; to absorb

He made it his life's work to *assimilate* the teachings of Plato.

It is often hard for students to *assimilate* as much material as their teachers present.

assuage (uh SWAJE) *v.* to soothe; to make less severe; to satisfy, ease, lessen

Dr. Moore was able to *assuage* the fear of his patient by predicting successful treatment.

Many athletes drink Gatorade to *assuage* their thirst and assimilate vital nutrients they lose during exercise.

astringent (uh STRIN junt) *adj.* stern, harsh, or severe

Everyone fears the General's *astringent* criticism because their promotions are dependent upon his approval.

The critic's *astringent* review of the play caused the author to have a fainting spell.

astute (uh STOOT) *adj.* shrewd, clever, keen

Louisa has a natural *astuteness* in dealing with angry people and winning them over to her view. (*n.*)

Mary was known to be a very *astute* bargainer when it came to buying cars.

asunder (uh SUN dur) *adj.* in separate parts or widely separated

When the earthquake stopped, we found the trees on our farm had been uprooted and torn *asunder*.

The views of the settlers and the Indians were as far *asunder* as the North Pole is from the South.

asylum (uh SYE lum) n. a place of safety, as for political refugees; also an institution for the care of the ill

The defector's family appealed to the courts to give him *asylum* in this country, but the appeal was denied, and he had to return to his country.

People with certain types of severe mental problems are often committed to *asylums* for the mentally ill.

atavistic (at uh VIS tic) *adj.* having characteristics relating to an earlier type; related to a throwback

Some peoples have the *atavistic* appearance of their ancestors from thousands of years ago.

The *atavistic* behavior of the street gang is a throwback to the days of cavemen.

atone (ah TONE) *v.* to make amends

Nothing the convicted murderer said to the victim's family could *atone* for his crime.

After *atoning* for his past indiscretions, the president quickly won back the support of the nation.

atrophy (AT ruh fee) *v.* to wither away

The *atrophic* condition of the ancient Egyptian mummy was apparent as soon as the tomb was opened. (*adj.*)

Because his leg was in a cast so long, the muscle was beginning to *atrophy*.

attenuate (uh TEN u wayt) *v.* to make thin in consistency; to weaken

Adding milk to the ice cream *attenuated* the thickness of the milk shake.

One of the council members made a motion to *attenuate* the Mayor's power, but the motion was voted down.

attest (uh TEST) *v.* to show or prove that something is true; to confirm or testify to

The notary *attested* to the signatures on the document.

The number of old Volkswagon cars still on the road *attests* to the excellence of their manufacturer.

attribute (uh TRIB yoot) *v.* to credit to; to assign; to ascribe to

A study by the Farmingham Health Group *attributes* the increase in acute asthma attacks to household dust.

Some people are lucky, and they *attribute* their success to being in the right place at the right time.

attrition (ah TRISH un) *n.* a gradual reduction or weakening; a rubbing away

Because our school has so many older teachers, the retirement *attrition* rate is high.

Washed ashore, the once jagged glass shard had become a smoothed gem due to the endless wave *attrition*.

atypical (ay TIP uh cull) *adj.* not typical; abnormal

A banana without a curve is *atypical* of the species.

It was *atypical* for Mrs. Moore to walk to work during the summer season without her umbrella and raincoat.

audacity (aw DAS uh tee) *n.* daring; boldness

Jennifer had the *audacity* to tell her friend Myrtle that she looked better before she had the face lift.

Wilber made the *audacious* decision to go over Niagra Falls in a waste basket. (*adj.*)

augment (awg MENT) *v.* to make or become greater

Jack's part time job did little to *augment* his family's income.

The sheriff *augmented* his credibility problem with the voters when he hired his three brothers as deputies.

augur (AW gur) *v.* to predict; to serve as a warning

It didn't *augur* well for a possible victory when the football team fumbled the ball the first five times they had it.

The *augury* practiced by TV fortune tellers is mostly unreliable. (*n.*)

auspices (AW spuh sez) *n.* sponsorship or protection; patronage; encouragement

The withdrawal of troops from Yugoslavia will be carried out under the *auspices* of the United Nations.

45

The Toys for Kids fund raiser this Christmas is being held under the *auspices* of the local banks.

auspicious (aw SPISH us) *adj.* favorable; promising for the future

Although our soccer team had a bad year, we are hoping for an *auspicious* start next year.

The weather was sunny and fair, *auspicious* weather for a picnic in the park.

austere (aw STEER) *adj.* stern, as in manner; unadorned; severely simple and plain

The chateau in Baigts, France was very *austere*, without furniture and with bare floors throughout.

The *austerity* of life in the village was understandable; many were jobless, and evidence of poverty was everywhere. (*n.*)

authentic (aw THEN tik) *adj.* real, *bona fide*, original

They found an *authentic* draft of the Declaration of Independence hidden in the closet of the farmhouse.

Jane was a truly *authentic* person; there was nothing false about her whatsoever.

authoritarian (uh THAWR uh tayr ee un) *n.* someone who believes in total obedience or subjection to authority figures

A true *authoritarian* is one who believes in dictatorships, many of which are still to be found in third world countries.

An owner needs to be an *authoritarian* to his dog if he expects him to learn obedience.

autism (AW tiz um) *n.* absorption in self-centered mental activity; withdrawal

Jerry always seemed to be in his own world; his condition was diagnosed as *autism*.

Helen's *autism* was characterized by daydreams, fantasies, and delusions.

autocratic (aw tuh KRAT ik) *adj.* tyrannical, despotic; ruling absolutely

Mrs. Jones is so *autocratic* her children have to make appointments to see her.

Mary Sue is an *autocratic* three-year-old who thinks she should get whatever it is she wants whenever she wants it.

autonomy (aw TAHN uh mee) *n.* freedom and independence; self-government

For years the Irish have been fighting to establish complete *autonomy* from Great Britain.

My daughter can't wait until she is eighteen when she feels she will be *autonomous*. (*adj.*)

auxiliary (awg ZIL yuh ree) *adj.* giving help or support; supplementary; additional

Volunteers are an important part of the hospital's *auxiliary* staff.

When the *Merry Widow* broke down at sea, Jake had to switch to his *auxiliary* engine to get back to the marina.

avail (uh VAYL) *v.* to be useful; be of value to; to serve

The doctors' efforts to save the man were of no *avail*; he died the next day. (*n.*)

The Colonel's preparations did not *avail* his troops, as the enemy struck in an unsuspected region of the front lines.

avant-garde (ah vahnt GAHRD) *adj.* describing the advanced group in any field, esp. the arts; dealing in experimental methods

Throughout his long art career, Picasso was *avant-garde,* always ahead of the pack with his experimental artwork.

Paris is the center of *avant-garde* fashion, where all the newest designs are displayed for the first time.

avarice (av UR IS) *n.* greed; extreme desire for wealth

Mr. Ford was a **philanthropist** without an ounce of *avarice* in his character.

Avarice ruled Scrooge's life because of his miserly desire to gain and hoard wealth.

aver (uh VER) *v.* to assert with confidence; to state as true

Clark, the defense's main witness, *averred* that the suspect was never at the crime scene at the time of the crime.

Ruth *averred* that her recipe for pineapple upside down cake was the best in the county.

averse (uh VERCE) *adj.* having a feeling of opposition, repugnance, or disinclination

Harry's wife says her husband is not *averse* to watching three football games on TV at the same time.

Jane decided not to become a surgical nurse because she has an *aversion* to the sight of blood. (*n.*)

avert (uh VERT) *v.* to turn aside or away; to prevent; avoid

She *averted* her glance so he wouldn't notice she was watching him.

The company *averted* heavy financial losses by coming out with a new line of toys that children liked.

avid (AV id) *adj.* characterized by great eagerness; an unbounded craving

Leslie always had an *avid* desire to become a TV journalist until she discovered she might have to get up at 4 a.m.

Elizabeth became an *avid* reader at the age of three.

avow (uh VOW) *v.* to claim; admit; declare

Stanley *avowed* his love for Stella even after she dropped him for a new beau.

The mayor *avowed* that he would make the city crime-free and safe for everyone to walk the streets at night.

avuncular (uh VUNG kyuh lur) *adj.* helpful; generous; understanding

The children's uncle was *avuncular,* while their father was quite domineering and difficult to get along with.

From all we have heard about the old geezer, Santa Claus must be an *avuncular* fellow indeed.

awe (AW) *n.* the emotion of respect mixed with fear; reverence

The sight of Notre Dame cathedral in France filled the tourists with *awe*.

The aborigines of New Guinea were *awed* upon seeing their first airplane fly over the jungle tree tops. (*v.*)

awry (uh RYE) *adj.* not according to plan; off course; not straight

Although we made detailed plans for our Canadian vacation, things began going *awry* when we had a flat tire not one mile from home.

Two things children learn about Robin Hood: he always beats up the

Sheriff of Nottingham, and his arrows never go *awry*.

axiom (AK see um) *n.* widely held belief

Our geometry teacher told our class the next homework assignment would be to memorize the *axioms* for triangles.

"The rich get richer and the poor get poorer," is an often heard *axiom*.

babble (BAB uhl) *v.* prattle; to talk foolishly; chatter

Our bridge club members *babbled* foolishly for hours, but afterwards I couldn't remember a word they said.

After dinner, Debra enjoys setting on her porch and listening to the soft sounds of the *babbling* brook.

bacchanal (BAK uh nul) *n.* any drunken party or riotous celebration

The Johnsons, who lived next door, had the reputation of throwing a wild *bacchanal* every weekend.

Bacchanals originated from the Greek god of wine and fertility, Bacchus, whose followers celebrated him with drink and riotous festivities.

badger (BAJ ur) *v.* to tease; annoy; harass persistently

Louis told his daughter not to *badger* him; he would take her to the mall when he finished work.

Harassment is common among teenagers who *badger* their younger siblings.

bagatelle (BAG ah til) *n.* something unimportant or insignificant; trifle

The pirates were proud of their booty until they realized it was all *bagatelle*.

Zach's uncle buys him *bagatelle* every year for his birthday, but Zach thanks him as if it were gold.

baleful (BAYL ful) *adj.* threatening; hurtful; malignant; ominous

The prisoner sat in *baleful* silence while the judge read his jail sentence.

The sky was *balefully* thick with clouds. (*adv.*)

balk (bawk) *v.* to stop short and refuse to proceed

The warden's security precautions *balked* the escape attempt of the prisoners.

Marcie was injured when her horse *balked* at the last jump in the steeplechase.

ballad (BAL id) *n.* narrative poem recited or sung, a folk song

Albert read the class several of Robert Burns's *ballads*.

We sat around the campfire while a guitar player sang old western *ballads* about cowboys and the Old West.

ballast (BAL uhst) *n.* heavy material used to balance ships; stabilizer

The old sailing ships carried tons of rocks in their holds to provide *ballast* so they wouldn't turn over in a storm.

In order to stabilize the ship during rough seas, the captain ordered his crew to take on more *ballast*.

ballistics (buh LISS ticks) *n.* the study of the dynamics or flight characteristics of projectiles

Most naval warships carry *ballistic* missiles.

Detective Culleton specializes in *ballistics* and is always called to a crime scene whenever a firearm is involved.

ballyhoo (BAL ee hoo) *n.* a lot of noise and activity, often with no real purpose; exaggerated advertising or publicity

With all the *ballyhoo* over the hula hoop, you'd think it the greatest invention since penicillin.

The newest anti-cancer pills were *ballyhooed* as a cure-all for any cancer. (*v.*)

balm (balm) *n.* something that soothes, heals or comforts; an oil or ointment

It was a *balmy* day, perfect for a game of golf or a trip to the beach. (*adj.*)

A soothing *balm* was applied to alleviate Jane's sunburn.

bamboozle (bam BOO zul) *v.* to cheat, dupe, hoodwink, trick

George was *bamboozled* out of his bank savings by a con man selling counterfeit gold bars.

Joel said his brother was trying to *bamboozle* him out of his turn to use the family car.

banal (buh NAL) *adj.* ordinary; not original; trite

The student's story was so *banal* that the teacher fell asleep while grading it.

It drives my father crazy when I have long, *banal* conversations with my friends on the phone.

bandy (BAN dee) *v.* to trade; to toss back and forth; to exchange

Mike's hobby is *bandying* baseball cards with his friends.

The two boxers *bandied* blows to the head and torso throughout the final round of the fight.

bane (bayn) *n.* cause of harm; torment; ruin

When we were young, my sister was the *bane* of my existence because she always wanted to be with me and my friends.

Some house plants are *baneful* to house pets. (*adj.*)

banter (BAN tur) *n.* a playful conversation; good-natured teasing

The professional baseball player carried on light-hearted *banter* with admiring teens who waited in line for his autograph.

He was a master of witty *banter*, always reducing his friends to tears of laughter.

baritone (BARE uh tone) *n.* a male singer who has a voice level below tenor but higher than bass

A powerful Italian *baritone* sang three unforgettable arias at the concert in the park.

He thought his voice level was bass, but his music teacher told him he was a natural *baritone*.

barometer (buh ROM uh ter) *n.* any device that measures air pressure for weather predictions

As the *barometer* continued to fall, we knew there was a good chance of rain.

Joe predicted dry weather for the weekend based on his *barometer* reading.

baroque (buh ROHK) *adj.* extravagantly decorated or ornate; flamboyant

Madelaine's paintings are *baroque* in style, reminiscent of the masters

51

of the 18th century.

Count Dracula's mansion in Transylvania looks scary because it is dark-looking and *baroque*.

barrage (bah RAHZH) *n.* a curtain of artillery fire; any overwhelming attack, as of words or blows

When Maria walked into the sorority house after her date, she was *barraged* with questions. (*v.*)

The boxer backed his opponent into the corner with a *barrage* of hammering punches.

barren (BAR uhn) *adj.* unproductive; lacking; sterile; desolate

The Sahara Desert in North Africa is *barren* of greenery except for an occasional oasis fringed with palm trees.

Jo Ann wanted children, but the doctor told her it would be impossible because she was *barren*.

bask (bask) *v.* to enjoy warmth or praise

The skiers *basked* by the fireplace after a long day of skiing in good snow conditions.

The new college graduate *basked* in his family's pride for his graduation with honors.

bastion (BAS chun) *n.* a projecting part of a fortress; stronghold; fortified place

The guerrilla band fled into the mountains and found a *bastion* of protection in a hidden cave.

The country drug store is a *bastion* for a bunch of tobacco-chewing seniors who sit on the porch and swap tales.

bathos (BATH os) *n.* triteness or triviality in style; overly sentimental, mawkish writing or emotion

The convention began on a high note but regrettably ended on a low ebb of common political speech-making *bathos*.

The book's plot, thrilling in the beginning, ended on a note of *bathos*, as the hero and heroine never married and neither seemed to care.

battery (BAT ter ee) *n.* act of beating or pounding; an emplacement for one or more pieces of artillery; an object designed to produce electric energy

Stan was arrested for assault and *battery* after the barroom fight.

The battleship focused its fire on the Japanese *batteries* along the beach.

The boy's toy car required two *batteries* in order for it to run.

bauble (BAW bul) *n.* a small, inexpensive trinket

Mixed among the precious gems in Jennifer's jewelry box were costume jewelry and other cheap *baubles*.

The child was delighted with the plastic and glass *bauble* she received from her aunt.

bazaar (buh ZAR) *n.* a marketplace or shopping quarter, esp. one in the Middle East

The hospital ran a *bazaar* in its parking lot to raise money for local medical charities.

In Istanbul, Turkey, there are said to be over 4,000 stalls selling assorted goods in the Grand *Bazaar*.

bedlam (BED lum) *n.* noise and confusion

Following the championship soccer match, the stadium was in a state of *bedlam*.

Bedlam broke out in the cafeteria after Bob was hit in the head by a flying meatloaf.

beget (bi GET) *v.* to give birth to; to create

Prior to the development of farm machinery, farmers would *beget* large families to help them run their farms.

The Wright Brothers didn't invent the airplane, but they were the *begetters* of the first heavier-than-air flying machine in the United States. (*n.*)

begrudge (bi GRUJ) *v.* to envy the good fortune of someone else

Linda *begrudged* Mary her band awards because Linda felt she was more deserving.

Jonathon *begrudged* paying so much for a motel room since the motel was practically empty.

behest (bi HEST) *n.* an order or command

Randy took the dog for a walk at his wife's *behest*.

The secretary typed the letters at the *behest* of her boss.

belated (bee LATE id) *adj.* too late; delayed; tardy

Absent-minded people are so abundant that stores now have a wide variety of *belated* birthday cards.

His brother used to send *belated* gifts, but now he sends nothing at all.

beleaguer (be LEE gur) *v.* to besiege; beset; surround; harass

In World War II, the Russian city of Stalingrad was *beleaguered* by the German Army for five months before it fell.

During his last year in office, Richard Nixon was *beleaguered* as president and struggled to fight off the Watergate scandal.

belie (bi LYE) *v.* to contradict; give a false impression

Although George acts like a gruff fellow, his tenderness toward children and animals *belies* his outward appearance.

Even though they tried to bribe Lisa, she refused to *belie* herself.

belittle (bi LIT ul) *v.* to put someone down; demean

Although the entire platoon worked hard digging the trenches, the Captain *belittled* their efforts as too little too late since the war had come to an end.

Because he constantly *belittles* his older sister, Pete's parents try to keep them apart as much as possible.

belligerent (buh LIJ ur unt) *adj.* quarrelsome; ready to fight

Josh is very *belligerent* when people try to prove they know more than he does about country music.

Eric is the nicest guy until he has a drink; then he becomes *belligerent*.

bemoan (bi MOHN) *v.* to complain about; to grieve over; lament

Researchers at universities traditionally *bemoan* their lack of funds.

General Wainright forever *bemoaned* the cruelty of the Japanese toward prisoners on the Bataan March of Death in World War II.

bemuse (bi MYOOZ) *v.* to cause to be confused; to muddle

Kevin was *bemused* by his blind date who refused to speak to him but sent him notes instead.

His parents were *bemused* when John's computer began smoking and making strange sounds.

(The word muse means to think about things. To be *bemused* is to think about something to the point of confusion.)

benchmark (BENCH mark) *n.* a point of reference; a standard by which to measure; a criterion

Four years of college is the *benchmark* for a basic college education.

The *benchmark* time which marathon runners try to achieve is two hours and ten minutes.

benediction (ben uh DIK shun) *n.* a blessing; a prayer asking for help and protection; an utterance of good wishes

Each Sunday for many years Father Fulton led the *benediction* services in his church on Sunday.

There was no family present to offer their *benediction* when Jack and Jill married quite unexpectedly in a Las Vegas marriage chapel.

benefactor (BEN uh fak tur) *n.* one who provides help to others

(The *benefactor* is the one who gives benefits. The *beneficiary* is the one who receives them.)

Diane became a *benefactor* of the United Way Fund when she made a financial contribution.

When Charles received aid from the United Way for his pet ranch, he became a *beneficiary*.

beneficent (buh NEF uh sent) *adj.* showing kindness resulting in benefit

Ian's father was the *beneficent* benefactor who sponsored the baseball team.

Jerry Lewis's *beneficent* telethon for MDA raised millions for research.

benevolent (buh NEV uh lunt) *adj.* kind; generous

Because Uncle Harry is so *benevolent,* he is the favorite uncle of all his nieces and nephews.

The United Way is a *benevolent* organization that supports many different charities.

benighted (be NI tid) *adj.* being in a state of intellectual darkness;

ignorant; unenlightened

Many *benighted* people never vote and don't realize how important their vote could be to their country.

Cameron had never read a book but was so *benighted* he did not realize he would never be accepted into Harvard.

benign (bi NYNE) *adj.* harmless; mild; kind

Because Charlie has a *benign* personality, he makes friends easily.

George was relieved when the doctor reported that his tumor was *benign*.

bequest (bi KWEST) *n.* the act of giving; something left to someone in a will

Hortensia's jewelry was a *bequest* from her mother for her graduation.

Tim's father *bequeathed* his business to his son in his will. (*v.*) (*Bequeath* is a verb meaning the act of leaving something in a will.)

bereave (buh REEV) *adj.* left alone; especially through the death of another

When their pony died, the *bereaved* children were told by their mother that everyone dies, and it was all right to cry and feel sad for a time.

The *bereaved* widow wore a black dress to her husband's funeral.

bereft (bah RIFT) *adj.* deprived, robbed, or devoid, as of life, hope, or happiness

She was *bereft* when she returned from college to learn that her beloved dog had died.

My grandmother was *bereft* after the death of her husband of over sixty years.

beset (bee SET) *v.* to harass; to surround

The hikers were *beset* by hordes of killer bees that came out of the woods.

When three of our aircraft crashed we knew we were *beset* with design problems we had yet to understand.

besiege (bih SEEJ) *v.* to close in or surround with hostile forces; beset

The Foreign Legionnaires were surrounded and *besieged* by Arab tribesmen.

Jacob *besieged* his girlfriend to marry him before he died of a broken heart.

besmirch (bee SMURCH) *v.* to make dirty; soil

Some high school girls make an effort to *besmirch* the reputations of their classmates.

When an American commits a crime abroad, this act *besmirches* the reputation of our country.

bestow (bi STOH) *v.* to give, as a gift or award; to confer

Many honors were *bestowed* on the teacher of the year at our school.

The George Cross is a decoration *bestowed* on British civilians for acts of great bravery.

betroth (bih TROTHED) *v.* to promise to marry; to become engaged

Nancy is *betrothed* to the captain of the basketball team.

Her *betrothed*, Jim, presented her with an engagement ring. (*n.*)

bevy (BEV ee) *n.* a group of animals; an assemblage

Bud's hunting dogs flushed out a *bevy* of quail.

A *bevy* of shoppers rushed into the store on opening day.

bias (BY us) *n.* a particular tendency or inclination; in a diagonal manner

Many people have a *bias* against foreigners because of the language barrier.

The design of a dress Martha was sewing required a *bias* cut from front to back. (*adj.*)

bibelot (BEE buh low) *n.* a small object of beauty or rarity

Many *bibelots* found in the sunken treasure proved to be emeralds and rubies.

Carl surprised Mary with an attractive golden *bibelot* to wear on her wrist.

biennial (bye EN ee yul) *adj.* occurring every two years

Our family takes *biennial* snow skiing trips to the mountains.

She planted *biennial* flowers in her garden.

bigot (BIG aht) *n.* a person who is strongly partial to his or her own group, race or religion

Members of the Ku Klux Klan are proud to be considered *bigots*.

My father says he is not a *bigot*, yet he got very upset when a black family moved into our neighborhood.

bilge (bilj) *n.* the lowest point of a ship's inner hull; nonsense, rubbish

The Senator said the newspaper articles about his crookedness were complete *bilge*.

The tanker's *bilge* was leaking oil at sea, creating an environmental hazard.

bilious (BIL yus) *adj.* in a bad mood; extremely unpleasant; ill-tempered

He was a *bilious* old man who griped and complained about everything.

The walls were painted a *bilious* shade of green which made the room dreary and unpleasant to enter.

bilk (bilk) *v.* swindle, cheat, defraud

Henry claimed he was *bilked* out of his inheritance by a group of thieving lawyers who handled his father's estate.

Zack's clothing store business *bilked* the state government of almost a million dollars for non-payment of sales tax.

biopsy (BIE op see) *n.* the removal of a sample of human body tissue for the purpose of examination

Dr. Child's *biopsy* report revealed that his prostate was not cancerous but only swollen as older men's prostates are frequently found to be.

The *biopsy* report of Mrs. Warner's breast revealed a small cancer in an early stage of growth.

bivouac (BIV wak) *n.* a temporary shelter or encampment, especially for military purposes

In worsening weather with darkness closing in, the climbers prepared a *bivouac* and settled down for the night.

The first platoon pulled back from the lines and *bivouaced* in a small valley for a week to rest. (*v.*)

bizarre (bih ZAR) *adj.* extremely unconventional or farfetched

As the medication began to take effect, Randolph's eyes took on a faraway look, and he muttered something *bizarre* about riding the pony one more time.

Mardi Gras in New Orleans is a *bizarre* affair during which people dance all night in the French Quarter and wear wild, colorful costumes.

blacklist (BLAK list) *v.* to place a person on a list under suspicion, disfavor, censure

In Senator McCarthy's witchhunt for American communists, his committee *blacklisted* many innocent people and often ruined their lives.

Jim was *blacklisted* from the casino and denied entrance because he was caught card counting while playing blackjack.

blanch (blanch) *v.* to remove color from; bleach; to make pale, as from illness or fear

It's easy to tell that Bill would never make it as a surgeon for his skin *blanches* at the sight of blood.

The leaves of the plant were *blanched* because they were out of the sunlight too long.

bland (bland) *adj.* lacking flavor or zest; dull

The doctor put Edgar on a *bland* diet of non-spicy foods in order to help heal his stomach ulcers.

Christopher's *bland* sense of humor was humorous in a smiling way more than a laughing way.

blandishment (BLAND ish munt) *n.* flattery; sweet talk

The teacher was unaffected by Johnny's daily *blandishments* of how he loved her course; she flunked him.

Arthur succumbed to the *blandishments* afforded a rock musician and came to think he could walk on water.

blasphemy (BLAS fuh mee) *n.* insult to anything sacred; profanity

The Royal Canadian Mounted Police consider it *blasphemy* for any of their officers to say anything bad about their organization.

It was nothing short of *blasphemy* for Carl to say George Washington never cut down a cherry tree and that he told many lies.

blatant (BLAYT unt) *adj.* offensively noisy; totally obtrusive

59

The coach was disappointed with the team's efforts and at half-time made a *blatant* display of his disapproval.

John *blatantly* turned up his stereo to disrupt his parent's dinner party.

blather (BLAH thur) *v.* to talk nonsensically

Mary and Kathy *blather* on the telephone every night.

Children have great imaginations, and they *blather* on endlessly about ghosts and goblins that enter their rooms and play with them.

bleak (bleek) *adj.* depressing, harsh, cold, barren

After Joy lost the first set 6-0, her chances of winning the girls tennis championship began to look *bleak*.

The thought of the *bleakness* of the Aleutian Islands, where the winds howl constantly, makes one shiver. (*n.*)

blight (blyte) *n.* anything that injures, destroys or prevents growth

A *blight* of grasshoppers took over the land and destroyed all the crops.

A depressing *blight* fell over the town when the factory closed and the workers lost their jobs.

bliss (blis) *n.* extreme happiness or joy

Coming from Norway, Hans's idea of pure *bliss* was two weeks lying on a sunny Florida beach.

(Anything that promotes a feeling of *bliss* can be said to be *blissful*.)

Henry and Jane thought their entire married life would be *blissful*. (*adj.*)

blithe (blyth) *adj.* cheerful; carefree

A *blithe* spirit is the most wonderful aspect of Jane's personality.

The children were *blithely* playing in the street and unaware of the danger of passing cars. (*adv.*)

bloc (BLOK) *n.* a coalition of factions; parties with a common interest or purpose

NATO began as a *bloc* of nations with the purpose of halting the rise of international communism.

Before the Civil War, the southern states formed a *bloc* of states that were called the Confederate States of America.

bludgeon (BLUD jun) *n./v.* a thick club; coerce, bully

Henry's *bludgeoning* accusations about his neighbor's dog caused his friend to break up their friendship. (*adj.*)

The police arrested the lumberjack on suspicion of striking a fellow lumberjack with a *bludgeon.*

blunt (blunt) *adj.* plain-spoken with lack of feeling; abrupt

My English teacher was very *blunt* when she told me I am not college material.

The doctor hated to be *blunt*, but he knew he had to tell the patient to get his affairs in order quickly.

bluster (BLUS tur) *v.* to act in a loud, boastful, or threatening way

Joan *blustered* so often at her children's misbehavior that they came to pay little attention to her.

A *blustering* wind blew in from the southwest, signaling a tropical storm was on its way. (*adj.*)

bogus (BOE guss) *adj.* not genuine; counterfeit

The bank confiscated Rick's twenty dollar bill, telling him it was *bogus* and that they would have to notify the U.S. Treasury Department.

The grocery clerk returned the *bogus* ID to the young teen and chided him for attempting to buy cigarettes when he was not a legal age.

bolster (BOHL ster) *v.* to support, as in a group

Jane *bolstered* the support of her fans by giving out autographed photographs.

The school had a pep rally in order the *bolster* their team before the big game.

bombard (bom BARD) *v.* to assail vigorously

The people of London sought protection in subway shelters during German air *bombardment* of that city during World War II. (n.)

The professor *bombarded* his class with questions about their upcoming exam.

bombast (BOM bast) *n.* high sounding use of language without much real meaning

To listen to his *bombast*, you would think Carl was the only person who ever got a speeding ticket.

Some people debate by shouting down their opponents with *bombastic* language. (*adj.*)

bon mot (bon moe) *n.* witticism or a clever reply

Oscar Wilde's writings were full of delicious *bon mots* that entertained and at the same time gave pause for serious thought.

John's pleasant *bon mot* about labor and management brought both sides together in agreement.

bon vivant (bon vih VAHNT) *n.* a person who enjoys life, esp. food and drink

Jackie's idea of a *bon vivant's* life was eating at fine restaurants every night.

Jacque's glamorous reputation preceded him as a playboy living a life of a *bon vivant*.

bona fide (BOH nuh fyde) *adj.* not counterfeit or phony; genuine; real

The accountant told his clients that *bona fide* charities would suffer if the new tax law passed.

The banks have means to determine when paper money is not *bona fide*.

bonhomie (bohn uh MEE) *n.* good natured; easy friendly disposition

Rice's *bonhomie* was seen in his genuine smile for his friends and co-workers.

The *bonhomous* young man made friends easily. (*adj.*)

boon (boon) *n.* a timely benefit; a blessing

The week-long rain was a *boon* to the farmers whose crops were withering from the drought.

The decline of interest rates proved a *boon* to the real estate market; more families could afford to buy homes.

boor (buur) *n.* a rude person; someone who is unrefined

She *boorishly* asked for a take-home bag at the wedding reception. (*adv.*)

Jake was not invited to the society dinner because everyone knew he was a *boor.*

bootleg (BOOT leg) *v.* to smuggle; to make, sell, or transport for sale illegally

Scott *bootlegged* illegal drugs across the border.

During liquor prohibition in the twenties, many gangsters were involved with *bootlegging* alcohol.

booty (BOO tee) *n.* loot; the spoils of war; goods or property seized by force; a valuable prize

Pirates kept their *booty* in chests which they sometimes buried on deserted beaches.

The burglars were apprehended before they could make off with the *booty.*

bosky (BOS kee) *adj.* covered with an abundance of trees or shrubs; wooded

The *bosky* area near the river hid the tributaries in its uncharted wilderness.

We paddled to a *bosky* island to set up camp.

botch (bahch) *v.* bungle; to spoil something by doing it badly

The funding was withdrawn after the tree frog scientists *botched* the first stage of the research.

Pauline's brother tried to decorate his bedroom but *botched* it so badly she had to do it over for him.

bouillabaisse (BOO yuh base) *n.* a stew made with several kinds of fish and shellfish; mixture of things

Captain Pete made *bouillabaisse* from clams, shrimp, and lobster.

The new play on Broadway is a *bouillabaisse* of comic routines in different humorous styles.

bourgeois (boor ZHWAH) *adj.* conventional; boringly middle class

Many writers of the 1920s moved to Paris, which they believed less *bourgeois*, and therefore more artistic, than the United States.

When she returned from college, she realized how *bourgeois* her home town was compared to the academic university atmosphere to which she had grown accustomed.

bovine (BOH vyne) *adj.* of, relating to, or resembling an animal such as an ox, cow or buffalo; solid; dull

The *bovine* features of the man scared the children.

Gateway Computer Company uses a unique *bovine* design on their computer packaging.

bowdlerize (BOWD lur ize) *v.* to omit, abridge, or modify a work of literature that is considered offensive

By *bowdlerizing Gone With the Wind,* the author made just another lackluster novel of the Deep South during the Civil War.

The producer wanted to *bowdlerize* the sexually oriented scenes in the script so the film wouldn't receive an adult rating.

bracing (BRAY sing) *adj.* invigorating; energizing; stimulating; healthy and fresh

The family took a *bracing* walk on the beach so they would have a good appetite for breakfast.

A *bracing* wind was blowing off the ocean, causing the surf to be higher than usual and making the conditions perfect for surfing.

brandish (BRAN dish) *v.* to wave or shake something in a threatening, agitated, or exciting manner; to flaunt

He rushed into the room happily *brandishing* a letter of acceptance from the college he applied to in California.

Jane was angry and *brandished* a saucepan at her little brother for licking icing from the freshly-baked cake.

brash (brash) *adj.* hasty and reckless; impetuous; unthinking

Sometimes one *brash* act is all it takes to cause a tragedy.

The *brash*, young driver endangered many as he ran the stop sign.

bravado (bruh VAH doh) *n.* a false, exaggerated, or boastful display of courage

It was an act of *bravado* when Josh volunteered to rescue the drowning man; everyone knew Josh couldn't swim.

With childish *bravado*, when his mother caught Bryan writing on the wall with a crayon, he told her it wasn't his fault; his brother Sam had done it.

brawn (brawn) *n.* large, solid muscles; great muscular strength

Myrtle went out with everybody on the wrestling team and told her friends she preferred guys with *brawn* instead of brains.

The old man didn't have the *brawn* to carry a heavy load up the hill to the factory.

brazen (BRAY zun) *adj.* bold, shameless; impudent; also like brass

Tiger Woods' *brazen* attempt to reach the green in two strokes paid off with a birdie.

The *brazen* cymbals worn by the dancers made metallic, melodious sounds.

brazier (BRAY zhur) *n.* a pan for holding burning coals

We toasted marshmallows over the open *brazier*.

In Mongolia the indigenous people cook much of their food on open *braziers*.

breach (breech) *n.* an act of breaking a law, promise, agreement or relationship; a violation

His refusal to work on a Sunday was a *breach* of contract.

There have been serious security *breaches* in the Central Intelligence Agency, revealing national security secrets to foreign powers.

breadth (bredth) *n.* distance from side to side; width; freedom from restraint

The *breadth* of the box was sixteen inches.

The *breadth* of the view of the Sahara from the Atlas Mountains is spectacular.

brevity (BREV i tee) *n.* briefness

We were all relieved that the speakers recognized the benefits of *brevity*.

The reception was marked by its *brevity*, as the bride and groom wished to leave for their honeymoon as soon as possible.

brigand (BRIG ahnd) *n.* a bandit or robber, usually one of an outlaw band

Jose Gaspar and his *brigands* pirated the western coast of Florida.

Billy the Kid was proud of his ability as a *brigand*.

brink (brink) *n.* edge

On the *brink* of disaster, Mike finally regained control of the skidding car.

Grandpa Ed was on the *brink* of death when the paramedics arrived and saved his life.

bristle (BRIS ul) *v.* to respond with anger; to be ready to fight back

The lightning struck so close to our house it made my hair *bristle*.

She *bristled* at the suggestion her new dress looked exactly like the dresses of three other women at the party.

broach (brohch) *v.* to bring up a subject for discussion

Because his father was out of work, Tim was careful not to *broach* the subject of money for a birthday present.

During lunch with his boss, Hal waited for the right time to broach the conversation about a raise.

brogue (BROAG) *n.* accent; regional dialect

Kenny was from Ireland, so his friends loved to hear him talk with his Irish *brogue*.

You can tell from the tennis players' *brogue* they are Australian.

bromide (BROH myde) *n.* dull, over familiar saying; cliché; a chemical compound used as a sedative

The lecture consisted of many *bromides* that the audience had heard before.

John took a *bromide* as a sedative to calm his nerves after meeting with his wife's divorce attorney.

brook (brook) *v.* to bear or tolerate; to put up with

Cynthia stormed from the room shouting she would no longer *brook* any of Sir Anthony's insults.

The substitute teacher could no longer brook the class's behavior so she sent everyone to the principal's office.

brouhaha (BROO hah hah) *n.* an uproar; hubbub

What began as a quiet party suddenly turned into a *brouhaha* when the party animals arrived.

My mother warned me that if the sleep-over turned into a *brouhaha*, she would send all my friends home.

brusque (brusk) *adj.* quick and rude in manner or speech; impolitely abrupt; curt

When Jerome called about the job vacancy, the secretary was *brusque* and told him the job was already taken.

A *brusque* welcome greeted his late night return from a poker night with the boys.

bucolic (byoo KAHL ik) *adj.* rural or rustic in nature, country-like

The art judges gave first prize to the painting of a *bucolic* landscape painted in greens and blues.

There is nothing *bucolic* about big city life; honking horns and bustling streets are neither peaceful nor rustic.

buffoon (buh FOON) *n.* a person who behaves comically; clown

Mary Ann doesn't realize what a *buffoon* she becomes when she tries to get attention at parties.

Leslie stopped dating Tom when she realized what a *buffoon* he really was.

bulwark (BULL wurk) *n.* a defensive wall; something serving as a principal defense

Quebec City is the only city in North America with a *bulwark* built entirely around it.

Our mother was a *bulwark* against bad times; no matter how bad things became, she always wore a smile and had a cheerful word.

bureaucracy (byoo RAHK ruh see) *n.* any large administrative system with numerous rules and regulations

Because of the *bureaucracy* involved, we were sure it would take over a year to get a building permit from the county government.

Government intervention into all aspects of personal life is *bureaucracy* at its worst.

burgeon (BUR jun) *v.* to flourish; expand

The *burgeoning* Roman Empire created by military expansion inevitable fell of its own degeneration. (*adj.*)

Weeds have *burgeoned* in my garden.

burlesque (bur LESK) *n.* exaggerated imitation

Saturday Night Live has performed *burlesques* of famous people for over twenty years.

Before movies were invented, Vaudeville actors were famous for their *burlesque* skits.

burnish (BER nish) *v.* to polish or rub to a high gloss

The silver bracelet was *burnished* to a bright finish.

Copper, brass, and silver are highly *burnishable*. (*adj.*)

butte (BYOOT) *n.* isolated hill or mountain with steep sides on a large plain.

We had a picnic on the *butte* outside of town overlooking a beautiful valley.

Butte, Montana, is named for its location.

buttress (BUT rus) *n.* support for a wall; encouragement or support for a person

The young attorney was warned by the judge to *buttress* his arguments with more facts before talking to the jury. (*v.*)

The east wall of the cathedral has a beautiful stone *buttress* supporting it.

Byzantine (BIZ un teen) *adj.* difficult to understand and complicated; characterized by the architectural style of the Byzantine Empire

Byzantine architecture is characterized by spires, domes, arches, and minarets.

To refer to something as *Byzantine* is to suggest it is complicated and intricate.

cabal (kuh BAL) *n.* a small group of people who plan a secret plot, especially political

There was an assassination attempt on Adolf Hitler by a *cabal* of people within his own regime.

The *cabal* of sophomore girls that Jill wanted to be part of constantly snubbed her.

cache (kash) *n.* a hiding place, or the objects hidden in a hiding place

Treasure hunters have searched for Blackbeard's treasure in Bahamian caves, but no one has yet found his *cache*.

When they could no longer carry their supplies, the hikers left them in a *cache* they would return to.

cachet (kah SHAY) *n.* a mark of prestige; a mark of approval

Courtesy is the daughter of Ambassador Douglas and is the *cachet* of good breeding.

The letter to the Three Musketeers was sealed with the royal *cachet*, which meant it came directly from the King of France.

cacophony (kuh KAFH uh nee) *n.* harsh sounds; jarring discordant sounds, dissonance

An unpleasant *cacophony* was produced as the orchestra tuned their instruments.

A *cacophony* in the classroom was created by everyone talking at once.

cadence (KAYD uns) *n.* the rise and fall of sound

The *cadence* of a cat's purr is very comforting.

The sergeant called "*cadence*," and the troops marched in step onto the parade grounds.

cajole (kuh JOHL) *v.* to wheedle, coax, or persuade someone to do something

Jack's sister *cajoled* him into entering the marathon just so she could get a free T-shirt.

Jeannie always sweet-talked and *cajoled* her parents into letting her go to Daytona Beach during spring break.

calamity (kuh LAM uh tee) *n.* an event causing extreme harm, suffering, or destruction; disaster

The factory closing was a *calamity* for the city, it left thousands unemployed.

Lately, Jake's life has been a series of *calamities*: a bitter divorce, loss of his job, and the bank repossession of his home.

callous (KAL uss) *adj.* unfeeling, insensitive

A *callous* remark about someone is a statement that does not take into consideration the feelings of another.

The doctor was alarmed at the *callousness* of the hospital medical staff on night duty. (*n.*)

callow (KAL oh) *adj.* immature and inexperienced

When rescued, the *callow* boater had neither a life preserver nor a radio aboard his sailboat.

Judy may have been *callow,* but we never saw a more enthusiastic, hard-working young lady at the glove factory.

calumny (KAL um nee) *n.* a harmful statement, known by the maker to be false

He was subjected to the most vicious *calumny* about his prison record, but he knew it would make matters worse to argue.

Donna resented the *calumnies* aimed at her and got even by tossing stink bombs into certain people's offices.

camaraderie (kah mah RAH der ee) *n.* comradeship; friendship

The sisters developed such a *camaraderie* in college that they remained friends for life.

People find their jobs more enjoyable if there is a sense of *camaraderie* among their fellow workers.

canard (kah NARD) *n.* a false story with the intention of misleading or doing harm

After they hit a tree, the boys concocted a *canard* about a dog running into the road.

As soon as I walked into the house and saw my mother's face, I knew that my *canard* was unsuccessful.

candor (CAN dur) *n.* truthfulness, sincere honesty

Speaking with *candor,* the governor called for police reforms throughout the state.

The coach told his team that *candor* means to speak honestly, and that to speak *candidly,* the team stunk. (*adv.*) (*Candid* is showing *candor.*)

canon (KAN un) *n.* a principle, decree, law or body of laws, especially in religion

The *canon* for lawyers is to treat their clients with fairness, honesty, and responsibility.

Josh's parents try hard to follow the *canons* of their church although they have been known to break a minor *canon* occasionally.

canopy (KAN uh pea) *n.* a covering from the weather; natural or man-made

The fierce storm windows blew the *canopy* away from the campsite and left the campers exposed to the heavy rain.

We sat quietly under the forest *canopy* and listened to all the beautiful bird calls.

cant (kant) *n.* insincere statements made to give one the appearance of goodness

When the preacher was asked a question he could not answer, he resorted to endless *cant* about the devil.

Cant is speech without sincerity or honesty about high ideals, goodness, or piety.

cantankerous (kan TANK er us) *adj.* difficult, ill tempered, and irritating to deal with

Baseball players become *cantankerous* whenever they are hit with a wild pitch.

The child became *cantankerous* when he did not get his milk on time.

canvass (KAN vus) *v.* to conduct a survey or poll; to make a survey

The neighbors were *canvassed* to see who was in favor of paying to put in new sidewalks.

The police *canvassed* the neighborhood, showing the photo of a suspected criminal and asking if he had been seen in the area.

capacious (kuh PAY shush) *adj.* spacious; roomy; able to hold much

The old castle has a *capacious* dining room large enough to seat a small army.

David's memory for jokes is *capacious*; he remembers them all.

capital (KAP ut ul) *n.* location of the center of government; money used to make more money

The *capital* of France is Paris.

We invested a great deal of *capital* so our business would succeed.

capitalism (KAP uh tuh liz um) *n.* economic system of free enterprise

71

Those who are firm believers in *capitalism* would not do well in an autocratic society.

Capitalism is a system of economy found in the United States.

capitol (KAP ih tul) *n.* a building where a state legislature or U.S. Congress meets

We needed passes to be admitted to the *capitol* building in Washington, D.C.

The budget hearing will be held at the *capitol*.

capitulate (kah PICH uh layt) *v.* to surrender under certain conditions; to give in

After continuous bombing, the enemy agreed to *capitulate*.

The workers *capitulated* when the company threatened to close down and fire all the workers.

capricious (kuh PRISH us) *adj.* unpredictable; impulsive

The weather is *capricious* in South Florida; the sun shines, and the next minute the sky turns black and the rains begin.

Joe's *capricious* attitude confounds his parents, one minute he's going to college, and the next he's joining the army.

captious (KAP shus) *adj.* quick to point out faults; critical

Mark is a *captious* member of the board of directors who finds fault with every new proposal from his fellow members.

Maria's mother is far too *captious* with her, so Maria is developing an inferiority complex.

captivate (KAP tuh vayt) *v.* hold the attention of someone by being interesting or charming

The singing of Frank Sinatra *captivated* audiences around the world for fifty years.

Mona *captivates* most men with her looks and flirtatious ways.

carapace (KAYR ah pays) *n.* a protective covering; shell

The Florida spiny lobster's *carapace* has many sharp horns for protection.

Captain Kirk's ray gun could not penetrate the alien's *carapace*.

carcinogenic (kahr sin uh JEN ik) *adj.* able or likely to cause cancer

Tests on laboratory rats determine that certain substances are *carcinogenic*, possibly causing cancer in humans.

The government requires warnings on cigarette packs stating that tobacco has been shown to be a *carcinogenic* substance.

cardiac (KAR dee ack) *adj.* relating to or affecting the heart

Horace had a heart attack and now takes a stress test yearly to determine his *cardiac* condition.

The patient suffered *cardiac* arrest, but the emergency room doctor started the heart beating again.

cardinal (KAHRD nul) *adj.* of great importance; chief

Finding food was the *cardinal* concern of the shipwrecked crew.

The *cardinal* rule of June's mom is "pick up your dirty clothes."

careen (kuh REEN) *v.* to move fast and unsteadily; to lurch while in motion

The car skidded and *careened* wildly across several lanes of traffic.

Billiard balls *careen* around a billiard table when the cue ball is hit effectively.

caricature (KAR uh kuh chur) *n.* an exaggerated portrait or description

When we were in Rome, a street artist did a *caricature* of Jason, exaggerating his mouth and nose.

Bill made his living drawing *caricatures* of tourists for ten dollars a piece.

carnage (KAR nij) *n.* a bloody and massive slaughter, especially in battle; a massacre

The *carnage* of World War I caused many to become disillusioned with war in general.

Absolute *carnage* took place in our back yard after my father discovered a nest of rats.

carnivore (KAR ni vour) *n.* a flesh-eating animal

Alligators and crocodiles are *carnivores*, so they eat only meat.

The most famous of the *carnivorous* dinosaurs was Tyrannosaurus

Rex. (*adj.*)

carp (KAWRP) *v.* to complain and find fault about unimportant things

Mom and my aunt don't get along well because my mother *carps* always about her sister.

Judy always gives me a *carping* replay of every disastrous dinner with her in-laws. (*adj.*)

carrion (KAIR ee un) *n.* dead and rotting flesh

After mauling its prey, the lion left the *carrion* to the hyenas.

For days after the battle, the battlefield was littered by the *carrion* of brave soldiers.

cartography (kahr TAHG ruh fee) *n.* the art or technique of producing maps and charts

Captain John Smith was renowned for his *cartography* of North America.

Governments have *cartography* departments to keep all the maps of their country updated with the latest roads and bridges.

cascade (kas KAYD) *n.* a waterfall; anything resembling a waterfall

Rachel's hair formed a beautiful *cascade* down her back.

A cloud of confetti *cascaded* down onto the crowd celebrating the New Year. (*v.*)

castigate (KASS tuh gate) *v.* to criticize harshly, usually with the intention of correcting wrongdoing

Jimmy's mother *castigated* him for tracking mud on the new living room carpet.

When *castigated* for behavior unbecoming a naval officer, Chief Petty Officer Peterson was denied shore-leave.

cataclysm (KAT ah kliz um) *n.* a violent upheaval or change

One of the United Nations' missions is to avoid the *cataclysm* of a third World War.

The sudden earthquake was *cataclysmic* in its destruction. (*adj.*)

catacomb (KAT uh kome) *n.* underground cemetery, esp. one with tunnels and tombs

The *catacombs* of Rome run for miles beneath the city.

The Egyptian pyramids have *catacombs* for those of royal birth.

catalyst (KAT uh list) *n.* something which causes reactions in other things without being affected itself

My mother is usually the *catalyst* of family arguments.

The shootings at Columbine High School were the *catalyst* for stricter security in public schools.

catapult (KAT uh pult) *n./v.* a device for hurtling things; to slingshot

Before the invention of cannons, *catapults* that hurtled stones were used to attack castles.

When the Dolphins beat the Steelers, the victory *catapulted* them into first place in their division.

cataract (KAT ah rakt) *n.* a large waterfall; a deluge; an eye abnormality

Niagara Falls is probably the most well-known *cataract* in North America.

The old dog developed cloudy *cataracts* on both his eyes.

categorical (kat uh GOR uh kul) *adj.* absolute; unconditional

The defendant *categorically* denied that he had stolen a six pack at the convenience store. (*adv.*)

O.J. Simpson's *categorical* denial of the murder of his wife made national news.

catharsis (kuh THAR sis) *n.* an emotional or psychological cleansing that brings relief or renewal

The companionship of domesticated pets can sometimes lead to a *catharsis* for mentally disturbed patients.

Returning to the French World War II battlefield he had known fifty years before, William found the experience *cathartic.* (*adj.*)

catheter (KATH uh tur) *n.* flexible tube inserted into a bodily channel to permit injection or withdrawal of fluids.

The doctor inserted a *catheter* into the patient's artery to inject a drug.

Because he was unable to get out of bed, the patient had to be *catheterized.* (*v.*)

catholic (KATH lik) *adj.* universal; embracing everything

Michaelangelo was a *catholic* artist who created everything from sculpture to murals.

Students attending Ivy League schools are usually very *catholic* in their outlook.

caucus (KAW kus) *n.* a meeting of leaders; esp. a local political group

Some delegates to political conventions are selected by vote in *caucuses*, while others are appointed.

A *caucus* was held to determine who would represent the union at the national conference.

caustic (KAW stik) *adj.* acidic; corrosive

Amy learned the hard way that soda is *caustic* to a car's finish.

Jennifer is known for her *caustic* comments about non-vegetarians.

cavalier (kav ah LEER) *adj./n.* showing arrogant disregard; a gallant gentleman; casual

Colonel Moore was disliked because of his *cavalier* attitude toward the troops in his command.

Darren was so *cavalier* that he always kissed a lady's hand when first introduced.

cavil (KAV ul) *v.* to quibble; to engage in trivial bickering

My father will *cavil* endlessly with merchants; he loves to bicker over prices.

My children *cavil* over things as trivial as on which end of the sofa each will sit.

cavort (kuh VORT) *v.* to strut; frolic; to prance

Jim's ponies constantly *cavort* in their corral.

Johnny and the neighborhood kids *cavorted* happily in the first snow of the year.

cede (seed) *v.* to withdraw; to give up, as by treaty

South Carolina *ceded* from the Union to join the Confederacy during the Civil War.

The United States *ceded* land to Russia at the Yalta Conference.

celerity (sah LER i tee) *n.* swiftness of action or motion; speed

Students who are slow to do their class work move with great *celerity* when the bell rings for dismissal.

David's *celerity* is improved when the coach is timing him.

celestial (se LES chul) *adj.* of or pertaining to heaven or the sky above

The moon is a *celestial* body.

My friend is very interested and involved in *celestial* studies.

celibacy (SEL uh buh see) *n.* abstinence from sex

The priest never married because he had taken a vow of *celibacy*.

The friends all swore they would remain *celibate* until married. (*adj.*)

censor (SEN sur) *n.* one who examines material to as ascertain whether it is objectionable

The *censor* rated the new French film suitable for mature adults only.

The book on Princess Diana was *censored* in England but sold well in the United States. (*v.*)

censure (SEN shur) *v.* to condemn severely for misconduct

The U.S. Congress sometimes *censures* members for misconduct unbecoming an elected official.

The Mayor was *censured* for his role in the cover up.

cerebellum (sare uh BELL um) *n.* part of the brain, between the cerebrum and brain stem, that controls muscle coordination and equilibrium

After the accident, Mary had loss of equilibrium caused by a damaged *cerebellum*.

Jack's loss of muscle coordination was related to an injured *cerebellum*.

cerebral (suh REE brul) *adj.* of or relating to the brain; describing an intellectual person

Dr. Clark was a *cerebral* Boy Scout leader. He would say, "Construct the canvas shelters in the proximity of the promontory," instead of saying, "Pitch the tents on the hill."

Finnegan's Wake is far too *cerebral* for third grade students.

certify (SUR te fi) *v.* to confirm formally; verify

cessation

Airline ticket personal must *certify* each passenger's identity with a picture ID.

Jack was a *certifiable* liar and crook, wanted in many countries by the authorities. (*adj.*)

cessation (se SAY shun) *n.* a stopping or ceasing, coming to an end

Her parents put a dead bolt lock on the door, putting a *cessation* to her coming in late at night.

Because the students could not handle the responsibility, the deans announced the *cessation* of the privilege.

chafe (chayf) *v.* to create friction; irritate; to rub

The horse was *chafing* at the bit, anxious for the race to start.

George *chafed* his hands holding onto the tug-of-war rope for so long.

chaff (chaf) *n.* anything worthless; the husks separated from grain

On the farm, the *chaff* is separated from the grain by a procedure called "threshing."

Billy's toy boxes have accumulated loads of *chaff*: legs, arms, and other useless pieces of toys.

chagrin (shuh GRIN) *n.* humiliation; disappointment

Susan was beside herself with *chagrin* when she entered the men's restroom by mistake.

Much to Max's *chagrin*, he tripped on stage and fell during graduation.

chalet (sha LAY) *n.* a kind of Swiss farmhouse with overhanging eaves

The first prize was a *chalet* on the edge of the mountain by the winding trail.

The injured hiker stopped to rest for the night in a deserted *chalet*.

chameleon (kuh MEEL yun) *n.* a lizard that changes colors; a highly changeable person

Our Senator is a political *chameleon*; he changes sides like a lizard changes colors.

In Florida, *chameleons* are popular yard critters because they eat roaches.

champion (CHAM pee un) *v.* to defend or fight for; advocate; to support

The Sierra Club *champions* protection of wildlife and the environment.

Martin Luther King, Jr., was a *champion* of civil rights for African-Americans.

channel (CHAN ul) *v.* to direct into a particular place or situation

A lot of money has been *channeled* into AIDS research.

She *channeled* her energies into providing for the homeless.

chanteuse (shan TEUZ) *n.* female singer in cabarets and night clubs

Edith Piaf was a famous French *chanteuse* who sang on the European night club circuit.

The *chanteuse* hopped on top of the piano to sing her finale.

charisma (kuh RIZ muh) *n.* ability to attract followers

Danielle's personal *charisma* and charm made her the perfect class president.

The con man had a *charisma* that helped him bilk hundreds of people of their life's savings.

charlatan (SHAR luh tun) *n.* quack; fraud

The *charlatan* sold an elixir guaranteed to give anyone eternal life for just $19.95.

Today there are many *charlatan* diet products offered on TV. (*adj.*)

chary (CHAR ee) *adj.* vigilant, careful, cautious, wary

Dave was *chary* of investing in computer chip companies.

Phillip was *chary* about donating to charities after he found out his last donation went to a charlatan organization.

chasm (KAZ um) *n.* a deep opening; a gorge

Chasms in the ice were formed by the slow moving glacier.

A rope bridge stretched across the *chasm*.

chaste (chayst) *adj.* morally pure; without obscenity

The main character in the romantic novel lives a *chaste*, uneventful life and marries a rich banker.

(To be *chaste* is to be in a state of chastity.) Jo Ann became a nun and lived a life of *chastity*.

chastise (chas TYZE) *v.* to discipline; punish

The teacher *chastised* the students for talking during the test.

Chastising our parrot never worked; he kept spitting seeds on the rug anytime he chose.

chateau (shat TOE) *n.* a French estate, manor, castle or large house in the country (chateaux – plural)

Marta and her family found a crumbling *chateau* in France where their grandfather had been born.

Many old *chateaux* in Europe are now historical museums.

chattel (chatel) *n.* an item of personal, movable property; slave

The bank held a *chattel* mortgage on all our office equipment, chairs, computers and even our electric clock.

Please do not order me around Lady Boswell, I am neither your servant nor your *chattel*.

check (chek) *n.* bring to a standstill, to stop to hold back, to block

Inflation must be held in *check* if the dollar is to have any value.

A system of *checks* and balances keeps any one of our three branches of government —legislative, judicial, executive—from dominating the other.

chemotherapy (kee mo THARE uh pee) *n.* use of chemical agents in the treatment of disease, esp. cancer

The *chemotherapy* prescribed by doctors is in proportion to the size and type of cancer to be destroyed.

She was aware of the side effects of *chemotherapy*, such as the temporary loss of her hair, but accepted the risk.

cherub (CHER ub) *n.* an angel represented in art as a beautiful, chubby child with small wings.

The wooden chest was overlaid with gold and painted with cute *cherubs*.

My niece is like a *cherub* as long as she gets what she wants.

chicanery (shi KAY nuh ree) *n.* deceitfulness; trickery

We suspected *chicanery* when six people held the same winning lottery ticket for the same car.

Halloween is a night when many children commit acts of *chicanery* if they are not given candy.

chide (chide) *v.* scold; reprove

Mom *chided* Glen for not cleaning his room.

When Bobby threw his toys against the wall, his father *chided* him for his bad temper.

chimerical (ki MAYR uh kul) *adj.* fanciful; imaginary; absurd

His hope for straight A's proved to be *chimerical* at best because he was a straight D student.

Lou had some *chimerical* scheme to make diamonds by crushing soda bottles.

chintzy (CHINT see) *adj.* gaudy; cheap; tacky

The hat looked *chintzy* but received the same admiration from prospective buyers as the expensive one.

Bob was so *chintzy* he tipped waiters with wooden nickels.

chloroform (KLORE uh form) *n.* colorless, volatile, toxic liquid that produces anesthesia

The rags soaked with *chloroform* burst into flames and started the fire.

The doctor used *chloroform* on the dog, putting him to sleep in preparation for surgery.

choleric (kahl UR ik) *adj.* hot-tempered; quick to anger

When my dad gets in one of his *choleric* moods, everyone stays clear.

When guests come, the neighbor's *choleric* dog is kept chained to the tree.

chord (kord) *n.* three or four musical notes played together

The notes E, G sharp and B comprise a *chord*.

The teacher instructed the student to play major and minor *chords* on the piano.

chortle (COR tul) *v.* to express with a snorting chuckle; to laugh with pleasure and glee

Every time my brother beats me in a game, he *chortles* in a most irritating way.

The children *chortled* under the covers, and their mom knew they would not soon fall asleep.

chronic (KRAHN ik) *adj.* continuing for a long time; continuous

When lower back pain becomes *chronic*, it's time to see a doctor.

Her *chronic* gossiping led to her being kicked out of the Garden Club.

chronicle (KRAHN uh kul) *n.* a history; record of events

Our literature book has a *chronicle* of each period of American literature.

My sister is the historian of our family; she has a *chronicle* of all the important events of our youth.

chronology (krah NOL uh gee) *n.* an order of events from the earliest to the latest

Though sketchy, geology can give clues of Earth's *chronology*.

Josephine put the biographies of famous Americans in *chronological* order. (*adj.*)

churl (churl) *n.* a rude or vulgar person; a crude or illiterate peasant or yokel

Jim is such a *churl*, always rude, drunk and insensitive.

(To be a *churl* is to be *churlish*.) Rex's *churlish* behavior at the wedding made him unwelcome. His *churlishness* offended the bride and groom.

chutzpah (HUT spuh) *n.* brazen, audacious behavior that is sometimes admired but often rude

Herb had a lot of *chutzpah* for attending his ex-wife's wedding and kissing the bride.

Put a little *chutzpah* into your efforts, and act as if you know what you are doing!

cinematic (sin uh MAT ik) *adj.* related to making motion pictures

A new *cinematic* presentation of the old Zorro film series was well received by the public.

The present *cinematic* trend of violence in films disturbs many parents and teachers.

cipher (SYE fer) *n.* a zero; a thing that has no value; a code; the solution to a code

Phil was not surprised at the *cipher* he earned on his math test.

The secret message was written in *cipher.*

circa (SUR ka) *adv.* about; at an estimated historical time period

The exact date of the first Egyptian dynasty is not known, but it is believed to have occurred *circa* 3000 B.C.

Circa is another word for "about" or "more or less," and it always refers to an estimate time period or date.

circuitous (sur KYOO uh tus) *adj.* not following a direct path; round-about

The road leading to the castle was a *circuitous* one, steep with many twists and turns.

On our vacation, we love to take the *circuitous* route to our grand-mother's so we can visit the historical sites en route.

circumlocution (sur kum loh KYOO shun) *n.* indirect speech; talking around the facts

Politicians are notorious for *circumlocution,* talking much but saying little.

The driver's *circumlocution* concerning why his driver's license was out of date did not amuse the police officer.

circumnavigate (sur kum NAV uh gayt) *v.* to travel all the way around

Magellan was the Portuguese navigator who first *circumnavigated* the Cape of Good Hope in 1520.

Randolph carried the punch bowl across the crowded room, safely *circumnavigating* obstacles along the way.

circumscribe (SUR kum skrybe) *v.* to set the limits; to restrict

The prison walls *circumscribed* the territory in which the convicts were allowed to move.

The baby's limits were *circumscribed* by his playpen.

circumspect (SUR kum spekt) *adj.* cautious; heedful of situations and potential consequences

In his usual *circumspect* manner, Frank first insured himself against all losses before placing a bet.

Pat's five-year-old *circumspectly* looks both ways before crossing the street. (*adv.*)

circumvent (sur kum VENT) *v.* to surround; enclose; bypass

The taxi driver *circumvented* the evening rush traffic by taking a short-cut through the park.

The general *circumvented* the enemy forces by sending a battalion to their rear.

citadel (SIT uh dul) *n.* a fortress overlooking a city; a stronghold

Charlie was a *citadel* of strength, always there for his friends no matter what.

There are many ancient *citadels* in Spain; they are among the attractions most visited by tourists.

cite (site) *v.* quote by way example, call to attention

Joe's attorney *cited* DNA evidence to prove his client was not the guilty party.

The chairman *cited* a specific parliamentary procedure that would enable him to have the security guards toss out unruly members.

civil (SIV ul) *adj.* courteous; polite; civilized

Uncle Frank tries to be *civil* during family functions, but he always seems to upset someone.

Although the couple had a most unpleasant divorce, they were *civil* to each other for the sake of the children.

claimant (KLAY ment) *n.* a person making a claim

The judge awarded all six of the *claimants* an equal share of the insurance money.

Rosalie not only wanted the house in her divorce, but she also was the *claimant* for her husband's birdcage collection.

clairvoyant (klayr VOY unt) *adj.* having the ability to foresee things; having exceptional insight

Some psychics claim they are *clairvoyant* and can communicate with the dead.

Louise's mother seemed to be *clairvoyant* because she always knew when her daughter wasn't telling the truth.

clamor (KLAM er) *n.* uproar

The *clamor* of the street traffic gave Josh a headache.

The sailors *clamored* for shore-leave while their ship was in Honolulu. (*v.*)

clandestine (klan DES tin) *adj.* planned or occurring in a secret manner, especially for subversive or illicit purposes; done in secret

The three inmates held a *clandestine* meeting to discuss their prison break-out plans.

Jimmy and Sue had to meet *clandestinely* after school because they knew her parents didn't approve of their relationship. (*adv.*)

claque (KLAK) *n.* a group hired to applaud at an performance; anyone who bestows approval motivated by self-interest

The TV producer hired a *claque* to applaud when cue cards gave them the signal.

It is not illegal to hire a *claque* to vote for a political candidate.

clarify (KLAR uh fy) *v.* to make clear, refine, elucidate

The patient asked the doctor to *clarify* his statement: "Whoopie, your ailment is going to make medical history!"

Joe's explanation about the crazy taxi ride *clarified* the mystery of why he missed his own wedding.

cleave (kleev) v. to adhere to; fasten tightly; split or divide

The climbing ivy vines *cleaved* to the ancient castle walls.

Rosie *cleaved* to the belief in her innocence even after forty years in prison.

clemency (KLEM un see) *n.* forgiveness; mercy

The president granted *clemency* to those who had run off to Canada as a protest against the Vietnam War.

The condemned man appealed to the governor for *clemency* for his horrific crime.

cliché (klee SHAY) *n.* an overused expression or idea; a commonplace

Fiction writers try to avoid *clichés* in order to keep their writing fresh and interesting.

Typical *clichés* one hears are "Have a nice day" and "An apple a day keeps the doctor away."

climactic (kleye MAK tik) *adj.* pertaining to the highest or most intense point

The *climactic* ending of the movie *Jaws* was when the shark was about to eat the hero.

The stadium was silent during the *climactic* point of the tennis match.

clinch (klinch) *v.* to make final; to settle; embrace

The Yankees *clinched* the World Series in four games against the Phillies.

Tom's offer to trade his favorite hog for Farmer Brown's bull *clinched* the deal.

clique (klik) *n.* a group bound together by a common interest

In the fall, the *clique* of players on the football team stick together as though they think they are some kind of special gift to mankind.

The women formed a writer's *clique* and each week gathered to discuss their writing.

cloister (KLOY stur) *n.* a covered walk; a tranquil, secluded place

To escape from the rain we ran to the *cloister* which led up to the building.

Seeking relaxation, Jim *cloistered* himself in his hotel room for the entire week of his vacation. (*v.*)

clone (klohn) *n.* a person or thing very much like another

John looks so much like his father he could be a *clone*.

McDonalds restaurants are *clones* of each other; they are exactly alike.

clout (klowt) *n.* power and influence over other people or events; a powerful blow or stroke

Kevin has *clout* with his teacher because his father is the principal of the school.

When John called Jim a name, Jim gave John a back-handed *clout* that bloodied his nose.

cloy (kloy) *v.* to become weary with an excess of something

A diet of ice cream and cake soon begins to *cloy* on the taste buds.

The new secretary became *cloying,* and her boss soon tired of her. (*adj.*)

coagulate (ko AG yoo late) *v.* to cause to become thickened, to form a solid mass

The doctor gave the patient a blood thinner to prevent his blood from *coagulating.*

After the rainy season, the *coagulation* of the muddy ditch into solid ground made it possible for vehicle traffic to pass once again. (*n.*)

coalesce (koh uh LES) *v.* to grow together; to unite; to fuse

The two lakes *coalesced* into one large lake.

The rhythm of the violins and the cello *coalesce* into a soothing sound.

coddle (KAHD ul) *v.* to overprotect someone or something; to pamper

The mother *coddled* her child as if the baby were a precious and fragile jewel.

The warden said he didn't support *coddling* criminals because doing so was not constructive for either the prisoner or society in general.

codger (KOD jur) *n.* a mildly eccentric and usually elderly man

Mr. Girard was an old *codger* who was always eavesdropping on our private conversations.

On the golf course, the young boys had to play through the old *codgers* who were playing very slowly.

coerce (koh URS) *v.* to force someone by threatening or physically overpowering him

The burglar claimed his confession was *coerced* by police brutality.

Elizabeth told her mother that her sister *coerced* her to take another cookie from the jar.

cogent (KOH junt) *adj.* very convincing

Matthew made a *cogent* argument about the benefits of wearing a helmet when biking.

The attorney's last piece of evidence was the most *cogent* one presented during the trial.

cogitate (KAHJ uh tayt) *v.* to think very carefully; to give careful consideration to

Barry said he was *cogitating* about the meaning of life, but we all knew he had really been asleep.

The scientist told his associates he would *cogitate* on the problem over the weekend.

cognitive (KAHG nu tiv) *adj.* dealing with our senses; cognition is knowing

Ben's poetry makes wonderful use of *cognitive* imagery.

The *cognitive* apparatus of older people is often not what is was when they were young.

cognizant (KAWG nu zunt) *adj.* conscious; aware

The patient did not appear to be *cognizant* because he would not respond to any stimuli.

Roger was *cognizant* of the dangers of sky-diving, but he was determined to give it a try anyway.

coherent (koh HEER unt) *adj.* making sense; holding together

The man the police pulled over for careless driving was surprisingly *coherent*.

Leslie gave a *coherent* and interesting explanation of the computer problem.

cohort (KOH hawrt) *n.* a friend or associate

Members of the 60s rock group *The Beatles* had all been *cohorts* before becoming famous.

The neighborhood bully and his many *cohorts* were always teasing and picking on the other children at the playground.

coiffure (kwa FYOOR) *n.* a hairdo; arrangement of hair

In the 18th century prior to the French Revolution, French royalty wore elegant *coiffures*.

Joan wanted her new *coiffure* to be exactly like that of her favorite movie star.

collate (KOE late) *v.* to assemble in proper order; to combine printed sheets to assemble in proper order

They have a copy machine that *collates* all the documents numerically after they are printed.

The attorney asked her secretary to *collate* the pages before leaving for the day.

collateral (kuh LAT uh rul) *n.* security offered for payment of a debt

The bank loaned Jim Morris $20,000 in cash, but he had to put up his house as *collateral* in case he didn't pay the loan back.

Harvey put up his Super Bowl ring as *collateral* for a $1,000 loan from a loan company.

colloquial (kul OH kwee ul) *n.* informality of language; street language

A sample *colloquial* expression commonly used is, "What's up, man." another is "cool."

The *colloquial* expressions are the hardest to learn when studying a foreign language because they don't always make sense to a non-native speaker.

collusion (kuh LOO zhun) *n.* a secret agreement; conspiracy

The owner of the New England Patriots accused the other team owner of *collusion*, forcing that owner to sell his ownership.

There was *collusion* among the office workers who secretly agreed not to join the union.

combustible (kum BUS tih bul) *adj.* capable of burning; easy to excite

Gasoline vapor is highly *combustible*.

The sign read, "Trucks carrying *combustibles* are not allowed to use this tunnel." (*n.*)

comity (KOM ih tee) *n.* social harmony, mutual courtesy

A period of national *comity* was experienced after the new president was elected.

The politician requested patience and *comity* from the crowd so the candidates could address the issues.

commemorate (kuh MEM uh rayt) *v.* to honor a memory in a special way; to serve as a reminder of or memorial to

The ceremony served to *commemorate* the 20th anniversary of the end of the Vietnam War.

The United States Postal Service printed a new stamp *commemorating* the U.S. Constitution.

commensurate (kuh MEN sur it) *adj.* proportionate; equal

In most companies pay is *commensurate* with experience.

Before the 1960s, pay for men and women was not *commensurate*.

commiserate (kuh MIZ uh rayt) *v.* to feel or express sympathy for someone's suffering or unhappiness

All the team members came to the funeral parlor to *commiserate* with John over his father's death.

Betty called Pete to *commiserate* over the closing of his factory and the loss of his job.

commodious (kuh MOD dee us) *adj.* spacious, roomy, capacious

The new airline seats, even in economy class, are much more *commodious* than before.

In Hong Kong, the government-built apartments are not very *commodious*, only about half the size of a small, two-bedroom apartment in the United States.

commodity (kuh MOD uh tee) *n.* a thing, something bought and sold

Wheat is a valuable *commodity* on the world-wide market.

A good reputation is a valuable *commodity* for everyone to have.

compassion (kum PASH un) *n.* the deep sorrow for the suffering of another along with an urge to help; pity

Even though we did not know the deceased, we attended the viewing to show our *compassion* for the family.

My friend sent a little gift to show her *compassion* when I was not chosen for the part.

compatible (kum PAT uh bul) *adj.* able to function in harmony with others

Joan and Cindy are *compatible*; they both like movies and boys, and boys and movies.

John's sister is not *compatible* with any members of her family since

Commoner a common person,

she became a famous New York model.

compelling (kum PEL ing) *adj.* forceful; urgently needing attention

The minister gave a *compelling* sermon about the importance of global brotherhood.

A *compelling* argument not to drive and drink can be found in the alarming national statistics on drunk driving accidents.

compendium (kum PEN dee um) *n.* a concise summary

The *compendium* on the back of the novel compelled Davis to want to read the book.

A *compendium* of books written by Ernest Hemingway can be found in most libraries.

compensate (KOM pun sayt) *v.* pay to in return for services rendered; offset; be equivalent to

The attorney offered his services pro-bono, asking no fiscal *compensation* for his work. (*n.*)

Jack *compensated* for his big ears with sharp wit and great personal charm.

competent (KAHM puh tunt) *adj.* having the skills or knowledge to do something well enough to meet a basic standard; qualified; capable

Jo Ann is not a genius, but she has proven to be *competent* managing the shop.

I don't think that Sondra will be a *competent* computer programmer because she can't type or spell and has no ambition.

compile (kum PYLE) *v.* to collect from a variety of sources and arrange together

Buster is *compiling* facts and figures as the basis for an article on the present Russian economy.

Mr. Moody *compiled* all the financial figures asked for by the tax inspector.

complacent (kum PLAY sunt) *adj.* self-satisfied; overly pleased with oneself

The *complacent* soldier failed to dig a foxhole, so when the bombing started this oversight resulted in his becoming a *complacent* dead soldier.

The *complacent* young girl never seemed to get a second date because all she would talk about was herself.

complaisant (kum PLAY zunt) *adj*. cordial, amenable, eager to please

The host's *complaisant* manner made everyone feel welcome.

Jeff was too *complaisant* about customer returns without a receipt.

complement (KAHM pluh munt) *v*. to complete; be the perfect counterpart

The dessert was a wonderful *complement* to the delicious dinner.

Jim and Sue are the perfect couple because they *complement* each other so well.

compliant (kum PLY unt) *adj*. willingness to adhere, acting in accordance

The company was *compliant* with the state agency's directives.

It is necessary to be *compliant* with the state traffic laws for your own safety.

complicity (kum PLIS uh tee) *n*. sharing in wrongdoing

The *complicity* of the two students on the test caused them both to fail.

Henry finally admitted his *complicity* in the senior prank.

compliment (KOM pluh munt) *n./v*. an admiring remark or the act of congratulating someone

Upon receiving the *compliment*, the young girl blushed and smiled.

George, the waiter, *complimented* Joan on her fluency in French.

comply (kum PLY) *v*. to obey an order, rule, or request; to act in agreement with a wish, or requirement

Mr. Morris has to *comply* with the judge's order to pay fifty dollars each week, or he could go to jail.

If my son would *comply* with one of my rules each day, I would consider myself blessed!

component (kum POH nunt) *n*. a part of; an element or ingredient

Water is the greatest *component* in human blood.

One *component* of getting into an Ivy League school is getting straight A's throughout high school.

composed (kum POHZD) *adj.* in a calm and collected state; serene; controlled; tranquil

She finally stopped crying and *composed* herself. (*v.*)

Because he had studied well, he was *composed* when the teacher handed out the test.

composure (kum POH zhur) *n.* the state of being calm and not emotional; self-possession; serenity

You may feel nervous, but don't lose your *composure* in front of the camera.

I was terrified during the storm, but I managed to keep my *composure* for my kids' sake.

compote (KAHM poat) *n.* dessert of fruit cooked in syrup, also the dish in which it is served

For dessert the hostess prepared a most unusual *compote* of tropical fruit.

The *compote* broke, spilling the variety of melons on the floor.

compound (kum POUND) *v.* to mix or combine so as to make a whole

He used the mixer to *compound* the cement.

Charlie chose not to date because he did not want to *compound* his problems.

comprehensive (kahm pruh HEN siv) *adj.* including everything

It is impossible to do a *comprehensive* study of American literature in just one semester.

Zachary's knowledge of the presidents was *comprehensive*; he could recite them in order without missing one.

comprise (kum PRYZE) *v.* to consist of; to include, to contain, to be made up of

A basketball team is *comprised* of five players and any number of substitutes.

The first aid kit was *comprised* of a bottle of aspirin, two gauze pads, and a pair of scissors.

compromise (KAHM pruh myze) *n.* a settlement of differences in which each side makes concessions

It is hoped that a *compromise* will be reached at today's meeting between the labor union and the company's administration.

My vote on this issue was a *compromise* of my principles, but I am satisfied with my decision.

compunction (kum PUNK shun) *n.* a slight feeling of guilt for something one has done; remorse

I don't have any *compunction* about telling my roommate to leave because he hasn't upheld his half of the responsibilities.

Robin Hood had no *compunction* about stealing because he felt that the wealthy could afford to give up some of their riches for the less fortunate.

concave (kahn KAYV) *adj.* curved inward like the interior of a sphere

You've lost so much weight that your stomach is almost *concave*!

It was obvious that my cake "fell" when I saw the *concave* shape of the top of it!

concede (kun SEED) *v.* to admit, often unwillingly, that something is true; to yield, as in a game or contest

With two players injured and three others removed from the game, the football team *conceded* defeat.

The government has *conceded* that the new tax policy has been a disaster, as we all had predicted.

concentric (kun SEN trik) *adj.* of circles or spheres having the same center

All of the rings around the bull's eye on a dart board are *concentric*.

All the coils of the spring are *concentric*.

concert (KAHN surt) *n.* a shared purpose; togetherness or cooperation; agreement

We must both act in *concert* to be successful.

The speaker said that the richer countries of the world should work in *concert* to help the poorer ones.

conciliatory (kun SIL ee uh tor ee) *adj.* making peace

The feuding family became *conciliatory* after the death of their grand-father.

The *conciliatory* handshake was a symbol that the opponents would try to get along.

concise (kun SYSE) *adj*. brief and to the point

When writing e-mail, it is best to be *concise*.

The doctor was *concise* when he reviewed the extent of his patient's injuries.

conclave (KON klave) *n*. gathering of a group, secret assembly

The *conclave* held its annual get-together for both business and vacation in Hawaii.

The political parties hold a *conclave* every four years for choosing a president.

concoct (kun KAHKT) *v*. to make by adding several different parts together; invent; contrive

He could *concoct* the most amazing dishes from all sorts of unlikely ingredients.

At the last minute, she *concocted* an unbelievable excuse for her absence.

concomitant (kun KAHM uh tunt) *adj*. accompanying; happening together and connected with; going along with

Old age and the *concomitant* loss of memory are part of a natural pro-gression.

The banana splits and the *concomitant* weight gain sent Mary into a tizzy when she couldn't fit into her new prom dress.

concord (KAHN kord) *n*. agreement; harmony

The uprising ended twelve years of *concord* in that country.

Recess is not always a time of *concord* because some kids are usually running around and yelling.

concur (kun KER) *v*. to coincide; to act together; cooperate

When my parents *concur*, I know I have to watch my step.

The second doctor *concurred* with the first, so I had my tonsils re-moved.

concurrent (kun KUR unt) *adj.* parallel; happening at the same time

Ryan's participation in three *concurrent* sports finally wore him out.

The criminal was given ten *concurrent* life sentences for his heinous crime.

condensed (kun DENSED) *adj.* shortened, reduced, compact

Campbell's makes many popular *condensed* soups.

To save time, Charlie read a *condensed* version of *Great Expectations.*

condescend (KAHN duh send) *v.* patronize; to lower oneself

The sorority's *condescending* attitude made me decide not to join. (*adj.*)

The teachers were all surprised when the superintendent *condescended* to talk to their representative.

condone (kun DOHN) *v.* to allow to happen; to purposely overlook

The kids loved their baby-sitter because she *condoned* behavior that their parents would never permit.

Although the school has a dress code, the dean *condones* many outlandish outfits.

conducive (kun DOO siv) *adj.* promoting; contributing

Strong study habits are *conducive* to good grades.

My mattress is always *conducive* to a good night's sleep.

confederate (kun FED ur ut) *n.* an accomplice; an ally

With the aid of my *confederates*, I will win this war.

The bully vandalized the entire neighborhood in one night with the help of his *confederates.*

confer (kun FER) *v.* to give, grant, or bestow

I should like some time to *confer* with my lawyer before I sign the contract.

The honor was *conferred* upon him for his bravery on the battlefield.

confidant (KAHN fu dahnt) *n.* a person with whom one can share feelings and secrets (female – confidante)

My best friend is my closest *confidante* because I can trust her not to tell my secrets.

Everyone should have a *confidant* because there always comes a time when one needs to be able to talk privately to someone he or she can trust.

configuration (kun fig yuh RAY shun) *n.* a particular arrangement or pattern of a group of related things

The *configuration* of the theater seating was such that everyone had a perfectly clear view of the entire screen and could clearly hear what was being said.

By *configuring* some of the wires on my motherboard, my son will be able to boost up the speed of my processing unit. (*v.*)

confiscate (KON fi skayt) *v.* to take or seize by authority, usually as punishment or penalty

The police raided the suspect's apartment and *confiscated* all his illegal drugs.

Ms. Henderson *confiscates* and reads every note she sees passed during her class.

conflagration (kahn fluh GRAY shun) *n.* a large destructive fire

New Mexico recently suffered a major *conflagration* that destroyed hundreds of homes and thousands of acres of land.

They say that a cow named Elsie was responsible for the *conflagration* that occurred in Chicago in the early 1900s.

confluence (KAHN floo uns) *n.* flowing together; place where rivers begin to flow together

The *confluence* of the instruments in Mozart's work is what makes it melodious.

The *confluence* of the two rivers forms the fertile valley.

conform (kun FORM) *v.* to bring into harmony; to make the same

Wearing uniforms to school is *conforming* to the system's policy.

Because of her magenta hair and various body piercings, she did not *conform* to the club's ideals.

confound (kun FOUND) *v.* to confuse and surprise; to perplex or bewilder; to amaze

The sudden drop in stock prices *confounded* my stock broker's predictions and left him paralyzed with amazement.

The athlete *confounded* his doctors when he won the gold medal in track after they said he would never walk again.

confraternity (kahn fruh TURN ih tee) *n.* a fraternal union; brotherhood

Commercial Travelers Union is a well known *confraternity* offering services to those who paid to belong.

The Kiwanis is a famous *confraternity* promoting good will in the community.

confront (kun FRUNT) *v.* to bring face to face; encounter

It was our plan to *confront* the other team with a show of strength.

My teacher doesn't usually *confront* students, but Justin gave her no choice.

congeal (kun JEEL) *v.* to change from a liquid or soft state to a thick or solid state; to coagulate; to jell

The blood will *congeal* and form a clot shortly after it is exposed to air.

According to the directions, it takes about three hours for the Jello to *congeal* before it is ready to serve.

congenial (kun JEAN ee ul) *adj.* pleasant to be around; social; agreeable

Miss Texas was voted Miss *Congeniality* in the Miss America pageant.

The atmosphere at the property appraiser's office is *congenial*; everyone enjoys his job, and visitors are welcome at any time.

congenital (kun JEN uh tul) *adj.* hereditary

Because the defect was *congenital*, the doctors anticipated it and treated it immediately.

All of my sisters have blue eyes, is a *congenital* trait.

congruent (kun GROO unt) *adj.* equivalent, compatible, of the same shape

Gerry learned about *congruent* triangles in geometry.

After making a duplicate, I had a *congruent* key to my house.

conjecture (kun JEK chur) *v.* to guess; figure out with little evidence

Although the theory was purely *conjecture*, Greg fooled us into believing it was fact. (*n.*)

Many times, the weathermen *conjecture* their forecasts.

conjoin (kun JOYN) *v.* to join or act together

The United Way is an organization consisting of smaller charities who *conjoin* to raise funds.

In Florida the Unemployment Department *conjoined* with the Department of Labor.

conjugal (KAHN juh gul) *adj.* connected with marriage or the relationship between husband and wife

Some prisons allow the inmates to have *conjugal* visits with their spouses, especially if the inmates are incarcerated for a long time.

Mr. and Mrs. Smith just celebrated fifty years of *conjugal* bliss.

conjure (KAHN jur) *v.* to call forth using magic

The witches of the coven tried to *conjure* the devil.

I don't know how Doug was able to *conjure* up such a good research paper in just one night.

connive (kuh NYVE) *v.* to join secretly in a plot; conspire; to support a wrongdoing by ignoring or failing to report it

My kids are always *conniving* with each other, so I never feel I can trust them.

Renee *connived* in cheating her classmates but was angry when they got a much higher grade than she.

connoisseur (kahn uh SUR) *n.* an expert, particularly in matters of art and taste

My uncle is a *connoisseur* of fine wines.

Art dealer Jorge Guizar is a *connoisseur* of Mexican art of the 19th century.

connote (kuh NOTE) *v.* to convey, to imply, exact explicit meaning

Many companies use logos to *connote* their names.

The title "Doctor" does not always *connote* a medical degree.

connubial (kah NOO bee ul) *adj.* relating to marriage or the state of being married

Every society has its own ceremony for celebrating the *connubial* rite of passage.

After twenty years of marriage, they were still in a state of *connubial* bliss.

conscript (kun SKRIPT) *v.* to register, enlist, draft, induct, recruit

The armed forces did not *conscript* farmers until the war was nearly over.

All *conscripts* were ordered to report to the town square. (*n.*)

consecrate (KAHN suh krayt) *v.* to make or declare sacred

The Puritans believed that God had led them to *consecrated* ground. (*adj.*)

Many items in the Vatican have been *consecrated* by the Pope.

consensus (kun SEN sus) *n.* general agreement

The bill to legalize nude beaches failed to pass *consensus*.

A *consensus* is more than a majority; it means most everyone agrees.

conservatory (kun SER vuh tawr ee) *n.* a school for the teaching of music, acting, or art; a room, usually connected to a house, in which plants are grown and kept; a greenhouse

My sister wanted to learn to play the piano professionally, so Mom and Dad saved enough money to send her to a well known *conservatory* in New York.

The university's agricultural department boasts a wonderful *conservatory*, filled with more exotic and beautiful plants than any other in the country.

consign (kun SYNE) *v.* to deliver, transfer, entrust or give up

Uncle Jed's massive estate was *consigned* to my brother for dispersement according to his will.

They *consigned* the abandoned child to a foster home while they searched for her parents.

consolidate (kun SAHL uh dayt) *v.* to join together to become more effective; to become stronger; to combine into a whole; unify

The two firms *consolidated* to form a single, stronger company.

The recent success of their major product has *consolidated* the firm's position in this market.

consonant (KAHN suh nunt) *adj.* in agreement; harmonious

The marching band was *consonant*, playing a lovely rendition of "The Star Spangled Banner."

When Jack learned that his idea about marriage was *consonant* with Diane's, he proposed.

conspicuous (kun SPIK yoo us) *adj.* very noticeable; tending to attract attention; easily seen; prominent

In Mexico, where almost everyone has black hair, Debbie's blonde hair was *conspicuous*.

He was *conspicuous* by his absence, particularly since the party was in his honor.

conspiracy (kun SPEER uh see) *n.* a secret agreement, plot

The two men formed a *conspiracy* to take control of the company at the meeting.

The French Revolution was a *conspiracy* to overthrow the ruling royalty.

consternation (kahn stur NAY shun) *n.* a feeling of anxiety, shock or confusion; a state of dismay

There was general *consternation* as the crowd learned the terrifying news of the terrorist bombing.

To his *consternation*, as he started to board his plane he realized his passport was at home.

constituency (kun STICH oo un see) *n.* the body of voters from a district represented by an elected official; a group of supporters for anything

The politicians from the Kennedy family have a large *constituency* of Irish American citizens in New England.

The candidate and his *constituency* comprised of mostly women fought hard for women's rights.

construe (kun STROO) *v.* to interpret

Mona went to a psychologist to see if he could *construe* her nightmares.

The seniors *construed* the school rules as not pertaining to them.

consummate (KON sum it) *adj.* perfectly skillful, (KON sum ayt) *v.* to complete or perfect

David Copperfield is the *consummate* magician.

After finally getting the buyer and sell to sign the contract Chuck was happy to *consummate* the deal.

contempt (kum TEMPT) *n.* a strong feeling of combined dislike and lack of respect; scorn

The socialite made no attempt to conceal her *contempt* for anyone who was of lower social status than she was.

The judge had him removed and held him in *contempt* of the court because he deliberately and with malice disrupted the proceedings.

contemptuous (kun TEMP choo us) *adj.* feeling contempt; disdainful; scornful

Nancy is so *contemptuous* of the family that she sent each member a spiteful note.

Sometimes the child who is given the most by his parents turns out to be the most *contemptuous* adult.

contentious (kun TEN shus) *adj.* argumentative; quarrelsome

Curly is the most *contentious* character in *Of Mice and Men*; he is always trying to pick a fight.

Holly's stepfather is the most *contentious* man I've ever met; it is no wonder the kids try to stay out of his way.

contiguous (kun TIG yoo us) *adj.* adjoining; side by side

Our property is *contiguous* to our neighbor's.

The umpire did not see both outs because they were *contiguous*.

contingent (kun TIN junt) *adj.* dependent upon

Ellen said that going out on Saturday night was *contingent* upon her having a date.

The mother told the children that ordering dessert was *contingent* upon their cleaning their plates.

continuum (kun TIN yoo um) *n.* a continuous whole without clear division into parts

At the carnival, a *continuum* of weaving dancers moved in a seemingly endless chain.

Albert Einstein believed that space and time are not distinct dimensions, but a *continuum*, a belief which he called the Theory of Relativity.

contort (kun TORT) *v.* to twist or bend out of shape

The acrobats were able to *contort* their bodies in unbelievable ways.

Sally just began ballet, so she cannot yet *contort* herself like those who have been taking lessons for years.

contraband (KAHN truh band) *n.* goods smuggled into or out of a place where they are illegal; goods banned by law from being imported or exported

When going through customs at the border, Lucy was found to be carrying thousands of pounds worth of *contraband* and was immediately arrested.

The police had confiscated *contraband* from the criminals.

contravention (kon truh VEN shun) *n.* contrary, opposition of

David's report without documentation was a *contravention* to company policy.

The student rebellion appeared to be a *contravention* of school rules.

contretemps (KAHN truh tanh) *n.* an unlucky event, often happening in public and causing social embarrassment

We had a slight *contretemps* at the theater because someone tried to push in front of us and Richard got angry.

A silly *contretemps* at the party nearly destroyed their friendship, but they eventually kissed and made up.

contrite (kun TRITE) *adj.* grieving and expressing remorse, feeling sorrow for sins or faults; penitent for short comings; apologetic

Harry's *contrite* appeal to the group was accepted, and he was forgiven.

Mary's *contrite* message to her parents helped to alleviate their differences.

103

contrived (kun TRYVED) *adj.* false; artificial; not spontaneous; obviously planned

Everyone except her father could tell that Sally's tears were *contrived*.

Although it became a popular song, it seemed *contrived* to me.

controversial (kahn tra VUR shul or kahn tra VUR see ul) *adj.* debatable between opposing sides

The idea that their son could ever do anything wrong is a very *controversial* subject in that family.

To write a persuasive paper the topic must be *controversial*, or the paper will have no purpose.

controvert (KON truh vert) *v.* to dispute, oppose by reasoning, refute

The adolescent's desire to leave school was *controverted* by employment requirements.

The FDA *controverted* the use of the drug due to negative laboratory tests.

contumely (kun TOO muh lee) *adv.* contemptuous rudeness; arrogance; an insulting act or comment

The rude child *contumely* told his parents to shut up.

Phil *contumely* took his roommate's belongings and used them without asking first.

conundrum (kuh NUN drum) *n.* a dilemma; any problem or puzzle

In most mystery novels, the *conundrum* is solved by the novel's end.

During the long drive, Jean invented entertaining *conundrums* to help keep Jeff awake.

convene (kun VEEN) *v.* to gather together; to assemble, especially for a formal meeting

The council members will *convene* on the morning of July 25th.

A convention is a meeting of members of a group who *convene* to discuss events and exchange ideas.

conventional (kun VEN shun nul) *adj.* ordinary; common

Martha's writing is *conventional*; she will not win an award for creativity.

convent a community of persons devoted to religious life under a superior

104

My grandmother is full of *conventional* wisdom.

converge (kun VERJ) *v.* meet, focus, come together

The Mississippi and Missouri Rivers *converge* at St. Louis, Missouri.

Jeff looked through the lens and saw the light rays *converge*.

converse (KAHN vurs) *n.* opposite; reverse

I always seem to have the *converse* opinion of my parents.

She always takes the *converse* position from mine, so we constantly argue. (*adj.*)

convex (kon VEX) *adj.* curved or rounded like an exterior sphere or circle

The camera's close-up lens created the effect of a *convex* surface.

Looking into the *convex* mirror, the child laughed at his distorted appearance.

convey (kun VAY) *v.* to take or carry someone or something to a particular place; to communicate; express

The exported goods are usually *conveyed* by sea from one country to the other.

He put his finger to his lips to *convey* the idea that I shouldn't say anything.

conviction (kun VIK shun) *n.* a determined belief or fixed opinion; the process or act of finding a person guilty of a crime

It was my father's personal *conviction* that all murderers should be given the death penalty.

Ever since Chris's first *conviction* for burglary 10 years ago, he has been in jail more than he has been out.

convivial (kun VIV ee ul) *adj.* sociable

The food, drink, and conversation were extraordinary, making the evening a *convivial* occasion.

Jim is extremely *convivial* and has never turned down an invitation to a party.

convolution (kahn vuh LOO shun) *n.* a complexity of coils, twists, and folds

The movie is good, but the plot has so many *convolutions* that you really have to concentrate.

The small child tried to work out exactly how many snakes were hidden among the endless *convolutions* in the pattern.

copious (KOH pee us) *adj.* abundant; plentiful

Farmer Brown was overjoyed with his *copious* crop of tomatoes.

David gave *copious* reasons to explain why he should be allowed to stay home from school.

cordial (KOR jul) *adj.* friendly; welcoming; warm and gracious; courteous

Relations between the two leaders are said to be *cordial*, hopefully allowing them to reach an amicable solution.

I try to have a *cordial* relationship with my ex-husband, but when I hear his voice on the phone, my blood boils!

cornucopia (kor nyoo KOH pee uh) *n.* bounty, plenty, affluence, an abundance

The term *"Cornucopia,"* or "horn of plenty," came from the horn of the goat Amalthaea.

There was a *cornucopia* of food on the buffet table.

corollary (KAWR uh ler ee) *n.* something that results from something else; a natural result or consequence

That child's poor behavior is just a *corollary* to the way his parents spoil him.

Employee satisfaction is a direct *corollary* to an increase in their wages.

corporal (KOR puh rul) *adj.* affecting or related to the body as in punishment

Corporal punishment was administered to the prisoner.

The *corporal* treatment of slaves was depicted in the movie "Roots."

corporeal (kawr PAWR ee ul) *adj.* physical and not spiritual; tangible; material; palpable; having substance

His *corporeal* possessions were many, but his spiritual beliefs meant more to him.

I believe in having dreams and fantasies, but it is the *corporeal* things like my job and my paycheck that keep me going!

corpulent (KOR pew lent) *adj.* fat; obese

England's King Henry VIII was known for his *corpulent* build.

"*Corpulent*" is a euphemism for "fat."

correlation (kawr uh LAY shun) *n.* a connection between two or more things

There's a high *correlation* between smoking and lung cancer.

There's little *correlation* between wealth and happiness, so they say, but ask me my opinion after I get rich.

corroborate (kuh ROB uh rayt) *v.* to support; confirm

I can usually rely on my sister to *corroborate* the stories I tell.

Because Dirk showed up after the accident, he could not *corroborate* Alicia's account of it.

corrosive (kuh ROH siv) *adj.* causing something to be destroyed, rusted, or eaten away over a period of time

This acid is highly *corrosive* and will eat away at anything it touches, so you must be careful with it.

A parent's *corrosive* belittling of a child can cause irreparable psychological damage when the child reaches adulthood.

corrugated (KAWR uh gay tud) *adj.* having parallel rows of folds which look like a series of waves; shaped or bent into ridges

Some potato chips are *corrugated* and look like ruffles.

The computer was packed in a *corrugated* cardboard box.

corrupt (kuh RUPT) *adj.* dishonest, unethical, unprincipled

The *corrupt* politicians must be thrown out of office.

Charley's *corrupt* friends led him astray by cheating the IRS.

cosmic (KOZ mik) *adj.* relating to the universe in contrast to Earth alone

Cosmic rays enter the earth's atmosphere from outer space at the speed of light.

Radio noise in the *cosmic* atmosphere originates beyond the Milky

Way.

cosmopolitan (kahz muh PAHL uh tun) *adj.* sophisticated; confident in many places or situations

The opening of the art exhibit attracted a *cosmopolitan* crowd.

Dave is *cosmopolitan*, feeling at home wherever he travels.

coterie (KOH tuh ree) *n.* a circle of close associates or friends

Today's tennis stars rarely travel alone but surround themselves with a *coterie* of managers and coaches.

Rock stars have a *coterie* of fans who follow them from concert to concert.

council (KOWN sul) *n.* an assembly or meeting for consultation, advice, or discussion

Aston's *council* meets once a month discussing future developments of the city.

Our local *council* listened to the community about changes in the tax code.

counsel (KOWN sel) *n.* advice given as a result of consultation; a lawyer or group of lawyers representing a client

George became the *counsel* to the city council for legal matters.

Henry obtained *counsel* to handle his case in court.

countenance (KOWNT uh nanz) *n.* a person's face, especially the expression; calm control; composure

The old farmer's *countenance* showed many years of hard work.

The captain's *countenance* during the attack gave his troops confidence in the face of danger.

countervail (kown tur VAIL) *v.* to counteract; to be useful or successful

Coach Jim *countervailed* the defense with two quarterbacks in the backfield.

The president *countervailed* the passing of a law by veto.

coup (koo) *n.* the violent overthrow of a government by a small group; a victorious accomplishment

In this century alone there have been almost one hundred military *coups* in Latin America.

It was a real *coup* for James when his teammates elected him captain of the basket-weaving team.

coup de grace (koo duh GRAHCE) *n.* a decisive finishing blow, act or event

General Patton's *coup de grace* in Sicily caused Germany's defeat and Britain's embarrassment.

Joe Louis's *coup de grace* against Max Baer resulted in his retaining the heavyweight boxing crown.

couplet (KUP lut) *n.* two successive lines of verse forming a unit in poetry

Many early American poems were written in *couplets*.

Browning and her contemporaries utilized *couplets* to communicate their feeling about love.

courier (KUUR ee ur) *n.* a messenger

Frederick works as a *courier* for United Parcel Service.

The spy acted as a *courier*, carrying secret information between the United States and Europe.

couture (KOO chur) *n.* fashion, esp. high fashion

Jane works for a department store chain, and they sent her to Paris to study the latest *couture*.

For three years Henry studied the art of *couture* in the finest French design institutions.

covenant (KUV uh nunt) *n.* sworn agreement; a pledge

The settlers made a *covenant* with the Indians that they would assist each other in time of need.

The boys signed a *covenant* that they would never break the rules of their club.

covert (KOH vert) *adj.* secret; hidden; concealed

Sam carried out *covert* missions for the CIA in China during the Korean War.

The *covert* military operation was never discovered by the press.

(*Overt* is the opposite of *covert*. *Overt* means open or unconcealed.)

covet (KUV it) *v.* to desire; envy

> One of the *Ten Commandments* is "Thou shalt not *covet* thy neighbor's wife."

> Bruce *coveted* Steven's family life and wished that he had a big brother.

cower (KOW ur) *v.* to crouch or cringe in fear; huddle in fear

> Oh, stop *cowering*! I'm not going to hit you.

> The puppy seemed to realize she'd done something wrong because she was *cowering* in the corner.

coy (koy) *adj* modest, demure, timid, shyly flirtatious

> Frank always gets *coy* when asked to recite in class.

> Judy's *coy* behavior made her attractive to many men.

crag (KRAG) *n.* a steep, rugged rock or cliff

> Mt. McKinley is full of *crags,* causing it to be one of the most dangerous mountains to climb.

> The two huge *crags* were the entrance to the lost gold mines in Arizona.

cranny (KRAN ee) *n.* a small opening as in a wall or rock face

> The secret message was found stuffed into a small *cranny* in the courtyard wall next to the church.

> We searched the house from top to bottom and did not overlook a single nook or *cranny.*

crass (kras) *adj.* stupid; without consideration for how other people might feel; lacking in sensitivity or refinement; crude

> It is *crass* and rude to ask someone how much money she earns.

> He makes *crass,* mean comments about her worn-out clothes even though he knows she can't afford to buy any more.

craven (KRA ven) *adj.* cowardly

> To let his wife do his fighting for him was the act of a *craven* husband with no backbone.

> The *craven* act of the assassin John Wilkes Booth led to the death of President Lincoln.

creditable (KRED ih tuh bull) *adj.* worthy of belief and praise

David's work in fund raising as president of the United Way was extremely *creditable.*

The CEO's report was received as *creditable* since the stock rose fifty points.

creditor (KRED uh tor) *n.* a person to whom money is owed

Mr. Randolph's lawyer recommended he declare bankruptcy; he had too many *creditors* and not enough assets with which to pay.

The entire banking industry is based entirely on performing as a *creditor* for depositors, then turning around and becoming *creditors* for borrowers.

credulous (KREJ oo lus) *adj.* gullible; eager to believe

The *credulous* children believed that their teacher lived under her desk.

Riki was not so *credulous* as to believe that a tall, dark, and handsome stranger was waiting to sweep her off her feet.

crescendo (kruh SHEN doh) *n.* a gradual increase in loudness of music; a gradual increase in intensity or force of anything

A *crescendo* of cheers from the crowd grew to a deafening roar when we won the game.

There has been a rising *crescendo* of criticism which started last year and is now reaching a climax.

crestfallen (KREST fawl un) *adj.* disappointed and sad; downcast or depressed; dejected

The tennis player strode confidently out on to the court but returned *crestfallen*, having lost the first set.

The children were *crestfallen* when they learned their father was leaving.

crevice (KREV us) *n.* a small narrow crack or space; crack; fissure

A lizard darted into a *crevice* between two stones.

The harsh light revealed every *crevice* and wrinkle in his face.

cringe (KRINJ) *v.* to move away, to try to make oneself smaller in order to escape from something or someone; to crouch or shrink back in fear; to cower

He acts like he's about to be hit and just *cringes* in terror.

Most of us *cringed* with embarrassment at her terrible jokes.

criterion (kry TEER ee un) *n.* a standard or rule by which something can be judged; a basis for judgment (plural – criteria)

There is no special *criterion* for making a fortune, but some say the fastest way is to marry rich.

The physical *criteria* for a good basketball player include being seven feet tall and able to jump like a kangaroo.

critique (kruh TEEK) *n.* critical review or commentary

The delegate has given us the first formal *critique* of the current economic policy and how it has affected the people.

The reporter responded to the harsh *critique* of her performance by fleeing from the room in tears.

croissant (kruh SONT) *n.* a flaky, rich, crescent-shaped roll or pastry

I cannot eat *croissants* because of the butter in the mixture.

The French bakery is well known for its delectable *croissants* with fruit filling.

crony (KROH nee) *n.* a close friend or companion

Jim and his *cronies* go to the football games on Friday nights.

John Dillinger and his *cronies* robbed the First National Bank.

crux (KRUKS) *n.* main point; the heart of the matter

After Harry rambled on for hours, it was difficult to understand the *crux* of his speech.

The mechanic thought the *crux* of the car's problem was a bad water pump.

cryptic (KRIP tik) *adj.* having an ambiguous or hidden meaning

Breaking Germany's *cryptic* codes during World War II helped the Allies win the war.

While exploring the cave, we stumbled across a *cryptic* message written on the wall.

cuisine (kwi ZEEN) *n.* a style of cooking; type of cooking

The Chinese *cuisine* in the new restaurant is excellent.

When I asked Dad what *cuisine* he preferred for his birthday dinner, he said, "Home cooked."

culinary (KYOO luh ner ee) *adj.* relating to cooking

Her desire to create new recipes was fueled by her interest in entering the *culinary* contest.

James attended *culinary* school to fulfill his dream of becoming a chef.

cull (kul) *v.* to sort out or select; to choose or collect from varied sources

The book is a collection of fascinating stories *culled* from a lifetime of experience.

Here are all the facts and figures I've *culled* from last month's business reports.

culminate (KUL muh nayt) *v.* to reach full climax

Millie's thirty years of teaching *culminated* with her being named Teacher of the Year.

The Homecoming Dance is the *culmination* of the week's festivities. (*n.*)

culpable (KUL puh bul) *adj.* guilty; deserving blame

We all felt *culpable* for the child's illness because we hadn't reported how often she had been left alone.

Johnny was *culpable* for the theft of the Girl Scout cookies.

cultivate (KUHL tu vayt) *v.* enhance; enrich; to help grow, to farm

The Smith family moved to the country to *cultivate* the rich soil for profit.

Martha *cultivated* her mind by reading many books each week.

cumbersome (KUM bur sum) *adj.* difficult to handle because of size or weight; burdensome

Jame's backpack was *cumbersome* because it was filled with books.

The Christmas tree was *cumbersome* to get into the house, but it looked beautiful when it was set up.

cumulative (KYOO myoo lah tiv) *adj.* increasing in size, scope or quantity by successive additions

Because the final exam is *cumulative,* we have to study all our notes.

The *cumulative* effects of the accident are not yet known.

cupidity (kyoo PID ih tee) *n.* excessive greed, especially for money

A good politician should have little *cupidity* and an abundance of concern for his constituents.

The *cupidity* of the Roman upper class led to the demise of the Roman Empire.

curb (kurb) *v.* to restrain or control

She wore a patch to try to *curb* her addiction to nicotine.

By making them raise their hands, the new teacher *curbed* her students' tendency to shout out the answers.

curmudgeon (kur MUJ un) *n.* a bad-tempered or irritable person; a difficult person

Grandpa, you're turning into a complaining, cranky old *curmudgeon*!

To pay my kids back for all the hard times they gave me, I plan to age into a disagreeable, cane-carrying *curmudgeon*!

curriculum (kur RIK yuh lum) *n.* courses offered by an educational institution

First year *curriculum* in colleges is generalized classes introducing various courses of study.

It is common for students to reassess their *curriculum* after the sophomore year.

cursory (KUR suh ree) *adj.* rapid and superficial; performed with haste and scant attention to detail

The general berated the private for his *cursory* attempt to clean his locker.

The general contractor was so *cursory* in the construction of our home that he forgot to lay the plumbing lines.

curtail (ker TALE) *v.* to truncate or abridge; to lessen, usually by cutting away from

The chairman requested that we should *curtail* any further discussion of women's rights until the women arrived.

The factory bosses *curtailed* the employment of any more workers until the strike was over.

curvilinear (kurv ah LIN ee ur) *adj.* formed, bound, or characterized by curved lines

Squares and rectangles have no *curvilinear* lines.

Surveyors have special instruments to lay out *curvilinear* streets in subdivisions.

cusp (kusp) *n.* a point or pointed end

Betty was born on the *cusp* of the astrological sign of Leo, so she had some attributes of Virgo.

He rounded the *cusp* of the 200 meter race and then broke for the tape on the straightaway.

cynic (SIN ik) *n.* one who distrusts humans and their motives

Because of the negative experiences he had as a young sailor, Herman Melville grew ever more *cynical*. (*adj.*)

A *cynic* would believe that a philanthropic organization really keeps the money it collects, rather than giving it to the poor.

damper (DAM per) *n.* a depression or restraint

An eyewitness put a *damper* on the defendant's hopes when he identified him as the one who committed the crime.

Jack's father put a *damper* on their vacation plans when he informed the family there was no money to travel this year.

daub (dawb) *v.* to cover; to paint crudely or skillfully

Freddy *daubed* his shoes with brown polish to cover the scuff marks.

Jackie *daubed* the kitchen walls with paint and created an artistic flower effect.

daunt (dawnt) *v.* to scare; to intimidate

When the home team saw the large players for the visiting team emerge from the bus, they were *daunted* by the visitors' size.

Although most people are fearful of speaking on a stage, Jerry was *undaunted* and enjoyed the experience.

dawdle (DAW dull) *v.* to spend time idly; to delay

The boys *dawdled* for hours watching TV before they finally decided to clean up their room.

We asked the children not to *dawdle*, but they still took too much time to do their chores.

debris (duh BREE) *n.* the remains of something destroyed; scattered rubble or wreckage

When we passed the site of the wreck, the *debris* was still on the ground.

On Christmas morning we ripped into our gifts, leaving our *debris* all over the living room.

de facto (dih FAK toe) *adj.* in fact; actually existing, esp. without lawful authority

Javier became the *de facto* president when his troops captured the capital.

De facto religious segregation exists in many countries without the approval of the respective governments.

deadlock (DED lok) *v.* to reach an impasse; to halt progress

The fight results were *deadlocked* until the referee cast the final vote to determine the winner.

Contract negotiations were *deadlocked* over television rights for the basketball players which resulted in suspension of the playoffs.

dearth (durth) *n.* scarcity; lack

A *dearth* of rain last summer led to many failed crops, especially corn and cotton in the valley.

There always seems to be a *dearth* of cookies in the cookie jar after our granddaughter's visit.

debacle (di BAHK ul) *n.* a sudden calamitous downfall; collapse or failure

The bank declared bankruptcy as a result of a *debacle* created by the thieving board of directors.

A worse *debacle* you would never hope to see; it rained on the Easter parade.

debase (di BAYS) *v.* lower in quality, character, or value

The inflation in Brazil has so *debased* the value of money that people won't stoop to recover small coins in the street.

The judge sued the newspaper for *debasing* his character in an article which claimed he was too easy on criminals.

debauchery (di BAW shuh ree) *n.* excessive self-indulgence

Ernest Hemingway was often guilty of alcoholic *debauchery*, but he never let this affect his writing.

After the couple won the lottery, their *debauchery* was evident when they purchased eight automobiles of different colors.

debilitate (di BIL uh tayt) *v.* to cripple; to weaken

Although Mr. Smith had always been a strong man, his disease of the bones was becoming progressively *debilitating.* (*adj.*)

We thought our dog Rex would be *debilitated* after he was hit by the car, but he learned to walk quite well on only three legs.

debug (dee BUG) *v.* to eliminate errors or malfunctions

Bob tried to *debug* the satellite dish but instead made it worse.

The serviceman arrived and was able to *debug* the computer program in only a few minutes.

debunk (di BUNK) *v.* to expose the falseness or exaggerations of a claim

When Christopher Columbus completed his ocean voyage, he *debunked* the theory that the world was flat.

Ralph was determined to *debunk* his daughter's theory that he had a money tree in their backyard.

debutante (DEB yoo tont) *n.* a young woman making her formal entrance into society

Max checked the attendance list for his girlfriend's name at the *debtante* ball.

It was hard to believe that the old crone had once been a *debutante*.

decade (DEK ayd) *n.* a period of ten years

High school students have changed a great deal over the past *decade*.

In this *decade* we have seen vast technological changes.

decadence (DEK ayh dens) *n.* social decay; loss of moral values

The *decadence* of some New York City neighborhoods is frightening!

Many of society's problems stem from the moral *decadence* of modern times.

decanter (dih CAN ter) *n.* an ornamental glass bottle used for serving wine or liquids

In restaurants people often order *decanters* of wine to be served during dinner.

The cut glass *decanter* looks lovely in the china cabinet.

decapitate (dee KAP ah tayt) *v.* to sever the head; behead

Henry VIII planned to *decapitate* every wife who could not produce a son.

Before the guillotine, sharp swords were used to *decapitate* those who were disloyal.

decimate (DES uh mayt) *v.* to kill; largely destroy

The dust *decimated* the cotton fields of the south during the 1930s.

The Texans were *decimated* by the Mexicans at the Alamo in 1836.

decipher (dih CIE fur) *v.* to decode, to interpret the meaning

The scrolls from the Dead Sea were difficult to *decipher*, as they were written in ancient Greek and Hebrew language.

The detectives *deciphered* the clues at the crime scene which led them to the conclusion that the butler had done it.

declaim (dee KLAYM) *v.* to recite a speech, usually in a pompous or dramatic way

When Karen began to *declaim* her graduation address, her classmates began to yawn, stretch, and roll their eyes.

We all hate to ask questions of that professor because he will *declaim* rather than converse with us.

decorous (DEK ur us) *adj.* in good taste; proper

The audience at an opera can usually be counted on to be *decorously* dressed in gowns and formal attire. (*adv.*)

The chaperones were pleased to observe the polite, *decorous* behavior of their students at the prom.

decorum (di KOH rum) *n.* appropriateness of conduct or behavior; propriety

One of the most forgotten rules of *decorum* is for a gentleman to remove his hat when entering a building.

On the first day of school, the principal lectured on the proper *decorum* expected from all students.

decree (dih KREE) *n.* an order having the force of law

The *decree* by the city council that all dogs must be kept on a leash set off a bitter conflict among dog owners.

In Dodge City, during the days of the great cattle drives of the 1880s, Sheriff Wyatt Earp enforced the *decree* that all guns must be turned over to the sheriff's deputies before a man could ride into town.

decrepit (dee KREP it) *adj.* weakened by old age or illness; worn out

The old dog was so *decrepit* that we were forced to have her euthanized.

The *decrepit* old man could barely get out of bed.

decry (di KRY) *v.* to openly denounce

Mitchell *decried* the high rate of unemployment in the state.

Mrs. Potts *decried* the low grades made in her English class.

deduce (dee DOOS) *v.* to come to a conclusion by reason

When the doors to the living room were locked the day before Christmas, Peggy *deduced* her mother was wrapping her presents.

From the footprints in the snow, the search party *deduced* that the missing hikers had wandered in circles several days before disappearing entirely.

deem (deem) *v.* to consider or judge; to have an opinion

The President asked Congress for authority to take whatever steps he *deemed* necessary to quell the riots.

The ocean current was so strong the long-distance swim team *deemed* it too great a risk to go for a practice swim.

deface (dih FACE) *v.* to mar the external appearance; destroy

The morning after the game it was clear that someone had *defaced* the walls of the school with spray paint.

Rain, winds, and pollution will eventually *deface* any historical monument exposed to the elements.

defame (di FAYME) *v.* to libel or slander; take away a good name

Defamed and defeated, Napoleon was exiled to the Island of Elba.

False accusations by unscrupulous, lying men have *defamed* the reputations of many fair ladies.

defeatist (dih FEET ist) *adj.* characterized by acceptance or expectation of defeat

Their *defeatist* attitude shortened the battle by days and caused the downfall of the nation.

His *defeatist* comments set him up for a loss he was unable to handle.

defer (dih FUR) *v.* postpone, delay; yield, as in congress

Senator Barr *deferred* to his colleague from Florida to make a congressional address.

Judge Rose *deferred* a final ruling until more evidence could be submitted by both sides.

deference (DEF ur uns) *n.* respect for another's view or wishes

The family showed *deference* to their elderly grandmother's whim and agreed to have dinner at 4 p.m.

The woman in the check-out line with two cart loads of groceries stepped aside and showed *deference* to the lady with only one grocery item.

deficient (dih FISH unt) *adj.* lacking in some necessary quality or element

Flunking his last exam, Frank was *deficient* in credits for graduation.

The doctor suggested his patient was *deficient* in vitamin C and should take vitamin supplements.

deficit (DEF uh sit) *n.* inadequacy or insufficiency; shortage

The theater had been operating at a *deficit* of over $150,000 a year and finally closed.

Jake's monthly budget shows a *deficit* because he makes $1000, but his bills total $1400.

defile (di FYLE) *v.* to make dirty or filthy; to pollute; to corrupt

Careless littering of beer cans and paper bags *defiles* the beauty of our beaches.

Malicious rumors *defiled* his good name, so he lost respect from many of the citizens.

definitive (di FIN uh tiv) *adj,* conclusive; stating the last word

Tommy had a *definitive* answer for why he didn't believe in ghosts; he'd never seen any.

Fast food restaurants provide the *definitive* solution for eating on the run.

deflate (di FLAYT) *v.* to let the air out of; to diminish in size or importance

When the roads are icy, it is a good idea to *deflate* the tires to provide more traction.

The reprimand Joan received from her boss the first week on the job *deflated* her enthusiasm about her career choice.

deft (deft) *adj.* dexterous; skillful

The quarterback *deftly* avoided the linebacker's rush while calmly throwing a touchdown pass. (*adv.*)

In one *deft* move, with a flick of the wrist, the magician produced a live pigeon where one had not been.

defunct (dee FUNGKT) *adj.* dead or inactive; having ceased to exist

Latin is a *defunct* language kept alive only by some religions.

Although Shakespeare has been dead for centuries, his plays will never be *defunct*.

degenerate (di JEN uh rayt) *v.* to deteriorate; to break down

It is a shame that the old stately mansion has been allowed to *degenerate* into an eyesore.

By the afternoon nap time, the children's behavior had *degenerated* into chaotic crankiness.

degrade (di GRAYD) *v.* to reduce in status, rank, or grade; demote

Some bottles of wine in Henry's wine cellar had leaky corks, so the wine *degraded* into a bitter liquid.

The police officer felt *degraded* walking a beat again after being demoted from captain. (*adj.*)

deign (dayn) *v.* to believe something to be beneath one's dignity; to condescend

Mr. Morris did not *deign* to reply when a reporter asked him if he thought he should have been arrested for walking on the grass.

The salesman *deigned* no further discussion of price since the buyer was quite wealthy and would not want to haggle.

deity (DEE uh tee) *n.* a god or goddess; someone or something worshipped as a god

The Egyptians, Greeks, and Romans had not one, but many *deities* that they worshipped.

Some people's only *deity* is money, so they devote all their time and effort to making more.

dejected (di JEK tid) *adj.* lacking hope; in low spirits; depressed

William felt *dejected* because he had sprained his ankle and had to sit out the game.

Jennie was *dejected* when her kitten was lost; she sat around the house and moped all day.

delectable (di LEK tuh bul) *adj.* giving great pleasure; pleasing to the taste; delicious

That cake is so *delectable* that I will have another piece, please.

You look absolutely *delectable* in that dress; all the boys will want to dance with you.

delete (duh LEET) *v.* to wipe out; omit; destroy

The editor *deleted* the second paragraph in the article because it was not pertinent to the story.

In his speech the ex-president *deleted* all references to the election results, probably because he lost.

deleterious (del uh TIR ee us) *adj.* harmful or injurious to one's health or well-being

It is well known that smoking cigarettes has a *deleterious* effect on one's health, yet some people still smoke.

It is a proven fact that sunbathing is *deleterious* to a person's well-being.

deliberate (di LIB ur uht) *adj.* cautious; prudent (di LIB ur ayt) *v.* to think over

Charley's horse was old and cautious; he proceeded at a slow and *deliberate* pace up the mountain trail.

The judge said he would have to *deliberate* before making a decision.

delineate (di LIN ee ayt) *v.* to describe exactly; sketch out; depict

Jim *delineated* his plan about how he planned to renovate the house.

Before writing a novel, the author usually *delineates* his plot, deciding what will happen during the story.

delinquent (di LING kwent) *adj./n.* not paid on time; neglectful of a duty failing to do what the law requires; a person who is delinquent

Sue was *delinquent* in paying her mortgage payment, so the bank threatened to foreclose and take her house.

A juvenile *delinquent* is someone under the legal age of adulthood who has committed a crime.

delirious (du LEER ee us) *adj.* incoherent; mentally confused; hallucinating

The crowd became *delirious* with joy when the team scored the winning touchdown.

Carla became *delirious* after three days in bed with a high fever; she was so confused that at times she thought she was at the library.

dell (dell) *n.* secluded hollow or small valley; a glen, usually wooded

We built a new home in a private *dell* surrounded by wooded hills.

The farmer stood in the *dell* watching his livestock.

delude (di LOOD) *v.* to deceive; mislead; trick; to evade

Many young writers *delude* themselves into thinking that they are going to write the great American novel.

The charlatan *deluded* the old woman into believing he would put her money into the bank for her.

deluge (DEL yooj) *n.* inundation; flood

We were afraid the fireworks would be canceled because of the *deluge* that started right before sunset.

We were *deluged* by phone calls after putting the ad in the paper.

delve (delv) *v.* to search intensely for a thing or information

The pop music idol said she was tired of journalists *delving* into her private life.

The attorney general promised he would *delve* into the rash of robberies in the valley.

demagogue (DEM uh GAWG) *n.* a leader, esp. a rabble rouser

Historians agree that Hitler and Mussolini were *demagogues* greatly responsible for starting World War II.

Lawyers, politicians, and other authority figures who inflame the populace to further their own aims are said to be *demagogues* who engage in *demagoguery*.

demeanor (di MEE nur) *n.* behavior; deportment

The colonel's stern military *demeanor* makes his children frightened of him.

Judging from her *demeanor*, I would say she is very uncomfortable being here.

demerit (dih MER it) *n.* blame; penalty

Jerry had so many *demerits* he was called to the principal's office.

Kathy gave *demerits* to the workers who arrived late for their shift.

demise (di MIZE) *n.* death; the end

Chuck was devastated by the *demise* of his pet turtle.

General George Custer met his *demise* at Little Big Horn.

demography (di MAHG ruh fee) *n.* statistical study of human populations

Demography is the study of characteristics shared by groups of people.

A *demographic* study shows that the age children begin working increases during every five year period. (*adj.*)

demonic (dee MON ik) *adj.* working devilishly; persistent; evil

Jack's Olympic practice habits were *demonic*; six hours a day on the track was his norm.

The terrorist's *demonic* plan to poison the city's water supply was foiled by the police.

demote (dih MOHT) *v.* to lower in rank, degrade

The general *demoted* the corporal to the rank of private for insubordination.

The administrator was *demoted* to assistant for failing to reach his quota.

demur (dih MUR) *v.* to object; to make exception

Billy said he was appreciative but *demurred* when his friends wanted him to run for class president.

The mayor said he would not *demur* if asked to speak at the town rally.

demure (di MYOOR) *adj.* well behaved; quiet; shy; modest

Two *demure* little girls sat quietly near their mother with their hands in their laps.

Mary Louise was so *demure* she never raised her tone of voice, even when she hit her finger while hammering a nail.

denigrate (DEN ih grate) *v.* belittle; defame; attack one's reputation

Keith *denigrated* his opponent, attempting to show that she was unqualified to be the new dog catcher.

Jack's father would *denigrate* him for minor things when angry and then later apologize for the harsh things he had said.

denizen (DEN i zun) *n.* inhabitant

Sharks are often called *denizens* of the deep, even though their habitat is often in shallow waters near shore.

The neighborhood residents were frequent *denizens* of Joe's Bar and Grill down the street.

denomination (di nahm uh NAY shun) *n.* a classification or category; a religious group or sect composed of a number of congregations

Annie and Bill belonged to two different religious *denominations*; Annie was Baptist and Bill was Lutheran.

Our money is minted in many different *denominations*, from pennies up to hundred dollar bills.

denote (di NOHT) *v.* to represent; to mark; to indicate

His angry tone *denoted* extreme displeasure with what had been said behind her back at the party.

A flashing yellow light on the road ahead *denoted* a need for caution, so Randolph slowed down to be on the safe side.

denounce (di NOWNS) *v.* to condemn; to expose critically

As an act of conscience, the young terrorist *denounced* his fellow terrorists and confessed his criminal acts to the police.

The captured soldiers were asked to *denounce* their government and join in the revolution.

denunciation (dih NUN see ay shun) *n.* a strong, public criticism; a verbal attack or condemnation

The Russian leader gave a *denunciation* of the evils of the communist system.

The maestro's *denunciation* of his pianist's performance was terribly embarrassing to the musician in question.

depict (di PIKT) *v.* to represent or portray, as in a painting, sculpture, or written work

In his last novel, the author *depicted* the hero's wife as a computer wizard who stole millions through her technology skills.

The newspapers *depict* Bellamy's father as an alcoholic tyrant, but in reality he is a reformed alcoholic who is president of his local AA chapter.

deplete (di PLEET) *v.* to reduce in size or amount; to lessen drastically; exhaust

The disaster *depleted* the supply of blood plasma, so the American Red Cross flew in an emergency supply to replenish the supply.

Janet's savings account had been *depleted* by the time she finished her Christmas shopping.

deplore (di PLOHR) *v.* to show or have regret or sorrow about; to condemn

We *deplore* the recent outbreak of violence in our schools.

Many citizens *deplore* the amount of foreign aid the U.S. gives to other countries when there are Americans who are economically impoverished and in need of help.

deploy (di PLOY) *v.* to arrange strategically

The general's intelligent *deployment* of his troops along the eastern front won the battle. (*n.*)

By *deploying* all his resources, Phil was able to buy a new car.

depose (di POHZ) *v.* to deprive of rank or office; to remove

Margaret Thatcher was *deposed* as leader of the British Conservative Party in 1991.

The stockholders voted to *depose* the present CEO from his office because of falling company profits.

depravity (di PRAV ih tee) *n.* extreme wickedness

When Ed was arrested for shoplifting, his mother told the judge she attributed his *depravity* to violent movies and video games.

Adolf Hitler will forever be remembered in history for his *depravity* towards the Jewish people and humanity in general.

deprecate (DEP ri kayt) *v.* to express disapproval of

That comedian is best known for the way he *deprecates* himself and his family.

The teacher acted in a *deprecatory* manner when she found out that no one had completed the assignment on time. (*adj.*)

depredate (DEP ruh dayt) *v.* to plunder and pillage; to despoil; to prey upon; to ransack

During the L.A. riots, many people *depredated* the neighborhoods, stealing stereos, televisions, and clothing.

Some unsavory businesses *depredate* the elderly, robbing them of their life savings with false promises and get rich quick schemes.

derelict (DER uh likt) *adj.* not cared for; abandoned; neglectful; remiss

He was *derelict* in visiting his mother, and she often felt alone and unloved.

The old factory has become *derelict* and run down since it closed two years ago.

deride (di RYDE) *v.* to treat contemptuously; ridicule

Middle school boys often *deride* each other to get the attention of girls.

Opposing coaches *derided* our team because we hadn't won a game this entire season.

derivative (di RIV uh tiv) *adj.* unoriginal; coming from or based on something else

The word "atomic" is a *derivative* of the word "atom." (*n.*)

The *derivative* term paper Sammy turned in was rejected by the teacher because it was the same one she had seen from another student a year earlier.

derogatory (di RAHG uh tor ee) *adj.* degrading

Nancy heard the other girls whispering *derogatory* stories about her family living in a slum.

James often makes *derogatory* remarks about his friends, yet he does not seem to understand that his uncomplimentary words drive them away.

derring-do (DARE ing DOO) *n.* daring action and deeds

Evil Knievel's *derring-do* on the motorcycle made him famous as a daredevil.

James Bond films show many acts of *derring-do* performed by stunt actors dressed up to look like Bond.

disburse (dis BURSE) *v.* to make payment in settlement; expend; distribute

Our attorney *disbursed* the final amount due from the sale of our home.

The teacher *disbursed* the exam to all her students.

descry (dih SKRIE) *v.* to find out; catch sight of; discover

Peter *descried* natives on the far side of the island and went over to ask them to help his shipwrecked crew.

The astronomer had developed a new telescope which could *descry* universes never seen before outside of the Milky Way

desecrate (DES ih krayt) *v.* to violate the sacredness of; treat with disrespect

Vandals *desecrated* the temple, removing statues and marble columns.

The protesters were arrested for *desecrating* the flag by attempting to burn it.

desiccate (DESS ih kayt) *v.* to dry out; to preserve food; dehydrate

The package of fruit had been *desiccated* and packaged to be sold to campers.

It didn't rain for two months and all Emma's garden vegetables *desiccated.*

designate (DEZ ig nate) *v.* stipulate; to set apart for specific use

John was *designated* as captain of the football team for the game against Central High.

The closest parking space was *designated* for the handicap.

desist (di ZIST) *v.* to stop doing something; cease

Sue was politely asked by her neighbors to *desist* from playing music after 11 p.m. because it kept them awake.

Mary tried to *desist* from eating the remainder of the apple pie but finally gave in and gobbled it down.

despondent (di SPAHN dunt) *adj.* despairing; depressed

After Herman left her at the altar, Lilly was *despondent* for days.

Our dog Spot has been *despondent* ever since his friend, the neighbor's dog, died.

despot (DES puht) *n.* an absolute ruler

Fidel Castro is the *despotic* ruler of Cuba. (*adj.*)

My big brother is the *despot* of the family; he is always bossing my brothers and sisters around.

destitute (DES tuh toot) *adj.* extremely poor

Harry never bothered to buy life insurance, and when he died his wife and fourteen children were left *destitute.*

The *destitute* old man stood begging on the street corner.

desultory (DES ul tor ee) *adj.* random; without purpose

Because of Peter's *desultory* attitude, his sergeant refused to write a recommendation for him.

Rick made a few *desultory* attempts to get a job, but nothing came of them.

detain (dih TANE) *v.* to delay, restrain, esp. from proceeding

The travelers at the airport were *detained* due to a bomb scare.

The mail was *detained* at the post office until after the hurricane blew through.

deter (dee TUR) *v.* to discourage; to keep someone from doing something

Nothing could *deter* John from his ambition to be a doctor.

Bryan's broken leg *deterred* him from playing softball.

determined (di TUR mund) *adj.* firm of purpose; unwavering; unfaltering

The *determined* fire fighters smashed through the door to get to the fire.

Brad was *determined* to pass the SAT and spent all of his free time studying.

detrimental (deh trih MEN tul) *adj.* obviously harmful or damaging

Smoking is *detrimental* to your health.

Some toys are *detrimental* to young children because the children can injure themselves while playing with them.

deviate (DEE vee ate) *v.* to stray from an established course

Smith *deviated* from the main route and chose to travel on the back roads to avoid traffic.

The travelers *deviated* from the norm when they chose to walk to town rather than take a taxi.

devious (DEE vee us) *adj.* not open, honest, or straightforward; sneaky; underhanded

Cheating is a *devious* way to win a game.

When he told his wife he was working late but instead went to visit a girlfriend, Bob was being *devious*.

devoid (di VOID) *adj.* entirely without; lacking

The island was *devoid* of drinking water, so the shipwrecked sailors had to drink coconut milk.

Our football team is totally *devoid* of an offense; we haven't scored a touchdown in the last four games.

devotion (de VO shun) *n.* loyalty; profound dedication; fondness

Pat's *devotion* to his father, who was a lawyer, was the factor that encouraged him to study law in college.

Tom's *devotion* to his sport paid-off when he won the gold medal.

devout (di VOWT) *adj.* earnestly devoted to religion; pious; showing devotion

My friend's mother is a *devout* Catholic who never misses mass on Sunday.

Toni is a *devout* health fanatic who eats only organic foods and exercises for three hours every day.

dexterity (dek STARE ih tee) *n.* mental skill or adroitness; the ease in use of the body

Jerry is a tennis champion because of his *dexterity*, speed, and determination.

Magicians must develop superior manual *dexterity* in order to make their tricks appear to be magical.

dialect (DIE uh lekt) *n.* any special variety of a language

Jorge was raised in Spain and speaks in a Spanish *dialect*.

The Chinese language has many *dialects*.

dialectical (dye uh LEK ti kul) *adj.* relating to the rules and methods of reasoning

To determine a truth about something, the *dialectical* approach is to examine all the possibilities in order to find the more correct one.

Plato taught Aristotle his *dialectical* approach to philosophical analysis.

diatribe (DYE uh tryb) *n.* a bitter verbal attack

Coach Johnson's *diatribe* about the bad call was futile because he knew the referee would not reverse his decision.

The prosecuting attorney began his opening statement with a *diatribe* declaring the defendant to be a low-down, lying, scheming, no-good rat.

dichotomy (dye KAHT uh mee) *n.* the division into two parts that are usually contradictory

It is a *dichotomy* when parents tell their children never to lie but also never to hurt someone's feelings.

The minister spoke of the *dichotomy* between religious righteousness and bigotry, meaning that it is a sin to serve both masters.

dictum (DIK tum) *n.* short saying expressing truth

My mother's *dictum* was, "An apple a day keeps the doctor away."

"Times have changed" is usually the *dictum* that begins one of my grandfather's stories about how things used to be.

diffident (DIF ih dent) *adj.* lacking self-confidence; timid

In order to assuage her *diffidence*, Beth was persuaded to enroll in drama class. (*n.*)

The *diffident* kitten was stuck in the tree for hours and was afraid to come down.

diffuse (di FYOOZ) *v.* scatter; disperse; cause to spread in many directions

The rats *diffused* once the light was turned on.

The smoke *diffused* over such a large area that the smoke detectors weren't triggered.

digress (dye GRES) *v.* to stray from the topic

The novel became boring in spots because the author constantly *digressed* from the main story line.

The World War I veteran began telling of his war experiences but soon *digressed* to tales of his childhood.

dilapidated (di LAP uh day tid) *adj.* in bad condition and needing repair; fallen into disrepair or decay

We still use the *dilapidated* barn for storing tools, but it is no longer good for anything else.

Our farm tractor looks *dilapidated*, but it still plows the fields as well as when it was new.

dilate (dye LAYT) *v.* to make wider or more open; enlarge; to explain or discuss something at length

The doctor's drops in Ellen's eyes *dilated* her pupils so wide she needed sunglasses to go into sunlight.

When my father lectures me on my errors, he *dilates* the topic so much, I forget what I did wrong in the beginning.

dilemma (di LEM ma) *n.* a difficult situation; any problem or predicament

John faced the *dilemma* of either taking a cut in pay or losing his job.

It was a small *dilemma*, but Bill couldn't choose between pecan or cherry pie for dessert.

dilettante (DIL uh tahnt) *n.* an amateur

Amy wants to be an artist, be we all know she's a *dilettante* with little ability in painting.

The art instructor hopes her students will develop into more than *dilettantes*.

diligent (DIL uh gent) *adj.* persevering; hardworking; industrious

Barry was a *diligent* worker and deserved his promotion to manager.

The fire department volunteer was *diligent* and stayed on the job until the fire was entirely put out.

diminish (dih MIN ish) *v.* to make less; or cause to appear less; belittle

The company's funds *diminished* because of bad bookkeeping and overspending.

His chance for promotion *diminished* when an outsider was hired as CEO.

diminution (di muh NYOO shun) *n.* the act or process of diminishing; reduction

The crew of the crippled research submarine was concerned with the *diminution* of their air supply.

There was an obvious *diminution* of the temperature as the sun began to set.

din (DIN) *n.* loud, confused noise; uproar, commotion

As Jim caught the ball, a *din* from the crowd prevented him from hearing the announcer.

Because of the rioting, the *din* prevented an announcement from the police to be heard.

diorama (di uh RA mah) *n.* an exhibit of scenic presentation featuring a painted background and statues

The *diorama* featuring model railroads and towns was the center attraction at the mall.

Charlie's functional *diorama* of the volcano spewing lava attracted many adults as well as children.

dire (DYE ur) *adj.* disastrous; desperate

The hurricane struck the Florida Keys with *dire* results; many homes were destroyed.

Jeff's *dire* predictions about a stock market crash unfortunately came true.

dirge (DURJ) *n.* a song or hymn for a funeral or memorial for the dead; any mournful music

That folk song sounds more like a *dirge* than it does a poem.

The *dirge* the organist played at Aunt Bea's funeral was so sad there wasn't a dry eye in the church.

disaffect (dis uh FEKT) *v.* to cause to lose affection for; alienate; estrange

An abusive husband will soon *disaffect* his wife who may stay with him only out of fear, not love.

The dog became so cranky and mean that he *disaffected* the children who had adored him.

disarray (dis uh RAY) *n.* a disorderly or confused condition; a lack of organization

My house is in such *disarray* that I can't find my car keys.

The salesman's car was in such *disarray* that his products were lost in a sea of trash.

disavow (DIS uh vow) *v.* to deny, repudiate; contradict

Boone *disavowed* the stories that he was running for mayor of the town.

Jim's coach *disavowed* the reports that he was married to three different women.

discern (di SURN) *v.* to discriminate; to see things clearly

The psychologist was able to *discern* the child's problem before he spoke to the parents.

The ability to *discern* between truth and fiction is essential to being an informed person.

disciple (di SY pul) *n.* a person who embraces and assists in spreading the teachings of another

Disciples of some churches spread the word by going door to door.

Every professional football team has *disciples* who would never dream of missing a game.

disclaim (dis KLAYM) *v.* to deny any claim to; to denounce

He *disclaimed* all responsibility for the accounting mistakes and blamed a computer error.

A *disclaimer* (*n.*) is an act or statement that *disclaims*.

discombobulate (dis kam BOB yoo layt) *v.* to upset the composure of; to throw into a state of confusion

The pilot became *discombobulated* while flying through a thunderstorm.

The kids' bedroom was in a state of *discombobulation* after the sleepover party. (*n.*)

discomfit (dis KUM fit) *v.* to upset or confuse; frustrate

George felt bad that he had inconvenienced and *discomfited* whomever was bumped off the plane so he could get aboard.

The sheriff's badgering *discomfited* the suspect until she broke out into a sweat and started shaking.

disconcert (dis cun SURT) *v.* to disturb the composure of; upset; to frustrate; throw into disorder

Some students are *disconcerted* when they listen to music while studying.

A baby may be unaffected by familiar loud noises while the simplest new sound may *disconcert* her.

disconsolate (dis KON suh lut) *adj.* dejected; downcast; deep in grief or sorrow

Tony was *disconsolate* after losing the race and a position on the Olympic team.

The family of the injured child was so *disconsolate* that for a time they did not answer sympathy calls from their neighbors.

discordant (dis KOR dunt) *adj.* disagreeing;, quarrelsome; in conflict

The city council's *discordant* attitude discouraged those who wanted to correct community problems.

Every generation develops artists with a *discordant* style that later becomes fashionable and highly sought after.

discourse (DIS kawrs) *n.* thoughtful spoken or written discussion of a subject; conversation

The movie was a wonderful *discourse* on love and what it truly means.

The locker room *discourse* after the game became a shouting match about who did what wrong.

discreet (di SKREET) *adj.* prudent; thoughtfully reserved

Wilma's friends tell her all their secrets because they know she will be *discreet*.

Doctors are required to be *discreet* with any information their patients may not wish divulged.

discrepancy (dis KREP un see) *n.* difference; inconsistency

There always seems to be a *discrepancy* between what my big brother says I should do and what he does.

Why does there always seem to be a *discrepancy* between what my check book says and what the bank says?

discrete (di SKREET) *adj.* separate; distinct; disconnected

The success of the play was a result of many *discrete* performances.

Jack and Jill may look alike, but their personalities are *discrete*.

discriminate (di SKRIM uh nayt) *v.* to discern; to differentiate

The art critic could easily *discriminate* between the original and the fake copy.

(*Indiscriminate* (*adj.*) means not *discriminating*.)

George would eat anything and was *indiscriminate* in his choice of food.

discursive (dis KUR siv) *adj.* rambling on aimlessly

George's novel quickly becomes *discursive*, and the reader loses the story line completely.

J.D.'s speech was so *discursive* that we never could decide what point he was trying to make.

disdain (dis DAYN) *n.* scorn; contempt

Rita viewed the Brussels sprouts with *disdain* and refused to eat them.

The millionaire lottery winner treated her former friends with *disdain*.

disgruntle (dis GRUN tul) *v.* to make irritably dissatisfied or discontent

The company's refusal to make Veteran's Day a holiday *disgruntled* the workers to the point that they all called in sick on that day.

Jack was *disgruntled* over having to give Henry a handicap in their golf match.

dishevel (dis SHEV ul) *v.* to make untidy; to disarrange

A strong breeze *disheveled* Andrea's hair.

The hurricane *disheveled* our yard with broken branches and debris.

disinformation (dis in fer MAY shun) *n.* false information deliberately spread

During the Cold War the Russians disseminated *disinformation* to make America appear warlike.

Disinformation usually emanates from a source desiring to create a false impression.

disingenuous (diss in JEN yoo uss) *adj.* lacking in candor, insincere; giving a false appearance of frankness

The ex-criminal was *disingenuous* about his background when he applied for a job.

It was *disingenuous* of Harold to say he played football for Notre Dame when he really was only the team waterboy.

disinterested (dis IN truh stid) *adj.* unbiased; not taking sides

If you don't care, you are uninterested. That's not the same as being *disinterested*.

A referee must remain *disinterested* in the outcome of the game and not take sides.

dismal (DIZ mul) *adj.* sad; without hope; gloomy

The weather is so *dismal* today that I don't feel like doing anything but staying indoors.

The vacation was a *dismal* failure; it rained every day at the beach.

dismantle (dis MAN tul) *v.* to take apart; to tear down

The government voted to *dismantle* its nuclear warheads.

They *dismantled* the reviewing stand after the parade was over.

dismay (dis MAY) *v.* to fill with shock; to frighten or discourage; daunt

They enjoyed the meal in the expensive restaurant but the enormous bill dismayed them.

The scene of the terrible auto accident *dismayed* the police when they arrived and saw the carnage.

disparage (di SPAR ij) *v.* to belittle

John's wife *disparaged* his efforts to paint their house with a toothbrush and set a new world record.

Bill's writing teacher *disparaged* his story by saying the idea was not original.

disparate (DIS pur it) *adj.* unequal, different; incompatible

Our personalities were *disparate*; Janet liked to socialize, and I liked quiet times alone.

The *disparate* types of fish all found their way through the narrow channel pass to the ocean.

(The noun form of *disparate* is *disparity*)

The *disparity* between the genuine coin and the fake coin were obvious to the coin dealer.

dispassionate (dis PASH uh nut) *adj.* able to think clearly without strong feeling or bias; calm; impartial

The book about the Kennedy family history provides a more *dispassionate* understanding of the tragic events than one would not get in *National Enquirer* magazine.

The killer described his heinous criminal acts in a frighteningly *dispassionate* manner, with a blank stare on his face.

dispel (dis PELL) *v.* to drive away; to dissipate

After the police *dispelled* the crowd from the scene of the accident, the wreckers hauled away the tangled, wrecked automobiles.

An exorcist was called-in to *dispel* the evil spirits.

disperse (dis PURS) *v.* to scatter in various directions; distribute widely

Napoleon *dispersed* troops strategically along the mountain's ridge where they could fire down upon the Austrian army as it advanced up the hill.

The police arrived and *dispersed* the riotous crowd with threats of arrest if they did not leave the parade grounds.

dispirit (dis PIR ut) *v.* to take the spirit out of; discourage; depress

The town looked tired and *dispirited* as the cowboys rode toward it looking for a good time.

It had rained for three solid days, and the cows in the field were a *dispirited* bunch.

disposition (dis puh ZISH un) *n.* state of mind; a person's usual way of feeling

Roger always has such a cheerful *disposition* that we have asked him to be the neighborhood Santa Claus this year.

The *disposition* of the puppy was aggressive and untamed, so I didn't think she would do well around small children.

disproportionate (dis pruh PAWR shuh nut) *adj.* too great or too small when compared to something else; unbalanced

The mother gave her baby a *disproportionate* amount of milk, taking only a sip herself.

When I went over my monthly budget, I found there was a *disproportionate* amount of money spent on clothing as compared to that spent on food.

disquiet (dis KWYE ut) *v.* to cause anxiety or worry

Her unpredictability *disquiets* me because I never know how to approach her on any given day.

That horror movie *disquieted* my kids so much that they slept with me for a week afterwards!

dissemble (di SEM bul) *v.* to hide one's real intentions; to act or speak falsely in order to deceive

Parents frequently *dissemble* when speaking about the Easter Bunny and Santa Claus.

Michele often *dissembled* when she spoke about her grades, but we learned the truth when she got her report card.

disseminate (di SEM uh nayt) *v.* to spread; to scatter; to make widely known

The news media *disseminate* news, information, and entertainment on a daily basis.

News of the school bus accident quickly *disseminated* throughout the community.

dissent (di SENT) *v.* to disagree with or reject something; withhold approval

As a die-hard liberal, the Congressman frequently *dissented* from the court's majority opinion, which he felt was outdated.

There were no *dissenters* when Jack suggested the dive trip be cancelled because of large shark fins seen at the dive site. (*n.*)

disservice (di SUR vus) *n.* an unfair or harmful action; harm; injury

Calling the judge unfair is a great *disservice* as he is the most honest person I know.

Jeffrey did a great *disservice* to his sister when he used her credit card without her permission.

dissident (DIS uh dunt) *n.* a person who disagrees

Cuba, under Castro, responds to political *dissidents* by imprisoning them.

Sports *dissidents* paraded in Manhattan protesting the Yankees moving to Miami.

dissipate (DIS uh payt) *v.* to dissolve; to waste away

In the mountains, the morning fog rarely *dissipates* before noon.

The smoke *dissipated* when the windows were opened.

dissolution (dis uh LOO shun) *n.* the breaking up into parts; termination of a legal bond or contract

After the divorce, the *dissolution* of the family assets was handled by the attorneys.

The *dissolution* of the company left the employees wondering if they still had jobs.

dissonant (DIS uh nent) *adj.* discordant, inharmonious, in disagreement

Carl's *dissonant* friends always argued over who would be first at the video machines.

The violin section of the orchestra tuned their instruments before the performance so they would not be *dissonant*.

dissuade (di SWAYD) *v.* to persuade not to do something ("dissuade" is the opposite of "persuade")

The bad weather *dissuaded* us from going outdoors.

Our group hopes to *dissuade* Congress from cutting funds for much needed health programs.

distant (DIS tunt) *adj.* faraway, far-removed, unfriendly, uncommunicative

Joseph's *distant* relatives live in the city of Bialystok, Poland.

Sue was so *distant* with Mike, he thought she was angry.

distend (di STEND) *v.* to swell; to enlarge

Starvation caused the baby's stomach to *distend* grotesquely.

The doctor gently examined Joe's *distended* finger. (*adj.*)

distinct (di STINKT) *adj.* clearly separate and different; unmistakable or evident

Jane and Mary had the *distinction* of being the only twins to run for Congress. (*n.*)

Those two dogs are of *distinct* breeds; one is huge with short hair, and the other is tiny with long hair.

distinguish (di STING gwish) *v.* to tell apart; to cause to stand out

Their voices are so alike, it is hard to *distinguish* between them on the phone.

In art museums, I have trouble *distinguishing* Monet's work from that of Renoir.

distraught (dis TRAWT) *adj.* extremely anxious and upset; mentally disturbed or deranged

Mrs. May was *distraught* over the death of her little dog.

John Charles was not *distraught* over the sinking of his boat because it was heavily insured.

diurnal (dye UR nul) *adj.* occurring every day

Brad enjoys a *diurnal* cup of coffee while reading the newspaper.

Diurnal is the opposite of *nocturnal*, which means occurring during the night.

divergent (di VER jent) *adj.* separating, differing in opinion, deviating

Captain Clark's *divergent* opinions about where the land mines lay along the road made everyone feel uneasy.

The Christians and the Muslims have *divergent* opinions about deities.

diverse (di VURS) *adj.* different; varied

Humphrey's collection of *diverse* antique classic automobiles was the largest in the state.

Randy was very educated and had a *diverse* education with degrees in medicine, law, and business.

diversify (di VURS if eye) *v.* to make diverse; give variety to; to expand

A prudent investor always *diversifies* his stock portfolio by purchasing many different stocks.

Candy wanted to *diversify* her education while in college, so she took classes in business, psychology, physics, and literature.

divert (di VERT) *v.* to change the direction of; to alter the course of

During the hurricane, the airport control tower *diverted* all landing aircraft to the Tampa Airport.

The nurse tried to *divert* the little girl's attention while the doctor pricked her finger.

divine (di VYNE) *v.* to foretell; to prohesy; to infer, to guess

Stockbrokers make their living *divining* when to buy and when to sell stocks.

Old timers used to use a stick to *divine* where they should dig a well.

divulge (di VULJ) *v.* to make something known; to disclose; to reveal

The newspapers published stories which *divulged* that several senators were taking bribes.

There is a law that protects members of the press from having to *divulge* the names of their secret sources.

docile (DAHS ul) *adj.* easily taught; obedient, easy to handle

A desirable quality of basset hounds is that they are *docile* pets.

Cameron was a fierce professional wrestling competitor, but his wife said he was a sweet, *docile* husband.

doctrinaire (dahk truh NAYR) *adj* inflexible; dogmatic

Even though evolution is widely accepted, some people maintain a *doctrinaire* view of creationism.

The professor's *doctrinaire* views about gasoline power was scorned by his progressive colleagues who believe in the future of electric power.

document (DOK yuh ment) *v.* to support with evidence

The report *documents* various aspects of native American life during the period following the American Civil War.

Nurses in hospitals are required to carefully *document* all care given to patients assigned to them.

doddering (DAHD ur ing) *adj.* shaky, feeble, unsteady, as from old age

They put their grandmother in assisted living because she was becoming too *doddering* to live alone.

Although the minister has become *doddering*, he still preaches an inspiring sermon.

doff (dof) *v.* to take off; to remove; to put aside

A gentleman should *doff* his hat to a lady.

He *doffed* the invitation and promptly forgot to respond.

doggerel (DAW guh rul) *n.* poetic verse of generally poor quality

The editor returned Walter's poetry, saying that it was unpublishable *doggerel*.

Most greeting cards contain *doggerel* rather than real poetry.

dogmatic (dawg MAT ik) *adj.* characterized by an authoritative, often arrogant assertion of opinions or beliefs

Grandpa was always *dogmatic* about his views on the best way to grow corn.

The opinions or ideas vehemently asserted by a *dogmatic* person are know as dogma.

doldrums (DOHL drums) *n.* a period or condition of depression or inactivity

Jack is in the *doldrums*; ever since he lost his job, he has moped around unhappily.

For thirteen days we were becalmed in the Horse Latitude near the Equator, our ship drifting in the *doldrums* without the faintest breeze to fill the sails.

doleful (DOHL ful) *adj.* sorrowful; melancholy

The *doleful* expression on the dog's face suggested he thought he had been deserted by his owners.

When the doctor arrived to examine her ailing husband, Jessica *dolefully* opened the door to let him in. (*adv.*)

dolt (DOHLT) *n.* a stupid person

Only a *dolt* would put his shoes on backward.

Jonathan felt *doltish* because he was the only student to fail gym class. (*adj.*)

domain (doh MAYN) *n.* a territory over which one rules or over which one has influence or power

The African plain is the lion's *domain*.

The courtroom is the *domain* of attorneys and judges.

domestic (duh MES tik) *adj* pertaining to the household; of one's own country

Domestic violence is too prevalent in American households.

Domestic tequila is made in Mexico.

domicile (DAHM ah syl) *n.* a residence; home; dwelling

The most common *domicile* of college students is the dormitory.

The police had to visit the *domicile* because the neighbors had complained of loud music.

don (don) *v.* to put on

Ed took a deep breath, *donned* his parachute, and jumped out of the airplane.

As the storm intensified, Bill went below deck to *don* his foul weather gear.

dormant (DOR munt) *adj.* sleeping or inactive

Bears hibernate in caves and remain *dormant* throughout the winter.

The rain fell steadily over the *dormant* village as nightfall approached.

dossier (DAW see ay) *n.* a file of documents or records; a detailed report

Jim submitted a *dossier* of his work experiences to his new employer.

The FBI keeps a *dossier* on world terrorists.

dotage (DOH tij) *n.* foolishness; senility

Grandmother has reached her *dotage*; in her kitchen she keeps washing the same pot.

Although the minister is in his *dotage*, he delivers an inspiring service every Sunday.

dour (dowr) *adj.* severe; gloomy; stern

The garbage collector was a *dour* one-legged man with never a kind word for anyone.

The barren *dourness* of the infertile land made it impossible for Tim's family to make a living as farmers. (*n.*)

douse (dowce) *v.* to throw a liquid on, drench, plunge into water

The children *doused* each other with water as they played in the summer heat.

Bruce *doused* the campfire to make sure there would be no forest fires during the night.

downcast (DOWN kast) *adj.* depressed or sad

The team's *downcast* faces indicated they had lost the championship game.

The attendants at the funeral service were *downcast* throughout the ceremony.

downplay (DOWN play) *v.* to make something seem less important or not as bad

The sheriff tried to *downplay* his role in rescuing the children.

The doctor would not *downplay* the risk involved in the operation he felt necessary for his patient

downsize (DOWN size) *v.* to reduce in number; make a smaller number

> The merger of the Atom Company and the Exxon Company resulted in the loss of two thousand jobs as they *downsized* their plants.

> The Mackle Yacht Company has *downsized* its most popular model from thirty feet to twenty feet in length.

draconian (dray KOH nee un) *adj.* hard, severe, cruel

> Judge McNamara handed down a *draconian* sentence to the defendant: sixty years in jail for spitting on the sidewalk.

> The word "*draconian*" did not originate with the fictional character Count Dracula, but with an ancient Greek official named Dracula who created a harsh code of laws.

drawl (DRAWL) *n.* speech with drawn-out vowels; slow speech

> George spoke with a *drawl*, and it was sometimes difficult to understand him.

> His *drawl* gave Mike away as having been raised in a southern state.

dregs (dregs) *n.* the least valuable part of something; the sediment contained in liquids

> The *dregs* formed by tea in the bottom of the cup are sometimes used to predict the future.

> The occupants of the prison were the *dregs* of society: murderers, rapists, and thieves.

droll (drohl) *adj.* amusing in an unusual, humorous way

> The comedian's humor was so *droll* you had to think about the punch line a minute to understand the joke.

> The talk show host has a *droll* sence of humor that only his fans appreciate.

dromedary (DRO me dary) *n.* a one-humped domesticated camel

> The *dromedary* is widely used as a beast of burden in Northern Africa and Western Asia.

> A *dromedary* is also known as an Arabian camel.

drone (drohn) *n./v.* lazy person, loafer; to talk on and on in a dull way

> Beth was a *drone* who loafed on the job and took advantage of her co-workers' hard work.

146

droop *Sag, sink, bend or hang down* as from weakness exhaustion, or lack of support

The new air conditioner *droned* all night without letting up.

dross (drahs) *n.* something useless; rubbish; impurities formed on melted metal during production

So much of what's on TV is pure *dross* and not worth watching.

At the garage sale, we found some interesting items that someone had regarded as *dross*.

drudgery (DRUJ ur ee) *n.* hard, tiresome, boring work

The best way to aviod *drudgery* is to find a job you enjoy.

The young girls who think motherhood looks like fun should also consider the *drudgery* involved.

dubious (DOO bee us) *adj.* uncertain; full of doubt

Adam's parents were *dubious* about his potential as a scholar; however, he made the dean's list every semester.

The army is *dubious* about the effectiveness of a love bomb that showers flowers on the enemy.

dulcet (DULL set) *adj.* melodious, soft, soothing

Senator Kramer was a political campaigner who could hypnotize an audience with sweet words and *dulcet* tones.

Nothing was *dulcet* about the rock-and-roll music that shook the McCraken's house from their son's room every morning before school.

dupe (doop) *v.* to fool; trick; deceive

Clark's attempt to *dupe* the store owner with counterfeit bills resulted in his arrest.

The class attempted to *dupe* the substitute, but he knew better.

duplicity (doo PLIS uh tee) *n.* the act of deception; the act of being two faced

Anyone who tells a lie is engaging in an act of *duplicity*.

Used car salesmen often don't tell the truth about the condition of a used car, resorting to *duplicity* in order to make a sale.

durable (DUR uh bul) *adj.* sturdy, long-wearing, lasting, enduring

Blue jeans are constructed of denim, which is a very *durable* fabric.

John bought an antique table because it was *durable* and well constructed.

duress (duh RESS) *n.* hardship; restraint; confinement

The judge ruled the defendant's confession was obtained under police *duress* and could not be used as evidence.

Social scientists have come to understand that people laboring in competitive industries are often under emotional *duress*.

dwell (dwel) *v.* to make one's home; reside; to focus attention on

That book *dwells* on the need for better schools in urban areas.

Psychologists recommend that the mentally ill *dwell* on the positive, rather than the negative.

dwindle (DWIN dul) *v.* to become steadily less; shrink; decrease

The water supply *dwindled* as the caravan reached deeper into the barrens of the Sahara Desert.

Roy's bank account began to *dwindle* as soon as his wife received her own credit card.

ebb (eb) *v.* to become less or disappear; recede; to weaken or decline

He could feel his strength *ebbing* as he lost more and more blood.

As the morning wore on, we could see the tide *ebbing* farther and farther out from the high water mark.

ebullient (i BUL yunt) *adj.* boiling, bubbling with excitement

The *ebullient* audience impatiently awaited the star's appearance on stage.

Pam was *ebullient* when she told her friends about her first date.

eccentric (ek SEN trik) *adj.* irregular; not conventional

The professor was well-known for his *eccentric* antics.

Linda's *eccentric* aunt hides her jewelry in jelly jars.

ecclesiastical (i klee zee AS ti kul) *adj.* belonging to or connected with the Christian religion

Mrs. Brown was proud of her husband, the minister, until it was time to wash and iron his *ecclesiastical* garments.

The many churches in the old city gave it an *ecclesiastical* feeling.

eclectic (i KLEK tik) *adj.* drawn from many sources

Sally's home decor is *eclectic*; she likes a bit of everything, modern as well as antique.

Rescued at sea after days of peanut butter and jelly sandwiches, Hal enjoyed an *eclectic* menu of turkey, ham, chicken, and assorted vegetables.

eclipse (i KLIPS) *v.* to make obscure or darker; to surpass or outshine; to block the light of

The state of the economy has *eclipsed* all other issues during the election campaign.

The new basketball star *eclipsed* the team records for points scored in one game.

economical (ek uh NOM i kul) *adj.* frugal, thrifty, saving

Economical shoppers wait for the day after Thanksgiving to find the best values for items on sale.

Buying in volume is the most *economical* way to shop.

ecosystem (EK oh sis tum) *n.* a community of living things, together with their environment

Our local environmentalists are working to preserve the delicately balanced *ecosystem* of the wetlands.

A pond is an interesting *ecosystem* to study because it contains plants, mammals, reptiles, fish, and numerous microorganisms.

eddy (EDD ee) *n.* a current of water or air running contrary to the main current; a whirlpool

After the riots in the city were quelled, an *eddy* of protest began against the local police, with charges of police brutality.

The boys threw stones into the *eddy* and watched the fast whirlpool revolve in circles.

edict (EE dikt) *n.* a public order given by an authority

The judge enacted an *edict* stating there would be no cameras in the courtroom for the remainder of the trial.

The city council issued an *edict* making it illegal to spit on the sidewalk.

edifice (ED uh fis) *n.* a building, especially one of imposing appearance or size

The construction of one *edifice* led to another, and New York City became a skyline of enormous skyscrapers.

The Taj Mahal may not be the largest *edifice* ever constructed, but surely it is one of the most imposing in the world.

edify (ED uh fye) *v.* to instruct; to enlighten

To further *edify* his platoon, the sergeant gave instruction on cross-country marches using the hand compass.

The *edification* of their children on the danger of drugs was a priority with the Jones' parents. (*n.*)

efface (uh FACE) *v.* to rub away

Many ancient cemetery headstones have been *effaced* by the ravages of time and can no longer be read.

To assure that he left no clues, the thief *effaced* his fingerprints from the stolen car.

effectual (ih FECT choo ul) *adj.* having the power to bring about a result

Parents have yet to discover an *effectual* way to make small children like their spinach.

(The opposite of *effectual* is *ineffectual*.)

The police tried several ways to catch the thieves, all of them *ineffectual*.

effervescent (eff ur VES sunt) *adj.* producing bubbles of gas; foaming; full of energy

Champagne is so *effervescent* that bubbles jet out of the bottle when it is first opened.

She has one of those *effervescent* personalities that often characterize those who are chosen to participate on TV game shows.

efficacy (EF i kuh see) *n.* an ability to produce the intended result; effectiveness

They recently ran a series of tests to measure the *efficacy* of the new cancer drug.

The *efficacy* of the program has yet to be determined, as not quite all the results of the study have been documented.

effigy (EF uh jee) *n.* an object that represents someone who is not liked, usually created in order to express hatred of that person

The people gathered in the village square to throw stones at the king in *effigy*, using a dummy made of cloth and straw with an old tin cup representing his crown.

At the pep rally, our team burned the other team's mascot in *effigy*.

effrontery (e FRUNT ur ee) *n.* brazen boldness; audacity; presumptuousness

Only Holly had the *effrontery* to tell the teacher that he was wrong.

The royal family will tolerate no *effrontery*.

effusion (i FYOO zhun) *n.* pouring forth

There was a great *effusion* of relief when the astronauts were brought back safely.

The clown's entrance caused an *effusion* of laughter and good feelings in the children's ward of the hospital.

egalitarian (e gal uh TARE ee un) *adj./n.* advocating the doctrine of equal rights for all citizens; a person who advocates equal rights

The Communists preached an *egalitarian* philosophy, but in the end they were the same old fascists the world has known through the ages.

Dr. Martin Luther King, Jr. was a true *egalitarian*; he preached equal rights for citizens of all races and religions.

egg (eg) *v.* to encourage or incite to action

My friends *egged* me to try out for the tennis team.

Without the crowd *egging* me on, I don't think I could have finished running the marathon.

egocentric (ee goh SEN trik) *adj.* selfish; believing that one is the center of everything

Unless she changes her *egocentric* attitude, Trish's arrogance and self-centeredness will make her few friends.

The actor was so *egocentric* he could talk for hours using himself as the only subject.

egotist (EE goh tist) *n.* one who excessively speaks boastfully of oneself; one who is conceited

The fact that Mike is an *egotist* is not lost on anyone who talks to him.

Lance is an actor who is so *egotistic that* when he plays King Henry V, he thinks he really is the King. (*adj.*)

egregious (i GREE jus) *adj.* flagrant; extremely bad

Matthew's table manners were worse than bad; they were *egregious*.

Sue's three year-old boy was not just mischievous; he was an *egregious* terror.

egress (EE gress) *n./v.* a place or means of going out; exit

The fire department was concerned that they were too few *egresses* from the building.

A mouse-hole is a means of *egress* for visiting mice.

elaborate (i LAB ur aht) *adj.* clear, detailed carefully

The *elaborate* lighting system took months to install in the new auditorium.

The general refused to make a charge with his forces until he had further intelligence that *elaborated* the enemy's position. (*v.*)

elapse (ee LAPS) *v.* to pass or go by (said of time)

Two years *elapsed* before they were to meet again, but all the time Jonathan knew Annette was the girl he was going to marry.

Fours years *elapsed* between the time the Japanese attacked Pearl Harbor and the end of the war.

elation (i LAY shun) *n.* a feeling or condition of elevated spirits; great joy

When the doctor pronounced Julie cured of cancer, her *elation* knew no bounds.

Pete just bought his first car, and his feeling of *elation* is that of a child receiving his favorite toy for Christmas.

electorate (i LEK tuh rut) *n.* those who participate in an election; qualified voters

Each political candidate for office promises the *electorate* various things he will do for the voters when elected.

In our system, we have an *electorate* as well as a popular vote to elect the president.

elegance (ELL uh gants) *n.* grandeur; refinement; grace

The old mansion was furnished with *elegance*; expensive tapestries and paintings were displayed throughout.

John was a gentleman devoted to the pursuit of *elegance*: art, history, and gourmet dining.

elegy (EL uh jee) *n.* a sorrowful or mournful poem or musical composition, esp. mourning for the dead

The princess sang a beautiful *elegy* in memory of her slain prince.

The sad poem that she wrote was actually an *elegy* for her favorite plant, which died from over-watering.

elfin (EL fin) *adj.* small and sprightly; mischievous, fairylike

Jane is small and has an *elfin* charm until she starts to sing; then she sounds like a bullfrog in a pond.

The entire family had an *elfin* quality like the little people who belong in the Land of Lilliputians.

elicit (i LIS it) *v.* to bring out; to call forth

The beginning teacher found it hard to *elicit* responses from the class, so she tried a different technique.

The attorney attempted to *elicit* sympathy for the accused murderer by calling his mother as a witness.

elite (i LEET) *n.* the best or most skilled members of a group

Members of the school's academic teams are among the educational *elite* of the entire state.

The city was defended by an *elite* corps of the army's finest soldiers. (*adj.*)

elixir (e LIX ur) *n.* cure-all; medicinal concoction

Those who sell so-called *elixirs* sold on TV make fraudulent claims of cures that cannot be verified.

Coca-Cola was considered an *elixir* when first introduced to the market because at that time it contained the juice of coca leaves.

elliptical (i LIP ti kul) *adj.* oval; missing a word; obscure

An *elliptical* statement is one that is difficult to understand, either because there is something left out or because it is so obscure the audience doesn't understand.

She learned from the make-up artist that because her face is *elliptical*, she should apply make-up in a way that makes it look narrower and less square.

elocution (el oh KYOO shun) *n.* the art of public speaking

Classes in *elocution* are helpful to those who seek a career in politics because public speaking for politicians is very important.

Although the valedictorian's message was wonderful, his *elocution* was less than desirable.

eloquent (EL oh kwent) *adj.* extremely expressive in speech, writing, or movement

Stan gave a moving, *eloquent* speech on the virtues of gardening.

The dancers glided *eloquently* across the stage with practiced, graceful movements. (*adv.*)

elucidate (i LOO so dayt) *v.* to make clear and explain fully

Doctors should always *elucidate* test results to their patients.

Elementary school teachers, as a rule, *elucidate* their words more clearly than do college professors, who take for granted their students will understand anything they say.

elusive (i LOO siv) *adj.* evasive; hard to pin down

The scientist from Costa Rica dedicated his life to his search for the *elusive* buffalo butterfly.

The greased pigs were slippery and *elusive* in the children's catch-a-pig rodeo event.

emaciate (i MAY see ayt) *v.* to make extremely thin, usually by starvation or disease

Joan emaciated herself by losing so much weight on her crash diet.

It was sad to see the *emaciation* of the cattle that had not eaten in weeks during the winter dry spell. (*n.*)

emanate (EM uh nayt) *v.* to come from or out of; issue or emit

Raucous laughter *emanated* from the next room.

When Beatrice strolls into a room, everyone stares in awe because of the aura of beauty that *emanates* from her.

emancipate (i MAN suh payt) *v.* to free from some external control or constraint; to liberate

The invention of the dishwasher *emancipated* families from the drudgery of doing the dishes by hand.

The court declared Janice an *emancipated* minor, able to make all her own decisions and legally handle her own financial affairs.

emasculate (ee MASS kyoo late) *v.* to castrate, weaken; to deprive of strength and vigor

The disease *emasculated* the patient; he lost strength and could no longer walk alone.

The *emasculation* of Germany's military capabilities by the Allies in World War II brought the war to an end. (*n.*)

embargo (em BAHR goh) *n.* a government order to temporarily suspend foreign trade

The United States *embargo* on goods to and from Cuba has been controversial since it was first instituted.

Gasoline prices will increase if there is an *embargo* on oil imported from any of the oil-producing Arab nations.

embellish (im BEL ish) *v.* to beautify by adding ornaments; actual or fanciful

Every time Thomas caught a large fish, he would *embellish* the size until he made it sound as big as a whale.

Christmas trees are *embellished* with colored and lighted ornaments.

embezzle (im BEZ ul) *v.* to appropriate illegally

We want to choose a treasurer who will not be tempted to *embezzle* funds from the club.

The loan officer at the bank disappeared and, when an audit was made, it was discovered he had *embezzled* funds by making phony loans to himself.

embody (em BAH dee) *v.* to give bodily form to; to personify; to make part of a system

Virginia Satir was a wonderful therapist who *embodied* in her own life the loving principles she taught to her students.

The *embodiment* of basic Christian virtues is to be found in the Boy Scouts' oath which every scout must take to become a member. (*n.*)

embrace (em BRAYS) *v.* to hug, to accept; to adopt a cause, to include

Jody and Shirley *embraced* warmly when celebrating their twenty-fifth wedding anniversary.

The study *embraced* all aspects of the housing shortage problem.

embroil (im BROYL) *v.* to involve in argument or hostile action; to throw into disorder

Most of the civilized world was *embroiled* in conflict during World War II.

Once someone was hit on the side of the head by a clump of mash potatoes the whole cafeteria *embroiled* into a huge food fight.

embryonic (em bree AHN ik) *adj.* in an early stage of development; in an undeveloped stage; rudimentary

Nick's business is in an *embryonic* stage, but in a year he hopes to have a much larger business.

In our biology class we are studying the various stages of the birth of a pig, from *embryonic* conception to the actual birth.

emend (ee MEND) *v.* to correct by textual alterations; to edit

The author wanted to *emend* his book because he discovered some errors in the printing.

The book was not *emendable* because the publisher had already printed 10,000 copies and had them sent to bookstores. (*adj.*)

emigrant (EM uh grunt) *n.* one who leaves one's place of residence or country

The *emigrants* were stopped at the border.

The *emigrant* left Russia in search for a better life in the United States.

emigrate (EM uh grayt) *v.* to leave a place

Many Americans have grandparents who *emigrated* to this country.

Every day hundreds of retirees *emigrate* to Florida seeking a life in the sun.

eminent (EM ih nent) *adj.* standing out; renowned; distinguished

Michael Jordan is considered the most *eminent* basketball player of the

20th century.

The most *eminent* feature of the hammerhead shark is its hammer-shaped head.

emissary (EM uh ser ee) *n.* an agent sent to represent another person or group, especially a government

The peace talks were presided over by *emissaries* from all the countries involved.

When I get into trouble, my big sister acts as *emissary* to soften up my parents before they see me.

emit (ee MIT) *v.* to send or give out; to express, utter; to put in circulation as money

Bull frogs *emit* a low croaking sound.

The new federal laws on automobile *emissions* are directed at reducing pollution on our nation's highways. (*n.*)

empathy (EM puh thee) *n.* the ability to share someone else's feelings or experiences

He loves children and has a certain *empathy* with them because he vividly recalls what it was like when he was a child.

(To have *empathy* is to *empathsize*.)

I *empathize* with Kim because I can imagine how I would feel if I were in her position.

emphatic (em FAT ik) *adj.* forcibly expressive

The foreman was *emphatic* that no workers come to work on the construction site without wearing their steel helmets.

The sign *emphatically* warned visitors to keep their hands out of the gorilla cage. (*adv.*)

empirical (em PIR uh kul) *adj.* relying on observation or experience

In science class we do experiments so that we can base our findings on *empirical* evidence.

The class proved the hamburgers' deliciousness by the *empirical* method; we ate them.

empower (im POW ur) *v.* to give the power to do something; to permit, enable

157

When my mother was in the hospital, she *empowered* me to handle all her medical matters.

John's vast inheritance *empowered* him to dedicate his life to charitable organizations.

emulate (IM u late) *v.* to attempt to equal or surpass; especially through imitation

It always try to *emulate* may father's work ethic.

The famous golfer Tiger Woods has a golf swing that many golfers try to *emulate*.

en masse (ahn MASS) *adv.* in a body as a whole; as a group

Everyone in the county arrived *en masse* to hear the county commission's proposal to raise taxes.

University of Florida fans rushed *en masse* onto the field as their team beat Tennessee.

enclave (ON klave) *n.* a distinct territory surrounded by a foreign area; any distinct small group surrounded by a larger group

Luxemburg is a small *enclave* surrounded by larger countries.

In Guadalajara, Mexico, there are many *enclaves* of Americans.

encomium (en KOME ee um) *n.* glowing and warm praise, an enthusiastic tribute

At the award dinner, *encomiums* were lavishly bestowed on the winning female team.

The out-going resident received enthusiastic *encomiums* from both parties.

encore (ON kore) *n.* a demand by an audience for a repetition or an additional performance; an additional performance in response to the audience demand

The audience applauded endlessly as a traditional means of requesting an *encore*.

When the band was called back for an *encore*, they played their most famous song to satisfy the crowd.

encroach (en KROACH) *v.* to trespass

Signs were posted all around the nuclear plant warning against trespassers *encroaching* on the property.

The lobster poacher *encroached* upon everyone else's traps until he was caught by the marine patrol.

encumbrance (en KUM bruns) *n.* something that stands in the way or burdens; hindrance

Because he is a noble person, he has to free himself of past *encumbrances* before he can get romantically involved.

A large purse is usually an *encumbrance* when traveling.

endear (in DIR) *v.* to cause to be liked; to cause to be loved or cherished

Bill's fiery temper did not *endear* him to his co-workers.

Elizabeth's kind, generous manner *endeared* her to her friends and family.

endeavor (in DEV ur) *v.* to attempt to fulfill commitment; reach; strive

Thousands of runners *endeavor* to win the Boston Marathon, but only one can win.

The submarine *endeavored* to dive beneath a giant iceberg but became stuck and had to surface.

endemic (en DEM ik) *adj.* native, belonging to a specific region or people

Cacti are *endemic* to Arizona.

Spanish the *endemic* language to Mexico.

endow (en DOW) *v.* bestow; grant; to give, especially a large gift

Grandfather Samuel *endowed* each child with a trust fund.

Nature *endowed* her with extraordinary beauty and grace.

endurance (en DOOR ans) *n.* fortitude; staying power

Sailing in the Americas Cup races requires great *endurance* and agility.

Marathon races are run over a distance of slightly more than twenty-six miles and require great *endurance* on the part of the runners.

enervate (EN ur VAYT) *v.* to gradually drain of strength

After a day of school followed by five hours of work, I am *enervated* even before I start my homework.

The cancer *enervated* Tim, and we watched him grow weaker each day.

enfranchise (en FRAN chyze) *v.* to set free; liberate; to grant the privileges of citizenship

After living many years as an alien, Helen decided to become a citizen by taking the test and becoming *enfranchised*.

In this country, women were not *enfranchised* and could not vote until early in the twentieth century.

engaging (in GAY jing) *adj.* charming; pleasing; attractive

Phillip's *engaging* personality made him popular with his fellow students.

The movie was not *engaging*; it was boring from beginning to end.

engender (en JEN dur) *v.* to create; to cause to happen; to bring into existence

The family who refused to clean up their yard *engendered* hostility among the neighbors.

The oil slick *engendered* a fish kill in the bay.

engross (en GROHS) *v.* to occupy the entire attention of; absorb

Brenda's favorite novels are ones that fully *engross* her.

The children were so *engrossed* by the story teller that they forgot what time it was.

engulf (in GULF) *v.* to surround or enclose completely

The movie stars were *engulfed* by a swarm of paparazzi as they arrived at the Academy Awards ceremony.

The hurricane completely *engulfed* the town in a surge of wind and water.

enhance (en HANS) *v.* to improve; to intensify

Bob *enhanced* his race car's performance by installing a more powerful engine.

Since I *enhanced* my computer's modem, I am able to do research more quickly.

enigma (uh NIG muh) *n.* a mystery; puzzle

How twin boys could be so different is an *enigma* to their parents.

Agatha Christie's books always contain an *enigma* that makes the reader want to continue reading.

enlighten (en LYT ten) *v.* educate; apprise; to inform

The tourists who took the United Nations tour were *enlightened* as to the workings of the organization.

Zeke hoped the results of our research will *enlighten* our colleagues.

enmity (EN mi tee) *n.* hostility; deep-seated hatred

When she saw his new girlfriend, she found it was not easy to disguise her *enmity*.

The *enmity* between the feuding families is the basis of the conflict in the story.

ennui (AHN wee) *n.* boredom and dissatisfaction; lack of interest

The whole country seems to be affected by the *ennui* of the long winter, which allowed so few days of sunshine.

Ricardo's *ennui* caused him to fall asleep in the middle of class.

enormity (i NOR muh tee) *n.* immensity

The boys did not understand the *enormity* of their vandalism of the church until they found themselves in jail.

The *enormity* of the universe is hard to comprehend.

enrage (in RAGE) *v.* to put in a rage; infuriate, anger

It *enrages* my wife when it rains and I forget to wipe my feet before coming into the house.

Muriel *enraged* her boss when she departed on a Caribbean vacation and left a mountain of unfinished work on her desk.

enrapture (en RAP chur) *v.* to delight, to thrill or give pleasure

John and Mary were *enraptured* upon learning they had won a new car in the YMCA fundraising lottery.

The Beatle's performance *enraptured* the crowd.

ensemble (ahn SOM bul) *n.* a coordinated outfit or costume; a performing group

The popular *ensemble* for students today is blue jeans and a T-shirt.

An *ensemble* of actors in a movie usually consists of a number of stars all with more or less equal parts to play.

ensign (EN sin) *n.* a banner; a flag; a naval officer

The ship's *ensign* was flown at half mast to honor the dead.

The graduates at the U.S. Naval Academy are given the rank of *ensign* upon completion.

ensue (in SOO) *v.* to occur just after or as the result of another event

Panic *ensued* when police opened fire at the terrorists.

Rioting *ensued* after the home team lost the pennant.

entail (in TAYL) *v.* to involve or make necessary

Any financial investment *entails* some degree of risk.

Exactly what duties does this job *entail*?

enthrall (en THRAWL) *v.* hold under a spell; to thrill; to captivate

The Great Wallendas' dangerous high wire act without a net *enthralled* millions of circus fans.

It was *enthralling* to be present at the President's Inauguration Ball. (*adj.*)

entice (in TICE) *v.* to lure, attract; to tempt in a pleasing fashion

The delicious aroma of a hamburger stand often *entices* the passerby to stop for a snack.

Food, entertainment, and visits to foreign ports all contribute to the *enticement* of a cruise vacation. (*n.*)

entity (EN tuh tee) *n.* something that exists; something having its own independent existence

Although the two museum buildings are in separate locations, they are part of a single *entity*.

The internet is a separate *entity* in the world of communications.

entomb (in TOOM) *v.* to place in a tomb or a grave

The Egyptians *entombed* their kings in special burial chambers together with all their possessions needed in the afterlife.

In the Pittsburgh coal mine disaster of 1938, thirty-six coal miners were *entombed* in a tunnel for thirteen days.

entomology (IN toe MOL o gee) *n.* the scientific study of insects

One primary function of *entomologists* is to discover how to prevent insects from destroying crops.

Because I find farming fascinating, I want to major in *entomology*.

entourage (ON too rahj) *n.* one's attendants or associates

The princess's *entourage* consisted of her family and friends.

Rock stars have an *entourage* of body guards and assistants who travel with them when they are on the road performing.

entreat (en TREET) *v.* to ask earnestly; to implore, plead, beg

Roger said he would *entreat* Professor Jones to permit us to take the exam early so we could go on the road with the booster club.

Our entire family *entreated* our father to take us on a summer vacation to Europe.

entrepreneur (ahn truh pruh NOOR) *n.* someone who assumes the financial risk of beginning and operating one or more businesses; an independent business person

Peter is an *entrepreneur* who made his fortune with his computer software company.

Jack has become quite the *entrepreneur* since starting his first business in his basement ten years ago.

enumerate (i NOO muh rayt) *v.* to name things separately, one by one; to list

The salesman *enumerated* all the features of the car.

In their divorce, Mary Belle had no trouble *enumerating* all her husband's faults.

enunciate (ee NUN see ayt) *v.* to pronounce; to state definitely

Jackie must learn to *enunciate* if she hopes to become a public speaker.

When one clearly *enunciates* each syllable it is much easier to understand what he is saying.

envision (in VIZH un) *v.* to picture or visualize in the mind; imagine

He *envisioned* a partnership between business and government in the near future.

The company *envisions* adding at least five stores next year.

eon (EE on) *n.* a very long, indefinite period of time

Dinosaurs roamed the Earth *eons* ago.

Eons passed before life appeared on Earth.

epaulet (EP uh let) *n.* ornamental strip, loops or fringed shoulder piece sewn across the shoulder

The *epaulets* on a soldier's uniform most frequently signify his or her rank.

The police officer's uniform includes *epaulets* of a contrasting color.

ephemeral (i FEM ur al) *adj.* short-lived

The common housefly is an *ephemeral* insect.

Poets write poems about first love being sweet but *ephemeral*.

epic (EP ik) *adj.* of major proportions in size and scope

The discovery of DNA was an *epic* event, helping us interpret an individual's make up.

The Ten Commandments is an *epic* movie starring Charlton Heston.

epicure (EP i kyoor) *n.* a person who enjoys food and drink of a high quality, often having great knowledge of the subject

I get nervous when I cook for my mother because she is an *epicure* who won't hesitate to criticize what I did wrong.

My son has become an *epicure* of fine wines.

epigram (EP ih gram) *n.* a brief and usually witty saying

Greeting card companies make huge profits creating *epigrams* about love.

Sally's favorite *epigram* is, "A friend in need is a friend indeed."

epigraph (EP ih graff) *adj.* quotation set at the start of a literary writing; an engraved inscription

"Justice is blind" is a famous *epigraph* in some legal textbooks.

Our teacher gave a test which asked us to explain how the *epigraph* applies to the novel.

epilepsy (EP ih lep see) *n.* a condition caused by electrical impulses in the central nervous system

Julius Caesar and Albert Einstein were both victims of *epilepsy.*

Epilepsy is more treatable now than in the past.

epilogue (EP uh log) *n.* a short concluding section to a literary work or a play; often a summary

My role in the play is to present the *epilogue,* in which I explain the idea of the play and interpret the theme.

A book's *epilogue* is placed at the end of the book just before the index.

epistemology (i PIS tu mol uh jee) *n.* the study of what can be known

Epistemology is a branch of philosophy investigating the limits of knowledge.

Stanley studied *epistemology* to better understand the possibilities of educational systems.

epitaph (EP ih taf) *n.* writing on a tombstone; a short commemoration

Horace's *epitaph* lists him as ten years older than he had always claimed to be.

George wrote a brief *epitaph* to honor his departed friend.

epitome (i PIT uh mee) *n.* the perfect example

Benjamin Franklin was the *epitome* of the enlightened statesman.

Michael Jordan is the *epitome* of a basketball player.

epoch (EP uk) *n.* a distinct or notable period in history; a long period of time; an era

The 1960s was an *epoch* of turmoil and unrest that seemed to go on forever, but many great things came from that era.

The *epoch* of rock and roll began in the early 1950s but continues, ever evolving, to this day.

equable (EK wuh bull) *adj.* free from many changes or variations; even

Sam had an easy going *equable* temperament.

Southern Florida lays claim to a pleasant and *equable* temperature year-round.

equanimity (ek wuh NIM uh tee) *n.* calm; composure

The young soldier faced his death with *equanimity*.

The mayor's chief asset was that he was able to maintain his *equanimity* while turmoil raged around him.

equestrian (i KWES tree un) *adj.* connected with the riding of horses; of or concerning horsemanship

The American Indians of the West were born *equestrians* who began riding horses at an early age. (*n.*)

In the center of town they are going to erect an *equestrian* statue in honor of the late, great jockey who was born here.

equitable (EK wuh tuh bul) *adj.* fair

The public thought the teachers deserved an *equitable* salary.

Judges try to make *equitable* rulings, but sometimes people don't view them that way.

equivocal (i KWIV uh kul) *adj.* ambiguous; confusing

By Danny's *equivocal* letters home from summer camp, his parents couldn't tell if he liked it or not.

When Eli asked Maureen to the dance, her answer was so *equivocal* that he decided to ask someone else.

equivocate (ee KWIV oh kayt) *v.* to avoid giving a direct answer; to deceive; to be shifty

He *equivocated* in his report to the press neither denying or confirming the rumors.

The mayor was *equivocating* when he deliberately avoided telling the public how bad the city's finances had become.

eradicate (ee RAD i kayt) *v.* to get rid of; exterminate; destroy

We hoped to *eradicate* the bugs by fogging the house.

It is my father's mission to *eradicate* all weeds in our yard.

erratic (i RAT ik) *adj.* unstable; inconsistent; unpredictable

March comes in like a lion and goes out like a lamb; those are *erratic* conditions.

The boy's *erratic* behavior toward his dog—sometimes being attentive, sometimes ignoring his pet for days—worried his parents.

erroneous (ih RONE ee us) *adj.* fallacious; false

It is *erroneous* to assume the you won't have to work for what you get in life.

The *erroneous* date on the new coins will make them valuable as collectors items.

erstwhile (URST while) *adj.* having been previously; formerly

Dolphin fans dream of their *erstwhile* star Dan Marino and a Super Bowl victory had he not retired.

Jack's *erstwhile* friends joined together and gave him a welcome home party.

erudite (ER yoo dyte) *adj.* deeply learned; scholarly

Most professional speakers are *erudite*, understanding proper grammatical structure and using large vocabulary.

(To be *erudite* is to have *erudition*.)

The extent of Dr. Smith's library is an indication of his *erudition*. (*n.*)

eruption (ee RUP shun) *n.* a bursting out

Just as the students were settling down, an *eruption* from the loud speaker disrupted them.

The *eruption* of a volcano is beautiful yet deadly.

escalation (ES kah lay shun) *n.* an increase in intensity

Many Americans were unhappy with the *escalation* of the Vietnam War.

From first to second semester, we usually see an *escalation* of good grades.

escapade (ES kah payd) *n.* an adventurous, unconventional act

Joe and Alan's *escapade* at the beach during Spring Break is one they will never forget.

Hiking in the Rockies for three full days was our most recent family *escapade*.

eschew (ES choo) *v.* to avoid or shun

We were advised to *eschew* riding the subway at night in certain parts of the city.

Sally *eschews* anyone who uses bad language.

esoteric (es uh TER ik) *adj.* hard to understand

Abstract algebra is too *esoteric* for the average math student.

Steve uses *esoteric* vocabulary with his children; they don't understand what he is talking about.

esplanade (ESS pluh nahd) *n.* a level open stretch of paved land or grassy ground near water

The *esplanade* mall is near the Lazy River, with walkways in both directions.

In New Orleans, people stroll along the *esplanade* every afternoon.

espouse (eh SPOWZ) *v.* to adopt; to support

The candidate for governor *espoused* a one-cent sales tax to build a new stadium.

Because Barbara was always ready to *espouse* students' privileges, she was elected senior class president.

espy (i SPY) *v.* discover; to glimpse; to catch sight of

From Arthur's lofty vantage point, he *espied* the man o' war.

When Christopher Columbus and his men finally *espied* land, they thought they had reached India.

essential (i SEN schul) *adj.* important; vital; absolutely necessary

Water is *essential* to the growth of new communities and to progress.

Quiet is *essential* in the public library.

estimable (ES teh muh bul) *adj.* worthy of respect or admiration; capable of being estimated

For many years, she ran an *estimable* publishing house of which her publishing peers thought highly.

The young boxer was an *estimable* opponent for the champ, and he won the fight after a tough struggle.

estrange (eh STRANJ) *v.* to turn an affectionate attitude into an indifferent or unfriendly one

Lawrence feared his candid, negative views of the company would *estrange* him from his co-workers.

Hardly recognizing anyone, Ed felt *estranged* from his old high school classmates during their 25th reunion.

estuary (ESS choo ayre ee) *n.* a waterway where the ocean tide meets the river current

A branch of the sea or gulf at the lower end of the river is an *estuary*.

Some believe strip mining up river will ruin the *estuary* in Charlotte Harbor because of the chemical waste.

et al (et al) *n.* and others

The commissioners, sheriff, treasurer, *et al* waited for Judge Smith to join the meeting.

Books by Jones, Smith, Brown, *et al* were on sale at Barnes & Noble book store.

etching (ETCH ing) *n.* an engraving, a design or inscription into a hard surface, esp. printing

The *etching* on the glass bowl showed images of the twelve astrological signs.

The art show featured *etching* cut into ivory.

ethereal (ih THEER ee ul) *adj.* very light; delicate; heavenly

An *ethereal* mist covered the base of the hill at sunrise.

The *ethereal* scent of freshly baked apple pie permeated the kitchen.

ethics (ETH iks) *adj.* values pertaining to human conduct; moral philosophy

The *ethics* of the fight promoter were questionable; he willingly encouraged a brain-damaged boxer to take a bout that could maim or kill him.

The *ethics* of the tobacco business are under severe scrutiny because tobacco and cigarette smoking have been proven to cause cancer.

ethnocentricity (eth no sen TRISS ih tee) *n.* a belief that one's own group is superior

Hitler's *ethnocentricity* can be seen in his book *Mein Kempf*, which advocates the racial superiority of the Germanic race.

The Ku Klux Klan's downfall was based on the American people's rejection of *ethnocentric* prejudice. (*adj.*)

eulogy (YOO luh jee) *n.* great praise, especially for someone who has recently died; formal commendation

Tony knew my brother better than anyone, so I asked him to give my brother's *eulogy* at the memorial service.

When his granddaughter delivered the *eulogy*, the mourners became tearful.

euphemism (YOO fuh miz um) *adj.* pleasant expression used in place of an unpleasant one

Euphemisms are regularly used as polite ways to describe body parts and bodily functions.

The *euphemism* "passed away" is a more pleasant expression than the word "died."

euphonious (you PHONE ee us) *adj.* pleasing to the ear

Carla sings in the choir because she has a sweet, *euphonious* voice.

The low, *euphonious* croaking of the summer frogs was music to Jeff's ears.

euthanasia (YOO thu NAY zuh) *n.* an easy and painless death; the act or practice of causing death painlessly to end suffering

Dr. Kevorkian is famous for his practice of *euthanasia* on terminal patients.

The *euthanasia* of unwanted domestic animals has been the subject of moral debate in the United States for years.

euthanize (YOO thu niyz) *v.* to put to death

The old dog was so decrepit that we were forced to have her *euthanized*.

Many unwanted cats and dogs are *euthanized* each year.

evade (ee VADE) *v.* to elude or avoid by cunning; to flee from a pursuer

The escaped prisoners *evaded* the authorities by breaking into a church and disguising themselves as nuns.

Jane *evades* helping her sister wash dishes by claiming she has homework to do.

evaluate (ee VAL yoo ayt) *v.* to determine or judge the value or worth of

The supervisor was sent in to *evaluate* each member of the department.

The hardest job of the English teacher is to *evaluate* each student's writing.

evanescent (ev uh NES unt) *adj.* happening for a brief period

The young film star never realized that fame is *evanescent* until the movie producers lost interest in her.

House flies are *evanescent*, having life spans of only a few days.

eventuate (ee VEN choo ayt) *v.* to happen in the end; to result ultimately

It was obvious to many that World War I would *eventuate* in World War II.

All too often marriage *eventuates* in divorce.

evince (i VINS) *v.* to show or demonstrate clearly

The prince sang a song beneath her balcony to *evince* his love for the fair maiden.

The new billboard *evinced* a sales message promoting a new kind of soap.

evoke (ee VOKE) *v.* to summon forth; call to mind; suggest

A clap of thunder and a flash of lightning over the old castle *evoked* dark spirits for the villagers who remembered the night of the headless ghosts.

The gymnastics coach's demand that her gymnasts give up dating *evoked* a strike by the members of the team.

exacerbate (ig ZAS ur bayt) *v.* to make worse

The old man *exacerbated* his discipline problem when he started screaming at his students.

Not going to class *exacerbated* the likelihood of Elliot's failing American History.

exacting (ig ZAK ting) *adj.* demanding, difficult, requiring great care

In college, Henry came to realize that the *exacting* teachers he disliked in high school were the ones from whom he learned the most.

A good cosmetic surgeon must be *exacting* so that none of his surgical stitches will be detected when the scars heal.

exalt (ig ZAWLT) *v.* to raise high; glorify

The fireman was *exalted* by the press for saving the child from a burning building.

Elizabeth's parents *exalted* her when she scored 1600 on her SATs.

exasperate (ig ZAS puh rayt) *v.* to thoroughly annoy

The child's endless whining on the airplane exasperated all the passengers.

The students *exasperated* the teacher by not having their assignment completed.

excerpt (EK surpt) *n.* a selection, quote, or portion taken from a work of literature

An *excerpt* from my book was used in the newspaper article.

Magazines use headline-size *excerpts* of the most interesting part of a story to attract a reader's attention to that story.

excise (ek SYZE) *v.* to remove by cutting; to cut out

The surgeon *excised* a small tumor from Jack's leg and found the tumor to be benign.

The sculptor *excised* the unwanted material from the stone.

excoriate (ek SKOR ee ayt) *v.* to denounce strongly

The speaker came to *excoriate* the new and controversial decisions of the school board.

It is not appropriate to *excoriate* members of one's family in public.

excruciating (ek SKROO shee ayt eng) *adj.* very intense

After her fall, she was in *excruciating* pain until she was given medication.

Although the exam was *excruciating,* it separated those who had studied from those who had not.

execrable (ig ZEK ruh bul) *adj.* wretched, very bad, detestable

It was an unusually *execrable* winter; it snowed for weeks and the sun never shone.

The hostess demonstrated *execrable* taste by inviting all three of Ric's former wives to the party.

exemplar (ig ZEM pler) *n.* a model or original; an example

The littlest ballerina was cited as being an *exemplar* as a student.

George Washington is presented in American history as the *exemplar* of a true patriot.

exemplify (ig ZEM pluh fye) *v.* to serve as an example

Benjamin Franklin *exemplifies* the wisdom and strength of the founding fathers.

Christina *exemplifies* the model skydiver because she has had over 300 jumps with never a mishap.

exempt (ig ZEMPT) *adj.* not having to obey a rule or to do something usually necessary; excused

Unlike profitable businesses, charitable organizations are *exempt* from paying taxes.

Bertha was *exempt* from jury duty because she was in the hospital at the time she was summoned.

exert (ig ZURT) *v.* to expend effort; to bring to bear steadily or forcefully

The ship's captain *exerted* influence over all the sailors on his ship.

The child continually *exerted* pressure on his balloon until it burst and frightened him.

exhaustive (ig ZAWS tiv) *adj.* thorough, complete

Because the play is tomorrow, we had to have an *exhaustive* dress rehearsal this afternoon.

Sherlock Holmes has gone down in literature as a famous detective who solves his cases by virtue of an *exhaustive* search for clues.

exhilarate (ig ZILL uh rate) *v.* to make cheerful, enliven, excite, or stimulate

The millions of Brazilian soccer fans were *exhilarated* when their team scored the winning goal in overtime.

Fresh mountain air *exhilarates* outdoorsmen.

exhort (ig ZORT) *v.* to urge strongly

The union *exhorted* management to meet its demands.

My parents *exhorted* me to go to college after graduation.

exorbitant (ig ZOR bi TENT) *adj.* exceeding normal bounds; excessive, unfair

The undisclosed fees on our tour were *exorbitant*.

The airline fare was *exorbitant*, but I had no choice and had to pay it.

expatriate (eks PAY tree ayt) *v.* to exile, banish; leave one's country (either by force or by desire)

Ernest Hemingway was one of the first authors to *expatriate* during World War I.

Fidel Castro *expatriated* many of Cuba's former patriots who no longer agreed with him.

expedient (ik SPEE dee unt) *adj.* giving an immediate advantage; practical

The rescue worker knew it was *expedient* to use a tourniquet before his patient lost too much blood.

The teacher thought it *expedient* to solve the misunderstanding before it became a fist-fight.

expedite (EK spi dyte) *v.* to speed up

The manager opened another cash register to *expedite* the check-out process during the sale.

Our young accountant who understood the new laws, *expedited* the filing of our taxes.

expiate (EK spee ayt) *v.* to atone or make amends

Don bought flowers to *expiate* his thoughtfulness in forgetting Mary's birthday.

The woman *expiated* for hitting my dog; she paid all the vet bills and often stopped to check on him.

explicate (EK spli kayt) *v.* to explain in detail; to make clear or explain completely

This is a book which attempts to clearly *explicate* the differences in male/female psychology.

Barbara *explicated* to her father her reasons for taking his car without permission and bringing it home on the back of a tow truck.

explicit (ik SPLIS it) *adj.* clearly and frankly expressed

The directions on the computer are so *explicit* that anyone who can read can operate it.

Because of their *explicit* sexual material, many television shows are not aired until young children are in bed.

exposition (ek spuh ZISH un) *n.* a detailed statement intended to explain something difficult; a public exhibition

Fred put on a wonderful public *exposition* of African artifacts he had procured over a period of five years.

The computer technician gave me a long *exposition* on the components and structure of the motherboard, but I still don't understand it.

expostulate (ik SPAHS chu layt) *v.* to express disagreement or complaint; to argue earnestly with someone

The Minister of Defense *expostulated* angrily against the terrorist bombing.

Walter *expostulated* with the waiter about the amount of his bill.

expunge (ex PUNDG) *v.* to remove; to delete; to erase

The judge ordered the clerk to *expunge* the lawyer's statement from the record.

The wet and muddy footprints were *expunged* with soap and water.

expurgate (EX pur gate) *v.* to free from sins; to purify

A religious group tried to *expurgate* books they considered immoral from the school system.

Kansas schools once attempted to *expurgate* the teaching of Darwin's Theory of Evolution, but the voters rejected their efforts.

exquisite (EKS kwi zit) *adj.* especially beautiful; delicately or finely made; keenly felt; intense

Uncle Bob brought back the most *exquisite* Chinese embroideries, the beauty of which I have never seen elsewhere.

The father cried from *exquisite* love and wonder as he watched his child being born.

extant (EK stunt) *adj.* still existing; current; not extinct, destroyed, or lost

She is the author of the earliest *extant* volume of poetry by an African-American.

In years to come, the number of his *extant* paintings will decrease and their value will increase at the same rate.

extempore (iks TEM puh ray) *adj.* spoken, performed, or composed with little or no advanced preparation

The Congressman unexpectedly delivered an *extempore* speech about his campaign.

Winston unexpectedly stood at the podium and with ease spoke *extemporaneously* about the team. (*adv.*)

extensive (ek STEN siv) *adj.* huge; comprehensive; widespread

The Sahara Desert forms part of the *extensive* desert system in Africa.

David, the scholar, had an *extensive* knowledge of Arctic history.

extinct (ik STINKT) *adj.* no longer existing or living

Because she had been unsuccessful in love, Rachel thought the perfect man had become *extinct*.

Many species could become *extinct* within the next century.

extirpate (EK stir payt) *v.* to exterminate; to rip out, uproot, destroy

Most exterminators attempt to *extirpate* termites from homes.

Tom *extirpated* the weeds from his lawn with various weed killers.

extol (ik STOHL) *v.* to praise; to laud

Many financial advisors *extol* the value of frugality.

The President *extolled* the work of the police who, with their efforts, reduced the crime rate in the city.

extort (ik STAWRT) *v.* to obtain by force or threat, or illegally; to extract or obtain by abuse of authority

The gang is accused of *extorting* money from local store owners in exchange for protection from rival gangs.

The stock broker was convicted of *extorting* money from his clients' accounts.

extradition (eks tra DISH un) *n.* surrendering a criminal to another jurisdiction

Costa Rica has no *extradition* agreement with the USA; American criminals cannot be brought back for their crimes.

Germany *extradited* the banker to the U.S. to face formal charges. (*v.*)

extraneous (ik STRAY nee us) *adj.* unnecessary; extra

I did not enjoy the movie because there were too many *extraneous* characters who did not add to the plot.

The speaker did not appreciate the *extraneous* comments from the audience and stopped talking until everyone was silent.

extrapolate (ik STRAP uh layt) *v.* to deduce; to infer

After he was presented with all the evidence, the detective was able to *extrapolate* the location of the weapon.

The accused man *extrapolated* his fate by studying the expressions on the faces of the jury members.

extreme (ik STREEM) *adj.* intense, severe, excessive, exaggerated

Extreme cold is dangerous for heart patients.

Jill will go to any *extreme* to get Jack to do what she wants. (*n.*)

extremity (ik STREM uh tee) *n.* the furthest point; the greatest degree; the utmost extreme; a limb or appendage of the body

Key West, Florida, is the southernmost *extremity* of the United States.

I knew Sheila was in shock because her breathing was shallow, her pulse faint, and her *extremities* pale and cold.

extricate (EK struh kayt) *v.* to free from difficulty

Matthew's parents hired a lawyer to *extricate* him from the legal charges brought against him.

After the blizzard many in the city needed snow plows to *extricate* their cars from their driveways.

extrinsic (iks TRINZ ik) *adj.* not part of the essential nature of things

The historical information in the book was *extrinsic* to the actual plot.

Gary's good looks were completely *extrinsic* to his superb ability as a house painter.

extrovert (EKS truh vurt) *n.* an outgoing person

Jim was an *extrovert*, always talking and making everyone laugh with his remarks.

An *extrovert* should never get a job in a funeral parlor.

extrude (ik STROOD) *v.* to force out, as through a small opening

Toothpaste *extrudes* from the tube when you squeeze it.

Plastic bags are usually manufactured by large *extrusion* machines. (*n.*)

exuberant (ig ZOO buh runt) *adj.* very energetic; high-spirited

My children were so *exuberant* once we got to Disney World that I had no idea how I was going to keep up with them all day.

The Wright Brothers were tremendously *exuberant* the day their airplane flew for the first time.

exult (igz UHLT) *v.* to celebrate

The American ice hockey team *exulted* in its victory over the strong Canadian team.

The childless couple *exulted* in the news that their adoption had been approved.

exultation (igz ahl TAY shun) *n.* the act of rejoicing; jubilation

When she learned she had gotten the lead role, Kelly was in a state of *exultation*.

His parents could barely control their *exultation* as he walked across the stage to receive his doctoral degree.

fabrication (fab ruh KAY shun) *n.* a lie; something made up

Those who know Ruth are sure her story about dating Prince William is pure *fabrication*.

Although Tim's list of his qualifications was a total *fabrication*, he got the job and did well.

facade (fuh SAHD) *n.* the front of a building; outward appearance, especially if superficial or misleading

The *facade* of this townhouse is made of limestone.

Behind her *facade* of gentleness was a tough competitor.

facet (FAS it) *n.* one of the small, flat faces of a cut gemstone; one of the parts or features of something

That stone shines brilliantly because it has so many *facets* to catch the light.

There's always one *facet* of Jeff's life that isn't going smoothly.

facetious (fuh SEE shus) *adj.* not serious; humorous

Diana's *facetious* remark about Jessica made everyone laugh.

Our statement about the new dress code was completely *facetious*, but the dean took it seriously.

facile (FAS il) *adj.* skillful in an off-hand way

Many people believe the poems of Emily Dickinson are too *facile* to be judged among the best.

The motivational speaker who addressed us today is the most *facile* lecturer I have ever heard.

facilitate (fuh SILL uh tate) *v.* to make easier, to help bring about

In order to *facilitate* the sale of their home, George had it painted.

Pete was a *facilitator* at the institution, helping things run smoothly by expediting matters. (*n.*)

facsimile (fak SIM uh lee) *n.* something closely resembling another; imitation; reproduction

The antique Chinese vase was a *facsimile* of one from the Ming dynasty.

The bell from the tavern was an exact *facsimile* of Big Ben in London.

faction (FAK shun) *n.* a group, usually part of a larger group

The Salem witch trials began because a *faction* of the Puritans believed in witchcraft.

Although a *faction* in our class did not like their schedule changes, no options were discussed.

factitious (fak TISH us) *adj.* not real, genuine or natural; artificial

She loved her engagement ring until she learned that it was *factitious*.

The *factitious* appearance of the driver's license was the bouncer's reason for not allowing the boys to enter the adult establishment.

fallacy (FAL uh see) *n.* a false belief; false idea or notion

It is a common *fallacy* that only boys are good at math.

The old wives' tale about cats lying on babies to "steal" their breath is a *fallacy*.

fallow (FAL low) *adj.* not in use, inactive

> After his most successful novel, the author took an extensive vacation, allowing his writing talent to lie *fallow* for a two-year period.

> We allowed the over-worked land to lie *fallow* for several seasons.

falsetto (fawl SET oh) *n.* high singing voice

> Many modern artists who lack tenor voices sing *falsetto*.

> When Glen dressed as a woman for Halloween, he also spoke in a *falsetto*.

falter (FALL tur) *v.* stumble; hesitate in purpose or action

> Joey *faltered* at the altar when he discovered his bride-to-be had false teeth.

> The race horse *faltered* and fell in the back stretch, but fortunately neither the jockey nor the horse were seriously injured.

fanatic (fuh NAT ik) *n.* one extremely devoted to a cause or idea

> The *fanatics* were eager to die for the glory of their country.

> Green Bay Packer fans are *fanatics* for their team.

farce (farce) *n.* a false imitation; a mockery

> *Third Rock from the Sun* is a *farce* about aliens living on earth today.

> *Saturday Night Live* is a *farcical* TV program that pokes fun at American celebrities and events.   (*adj.*)

farrago (fuh RAG oh) *n.* a careless or confused mixture; hodge-podge

> Charlie ran from the burning building wearing a *farrago* of different shoes.

> The student roommates furnished their apartment with a *farrago* of furniture.

fastidious (fa STID ee us) *adj.* meticulous; picky

> Mr. Williams hired a *fastidious* secretary to overlook legal details in his office.

> My wife is a *fastidious* housekeeper who never lets dust settle on anything for five minutes.

fatalist (FAYT uh list) *n.* someone who believes fate is in control of everything that happens

The *fatalist* believes that he can do nothing to alter his circumstances in life.

The patient was a *fatalist* and refused treatment for his illness; whatever would happen would happen anyway, he believed.

fathom (FA thum) *v.* to understand fully; to penetrate the meaning of

The jury found it hard to *fathom* how the defendant could commit such a terrible crime.

(In nautical terms, *fathom* is six feet of water depth.)

We dropped anchor in four *fathoms* of water and made plans to stay for the night. (*n.*)

fatuous (FACH oo us) *adj.* silly; foolish

The high school boys were driven to *fatuous* acts for attention when the twenty-year-old girl announced that she was their substitute for the day.

The audience made *fatuous* comments during the serious play.

fauna (FAW nuh) *n.* animals of a specific region

On our vacation in Alaska, we saw much *fauna* that we'd never seen at home.

The *fauna* of Florida would never survive in New England.

faux (foh) *adj.* false; phony; fake

The facade on our townhouse is actually *faux* limestone, not real limestone at all.

Many fur coats are made of *faux* fur, not actual animal pelts.

fawn (fawn) *v.* exhibit affection; "suck up" to someone or something

Andrea's cat *fawns* her by rubbing along side her leg when she is hungry.

The grandmother *fawned* over her grandchild, tickling him and making "goo-goo" sounds.

feasible (FEE zub bul) *adj.* within reason, likely, able to be done

It is not *feasible* to drive to Charleston and return the same day.

To break the nicotine habit is *feasible*; millions have done it.

fecund (FEE kund) *adj.* fertile; productive

181

Leonardo Di Vinci's *fecund* artistic abilities have left the world many art treasures.

Our cat is so *fecund* that she once had three litters in one year.

feign (fayn) *v.* to give a false appearance; to pretend

Jeremy talked a good game, but he also *feigned* knowledge of space science he did not possess.

Elizabeth *feigned* illness in order to stay home from school the day of her final exam in math.

feint (faint) *v.* to trick by cunning

The defensive tackle *feinted* to the left, then charged to the right and tackled the quarterback.

The young boy *feinted* being sick in order to stay home from school.

felicity (fuh LIS uh tee) *n.* happiness; adeptness at expressing things

The immigrants had dreams of *felicity* in their new country.

Children with a good vocabulary have more *felicity* in communication than those without.

felony (FEH lon ee) *n.* a serious crime; a crime punishable by imprisonment for more than a year

Jay's burglary was a *felony* and got him three years in jail.

Judy's *felonious* attempt to steal a car was frustrated by an empty gas tank. (*adj.*)

femme fatale (femme fuh TAL) *n.* a woman who attracts men by her aura of charm and mystery

Mata Hari was a famous *femme fatale* who was a German spy during World War I.

In the play *Damn Yankees*, the character Lola was a *femme fatale* sent by the devil to entice a baseball player.

femur (FEE mur) *n.* largest bone in the body, thigh bone

Doctor George repaired the patient's broken left *femur* with a steel plate and four screws.

A biology professor waved the *femur*, saying, "This is the longest bone in the body."

ferment (FUR mint) *n.* a state of agitation

Mrs. Jones' *ferment* was clear when she kicked Scott out of the class.

The *ferment* between the nations led to the eventual war.

ferret (FARE ut) *v.* to force out of hiding

The Mexican general declared that he would *ferret* Zorro out no matter where he attempted to hide.

The fox ran into a hole, and the hunting dogs tried to *ferret* him out.

ferrous (FAIR us) *adj.* relating to iron and its properties

Rose plants are affected by *ferrous* compounds in the soil that determine their degree of color.

To prevent anemia the doctor prescribed a B-12 vitamin instead of *ferrous* vitamin supplements.

fertile (FUR tuhl) *adj.* productive, resourceful, fruitful

Mary was delighted she was able to grow eggplant in her garden, and she attributed her success to the *fertile* soil.

Mark's *fertile* mind keeps churning out new inventions by the dozens.

fervid (FUR vid) *adj.* extremely hot; with great passion

He was *fervid* in his belief that professional wrestling is a legitimate sport.

Everyone sitting in his section at the game could see that Jim was a most *fervid* Miami Dolphins fan.

fervor (FUR vur) *n.* great ardor or zeal

On Super Bowl Sunday the *fervor* of the fans is unbounded.

Michael Jordan's *fervor* for the game of basketball was obvious each time he stepped onto the court.

fester (FES tur) *v.* to generate pus; to cause resentment or irritation

Diane's resentments towards her boss's unkind remarks about her work *festered* until they finally drove her to quit her job.

Private Sholley's wound *festered* for so long it was impossible for the surgeons to save his leg.

fetish (FET ish) *n.* an object of unreasonable, obsessive reverence or attention

Her psychologist said the reason Darlene had a *fetish* for washing her hands a dozen times a day was that she had a guilt complex about something in her past life, and she was trying to wash the guilt away.

Chocolate was more than a *fetish* with Mary; she had to have a chocolate fix several times a day.

fetter (FET ur) *v.* to restrain; to hamper

The prisoners were *fettered* by shackles around their ankles.

The cowboy *fettered* his horse so it would be there when he returned.

fiasco (fee AS koh) *n.* a complete or humiliating failure

The children's plan to release all the animals at the Humane Society was an utter *fiasco*.

Teresa ordered $300 worth of Girl Scout cookies, and her parents had to pay for the *fiasco*.

fiat (FYE ut) *n.* an authoritative, often arbitrary, decree or order

The general ruled by *fiat* for eight years after seizing power.

The new administrator handed down a *fiat* that disallowed any breaks, other than 30 minutes for lunch each day.

fibrous (FIE bruss) *adj.* containing or relating to fibers

Bran cereal contains a large quantity of *fibrous* wheat, believed to be beneficial.

The advantage of *fibrous* paper towels is that they absorb liquid and are handy in kitchen use.

fickle (FIK ul) *adj.* not loyal or consistent

Summer weather is *fickle*; each morning the sun shines, but when you are ready to play golf, it starts to rain.

Mary Jane's *fickle* nature was well known by her boyfriends; she told each he was her favorite.

fidelity (fuh DEL uh tee) *n.* faithfulness; loyalty

My parents have shown their *fidelity* to each other through thick and thin for almost fifty years.

Bootleg music tapes often do not have the *fidelity* of the originals.

fiefdom (FEEF dum) *n.* something one has rights over

If any *fiefdom* controlled the hydrogen bomb, it could well control the world.

A man's home is his *fiefdom*, and he makes his own policy.

figment (FIG munt) *n.* something imaginary or invented; a fabrication

The ghosts Jimmy saw in his bedroom were *figments* of his imagination.

Many children have imaginary friends which are only *figments and* which usually disappear with age.

figurative (FIG yur uh tiv) *adj.* expressing something as a figure of speech

Strong poetry is usually full of *figurative* language.

When Bob told Rita she was as dumb as a brick, he was speaking *figuratively*. (*adv.*)

filial (FILL ee ull) *adj.* having the relationship of a child to a parent

Before Jan's children could go to school, they had a *filial* responsibility to make their beds.

Father assumed I would take over the family business as my *filial* responsibility.

filibuster (FILL ih buss ter) *n.* the attempt to delay or prevent action; legislative tactic

In their Congressional *filibuster* against medical insurance, the opponents talked for six straight days to prevent the issue from coming to a vote.

The class attempted a *filibuster* so the teacher would forget to assign homework.

filigree (FIL uh gree) *n.* anything delicate or fanciful

A *filigree* of light patches of snow covered the road to the farmhouse.

Teddy wore a large pin of diamonds laced with gold *filigree*.

finagle (fih NAY gul) *v.* obtain by trickery; to use devious or dishonest methods

Jim *finagled* his way into the private party by entering through the kitchen when no one was looking.

Horace's construction company *finagled* a look at the bids of their competitors in order to become the lowest bidder.

finesse (fi NES) *n.* skillfulness; subtlety; craftiness

The ice skater skates with *finesse*, leaping and twirling with graceful abandon.

The prosecuting attorney *finessed* the witness into admitting that she had not been telling the truth. (*v.*)

finis (fih NEE) *n.* the end or conclusion

The *finis* to the show was when the actors took their final bow and the curtain came down.

The Nuremburg Trials of Nazi war criminals marked a symbolic *finis* to World War II.

fiscal (FIS kul) *adj.* relating to public money or other financial matters; monetary

Financial planners assume the *fiscal* responsibility of their clients, hoping to make them more money.

A *fiscal* year is a period of twelve months, but not always January 1st to December 31st; it can be any 12-month consecutive period.

fitful (FIT ful) *adj.* occurring at irregular intervals; spasmodic; restless

Mr. Claymore spent a *fitful*, sleepless night when his wife entered the hospital because of chest pains.

The coach flew into a *fitful* rage when his star player failed to arrive for the game.

fjord (fyord) *n.* a long narrow inlet from the sea between steep cliffs or hills

Norway and New Zealand are two countries noted for having the most scenic *fjords* in the world.

The ship took us to the *fjords* to examine the distinctive flora and fauna.

flabbergasted (FLAB er gast id) *adj.* astounded or amazed

After the first game, the fans were *flabbergasted* to realize how much their team had changed in the last year.

Jessica was *flabbergasted* by the unexpected gift.

flaccid (FLASS id) *adj.* not firm or stiff

> After a long sickness the athlete's muscles became *flaccid*, suffering a considerable loss of strength.

> The over-ripe celery stalks lost their freshness and became *flaccid* when they were left in the sun for several days.

flagellate (FLADGE uh late) *v.* scourge; to drive or punish as if by whipping

> In some religions, practitioners *flagellate* themselves with whips as a form of penance.

> In biological terms, a class of unicellular organisms are called *flagellates* because of their whip-like shape. (*n.*)

flagrant (FLAY grunt) *adj.* blatantly bad; scandalous

> Brian's *flagrant* disregard for Shelia's feelings is what upset her the most.

> The professor gave the otherwise acceptable essay a poor grade because it was filled with *flagrant* spelling errors.

flamboyant (flam BOY ant) *adj.* excessively showy, ornate; highly elaborate

> The Palace of Versailles is one of the most *flamboyant* edifices ever constructed.

> After they win the lottery, many people become *flamboyant* with their newly found wealth.

flak (flak) *n.* criticism; opposition; anti-aircraft shells

> Heavy *flak* filled the air as the bombers flew over the city.

> The attorney took a lot of *flak* from the media when he agreed to defend a suspected serial killer.

flashback (FLASH back) *n.* a past incident recurring vividly in the mind

> Jim's *flashback* of his wedding day brought him pleasant memories.

> Joan's *flashback* of her auto accident frightened her.

flaunt (flawnt) *v.* to show off

> The lottery winner *flaunted* his new wealth by tipping waiters with hundred dollar bills.

Newly rich people tend to *flaunt* their wealth more than those who have always had money.

flaxen (FLAK sun) *adj.* resembling flax; yellowish in color

She had long braids of *flaxen* hair.

The *flaxen* tablecloth adorning the table was handed down to Joy by her grandmother.

flay (flay) *v.* to attack or scold with stinging criticism

While the professor distributed the papers, he *flayed* the class for doing such a mediocre job on them.

The assistant principal *flays* any student who is sent to him for misbehaving in class.

fledgling (FLEJ ling) *adj.* new, young, inexperienced

Still in his teens, John pursued his *fledgling* career in aviation by building his own airplane.

A *fledgling* bird is one reluctant to leave the nest and to try his wings.

fleece (fleece) *v./n.* to defraud, swindle; also the wool of a sheep

Jim was a crooked salesman and would sooner *fleece* a customer than make an honest deal.

The sheep's *fleece* keeps it warm in the winter.

flimsy (FLIM zee) *adj.* having little substance or significance; not believable

The cheerleaders arrived with a *flimsy* excuse for being held up in traffic.

Checking out the merchandise, we discovered the umbrellas to be *flimsy* and of inferior material.

flippant (FLIP unt) *adj.* showing a rude attitude; shallowly humorous; disrespectful

Henry lost thousands of dollars at bingo, so he did not appreciate the *flippant* remark from a friend who said, "Better luck next time."

Flippant with the judge in traffic court, Charlie was charged with contempt of court.

floe (FLOW) *n.* ice floating in sheets on the surface of a body of water

We watched the polar bear amble across the ice *floe*.

The ice breaker cut through many ice *floes* before opening up a channel for normal ship traffic.

florid (FLAWR id) *adj*. red or ruddy in color; flushed

The scoutmaster could tell by her *florid* complexion that the girl scout was suffering from heat exhaustion.

A newborn baby's complexion, often *florid* at birth, lightens to a more normal complexion in a few days.

flotilla (floe TILL uh) *n*. an indefinite large number of boats

Admiral Nimitz was in charge of the American *flotilla* in the Pacific during World War II.

Columbus sailed to find the new world in a *flotilla* of three Spanish ships.

flotsam (FLOT sum) *n*. floating wreckage of a ship; debris

When the *flotsam* floated ashore, it became evident that a small freighter had wrecked during the storm.

The *flotsam* floating in the river was dangerous to small boats that might run into it.

flounder (FLOWN dur) *v./n*. to move about in a clumsy manner; a fish

Sarah *floundered* with the new dance and fell on the floor in a awkward heap.

Henry served *flounder* stuffed with crab.

flourish (FLOOR ish) *v*. prosper, thrive, to grow strong; boasting

Walt's air conditioning business *flourishes* in Florida where the weather is warm most of the year.

The Roman Armies advanced on the barbarians with a *flourish* of swords and spears. (*n*.)

flout (flowt) *v*. to disregard out of disrespect, to mock or scoff at

Steve *flouted* the school dress code by wearing a dirty T-shirt and blue jeans with huge holes in the knees instead of the school uniform.

The rude neighbor *flouted* my new car by bragging about his new Lexus.

fluctuate (FLUK choo ate) *v*. to shift back and forth uncertainly

189

The stock market *fluctuates* like a bouncing ball that never stops bouncing.

The baby's temperature *fluctuated* between 99 and 102 degrees.

fluency (FLOO un see) *n.* facility or polish in speech

President Kennedy's *fluency* in the English language made him a great orator.

You must have *fluency* in certain foreign languages to become an ambassador.

fluke (FLOOK) *n.* unlikely windfall; a chance event; a fish

By some *fluke* Jesse was hired because he arrived early for the interview.

Tim caught thirty *fluke* on his birthday.

fob (FOB) *v./n.* foist, to force another to accept, esp. by deceit or stealth; a pocket watch

Web site companies sometimes try to *fob* off items which are copies of originals.

The *fob* was attached to a short gold chain and kept in his pocket.

fodder (FAHD ur) *n.* food given to cows, horses, and other farm animals; raw material

The scandalous activities in the White House were *fodder* for the news media and gossip mongers for months on end.

My father is trying a new mixture of *fodder* for the animals, and so far, they are eating twice as much as they had been.

foible (FOY bul) *n.* a minor character flaw

Greg's *foibles* include a tendency to go back to the free buffet one too many times.

In an election year, we always tend to dwell on the candidates' *foibles*.

foliage (FOLE ee udge) *n.* a cluster of leaves, flowers and branches

The *foliage* in the fall displays multiple colors that blend into one beautiful painting.

Beautiful, luxuriant, green *foliage* dots the south with many exotic plants.

folly (FAHL ee) *n.* lack of common sense or of good judgment; foolishness, or a foolish action or belief; rash behavior

It would be *folly* to attempt a trip through the mountains in this snow storm.

It was pure *folly* for Marsha to think she could pay for a $70,000 car on a minimum wage salary.

foment (foh MENT) *v.* to instigate

The news of the merger *fomented* a heavy trading day on Wall Street.

Agitators were sent into the crowd to *foment* discontent.

foolhardy (FOOL har dee) *adj.* foolishly adventurous and bold

Jack's *foolhardy* shot in the last seconds of the game resulted in a loss.

Harry's decision was *foolhardy,* causing him to receive a demotion.

foppish (FOP ish) *adj.* gaudy; ornate; overly dressed

Bill wears such *foppish* clothes his peers make fun of him.

Jean's *foppish* green hair made her the talk of the town.

forage (FOR uj) *v.* to search or hunt for food and provision

When the last of our provisions was gone, we decided that two men would take our only rifle and go *foraging* for game.

We *foraged* through the shed for plywood, tin sheets, and boards, anything with which to board up the windows and doors before the full force of the hurricane struck.

foray (FAWR ay) *n.* a quick raid or sudden advance; a new venture

The small group of soldiers attempted a *foray* into the village but were surprised to be met by a large enemy patrol.

The model's *foray* into acting proved very lucrative for her, as she seemed to be a born movie star.

forbear (for BAYR) *v.* to refrain from; to abstain; to be patient or tolerant

To *forbear* giving your opinion on any controversial matter until you have first heard all the facts is generally the wisest course of action.

The captain told his crew to *forbear* smoking in the cockpit.

forbearance (for BAYR ans) *n.* patience

The hunter showed great *forbearance* by sitting in the tree stand all day long.

Social workers must possess *forbearance* to deal with their difficult clients.

forcible (FORCE ih bul) *adj.* accomplished by force; powerful; violent

Everyone was shocked by the *forcible* entry of the police into the wrong house.

The policeman's *forcible* grip on the frail man caused a broken arm and muscle damage.

forebode (for BODE) *v.* to predict or foretell

The man's purple face and clenched fists *forebode* his anger.

(A *foreboding* (*n.*) is the feeling that something is about to happen.)

We had a *foreboding* that rain was coming.

foreclose (fawr KLOHZ) *v.* to take control of property because the buyers did not pay back the money borrowed to pay for it; to bar or rule out

It wasn't long after Sandy's dad lost his job that the bank *foreclosed* on their house and they had to move.

If a young lady has been married or had children, she was *foreclosed* from entering the Miss America Beauty Pageant.

forensic (fuh REN sik) *adj.* using the methods of science to provide information; pertaining to or used in legal proceedings

Forensic medicine is the use of medical facts and findings that can provide information relating to a crime.

The court found the defendant criminally insane and sentenced him to a facility of *forensic* psychology for mental evaluation.

foreordained (fore or DANED) *adj.* determined in advance; fated; pre-destined

Prince Charles's role as future King of England is *foreordained* since he's heir apparent.

The prince's bride was *foreordained* at an early age.

forestall (fawr STAWL) *v.* to prevent something from happening; to hinder by taking action beforehand; to get ahead of or head off

Many doctors prescribe aspirin to *forestall* heart attacks because it keeps the blood thin and prevents clotting.

Let's *forestall* the possibility of our electricity being turned off by paying the bill on time.

forfeit (FOR fit) *v.* to give up something, esp. as a penalty

Our team had to *forfeit* the game since we didn't have enough players.

Burt *forfeited* his scholarship when he went shopping with an agent.

forge (forj) *n./v.* a furnace where metal is heated and wrought; to shape, break, or flatten with blows; to counterfeit

He placed the two metals into the *forge.*

They *forged* plates to print counterfeit dollar bills.

forgo (for GO) *v.* to do without

Because we had eaten so much for dinner, we had to *forgo* dessert.

In order to make up her English exam, Lisa was forced to *forgo* the baseball game.

forlorn (for LORN) *adj.* desolate or unhappy; left alone and neglected; hopeless

As I left little Bobby on his first day of school, he gave me such a *forlorn* look.

Feeling *forlorn* and destitute, I sat on the curb and sobbed next to my broken-down truck.

formal (FOR mul) *adj.* strictly following traditions or conventions, stiff, rigid, prescribed

Lee offered his sword to General Grant in the *formal* gesture of surrender.

Ruth's signature on the lease will make our agreement *formal.*

formidable (FOOR muh dih bul) *adj.* exceptionally difficult; fearsome or intimidating

There were *formidable* obstacles to reaching an early settlement in the lawsuit.

The young fighter was worried about facing his *formidable* opponent in the ring.

193

forsake (for SAYK) *v.* to abandon, to give up, to renounce

> The parents urged their daughter to *forsake* her life as a model and return home to become a school teacher.

> All the general's troops had *forsaken* him, and he had no choice but to allow them to return to safe ground.

forswear (fawr SWER) *v.* to make a serious decision to stop doing something; to give up or renounce

> I will *forswear* smoking if I find out that I am pregnant.

> When Joan found the receipt for money David spent foolishly, he had to *forswear* his original statement that he did not get paid and come up with his share of the rent anyway.

forte (for TAY) *n.* something in which a person excels

> Spelling has always been Zachary's *forte*.

> Tanya is a born actress, so the director highlighted her *forte* by giving her the lead in the play.

forthright (FOWRTH ryt) *adj.* frank; going straight to the point

> The boss asked everyone to be *forthright* at the company meeting.

> When Kathy asked Mark if her dress made her look fat, she wasn't expecting his answer to be so *forthright*.

fortuitous (for TWO uh tus) *adj.* occurring by accident or chance

> Arriving at the opera at the last moment, we agreed it was *fortuitous* there were seats available for the two of us.

> "The most *fortuitous* event of my entire life," said President Roosevelt, "was meeting my wife, Eleanor."

forum (FOR um) *n.* a public meeting place for open discussion; a public meeting

> The Roman Senate held a *forum* to discuss the benefits of installing a public sewer system.

> The Presidential *forum* is held on TV to allow maximun public viewing.

foster (FAWS tur) *v.* to encourage the development or growth of; to nurture

> The old professor *fostered* an appreciation for classical music in his

students in spite of their devotion to rock and roll.

Living in Arizona's dry climate has *fostered* my grandmother's victory over her allergies and asthma.

founder (FOWN dur) *v.* to fail; to sink

The Titanic began to *founder* after hitting the iceberg.

The witness began to *founder* with his answers as the attorney became more direct with his questioning.

foyer (FOY ur) *n.* an entrance way or lobby, esp. in theaters or hotels

The *foyer* contains ornate wooden furniture made of teak and rose-wood.

The mansion had a marble *foyer* brightly lit by a crystal chandelier.

fracas (FRAK us) *n.* noisy quarrel, brawl

Buster created a *fracas* in the hotel lobby, and the police were called.

The *fracas* in the schoolyard resulted in two students being suspended.

fragmentary (FRAG mun tar ee) *adj.* existing only in small parts; not complete; incomplete or disconnected

All the evidence was *fragmentary* and not sufficient to bring in a guilty verdict.

Tom talks in such a fast and *fragmentary* manner that it is almost impossible to follow or understand anything he tries to explain.

frail (frayl) *adj.* weak; slender; delicate; fragile

Although she has always been a healthy woman, she appears *frail* since her surgery.

The *frail*, old cat placed itself on the bed very gingerly.

frank (frangk) *adj.* straightforward; open and sincere in expression

Jim's *frank* remark about Marge's weight made her cry.

The boss encouraged us to speak *frankly* at the meeting even if we were critical of the way he ran the company. (*adv.*)

fraternal (fruh TUR nul) *adj.* related to brothers

The *fraternal* organization did all they could to help the family of their deceased member.

The war veterans who served together formed a *fraternal* support group.

fraught (fraught) *adj.* teeming with; laden; full; involving

Although Mark Twain's books were *fraught* with humor, they nevertheless drove home good advice for their readers, young and old.

Fraught with guilt about losing her temper with the children, Mary treated them to ice cream after supper.

fray (fray) *n.* fight or scuffle; brawl

A *fray* occurred in the cafeteria when Kirk spilled his lunch on Jody.

After Mark was beaned by the pitcher, a *fray* ensued between the teams.

frenetic (fruh NET ik) *adj.* frantic; frenzied

Before the publication of the daily newspaper, the editorial room was filled with *frenetic* activity.

The cheerleaders made a *frenetic* display of school spirit as the team took the field.

frenzy (FREN zee) *n.* state of extreme excitement, confusion or agitation

Airline customers were in a *frenzy* because of the long delays created by the weather.

George was in a virtual *frenzy* after he lost the winning lottery ticket.

frowzy (FROW zee) *adj.* having a slovenly or unkempt appearance

Harvey's *frowzy*, oversized clothing is typical of this generation and distinguishes it from generations past.

Jim's *frowzy* look caused some people to go home and wash up.

frugal (FROO gul) *adj.* penny-pinching; stingy; careful with money

Kevin is so *frugal* that he orders children's portions when he goes through the fast food window.

In our club, we chose the most *frugal* person to be the treasurer.

fruitless (FROOT lis) *adj.* unproductive; without results; unsuccessful

Eric has been writing for years, but his attempt to write the great American novel is still *fruitless*.

Since she has three large dogs, Sally's attempts to clean the house are usually *fruitless*.

fruitful (FROOT ful) *adj.* producing good results; successful; productive

He had a long and *fruitful* career as a research chemist, discovering and inventing many helpful compounds.

Joshua's investment in IBM proved very *fruitful,* and he is now a millionaire.

fuel (fyool) *v.* to provide or add to; renewed energy to stimulate

The heating system in their home is *fueled* by natural gas.

The more she talked, the more she *fueled* his anger, and the louder he yelled.

fulcrum (FUL krum) *n.* the support about which a lever turns; any prop or support

The knee could be considered the *fulcrum* of the leg.

We used a *fulcrum* to lift the bolder.

fulminate (FUL muh nayt) *v.* to criticize strongly or express strong opposition or opinion; to vehemently denounce or criticize

Uncle Ted is always *fulminating* about the youth of today and how irresponsible and disrespectful he thinks they are compared to young people in the old days.

The governor's speech *fulminated* against political corruption and addressed what he plans to do to halt it.

fulsome (FUL sum) *adj.* generous in amount, extent, or spirit; abundant, copious

Politicians who always greet voters with *fulsome* exchanges make one wonder about their sincerity.

This critic gave a *fulsome* review of the new play, which helped make it a smash hit on Broadway.

fumigate (FYOO mih gate) *v.* to apply a chemical vapor, generally gases, to destroy insects and pests

Ace Pest Control *fumigated* the building to prevent the spread of cockroaches and ants.

The *fumigated* building had to be covered with a tent to prevent the gases from escaping. (*adj.*)

furlough (FUR low) *n.* a leave of absence

After basic training the new recruits received a *furlough* before reporting for active duty.

Private Jones asked for a weekend *furlough* so he could visit his wife.

furor (FYOOR ur) *n.* maniacal act; violence, unrestrained anger

The sale of fake ID's to teens caused a *furor* when discovered by the public.

A *furor* ensued when my father learned that I wrecked his car.

furtive (FUR tiv) *adj.* secretive; sly

Our cat always makes *furtive* attempts to hide when a stranger comes to the house.

When Ronny comes home after his parents' curfew, he *furtively* sneaks in the window so they won't see him. (*adv.*)

fusillade (FYOO se lahd) *n.* a rapid outburst or barrage

A *fusillade* of machine-gun fire tore through the plane's right wing.

As soon as the president reached the podium a *fusillade* of questions was hurled at him by the mass of reporters.

futile (FYOOT ul) *adj* useless; hopeless

Romeo made a *futile* attempt to awaken Juliet from her sleep.

After taking poison, Romeo took one last *futile* breath before he died.

gadfly (GAD fly) *n.* a person who annoys by persistent criticism; an insect

A person who does not have a good word for anyone is considered a *gadfly*.

The horse flew past the finish line with a *gadfly* attached to his nose.

gaffe (gaf) *n.* an embarrassing mistake; a crude social error; blunder; a faux pas

His failure to consult with the county's Hispanic leadership was a major *gaffe* and may have cost him the election.

When Susie showed up at the formal ball in jeans and a T-shirt, she was so embarrassed by her fashion *gaffe* that she never attended another public activity.

gainsay (gayn SAY) *v.* to deny; to contradict; to speak against; oppose

With all the evidence, it was impossible for the defendant to *gainsay* the fact that he was at the crime scene on the night of the murders.

The newspaper article gainsaid what was reported on TV the night before.

galore (gah LORE) *adj.* copious; characterized by abundance, plentiful

Champagne *galore* bubbled out of the fountain at the wedding.

At the banquet, there was food *galore* beyond one's imagination.

galvanize (GAL vuh nyze) *v.* to subject to or stimulate by an electric current; to stimulate into awareness or activity; to cause to suddenly take action

Why not involve the media to *galvanize* the community into action against the misuse of government funds?

The impending war *galvanized* the nation's industries, causing them to produce and sell their goods at a much faster rate.

gambit (GAM bit) *n.* a risk taken for some advantage

The general's *gambit* paid off when his troops won the battle.

The employee's daring *gambit* won him a raise from his boss.

gamesome (GAIM sum) *adj.* merry, frolicsome

The children were *gamesome* at the maypole and leaped about play-fully.

When the clock struck midnight on New Year's Eve, everyone was *gamesome* and full of life.

gamin (GAM in) *n.* a neglected boy left to run about in the streets

In India, everywhere our tour bus stopped, there would be a gang of *gamins* begging for money.

In the novel *Oliver Twist*, we learn of the intolerable living conditions in English orphanages of the nineteenth century and the life of the many homeless, streetwise *gamins*.

gamut (GAM ut) *n.* the whole range of things that can be included in something

Her stories caused me to experience the *gamut* of emotions from joy to despair.

My daughter gave me the *gamut* of excuses for not cleaning her room, from, "I forgot," to "I think I am dying!"

garbled (GAR buld) *adj.* confused and unclear; mixed up; distorted

He left a *garbled* message on my answering machine.

He was so sleepy that his speech had become *garbled*.

garner (GAHR nur) *v.* to gather or store

Maria worked to *garner* all the information she could before she started writing her report.

Throughout her lifetime, Bernice *garnered* enough antique furniture to fill five houses.

garret (GARE ut) *n.* watchtower; refuge; unfinished part of the house just under the roof

Jane went to the *garret* and found unpublished books of a famous cousin.

He entered the *garret* and took up the midnight duty watch.

garrulous (GAR uh lus) *adj.* overly talkative

Uncle Tom is so *garrulous* that we know we have to set aside a full hour every time he calls.

Our *garrulous* neighbor never asked much about us, but we knew her whole life's story.

gastronomy (ga STRON ah mee) *n.* the art of good eating

One can learn a great deal about a country by studying its *gastronomy*.

The feast was a *gastronomic* delight with every gourmet dish imaginable. (*adj.*)

gauche (GOHSH) *adj.* unpolished; ill-bred; unsophisticated; inelegant; unmannerly

Gerald's so *gauche* he even addresses the Mayor as "old buddy."

Nancy's *gauche* behavior shocked everyone at the senator's reception.

gaudy (GAW dee) *adj.* too showy; lacking good taste

Country performers used to be known for their *gaudy* clothing.

The rhinestone jewelry was far too *gaudy* to wear to work.

gaunt (gawnt) *adj.* excessively thin and angular, physically haggard

200

geezer an odd or eccentric man

Those who lived after the Holocaust were _gaunt_ from months of torture.

Many of the models today maintain _gaunt_ bodies in order to preserve their jobs.

gazebo (guh ZEE boe) _n._ an outdoor structure with a roof and open sides

The _gazebo_ in the mission courtyard was used for weddings in the summer, but in the winter, goats would come and huddle together to stay warm and out of the rainy weather.

On Sunday afternoons the family gathers together in the shade of our backyard _gazebo_.

gazetteer (gah zih TEER) _n._ geographical dictionary; journalist, publicist

Marvin opened the _gazetteer_ to find Lichenstein and the surrounding countries.

The World Atlas is a well known _gazetteer_ utilized by many.

gemology (jeh MALL ah gee) _n._ the science dealing with gemstones

In the study of _gemology,_ one learns the differences between real and synthetic items.

Bennie, the _gemologist,_ examined the diamond to check for color and clarity.

generalize (GIN er ul ize) _v._ to be general rather than specific; to form a general conclusion

Wilma always _generalized_; everything was either always bad or always good.

Our teacher asked us to be specific in our criticism and to avoid _generalizations. (n.)_

generic (je NER ik) _adj._ not specific to any particular thing; produced or sold without a brand name; general; common; not protected by trademark

I usually prefer to buy _generic_ products because they are cheaper and generally the same.

Christmas has become a sort of _generic_ holiday, celebrated by people of all religions.

genesis (JEN uh sis) _n._ the time when something came into existence;

the beginning or origin; creation

The book of *Genesi,* is about the creation of the earth and of man.

Unfortunately, your first cigarette can be the *genesis* of a life-long habit that is very hard to break.

genial (JEE nee uhl) *adj.* cheerful and pleasant, friendly, helpful

The host's *genial* manner put everyone at ease at the party.

The interviewer's *genial* personality made her guest feel comfortable at the meeting.

genocide (JEN uh syde) *n.* the extermination of all members of a certain race, nationality, religious or ethnic group

Adolph Hitler's attempt at *genocide* has made him one of the most hated and disrespected figures in history.

It is hard to believe that *genocide* is still being practiced in some third world countries.

genre (ZHAHN ruh) *n.* type or category

Of all the *genres* of literature, my favorite is poetry.

Many artists choose one *genre* and then stay with it rather than creating in other media.

genteel (jen TEEL) *adj.* refined; polished

Lisa is not at all *genteel*, but she does know how to have a good time.

Joan's grandmother was too *genteel* to go to the hockey game.

germane (jur MAYN) *adj.* connected with and important to a particular subject or situation; relevant

I don't think a question about funds is really *germane* to a discussion about why we have to protect our children.

I think hiring more school crossing guards is *germane* to the children's safety, considering the increase in traffic in the area.

gesticulate (jes TIK yuh layt) *v.* to make gestures with the hands

The lifeguards *gesticulated* wildly on the shore to get the attention of the swimmers.

Good speakers usually *gesticulate* to add emphasis to their words.

ghastly (GAST lee) *adj.* frightening and shocking; inducing fear;

terrifying; having a deathlike color or appearance; pale; ghostlike

It was a *ghastly* crime, very bloody and cruel.

Mr. Peabody's appearance was so *ghastly* that he looked like the Ghost of Christmas Past.

gibber (JIB bur) *v.* to speak rapidly, incoherently, or indistinctly

Sally, being nervous, could hardly *gibber* when addressing the workforce.

The mechanic *gibbered* about how he fixed the engine then handed Amy an exorbitant bill.

giddy (GIDD ee) *adj.* light-headed; dizzy, frivolous

After Sue Ellen won the beauty contest, she was absolutely *giddy* with joy.

Jackie didn't faint, but she said the sun was so hot she felt *giddy*.

gild (gild) *v.* to overlay with a thin coating of gold; to give a superficial bright aspect

To "*gild* the lily" is an adage used when something is unnecessarily overdone by an individual.

Charlie *gilded* his offer to purchase the land with half truths.

gird (gyrd) *v.* to encircle as with a belt; to prepare as for action

A size 54 belt was needed to *gird* the large man.

Girded for action, the tanks moved forward into battle formation.

girth (girth) *n.* the distance around something; something that encircles

Jonathan placed the saddle on top of the horse and fastened the *girth*.

The *girth* of the planet Earth is about twenty-five thousand miles.

gist (jist) *n.* central and material part, essence

The *gist* of the report was based on unsubstantiated records, audits, and facts.

The *gist* of her book report on World War II was how the United States entered the war.

glaucoma (glaw KOE muh) *n.* a disease of the ocular (eye) system, increased pressure on the eyeball, causing damage

The doctor checked the eye pressure to determine if his patient had *glaucoma.*

Glaucoma caused Carl's loss of eyesight in the left eye after years of neglect.

glean (gleen) *v.* to gather information or material slowly, search for relevant articles

The night supervisor had to *glean* any article that was political from all newspapers.

Max *gleaned* articles from foreign countries to continue his chemical research.

glib (glib) *adj.* nonchalant, insincere, superficial, readily fluent

Charlie's *glib* attitude caused everyone to think before answering any question.

The politician's *glib* remarks had no effect on the audience because they were unbelievable.

gloat (gloat) *v.* to brag greatly

For years she *gloated* over the marriage of her daughter to the most eligible bachelor in town.

My big sister always *gloats* on how she always beats me in checkers.

glower (GLOU ur) *v.* to stare fixedly and angrily; frown

The coach *glowered* at the football players who arrived late for practice.

Mickey *glowered* at his former boss after being fired for joking around.

glut (glut) *n.* surplus; overabundance

At tax time, charities usually get a *glut* of contributions.

Our choir has a *glut* of sopranos but very few altos.

glutton (GLUT en) *n.* one who eats or consumes a great deal; a person having the capacity to receive or withstand something

Every day at school lunch the Pitts children behave in a *gluttonous* manner; so much so, it made one wonder if they were ever fed at home. (*adj.*)

Jack was a *glutton* for punishment; no matter how many times he was knocked down in the fight, he kept getting up.

gnash (nash) *v.* to rub together noisily

The victim lay on the ground *gnashing* her teeth in an epileptic seizure.

Lannie had a habit of *gnashing* his teeth when upset by terrible news.

goad (GOHD) *v.* to urge forcefully, to taunt someone into doing something

The cowboys *goaded* the herd along by shouting loudly.

Being the youngest child, she was *goaded* by expectations of the family.

gossamer (GOSS uh mer) *n.* delicate floating cobwebs; a sheer gauzy fabric; something delicate, light

The bride wore a white silk wedding dress which touched the floor; as she proceeded up the aisle to the altar, the *gossamer* of fine Italian lace gently touched her face.

Between the audience and the actors on stage hung a fabric as thin as *gossamer*, heightening the feeling that the actors were in a dream-like setting.

gouge (GOWJ) *v.* to cut or scoop out, to swindle, over charge

The little boy *gouged* into the birthday cake with his finger, then licked his finger clean.

The oil companies are *gouging* the people at the gasoline pumps.

gourmand (GOOR mahnd) *n.* one who is excessively fond of good food and drink

Joey, being a *gourmand*, was asked the best place to dine.

Jill was ordered by the doctor to stop being such a *gourmand* and watch fat consumption.

gradient (GRAY dee unt) *n.* a rate of inclination; a slope

The steep *gradient* up the hill made it difficult to pedal my bike.

The *gradient* of metabolism is important in the field of biology.

grandiloquent (gran DIL uh kwunt) *adj.* attempting to impress with big words or grand gestures

It was another *grandiloquent* political affair, with the candidates making the same old promises to lower taxes and increase free services.

The new teacher's *grandiloquence* didn't fool the class one bit; she really knew very little about South American history. (*n.*)

grandiose (GRAN dee ohs) *adj.* grand and impressive, especially flashy and showy

Our coach had a *grandiose* plan to beat the Dallas Cowboys, but he didn't count on the fact they had a *grandiose* plan of their own.

In all respects it was a simple enough house, but the one exception was the *grandiose* fireplace in the family room; it was big enough to drive a truck through.

grapple (GRAP ul) *v.* to seize firmly or hold onto something, wrestle

Jim *grappled* with Carl for the wrestling crown of the heavyweight division.

As Steve slid down the hill, he *grappled* a small bush just before the edge of the cliff.

gratis (GRA tus) *adj.* free; without charge; not costing anything

All our drinks were *gratis* because Joel lost the bet and had to pay the tab.

Since I rented the car for the whole week, mileage was *gratis*, which saved me a great deal of money.

gratuitous (gruh TOO uh tus) *adj.* given freely; unjustified; uncalled for

The attack upon the children at the park was *gratuitous*.

Many current movies contain far too much *gratuitous* violence for the average movie-goer.

gratuity (gruh TOO ih tee) *n.* voluntary gift for services rendered

It has become a way of life to leave a *gratuity* after dining services are completed.

At some restaurants the maitre d' expects a *gratuity* for special service.

gravity (GRAV i tee) *n.* seriousness or importance

Young children don't understand the *gravity* of playing with matches.

We didn't realize the *gravity* of Steven's drug addiction until it was too late.

gregarious (gruh GAIR ee us) *adj.* seeking and enjoying the company of others; sociable

Paige was so *gregarious* that she hated to be alone.

Bernard's *gregarious* nature made him an enjoyable person.

grievous (GREE vus) *adj.* causing emotional or physical suffering; painful; grave and deplorable; heinous; expressing or full of grief; anguished

The family's loss of income was a *grievous* situation; they lost their home, their cars, everything!

The end of the war left the country in a *grievous* condition; all buildings were destroyed, farm animals were killed, and little food and no fresh water were left.

grill (gril) *v.* to query, to question aggressively; to broil, cook, griddle

The police *grilled* the suspect about the missing cars.

Let's *grill* the steaks over the charcoal for dinner.

grimace (GRIM is) *v.* to make a contorted facial expression that shows pain, disgust, or contempt

He *grimaced* in pain as the surgeon removed his bandages and ripped his hair out.

Watch the kids *grimace* when I run my nails down the blackboard!

grisly (GRIZ lee) *adj.* shockingly repellent, ghastly, horrid, macabre

Poe is renowned for telling *grisly* tales in many of his works.

The police officer turned his face from the *grisly* scene of the automobile accident.

grotesque (groh TESK) *adj.* bizarre or outlandish, as in character or appearance

Jose's *grotesque* impersonation of the preacher was totally inappropriate.

Many of Edgar Allan Poe's short stories are *grotesque* in nature.

grovel (GRUV ul) *v.* to beg persistently, be servile, fawn

Mary hates to see men *grovel* over important people.

John Jones makes his employees *grovel* if they want to leave just five minutes early.

guffaw (guh FAW) *n.* a loud or boisterous burst of laughter

Joey's whistles and *guffaws* while the principal was speaking resulted in everyone laughing.

John's *guffaws* in the midst of a serious speech helped to release tension in the audience.

guild (gild) *n.* a group of people united with a common goal

Charley joined the *guild* for health insurance because it was less expensive than individual insurance.

Jill joined the Animal Rights *Guild* to protest with others about animal testing.

guile (gyle) *n.* skill in treachery, deceit

Few people realized that Bob's reputation as a shrewd businessman was due to his *guile*.

(Beguile is the action of *guile*, verb.)

Butch *beguiled* his friends out of their lunch money.

guise (gyze) *n.* outward appearance, semblance; false appearance

Every night the undercover detective would enter the toughest part of town in the *guise* of a junkie, uncovering the identity of many drug pushers.

Amy was extremely cautious of advances made toward her by Harold because, as she put it, he had the *guise* of an angel but the intentions of a devil.

gullible (GUL ih bul) *adj.* easily cheated or fooled

Joel could not believe he had been so *gullible* as to believe his friend's wild story.

In order to take money from their victims, con artists rely on the *gullibility* of people. (*n.*)

guru (GOO roo) *n.* expert, chief proponent, a leader

The elder congressman was his political *guru*.

The old martial arts teacher was considered a *guru* by his students.

gusto (GUS toh) *n.* enthusiastic enjoyment; zest

After playing a rough first half, the team quaffed the water with *gusto*.

Jim greets each new day with *gusto.*

guttural (GUTT er ul) *adj.* disagreeable, marked by utterance that is strange or unpleasant

The carpenter let out a loud *guttural* scream as the hammer fell on his foot.

Wanting to get out of the cage, the parrot let out a low *guttural* screech.

gyrate (JIE rate) *v.* to rotate rapidly, to spin, to wind or coil

Jill's body *gyrates* when she belly-dances.

When the pilot cut the engine, the propeller stopped *gyrating.*

habitat (HAB i tat) *n.* a place where a person, animal, or thing is most likely to be found

Southwest Florida is the natural *habitat* for manatees.

We replicated the turtle's *habitat* in our aquarium.

habituate (huh BICH oo wayt) *v.* to make accustomed to; to train

Since moving five times in the past year, he was *habituated* to the idea of moving again next month.

My mother *habituated* herself to going to the cafe every afternoon for lunch.

hacienda (ha see EN duh) *n.* large estate, esp. in a Spanish speaking country

In Caracas many oversized *haciendas* line the more expensive area of the country.

The tour in Spain included a visit to the *haciendas,* which could be compared to American plantations.

hackneyed (HAK need) *adj.* overused; cliché

A strong writer always avoids *hackneyed* expressions.

Although the adult viewers found the film's dialogue *hackneyed,* most of the children thought the dialogue was funny.

haggle (HAG ul) *v.* to argue about the term; dicker

I like to *haggle* using American dollars overseas to get the best buy.

When buying a car, everyone attempts to *haggle* over the trade-in allowance and final price.

halcyon (HAL see un) *adj.* tranquil; peaceful; calm; happy and carefree

Father would look back fondly on those *halcyon* days at college when he hadn't a care in the world.

I just love the *halcyon* atmosphere of a quiet, warm cabin in the woods during a snowstorm.

hale (hale) *adj.* having good health, vigorous

Dr. Wing's prognosis was that I would be *hale* and able to resume a full schedule.

The team physician expects all players to be *hale* by the time of the starting whistle.

hamper (HAM pur) *v.* to prevent the free movement, action, or progress of; to hinder or impede

Not routinely changing the car's oil will *hamper* its performance.

A thunderstorm *hampered* our plans for going to the beach.

haphazard (HAP haz urd) *adj.* lacking order or purpose; not planned; random

Larry's *haphazard* attempt to fix the leaking roof only made the problem worse.

Sam's *haphazard* painting actually turned out to be pretty good. His art teacher said it was a good example of modern art.

hapless (HAP lis) *adj.* unlucky

The *hapless* individual stood on the corner, hoping to collect enough money to buy supper for his family.

Sam's *hapless* game of blackjack cost him $200.

harangue (huh RANG) *v./n.* to lecture, berate; a long bombastic speech

Our neighbor is a farmer who goes to town once a week on Saturdays and *harangues* everyone he meets about how bad the government treats farmers.

A perpetual *haranguer*, Jeannie was a feminist who believed everyone who didn't believe as she did was anti-feminist.

harass (HAR ras) *v.* to annoy or trouble repeatedly or persistently; to hinder or exhaust by repeated attacks

She felt she was being *harassed* by his constant, non-stop phone calls.

Hecklers *harassed* the comic until he couldn't take any more and walked off stage.

harbinger (HAR bin jur) *n.* something that shows what will happen in the future; an indication; an omen

The latest financial figures are seen by many to be *harbingers* of future financial doom.

The robin is a *harbinger* of spring.

harlequin (HAR luh kwin) *n.* a buffoon, in comedy, wearing masked face and variegated tights

In the opera *Pagliacci,* Beppe is a *harlequin.*

Jackson dressed as a *harlequin* in Italian tradition for the New Year's Eve party.

harmony (HAR mu nee) *n.* friendship, accord, pleasant agreement, like-mindedness

At the factory, Jack and Jill worked together in *harmony* for years.

The interior decorator chose a color scheme which is in *harmony* with the house.

harp (harp) *v.* to repeat or complain about something repeatedly in an annoying way; to go on and on

I'm annoyed with these people who keep *harping* about what is wrong with the country.

He was always *harping* about his lack of money but didn't seem to want to work.

harried (HARE eed) *adj.* beset by problems or harassed

The *harried* voters became distressed by the long ballot and voted for the first names they came to.

Tom was *harried* by constant doubts about trading his car for a new one.

harrowing (HARE oh ing) *adj.* extremely distressing; disturbing or frightening

After the *harrowing* experience when Eddie's main parachute didn't open, and his emergency chute saved him only at the last minute, he vowed never to jump again.

After the *harrowing* roller coaster ride, Jill thought she was going to get sick.

harry (HAR ee) *v.* to attack or annoy repeatedly or constantly; harass

She *harried* the authorities with her cause, writing letters and getting up petitions.

The Japanese dive bombers *harried* the U.S. fleet for over two hours.

harsh (HARSH) *adj.* discordant, unpleasant, severe, demanding, caustic, abusive

Snow White received *harsh* treatment from her stepmother, who tried to kill her.

The critics had nothing but *harsh* words for the new play on its opening night.

hasten (HAY sen) *v.* scamper, expedite, quicken, speed up, accelerate

Tony gobbled down dinner and *hastened* to his evening appointment.

A computer in the place of an electric typewriter would *hasten* the office work.

haughty (HAUT ee) *adj.* overly convinced of one's importance and superiority; arrogant

The hostess welcomed her guest warmly, but she received a cold, *haughty* reply.

Sue was devastated by the *haughty* look and cold greeting from her fiance's parents.

halyard (HAL yurd) *n.* a tackle or rope used on a ship to hoist and lower

In the Americas Cup, experts are needed to handle the *halyards* under everyday conditions.

Because of the high winds, Dennis was told to slacken the *halyards* to make sailing easier.

haven (HAY vin) *n.* any shelter or safe place; refuge

Churches and hospitals are usually considered safe *havens*.

The convict sought *haven* in a barn after his escape from prison.

havoc (HAV ahk) *n.* disorder or chaos; great destruction

The students wrecked *havoc* the day the substitute arrived.

John's notebook was in a state of *havoc*; no wonder he failed the exam.

hearten (HAHR tn) *v.* to give strength, courage, or hope; to encourage

The family received *heartening* words of encouragement from the priest. (*adj.*)

The coach *heartened* his team at half-time with his usual pep talk.

hedonist (HI duhn ist) *n.* one who lives by the belief that pleasure-seeking is the primary goal of life

Peter's life as a *hedonist* was not compatible with his budget!

Mary's boyfriend was too much of a *hedonist* to care about her wants and hopes.

heed (heed) *v.* pay careful attention, notice, observe

Bill *heeded* Tom's tip to purchase high tech stock, and he prospered.

Heed the teacher's advice to study, and you'll pass the examination.

hegemony (hi JEM uh nee) *n.* leadership of one nation or group over another

In the 1920s America was unchallenged in financial *hegemony*.

The *hegemony* of the Nazi party lasted far longer than it should have.

heinous (HAY nus) *adj.* extremely bad or evil; despicable; atrocious

We were shocked to read about the *heinous* murders committed by the Manson family.

Our neighbor was arrested for the *heinous* treatment of his dogs; he left them tied in the hot sun all day with no shade and no water.

heirloom (AIR loom) *n.* family possession handed down from generation to generation

The Chinese vase was an *heirloom* until Chris broke it into a hundred pieces.

From her grandmother, Kathy received a mink coat which was a family *heirloom*.

helter-skelter (HEL tur SKEL tur) *adv.* tumultuously, disorderly, haphazardly, in a confused manner

The delegates were running *helter-skelter* at the convention trying to meet the candidates.

The children ran *helter-skelter* all over the house playing blind man's bluff.

herald (HER uld) *n.* a person who conveys or announces official news; messenger; a person or thing that signals the beginning or approach of something

The daffodil blooming is a *herald* of spring.

Paul Revere was a *herald*, announcing the coming of the British.

herbicide (HERB uh side) *n.* a substance used to destroy plants, especially weeds

Environmentalists have proven that *herbicidal* runoffs from farmland pollute our rivers, streams, and oceans. (*adj.*)

Ed completely destroyed his lawn after he mistook *herbicide* for fertilizer.

hereditary (huh RED ih tare ee) *adj.* from one's ancestor, possessed at birth

Blue eyes are a *hereditary* trait in our family.

The doctor diagnosed a *hereditary* defect in the young boy's heart.

heresy (HER uh see) *n.* belief that is opposed by the establishment

The Catholic Church used to consider it *heresy* to eat meat on Friday.

Many visionaries commit *heresy* with ideas that are not traditional.

heretic (HEH ruh tik) *n.* one who maintains unorthodox religious opinions or beliefs; one who dissents from official church doctrines

The movie *The Exorcist* is about a young *heretic* named Regan.

The priest was thought to be a *heretic* and was asked to leave the order.

hermetic (hur MET ik) *adj.* airtight; not influenced by the outside

Many film stars want their children to lead *hermetic* existences.

The solution was *hermetically* sealed, but we still called Poison Control. (*adv.*)

heterodoxy (HET ur uh daks ee) *n.* unconventionality; unorthodox

Jeff's *heterodoxy* was well known among his contemporaries.

The priest's *heterodoxy* caused him to be removed from his position.

heterogeneous (het ur ah JEE nee us) *adj.* having dissimilar parts or elements

Students of all abilities were in the same class, making a *heterogeneous* group.

The elements in that concoction are *heterogeneous*.

heyday (HAY day) *n.* glory days; prime

In his *heyday*, Uncle John was an Olympic gold medalist.

It is hard to believe that in our parents' *heyday* they did some of the same silly things we do today.

hiatus (hye AY`tus) *n.* a gap or interruption in space, time, or continuity; a break

Emily looked to Christmas vacation as a welcome *hiatus* from the drudgery of school work.

After reviewing the tax plat, Richard found a *hiatus* of ownership between his property and his neighbor's.

hibachi (hih BOCH ee) *n.* a small Japanese style charcoal brazier, outdoor grill

We used the *hibachi* to cook steaks and corn on the cob outside on the lawn.

We have a special area at the condo near the pool for *hibachi* cooking.

hierarchy (HYE eh rahr kee) *n.* categorization of a group according to ability or status

Ed was very low on the company's *hierarchy*; he only delivered the mail and emptied trash.

Chief Sitting Bull was at the top of the tribe's *hierarchy*.

hieroglyphics (HY ur u GLIF iks) *n.* illegible or incomprehensible symbols, illegible writing

Egyptian *hieroglyphics* have been deciphered by Egyptologists.

The doctor's handwriting on the prescription looks like *hieroglyphics*.

highbrow (HIE brow) *n.* a person of superior intellectual interest and taste

The *highbrows* met at the opera house to view *Dr. Faustus* sung in high German.

The minimum acceptable IQ necessary to join that *highbrow* club is 135. (*adj.*)

hindrance (HIN drens) *n.* an obstruction, an annoying interference or delay

In today's world, a lack of education is a *hindrance* to one's career.

The obstructions built into the pyramids are *hindrances* to looters.

hinterlands (HIN tur lands) *n.* the remote or lesser developed areas of any country

The *hinterlands* are much more picturesque than urban areas.

As children, we disappeared into the *hinterlands* to avoid the crowds of the city.

hippodrome (HIP uh drome) *n.* any structure or arena for equestrian and other spectacles

The *Hippodrome* in England hosted the Beatles many times for their concerts.

The indoor track finals were staged at the *hippodrome* to allow room for the participants and spectators.

hirsute (HUR soot) *adj.* covered with hair, shaggy

Jeanie could not believe her sister could be attracted to such a *hirsute* man.

Jerry's English sheep dog was *hirsute*; he looked like a large ball of fur.

histrionic (his tree AHN ik) *adj.* overly dramatic, theatrical

The little boys *histrionic* cries after scrapping his figure got everyone's attention.

Everything Michael said was on the swaggering, *histrionic* side, as if he were the coolest guy on campus.

hoard (hoard) *v.* to accumulate for future use; stockpile

Whenever there is a hint of a gold shortage, people will *hoard* the precious metal.

The government announced rationing to prevent people from *hoarding* necessary goods.

hoarfrost (HOAR frost) *n.* a covering of minute ice needles on the ground

The children love to break the *hoarfrost* as it forms on the puddles.

The *hoarfrost* covered the ground, so we could not tell the lake from the fields.

hoary (HOHR ee) *adj.* very old and white with age; grey-haired; of great age; ancient

A *hoary* butler slowly opened the creaking door of the old, dilapidated house.

Dr. Jones blew the dust of the *hoary* map he found in the mummy's tomb.

hoax (hohks) *n.* a trick; practical joke; fraud

He didn't understand that he was the object of the *hoax* until everyone started laughing.

We knew him for years before we learned that his identity was a *hoax*.

hologram (HOLL uh gram) *n.* a three-dimensional image created by laser beams

Tampa Museum has a *hologram* display which produces many ghostly images.

The *hologram* of the dead man projected on the wall caused everyone to leave the building.

homage (AHM ij) *n.* an expression of great respect and honor

We paid *homage* to him for his achievements in medical research.

The city is going to pay *homage* to the great football star by naming a major highway after him.

homeopathy (ho me AHP uh thee) *n.* a system of natural healing

Herbs can be used as a method of *homeopathy* for healing.

Homeopathy is considered a form of alternative medicine.

homily (HAHM uh lee) *n.* story with a message

Our minister gives a special *homily* every Sunday just for the children.

At camp we sat around the campfire while our counselor gave the daily *homily*.

homogeneous (hoh muh JEE nee us) *adj.* consisting entirely of one thing or quality

> The gifted class is very *homogeneous*; everyone in it has a high IQ.

> My taste in candy is *homogeneous*; I like only chocolate.

hone (hon) *n./v.* a tool for sharpening or to sharpen

> Frank *honed* his knife down to a precise instrument.

> Sam *honed* his tennis game by playing four times a week.

horde (hord) *n.* an enormous number of persons gathering together; crowd

> Outside the stadium, *hordes* of happy alumni waited in line for the ticket sale.

> As the golfers approached the 18th green, *hordes* of spectators marched behind them.

horrific (hor RIFF ik) *adj.* causing great horror, scary, terrifying

> The *horrific* Holocaust was caused by the idea of racial superiority.

> Plane crashes are *horrific* and increase public concern for safety.

hostile (HAUS tile) *adj.* having or showing ill will

> The wild dog's *hostile* actions scared the children.

> The *hostile* crowd began to throw rocks at the building.

hovel (HUV ul) *n.* a small, miserable dwelling; an open, low shed

> In the famous play *Tobacco Road*, the characters are poor tobacco farmers who live in *hovels* made of cardboard and discarded wooden boxes.

> Compared to the Summertons' palatial estate on Long Island, Jane said her apartment in the Bronx was a *hovel*.

hubris (HYOO bris) *n.* very great pride and belief in one's own importance; arrogance; excessive pride considered as sin

> It was *hubris* that led them to believe that they could take over the business without any opposition at all.

> He was publicly shamed and shunned for his *hubris*.

humility (hyoo MIL uh tee) *n.* modesty, lack of pride; unpretentiousness

With *humility* Thomas thanked everyone who helped him win the election.

Most people accept the Noble Prize with *humility* and pride.

husbandry (HUZ bun dree) *n.* management of resources, especially in agriculture

The nation's *husbandry* of natural resources is crucial in assuring their availability for future generations.

(*Husbandry* is the practice of conserving resources; to *husband* is to economize.)

Experts say the world's oil resources will soon be exhausted, and we must soon begin to *husband* oil. (*v.*)

hydraulic (hie DROLL ik) *adj.* operated, moved or effected by means of water

The flood waters produce *hydraulic* motion sweeping away homes in their path.

The water in Florida provides *hydraulic* power for FPL's enormous electrical output.

hybrid (HIE brid) *n.* an offspring of two different species, whether animal or plant

George's *hybrid* of roses and tiger lilies sold out on the first day.

A tangelo is a *hybrid* fruit derived from tangerines and oranges on a new plant.

hyperbole (hye PUR buh lee) *n.* extreme exaggeration

Henry says he works out sixteen hours a day, but we know he's using *hyperbole*.

Many jokes are based upon *hyperbole*.

hypercritical (HIP ir KRIT ih kul) *adj.* severely critical; inclined to judge severely and find fault; hard to please

Our English teacher was so *hypercritical* when grading our mid-term papers, the highest grade in the class was a C+.

The *hypercritical* coach made the whole team stay after practice and run through more plays.

hypocrisy (hi PAHK ruh see) *n.* pretending to be what you are not, or pretending to believe something that you do not; insincerity

I think going to church is *hypocrisy* for many because they only use it as a social time or gossip hour.

The political critics are accusing the candidate of *hypocrisy* and deceit.

hypothesis (hie POTH uh suss) *n.* a proposition assumed as a premise in research, argument, or conversation

After years of research marine biologists have reached a *hypothesis* that whales do communicate with each other using a variety of clicking sounds.

The scientists conducted many experiments hoping to prove their *hypothesis*.

hypothetical (hye puh THET uh kul) *adj.* unproven

The teacher gave us a *hypothetical* situation and told us to role play.

Several *hypothetical* explanations exist, but none has ever been proven.

iconoclast (eye CON oh klast) *n.* one who attacks and seeks to overthrow traditional or popular ideas or institutions

Troy's *iconoclastic* views were not popular with his parents. (*adj.*)

Thomas Edison was a great *iconoclast*; without his *iconoclastic* views we might still be sitting in the dark.

ideogram (ID ee gram) *n.* a written symbol representing an idea rather than a word

Many *ideograms* appear in general use, for example the "&" means the word "and."

The "$" sign is an *ideogram* for the monetary term "dollar."

ideology (eye dee AHL uh jee) *n.* a system of ideas

Capitalism and communism are opposing *ideologies*.

The candidate's platform had more to do with *ideology* than it did with political facts.

idiom (ID ee um) *n.* a language or style of speaking peculiar to a people

"Shoot yourself in the foot" is an *idiom* that refers to doing something that hurts yourself.

Curse words simply aren't a part of John's usual *idiom*.

idiosyncrasy (id dee oh SINK ruh see) *n.* a behavioral quirk

Harriet had a way of smacking her lips every time she was asked a question, a harmless enough *idiosyncrasy*, only it drove everyone crazy after a while.

Jimmy Chen's habit of eating soup as a last course is no *idiosyncrasy*; most Chinese have soup last instead of first as is the American custom.

idol (EYE dul) *n.* an image representing a deity, object of devotion

Isis, an *idol* of ancient Egypt, was the goddess of fertility.

Valentino, a matinee *idol*, became the object of devotion to many women.

idolatry (eye DOLL ah tree) *n.* blind or excessive devotion to something

Ben's parents worried about his *idolatry* toward the occult.

Elvis's *idolatrous* fans stormed Graceland. (*adj.*)

idyllic (eye DIL ik) *adj.* charming in a rustic way; naturally peaceful

Chuck and Cathy bought an *idyllic* cabin in the Smoky Mountains.

Uncle Frank likes to paint *idyllic* seascapes.

ignominy (IG nuh min ee) *n.* deep disgrace

In *The Scarlet Letter*, Hester Prynne's sin is an *ignominy*.

Once the mob was broken up, the former gangsters lived a life of *ignominy*.

illicit (i LIS it) *adj.* illegal

The gang made most of its money from the sale of *illicit* drugs.

We hoped the *illicit* activities would not come to our little town.

imbecility (im buh SILL ih tee) *n.* stupidity, silliness, absurdity, simplemindedness

Joey's *imbecility* caused him to be the brunt of mistreatment by others.

Years ago people in the state of *imbecility* were assumed to be mentally ill.

imbibe (im BAYB) *v.* to drink or absorb

Young adults tend to *imbibe* too much.

The scholar intended to *imbibe* every bit of wisdom that his teachers placed before him.

imbue (im BYOO) *v.* to fill with a certain quality or feeling; to inspire or permeate, as with an idea or emotion; deeply influence

Her poetry was *imbued* with a love of the outdoors.

He was *imbued* with guilt, knowing he had hurt her so badly.

immaterial (IM uh teer ee ul) *adj.* not likely to make a difference; irrelevant

It's *immaterial* whether the trial is held in San Diego or Los Angeles.

Your complaint is *immaterial* to the issue at hand.

immersed (im MURCED) *adj.* involved deeply, absorbed

Jane was *immersed* in the textbook and was oblivious to the phone ringing.

The gold doubloons *immersed* in salt water for 100 years had no physical change. (*v.*)

imminent (IM uh nunt) *adj.* just about to happen

The clouds made us sure that a thunderstorm was *imminent*.

We saw the little girl fall off her bike and knew the crying was *imminent*.

immutable (i MYOO tuh bul) *adj.* unchangeable

Those who believe in fate believe their destiny is *immutable*.

The Rocky Mountains appear *immutable*; however, they are changing all the time.

impair (im PAIR) v. to cause to diminish, as in strength, value, or quality

An overly aggressive negotiator can often *impair* negotiations.

Our best soccer player was *impaired* when he hurt his knee.

impale (im PALE) *v.* to pierce with anything pointed

In the stable, Henry was *impaled* by the metal prongs of a pitchfork.

Dueling with epees, Richard and George *impaled* each other.

impartial (im PAHR shul) *adj.* fair; unbiased

Mrs. Greene tries to be *impartial*, but it is impossible with her son in the class.

We searched for an *impartial* judge for the science fair.

impasse (IM pas) *n.* a point in a process at which further progress is blocked; stalemate

We have reached an *impasse* in the negotiations; neither side will budge.

A "Mexican standoff" is slang for *impasse*, referring to the Alamo and neither side conceding.

impassive (im PASS iv) *adj.* not showing or feeling any emotion; insensate

Nick kept his face *impassive*, but his mind was racing.

The criminal seemed *impassive* even as the guilty verdict was read.

impeach (im PEECH) *v.* to formally accuse of a serious crime in connection with one's job; to accuse of or charge with misconduct of public office; to cast doubt or discredit

President Clinton was *impeached* due to his inappropriate relationship with an intern.

The magazine article *impeaches* the mayor's honor because of his questionable financial dealings.

impeccable (im PEK uh bul) *adj.* flawless

Miss America was *impeccable* as she waltzed down the walkway.

My mother is so *impeccable* that she cleans before the housekeeper arrives.

impecunious (im pi KYOO nee us) *adj.* poor; having very little money; lacking funds; penniless

I first knew him as an *impecunious* student living in one small room; now he is rich and famous.

Right now I am *impecunious*, but when I finish college, I will have a very profitable career and be comfortable in no time.

impede (im PEED) *v.* to obstruct or interfere with; to delay

He was only my uncle, but he always told me no matter what, not to let anyone *impede* my ambition to go to medical school.

(Something that impedes is an *impediment*.)

As a hopeful runner on the school track team, James Carver's biggest *impediment* to his foot speed was his short legs. (*n.*)

impending (im PEND ing) *adj.* about to happen soon; about to occur or appear

The *impending* crisis over trade made everyone nervous.

Our windows were boarded up and we had all our supplies, so we watched TV and waited for the *impending* hurricane.

impenetrable (im PEN uh truh bul) *adj.* impossible to enter or go through; impossible to influence; immovable; impervious

The castle was so heavily guarded and protected that it was *impenetrable* to unwelcome visitors.

Jeff's mood was so *impenetrable* that all my jokes and antics wouldn't even put a smile on his face.

imperative (im PER uh tiv) *adj.* extremely important or urgent; unavoidable

It is *imperative* that sales of cigarettes to children be prevented.

It is *imperative* that you return the movies on time because we don't have enough money to pay late charges.

imperceptible (im pur SEP tah bul) *adj.* difficult to understand or perceive; not plain

At college, Lester learned that he was not nearly as smart as he had thought; many concepts were *imperceptible* to him.

No aspect of the law should be *imperceptible* to an astute lawyer.

imperial (im PEER ee ul) *adj.* like an emperor

The Vatican is decorated with *imperial* splendor.

My older sister's *imperial* attitude is the most annoying thing about her.

imperil (im PARE ul) *v.* to put in danger, jeopardize

The soldiers lives were *imperiled* when on a secret mission behind the lines.

Abusing the use of credit cards *imperils* control of one's finances.

imperturbable (im pur TURB uh bul) *adj.* not easily excited or disturbed; calm

The lifeguard was *imperturbable* in a crisis.

No matter how many times I disobeyed him, my father was *imperturbable.*

impervious (im PUR vee us) *adj.* impenetrable

Joe's new watch was very expensive because it is *impervious* to water.

Some students do not want to improve themselves; they are *impervious* to instruction.

impetuous (im PECH oo wus) *adj.* without much thought; sudden and impulsive; rash

Grandma *impetuously* jumped out of the car and tapped the bear on the head with a shovel. (*adv.*)

I regret my *impetuous* decision to buy the car when I lost my job and couldn't pay for it.

impious (IM pee us) *adj.* lacking respect or reverence; not pious

Shouting in a church is *impious* behavior.

The criminal appeared on *Sixty Minutes* espousing his *impious* ideas.

implacable (im PLAK uh bul) *adj.* unable to be pleased, inflexible

It was impossible to negotiate with an *implacable* union.

Sally was so *implacable* that everyone left her to fend for herself.

implausible (im PLAWZ uh bul) *adj.* hard to believe or credit; not probable

The plot of the movie involving a 20-year-old brain surgeon is *implausible.*

The teacher did not believe Josh's *implausible* excuse for being late.

implement (IM pluh munt) *v.* to carry through

Sam was able to *implement* her new study schedule and got all A's for the semester.

The state recently *implemented* a new motorcycle helmet law.

implication (im pluh KAY shun) *n.* a suggestion of something that is made without saying it directly; something implied or suggested

There was no *implication* that they were divorcing, as they always seemed so happy together.

The decision to quit school has serious, negative *implications* for your future as a successful businessman.

impolitic (im PAWL i tick) *adj*. lacking sensitivity and skill in dealing with others; not wise, tactless

Greg's *impolitic* statements concerning junk bonds caused personal resentment.

Bill's *impolitic* remarks about the other candidates cost him votes.

implore (im PLOHR) *v*. to beg or appeal for; to urge

To no avail, the teacher *implored* the class to do their homework.

The mother *implored* the child to always wear his helmet while riding his bike.

importune (im pawr TOON) *v*. to make repeated forceful requests for something, usually in a way that is annoying or inconvenient; to pester with insistent demands or requests; to trouble

As a tourist, you are *importuned* for money by peddlers of all ages the moment you step outside your hotel.

My children are constantly *importuning* me to take them to the toy store; however, I don't have enough money.

imposition (im puh ZISH un) *n*. instance of inconvenience, unwelcome burden

Unannounced house guests are an *imposition* on the hostess.

Johnny picked up the package which was an *imposition* as the errand took him was out of his way.

impotent (IM puh tunt) *adj*. powerless; helpless

Our team was *impotent* against the state champs.

The revolutionaries became an *impotent* force when their leader was killed.

impoverish (im PAH vrish) *v*. to make poor and without money or to make worse in quality; cause to live in poverty; to exhaust the natural richness or strength of

Tim's constant gambling *impoverished* his family, forcing them to live in the streets and wear rags.

Lack of fertilizer *impoverished* the soil and left us with a very poor crop this year.

impregnable (im PREG nuh bul) *adj.* so strongly made that it cannot be broken into or taken by force; able to withstand any attack; absolutely secure, as a point or position in a debate

The fortress was built so strongly that it was *impregnable* to the enemy troops, no matter what tactics or weapons they used.

My father's attitude is *impregnable* to my pleas, and he won't let me go on a date until I am 16 years old.

impresario (im pruh SAHR ee oh) *n.* a person who arranges public entertainment; any manager or producer

Mr. Shaw has become one of New York's leading theatrical *impresarios*, handling some of the biggest names in entertainment.

Dave sees himself as a great *impresario*, trying to become agent and manager of all the high school bands and hoping that he will make one of them famous.

imprimatur (im pruh MAH ter) *n.* sanction or approval, support

Our plan has the company president's *imprimatur* for a company holiday party.

The director of the meet gave his *imprimatur* to admit unregistered members.

impromptu (im PRAHMP too) *adj.* done or said without earlier planning or preparation; spontaneous or improvised

Tanya did very well on a moment's notice, giving an *impromptu* performance at the piano.

The actress was totally unprepared for winning the award, but her *impromptu* acceptance speech was very appropriate and touching.

improvident (im PRAV uh dent) *adj.* lacking prudent foresight, careless, wasteful

The *improvident* heir quickly spent the family fortune and became broke.

Underwater adventures that are *improvident* can be dangerous recreational pastimes.

improvise (IM pruh vyze) *v.* to invent or provide something at the time when it is needed without previous planning; to construct or compose from whatever materials are available or handy

We had very little furniture, but we *improvised* a mattress from a pile of blankets.

The drama coach encourages young actors to *improvise* during rehearsals to exercise their creativity.

impudent (IM pew dent) *adj.* bold, impertinent, rude, insolent

Chuck's *impudent* language brought a defamation of character law suit.

Sheila, the *impudent* child, antagonized her mother at bedtime.

impugn (im PYOON) *v.* to attack the goodness of something

In his column, the critic *impugned* the movie before he had seen it.

In an election year, candidates attempt to *impugn* each other's integrity.

impulsive (im PUL siv) *adj.* tending to act thoughtlessly, impelling, spur-of-the-moment

The *impulsive* teenagers jumped into the pool fully clothed.

The *impulsive* youth purchased a car over the internet even though he lacked a driver's license.

impunity (im PYOO nuh tee) *n.* freedom from punishment; immunity from harm, punishment or retribution

Drug dealing was carried on with *impunity* in broad daylight because even the police were afraid to be in that neighborhood.

Because he is a recognized hero and has served his country tirelessly, he can speak with *impunity* about his country's shortcomings.

inadvertent (in ad VUR tunt) *adj.* done or happening unintentionally; not planned; inattentive, or resulting from inattention

It was an *inadvertent* mistake to throw the term paper away when I was in a hurry to clean before company arrived.

I *inadvertently* put the wrong gas in the car because I was too involved in a conversation with someone at the pumps. (*adv.*)

inalienable (in AY lee un uh bul) *adj.* not subject to transfer, surrender, or removal; sacred

Inalienable rights are freedoms that cannot be taken away from a United States citizen.

The right to survival has to be the first on any list of *inalienable* rights for every human being.

inane (i NAYN) *adj.* silly; senseless

Todd's *inane* comments were amusing to the class and irritating to the teacher.

The film has some funny lines, but for the most part it is *inane*.

inanimate (in AN ih mutt) *adj.* lifeless, sluggish, dull, spiritless

An *inanimate* body was found in the high grass by a jogger.

Disney was famous for *inanimate* creatures he brought to life on film.

inaugurate (in AW gyuh rayt) *v.* to begin officially

We will *inaugurate* the new school year with a special assembly.

A new president is *inaugurated* every four or eight years.

inauspicious (in oss PISH uss) *adj.* bringing, predicting, or character-ized by misfortune

The *inauspicious* ending of the Dolphin's season caused the resigna-tion of the coach.

British *inauspicious* losses in the South caused the Americans to win.

inborn (IN born) *adj.* present at birth, as opposed to something acquired; inherent, hereditary

Children seem to have an *inborn* love of music.

Newborns have an *inborn* resistance to certain diseases for a short time.

incandescent (in kun DES unt) *adj.* bright; giving off light

Thomas Edison invented the *incandescent* light bulb.

Chloe has an *incandescent* personality that can light up a whole room.

incantation (in kan TAY shun) *n.* a chant

The witch's *incantation* turned the prince into a frog.

The coach's *incantations* seemed to have no effect on his losing team.

incapacitate (in kuh PASS ih tate) *v.* to make unfit, to deprive of physical and mental qualities, to handicap

Although the Special Olympics contestants have been *incapacitated* all have the will to win.

John's heart attack and pneumonia *incapacitated* him for one year.

incarnation (in kahr NAY shun) *n.* an embodiment, as of a god, idea, or quality; the human form of a spirit, or the human representation of a principle or idea

He dances so effortlessly and smoothly, he is the *incarnation* of gracefulness.

The guard said that the inmate was so mean and devious that he was the *incarnation* of the devil.

incendiary (in SEN dee er ee) *adj.* of or relating to objects that produce intense heat and fire when ignited; inflammatory; likely to cause violence or strong feelings of anger and strife

Thai food is usually so spicy and hot that it is *incendiary*!

He gave an *incendiary* speech at last night's rally, and the crowds rioted as a result.

incense (in SENS) *v.* to make very angry

The behavior of the parents *incensed* the umpire was so *much* that he walked off the field.

The publishers *incensed* the author by misspelling his name on the book's cover.

incessant (in SES unt) *adj.* continuing without interruption; nonstop

The teacher gave Allison and Karen a detention for their *incessant* chatter in class.

Their *incessant* bickering drove Mike and Barbara to divorce.

inchoate (in KOH it) *adj.* just begun; in an initial or early stage

Because the cancer was *inchoate*, the doctors were able to stop its spread.

Her pregnancy was *inchoate*; even she did not know about it yet.

incidental (in suh DENT ul) *adj.* occurring accidentally, of less importance

The *incidental* costs for the care of a car add up to a large amount of money.

The small valise containing *incidentals* was being checked by customs. (*n.*)

incipient (in SIP ee unt) *adj.* beginning

We heard the *incipient* crackling and knew the chicks were almost out of their shells.

Support for the mayor was *incipient*, but we all knew it would grow.

incisive (in SYE siv) *adj.* cutting to the heart of the matter

David's *incisive* comments proved that he understood the novel.

His letters to the editor are always *incisive* and current.

incite (en SIGHT) *v.* to arouse to action

The mob was *incited* to riot when the police arrived and began hitting people with their nightsticks.

Waving a stick at Jerry's dog only *incites* him and increases the chance he will bite you.

inclement (in KLEM unt) *adj.* stormy; rough; severe

Many areas of the country are forced to close schools for *inclement* weather.

While we were on a cruise, the waters became *inclement* and most of us became seasick.

inclination (in kluh NAY shun) *n.* a preference or tendency, or a feeling that makes a person want to do something; liking

If I were as unhappy and insecure with my employer as you are with yours, my *inclination* would be to look for another job.

I so want to impress Dan on our first date that my *inclination* is to buy a new dress for the occasion.

incoherent (in ko HER ent) *adj.* jumbled, chaotic, hard to understand

Herb's account of the bank robbery was hysterical and *incoherent*.

Angie was *incoherent* when explaining what happened in the cafeteria.

incompatible (in kum PAT ah bul) *adj.* incapable of associating or blending; inharmonious

The sound of bagpipes is *incompatible* with that of most other instruments.

Many high school couples are *incompatible*, yet they stay together.

incongruous (in KAHN groo us) *adj.* not harmonious, not appropriate, out of place

Bathing suits look *incongruous* on a ski slope in Alaska.

The witness's *incongruous* testimony damaged his credibility for the defense.

incontrovertible (in kon trah VUR tih bul) *adj.* not able to be "turned against" or disputed; certain; indisputable

It is *incontrovertible* that two plus two equals four.

The suspect's fingerprints on the window were considered *incontrovertible* evidence of his participation in the robbery.

incorrigible (in KOR uh juh bul) *adj.* incapable of being reformed

When it comes to playing practical jokes, my father is *incorrigible*.

The convict proved that he was *incorrigible*, so he was sent back to prison.

incredible (in KRED ih bull) *adj.* not plausible or believable

Since she was only eight, her *incredible* violin performance had everyone talking.

His solution to math problem was *incredible* but correct.

incredulous (in KRED yoo luss) *adj.* refusing or reluctant to believe

Sam tried to reassure his *incredulous* customers that the meat was beef not horse meat.

Charlie was *incredulous* when advised he was accepted to West Point.

increments (IN cruh munts) *n.* increasing units

As he got older, his allowance was raised in *increments*.

We climbed the mountain in small *increments* so that we could save our energy.

inculcate (in KUL kayt) *v.* to cause someone to have particular beliefs or values by repeating them frequently; to implant in someone's mind by earnest and frequent repetition; instill

The goal is to *inculcate* in students a tolerance for people of other religions and races by educating them in those areas.

Religious cults entrap people by isolating them and *inculcating* the beliefs of the cult by brainwashing.

incumbent (in KUM bunt) *adj.* presently holding a particular office or position; required or obligatory; necessary to do something

Arnold Smith, the *incumbent* mayor, faces a tough fight for reelection next year.

As your supervisor and preceptor, it is *incumbent* upon me to instruct you in your duties and to teach you our policies.

incursion (in KUR zhun) *n.* a sudden and unwanted entrance to a place or area; a raid or sudden invasion

Sally led an *incursion* in the cafeteria hoping to overtake our lunch table.

Our troops led an *incursion* on the small, unprotected village, looting and plundering as we went.

indefatigable (in duh fah TEEG uh bul) *adj.* never becoming tired; not subject to fatigue

For many years Annie has been an *indefatigable* campaigner for human rights.

Sasha's *indefatigable* pleas for a kitten are wearing me out!

indict (in DYTE) *v.* to officially accuse of a crime; to bring a formal charge against

Five people were *indicted* on drug charges at yesterday's court hearings.

Although the man professed his innocence, the evidence left the judge no choice but to *indict* him on charges of terrorism.

indifferent (in DIF ur unt) *adj.* apathetic; ambivalent

Lois grew so *indifferent* that she could find little to interest her.

A stoic is *indifferent* to pleasure or pain.

indigenous (in DIJ uh nus) *adj.* native to an area

The sabal palm is *indigenous* to Florida.

We couldn't be sure that the tomatoes were *indigenous*, but they tasted great.

indigent (IN di junt) *adj.* poor

The *indigent* family was forced to seek assistance in a shelter.

After his business collapsed, Pete became *indigent* and lived on the streets.

indignant (in DIG nunt) adj. angry as a result of insult

The teens became *indignant* when the security guard started to follow them around the store.

Pat became *indignant* when she learned of the rumors that had been spread about her.

indoctrinate (in DOCK truh nate) v. to instruct in a body of doctrine or belief, to inculcate

Parents try to *indoctrinate* children at a young age to learn decorum.

Political parties *indoctrinate* anyone willing to listen as they pander for their votes.

indolent (IN duh lunt) *adj.* lazy

The *indolent* students never got up in time to attend their first period class.

After they won the lottery, the couple became even more *indolent* and quit their part-time jobs.

indomitable (in DOM i tu bul) *adj.* invincible, unconquerable, indefatigable

The coach's *indomitable* spirit helped the team to victory.

The *indomitable* spirit of the colonies resulted in the Declaration of Independence.

induce (in DOOS) v. to persuade to do something; to cause to happen; to influence; to stimulate

They *induced* her to take the job by offering her a large bonus.

If doctors *induce* labor in a pregnant woman, they cause a baby to be born before its natural time.

induct (in DUCT) v. to admit formally into office or membership, as with ritual

In 2001 the new president was *inducted* into office in Washington, DC.

McGwire will be *inducted* into the Baseball Hall of Fame after retiring.

indulgent (in DUL junt) *adj.* lenient

My parents are too *indulgent* with my youngest sister, who is turning into a brat.

Glen knows that he is his grandmother's favorite because she is so *indulgent* with him.

inebriated (in EEBREE ayt id) *adj.* intoxicated; drunk

Too many parents allow their teenagers to get *inebriated* at their homes.

Although Hemingway was *inebriated* much of the time, he never allowed this to interfere with his writing.

ineffable (in EF uh bul) *adj.* incapable of being expressed or described

When we snorkeled on the reef, we experienced the *ineffable* beauty of the sea.

The sun rising over the Rocky Mountains is an *ineffable* spectacle that I will always cherish.

ineffectual (in e FEK choo el) *adj.* not able to produce a desired effect; useless

The child tried to berate his father, but the attempt was *ineffectual*.

We now know that leeching is an *ineffectual* way to reduce a fever.

ineluctable (in uh LUK tuh bul) *adj.* impossible to be avoided or resisted; inescapable

Pamela found it hard to say no to Ralph's *ineluctable* charm when he asked her to marry him.

I struggle daily against the *ineluctable* energy my children seem to have.

inept (in EPT) *adj.* clumsy; incompetent

Zelda was an *inept* dancer who liked to think of herself as a ballerina.

My father's *inept* attempt at humor was an embarrassment to the whole family.

ineradicable (in uh RAD uh kuh bul) *adj.* not able to be removed; impossible to wipe out of existence, memory

He spoke in such a commanding way that he left us with the *ineradicable* impression that we had been listening to a future leader.

After Sheila married him, she grew tired of looking at the *ineradicable* tattoo that screamed, "Betsy" across his chest.

inert (in URT) *adj.* inactive

After we had finished Thanksgiving dinner, everyone was *inert* in front of the television set.

Even though they had been lively at the pep rally, the team was *inert* on the field.

inevitable (in EV i tuh buhl) *adj.* unavoidable, bound to happen

In Los Angeles, traffic delays are *inevitable* every day of the year.

Two things are *inevitable*: death and taxes.

inexorable (in EK sur uh bul) *adj.* inevitable; unavoidable

Walter bowed to the *inexorable* truth that he would never be a major film star.

The *inexorable* winds pulled the trees from the ground.

infallible (in FAL ah bul) *adj.* never wrong; incapable of failing

Many students believe that they are *infallible*, until they go to college.

My team was *infallible* this year, so we won the championship.

infamous (IN fuh mus) *adj.* having a very bad reputation

Billy the Kid is one of the most *infamous* bank robbers of all time.

In London we visited the *infamous* torture chamber, which still houses some gruesome reminders of the past.

infamy (In fa mee) *n.* evil reputation; extreme disgrace

Western outlaws such as Jesse and Frank James have been made heroes in movies, but in reality their *infamy* is what should be remembered.

The *infamy* of Germany's Adolph Hitler will live for eternity.

infatuated (in FACH oo ay tid) *adj.* foolishly in love

Joey was so *infatuated* with the little girl who sat in the first row that he stammered when he tried to speak to her.

Although we liked the candidate at first, it soon became clear that he was *infatuated* with the position of power, and not with serving the people.

infer (in FUR) *v.* to conclude; to deduce

Melissa was able to *infer* by Jason's attitude when he dropped her off that she would not be hearing from him again.

Because there was no turkey or any other meat on the Thanksgiving table, I *inferred* that the family was vegetarian.

infinitesimal (in fin uh TES uh mul) *adj.* extremely small

Even an *infinitesimal* amount of bacteria may cause food poisoning.

Alex thinks he looks exactly like Mel Gibson, but I can see only an *infinitesimal* similarity.

inflammatory (in FLAM uh taw ree) *adj.* likely to excite strong feelings, especially of anger; tending to arouse and excite the emotions; fiery

The drunken man's *inflammatory* remarks made the bartender so furious that he threw the drunk outside.

The actress was very perturbed by the reporter's *inflammatory* headline, "Black Widow Weds Another Victim."

influenza (in floo EN zuh) *n.* an epidemic disease caused by a virus, respiratory infection

Influenza shots will be scarce this fall, making the disease of utmost concern in doctors' minds.

Irene was diagnosed with a virus, fever, aches and pains probably related to *influenza*.

influx (IN fluks) *n.* a mass arrival or incoming; a continuous coming

South Florida has an *influx* of northern tourists every winter.

We will have to build an addition to the school because of the *influx* of new students.

infraction (in FRAK shun) *n.* a breaking of a rule or law; violation or breach

My son already had two bus referrals, and he was warned that one more *infraction* of the rules would get him kicked off the bus.

When I got home a half hour late, Mom grounded me for *infraction* of curfew.

infrastructure (IN fruh struk chur) *n.* the basic structure of an organization or system; foundation

The *infrastructure* of the building was so weak that the engineers didn't think it would stand under the stress of an earthquake.

The new building codes dictate that the *infrastructure* of new houses must be able to withstand hurricane force winds.

infringe (in FRINJ) *v.* to cross established limits; encroach; trespass

Unauthorized copying of videos *infringes* copyright law, and the culprit could be jailed or fined.

Censorship *infringes* on our right to free speech.

infuse (in FYOOZ) *v.* cause to take in and be filled with; instill; to introduce into

His landscape paintings were *infused* with a warm, subtle light.

The teacher *infused* knowledge into her students.

ingenue (ON zhuh noo) *n.* a guileless unsophisticated person

Faye was signed to a contract to play the part of an *ingenue* on Broadway.

A novice can be considered an *ingenue* in the arts.

ingenuous (in JEN yoo us) *adj.* frank; simple; charmingly naive

The *ingenuous* little boy was a breath of fresh air; he answered every question honestly and from the heart.

Molly was *ingenuous* when she moved to Los Angeles, but she learned quickly not to trust everyone she met.

ingot (ING gut) *n.* a mass of metal casting, a bar

Fort Knox has gold *ingots* stored there for protection.

Gold *ingots* were found on many Spanish ships sunk by inclement weather.

ingratiate (in GRAY shee ayt) *v.* to try to make especially pleasant in order to get approval; to seek or secure another's favor or approval for

He tries to *ingratiate* himself with the boss by saying that all her ideas are brilliant and by waiting on her hand and foot.

She did everything right to *ingratiate* herself with important people, so she benefitted from their influence.

inherent (in HAYR unt) *adj.* intrinsic; part of the basic nature of something

It is an *inherent* property of Earth to rotate around the Sun.

In the mountains we could feel the *inherent* sweetness of the brisk, clean air.

inhibit (in HIB it) v. hinder, repress, prevent; to hold back, to restrain

The antibiotic *inhibited* the spread of the bacterial infection.

The highway patrol barrier *inhibited* traffic flow, causing a backup for miles.

inimical (i NIM i kul) *adj.* like an enemy; hostile; harmful or adverse; having or tending to have a bad effect

Newspaper editors regard any restrictions on them as being *inimical* to free speech and a hindrance of their ability to make the public aware.

Excess of control is *inimical* to creative expression because it stops the flow of one's imagination.

inimitable (i NIM i tuh bul) *adj.* impossible to copy because of being of very high quality or a particular style; incomparable; matchless

Louis Armstrong's gravelly voice is *inimitable*.

To me, the sunset on the Gulf of Mexico has an *inimitable* beauty and peacefulness that I find nowhere else on Earth.

iniquitous (i NIK wi tus) *adj.* unrighteous, evil, unjust, infamous

The corrupt company's *iniquitous* practices should not go unpunished.

Jed's false testimony was *iniquitous* and hedged on perjury.

initiate (i NISH ee ayt) v. to take the first step in doing something; to bring into practice

I'll never forget the day I was *initiated* into National Honor Society.

It was up to the club's president to *initiate* the new rules.

injunction (in JUNGK shun) *n.* command or order, usually having to do with the court

Randy was served with an *injunction* that said he must keep his dog on a leash.

As Lois finished the chocolate fudge sundae, she recalled her doctor's *injunction* that she must cut down on her intake of sugar.

innate (i NAYT) *adj.* inherent; inborn

Scott has an *innate* ability to run quickly; his coaches first noticed it when he was still in pre-school.

Eric has an *innate* charm which makes it impossible for anyone to dislike him.

innocuous (i NAHK yoo us) *adj.* harmless; banal

Lennie's *innocuous* smile causes people to trust him immediately.

Some movies that seem *innocuous* to us seem scandalous to our grandparents.

innovate (IN uh vayt) *v.* to be creative, to introduce something new

The *innovation* of space shuttles has made the universe seem to shrink. (*n.*)

Microsoft *innovated* the next generation of Windows with the Millennium Edition.

innuendo (in yoo EN doh) *n.* a remark that suggests something but does not refer to it directly; an indirect hint, implication, or insinuation

In the work place, sexual *innuendoes*, no matter how innocent or covert, can be interpreted as sexual harassment.

I caught Dad's little *innuendo* about the scratch on his car, so I know he thinks that I did it.

innumerable (in NOOM ur uh bul) *adj.* too great to be calculated

Sharon requested a product report *innumerable* times, but she has yet to receive it.

His poor record keeping caused *innumerable* errors and made his taxes impossible to audit.

inordinate (in OR den it) *adj.* exceeding a reasonable or normal amount

Basketball players' salaries are *inordinate* compared to the average layman's wage.

Tom worked *inordinate* hours of overtime and was seldom home with his family.

inquire (in KWIRE) *v.* to seek information; ask questions

My mother *inquired* us to where we were last night.

The court intervened to *inquire* whether the witness is credible.

inquiry (in KWIRE ee) *n.* the act of inquiring

An *inquiry* into the cause of the accident has begun.

The *inquiry* into the robbery revealed many clues.

inquisition (in kwi ZISH un) *n.* a detailed questioning; an official inquiry; an inquest or other legal investigation; questioning that is prolonged, unrelenting, or brutal

I don't want to be late because I can't stand my father's inevitable, endless *inquisition*.

The harsh *inquisition* imposed on the captured soldier wasn't enough to make him talk.

inquisitive (in KWIZ i tiv) *adj.* prying, snooping, curious, eager for knowledge

The young student is bright and *inquisitive*, traits we admire in education.

The *inquisitive* woman spread rumors about her neighbor.

insatiable (in SAY shah bul) *adj.* impossible to satisfy; constantly wanting more

Most teenage boys tend to have *insatiable* appetites.

The starving puppy was *insatiable*.

inscrutable (in SKROO tuh bul) *adj.* impossible to comprehend or interpret; mysterious

He believes that a certain part of his life must remain *inscrutable* and private.

His expression was *inscrutable* as I told him my story.

insidious (in SID ee us) *adj.* intended to trap or beguile, cunning

The linebacker's *insidious* moves lulled the defense into exposing the quarterback.

The *insidious* Bubonic Plague of 1665 killed about 15% of London's population.

insinuate (in SIN yoo ayt) *v.* to suggest or hint slyly, convey an idea by indirect, subtle means

He *insinuated* that the girls were lying concerning their whereabouts.

They *insinuated* that Carole was the other woman in the romantic triangle.

insipid (in SIP id) *adj.* dull; bland

Our math teacher tells the most *insipid* jokes, but we all laugh because he is such a nice guy.

Because the fraternity party was attended by only the most *insipid* people, I took my leave as soon as I was able.

insolent (IN suh lunt) *adj.* arrogant; insulting

Because the parents were afraid to discipline their children in public, the whole theater had to endure the children's *insolent* behavior.

The *insolent* sales clerk refused to offer help, even after we requested it.

insolvent (in SAWL vunt) *adj.* in a state in which one's financial liabilities exceed one's assets

ABC Company was *insolvent* because all three owners drew large salaries.

Over using of credit cards is the easiest way to become *insolvent*.

insouciant (in SOO see unt) *adj.* calm and carefree; lighthearted

Children play *insouciantly*, as if they did not have a care in the world. (*adv.*)

Jake's *insouciant* behavior was inappropriate at his grandfather's funeral, showing lack of respect for his memory.

inspire (in SPYR) *v.* arouse, to encourage, to give hope to, stimulate

Shakespeare has *inspired* generations of playwrights and authors.

The chance to win the gold medal at the Olympics *inspires* many athletes to excel.

instigate (IN stuh gayt) *v.* to provoke; to stir up

My brother *instigated* the bad behavior, but I got in trouble for it.

Joshua was so upset about the teacher's decision that I thought he would try to *instigate* a riot in the classroom.

insufferable (in SUF ur uh bul) *adj.* extremely unpleasant and therefore difficult to bear; unbearable; intolerable

George is an *insufferable* bore, and I don't know how you can tolerate spending so much time with him.

During the summer months, the heat is so *insufferable* that hardly anyone goes outside.

insular (IN suh lur) *adj.* isolated; related to an island

Coronado is an *insular* community located off the coast of San Diego.

I believed the only way I could succeed in college was to stay away from parties and lead an *insular* existence.

insuperable (in SOO pur uh bul) *adj.* not able to be conquered or overcome; extremely great or severe; overwhelming

Hospitals now face *insuperable* difficulties with too few staff members and too little money.

Because of her recent diagnosis of cancer, she battled against seemingly *insuperable* odds to win, and she did it!

insurgent (in SUR junt) *n.* a rebel; someone who revolts against a government

The governments of some small countries are dependant on *insurgents*.

Jeremy is an *insurgent* who prides himself on being unique.

insurrection (in sur EK shun) *n.* an act or instance of open rebellion against a government or other authority; uprising; a revolt

If the leaders try to take away our right to vote, the inevitable *insurrection* will be so large and violent that they will undoubtedly change their minds.

I tried to take away phone privileges during the week but the ensuing *insurrection* of my four teenage daughters was more than I could bear.

intangible (in TAN juh bul) *adj.* incapable of being apprehended by the mind or senses

Intangibles in a good government are difficult to evaluate. (*n.*)

Goodwill is an *intangible* asset in any business and it is difficult to place a value.

integral (IN tuh grul) *adj.* essential

> Charlie is an *integral* member of our school's Math Team.

> Most children agree that chocolate should be an *integral* part of everyone's diet.

integrity (in TEG ri tee) *n.* moral stature, honesty, trustworthiness, structural soundness

> The officer's *integrity* is unquestionable, as she has a flawless record.

> The *integrity* of a building depends on a sound foundation.

intemperate (in TEMP ur ut) *adj.* lacking restraint or self-control; excessive, overindulgent

> The governor said he would not be provoked into *intemperate* action.

> The leader was accused of using *intemperate* language to stir up anger in the crowd.

intensify (in TEN su fy) *v.* to increase the strength, size, or force of; accelerate; escalate

> The desert heat *intensified* the discomfort of the troops marching back to their base.

> The artillery shelling *intensified* before the major attack on the village.

intercede (in tur SEED) *v.* intervene, act as an intermediate agent

> Smith was appointed to *intercede* in negotiations to settle the contract.

> The referee *interceded* in the boxing match to prevent serious injury.

interim (IN tur im) *n.* a short period of time; the interval of time between two events; meantime

> I started writing about that two years ago, but unfortunately, other books on the subject have come out in the *interim*.

> Yesterday we presented our case to the principal, but in the *interim* we shall just have to wait for his decision.

interject (in tur JEKT) *v.* to interrupt with; insert in between

> Sally is known to *interject* her own thoughts at inappropriate times.

> I would never have believed that such a meek person could *interject* so vehemently.

interloper (in tur LOH pur) *n.* someone who becomes involved without being asked or wanted; someone who enters a place without being allowed; meddler

We felt like *interlopers* when we tried to join the game because we were obviously unwelcome.

Raccoons are cute, but they are unwelcome *interlopers* when they tear my trash apart in the driveway.

interlude (IN tur lood) *n.* a period or event that comes between two others; a pause or space; interval

The ferry trip across the sound was a relaxing *interlude* during the drive.

An hour with the masseuse was a wonderful *interlude* in the middle of my hectic work day.

interminable (in TUR muh nuh bul) *adj.* continuing for too long and seeming never to end; endless or seemingly endless; monotonously long

When I wrecked the car, Larry's *interminable* tirade went on for hours.

The professor's *interminable* lecture droned on for so long that Jack fell fast asleep.

intermittent (in tur MIT unt) *adj.* not happening regularly or continuously; stopping and starting repeatedly; occurring at intervals

The rain was *intermittent* with sunshine all day long.

Good reception on our TV is *intermittent*, depending on how clear the weather is.

internecine (in tur NEE sin) *adj.* mutually harmful or destructive; deadly to both sides

The atomic bomb was the most *internecine* occurrence in the last century.

The gang violence is *internecine* and must be ended.

interregnum (in tur REG num) *n.* the period between two successive governments

After the shooting of President Reagan the leader in the *interregnum* was Al Haig.

The policy regarding an *interregnum* is set up by law regarding presidential succession.

interrogate (in TER uh gayt) *v.* to examine or ask questions formally

The prosecutor was called upon to *interrogate* the witness.

The teacher felt she had a right to *interrogate* the student concerning the authenticity of the paper.

intersperse (in tur SPURS) *v.* to put in different parts or places; to place or scatter among other things

Framed pictures of her children were *interspersed* among the books in the bookcase.

The real eggs were *interspersed* among the plastic prize eggs all over the yard.

interstellar (in tur STEL lur) *adj.* situated or occurring between the stars

The *interstellar* sky lab will make deep space travel more convenient.

Many *interstellar* studies of medicine will take place in the new space village.

interstice (in TUR stis) *n.* an intervening space, a crack or crevice

Harvey caught his foot in an *interstice* while climbing the mountain.

The broken necklace settled in the *interstice* between the two rocks.

intervene (in tur VEEN) *v.* to come between; to mediate, to occur between times

Harold and his brother might have argued all day, but their father *intervened* and said if they couldn't decide who would ride in the front seat, they could both sit in the back.

So much had happened to the family in the *intervening* years since Brett had gone off to college. (*adj.*)

intimate (IN tuh mayt) *v.* to suggest without saying directly; to make known with a hint; to imply

He *intimated* that he was going to propose to her when he said he was planning a honeymoon trip.

If you don't love me, then don't *intimate* that you do by getting jealous if I date someone else.

intimidate (in TIM uh dayt) *v.* to make afraid or timid

On the first day of school, many students try to *intimidate* their teachers.

The fifth grade bully tried to *intimidate* all the other kids in the school.

intractable (in TRAK tuh bul) *adj.* stubborn; uncontrollable; disobedient

Matthew's parents finally decided to send him to military school when they realized he was *intractable*.

The new disease is *intractable*; no antibiotic has any effect upon it.

intransigent (in TRAN suh junt) *adj.* uncompromising; stubborn

One member of the jury was *intransigent* in his views of the crime, so a mistrial was finally called.

Lucy was *intransigent* about not wanting to go to school on the first day.

intrepid (in TREP id) *adj.* fearless; bold

The bullfighter was *intrepid* as he stood in the arena before the fierce bull.

The Green Berets have always been known for their *intrepidity*. (*n.*)

intricate (IN truh kit) *adj.* difficult to understand in detail; having many complexly interrelated parts, angles, or aspects; involved; elaborate

The novel's *intricate* plot will not be easy to translate into a movie.

That is an extremely *intricate* model of a car engine, with hundreds of tiny parts to place correctly.

intrigue (IN treeg) *n.* a secret or crafty scheme or plot

The tale of political *intrigue* explained the underhanded dealings of a corrupt government and its plan to overthrow the present ruler.

The fictional espionage agent James Bond is driven by *intrigue* in all aspects of his life.

intrinsic (in TRIN sik) *adj.* inherent; part of the essential nature of something

Juliet gets away with so much because of her *intrinsic* charm.

An *intrinsic* characteristic of the tiger shark is that it will eat just about anything, including garbage.

247

introspective (in truh SPEC tiv) *adj.* examining one's own feelings

> After the divorce, Jeff became much more *introspective*, realizing that he must not cause the same problems in a new relationship.

> When she was young Melissa was an out-going child, but after entering high school she became very *introspective*.

inundate (IN un dayt) *v.* to overwhelm with abundance or excess; flood

> During final exams, we are so *inundated* with school work that we have no time for fun.

> Jack's father used to *inundate* the front yard in the winter so all his friends could ice skate.

inure (IN yoor) *v.* to get used to something undesirable; harden

> Bob *inured* the hardships of prison life after his first year.

> After thirty days at sea, Bob was *inured* to life in a life raft.

invalidate (in VAL uh dayt) *v.* to nullify; to make invalid

> After his speeding ticket, Doug was unhappy to learn that the state had *invalidated* his license.

> The teacher chose to *invalidate* all the tests because one was missing from her classroom.

invective (in VEK tiv) *n.* insulting or abusive speech

> Bill's speech about his opponent was full of *invective*.

> The subtleties of *invective* in his writing are clever yet mean.

inveigh (in VAY) *v.* to vent anger verbally or write bitterly

> When Louis went to court, he *inveighed* against the police, citing all reasons he believed he had been mistreated by them.

> Many people write letters to the editor to *inveigh* their anger against inequities.

inveigle (in VAY gul) *v.* to tempt or persuade by using deception or flattery

> My brother Ryan *inveigled* me into doing his chemistry homework by promising to take my turn washing dishes for the next week.

> New York City street vendors *inveigle* people into purchasing counterfeit Rolex watches for many times what they are worth.

invert (in VURT) *v.* to change to the opposite position, direction, or course

The auditor found the mistake; the numbers had been *inverted.*

The quarterback *inverted* the planned direction of the play and scored a touchdown.

inveterate (in VET ur it) *adj.* deeply rooted; habitual

When it comes to playing golf, Jordan is an *inveterate* cheater.

After hearing Michael's latest story, we are convinced that he is an *inveterate* liar.

invidious (in VID ee us) *adj.* likely to cause unhappiness or offense; tending to arouse feelings of resentment or animosity; offensive or discriminatory

He offended the kindergarten teacher when he made an *invidious* comparison of children to pigs.

One candidate made an *invidious* comparison of his opponent to a bowling ball.

inviolate (in VYE uh lit) *adj.* not violated, injured, disturbed, or profaned; pure or intact

For centuries the tomb lay *inviolate* until, by accident, it was discovered when a peddler's donkey fell through the dry ground and into the tomb.

The wedding cake remained *inviolate* all day, until the boy tripped and fell while carrying it to the table.

invoke (in VOHK) *v.* to ask for help; to call out to for help, support, protection, or inspiration; to ask for earnestly, as in prayer; solicit

Barry repeatedly *invoked* God during his discussion of his alcoholism and his attempts to defeat it.

She *invoked* her reputation of honesty and purity as a way of convincing him to trust her.

iota (eye OH tuh) *n.* a tiny amount, the least bit

I woke up very tired after sleeping just an *iota* the night before.

Lance was still hungry after only eating an *iota* of dinner.

irascible (i RAS uh bul) *adj.* easily angered, irritable

Normally, Rose was a pleasant wife and mother, but if a member of her family prevented her from watching her favorite "soaps," she could become quite *irascible*.

Uncle Tim was a real grouch; even on his birthday he would find a way to become as *irascible* as a spoiled child.

irate (eye RAYT) *adj.* extremely angry, irritated

The long wait at the checkout counters made shoppers *irate*.

Joe wrote an *irate* letter to the editor about school sports.

iridescent (ir i DES unt) *adj.* showing many bright colors which change with movement; shiny, lustrous, or brightly colored

Her latest fashion collection features *iridescent* materials which make the models seem to be clothed in a liquid rainbow.

The toothpaste ad promises you an *iridescent*, sparkling white smile.

ironic (eye RAHN ik) *adj.* meaning the opposite of what is said or expressed; incongruous

It is *ironic* that Eric can't swim and lives on an island.

We thought it was *ironic* that Brad, who is afraid of heights, lives on the 50th floor.

irrational (i RASH uh nal) *adj.* incoherent, illogical, without apparent reason

Herb's *irrational* behavior made him undesirable to all the colleges.

The attorney's *irrational* attempt to sway the jury was unsuccessful.

irrefutable (ih ruh FYOOT uh bul) *adj.* impossible to refute or disprove; indisputable

The man didn't have a chance against the traffic cop's *irrefutable* evidence against him.

It is an *irrefutable* fact that dinosaurs existed millions of years ago.

irrelevant (ih RELL uh vunt) *adj.* not related to the subject at hand

Those documents are totally *irrelevant* to the investigation.

Your reasoning is totally *irrelevant* to the debate.

irrevocable (i REV oh kuh bul) *adj.* irreversible

The judge had the last word, and it was *irrevocable*.

Because the store is going out of business, all sales are *irrevocable*.

isolated (EYE suh lay ted) *adj.* separate, set apart; unconnected, sequestered

The researchers in the lab *isolated* and attempted to identify the virus. (*v.*)

The patient with pneumonia was put into an *isolated* room.

isthmus (ISS mus) *n.* a narrow strip of land, with water on both sides, which connects two larger bodies of land

The *isthmus* at Istanbul connects Europe and Asia.

The *isthmus* of Panama is bounded by the Caribbean Sea and the Pacific Ocean.

itinerant (eye TIN ur unt) *adj.* moving from place to place

James Michner was an *itinerant* writer who moved to each place about which he planned to write.

Monica told Jose that if he hoped to marry her, he would have to put down roots and put an end to his *itinerant* lifestyle.

itinerary (eye TIN uh rare ee) *n.* detailed plan, a list of places to visit

Our *itinerary* included hearing a speech from the visiting congress-man.

Joey's *itinerary* led him to Boston, New York, and Washington, DC.

jaded (JAY dud) *adj.* worn out or wearied as by overwork or overuse

The rich child was *jaded* with luxuries to the point of not enjoying anything.

Working sixteen hours a day he was *jaded*, exhausted, and in need of sleep.

jargon (JAHR gun) *n.* words and phrases used by particular groups of people, in their work or trade, that are not generally understood; any confusing, pretentious, or meaningless words or language; gibberish

I need to take a computer course so I can understand all the *jargon* that my co-workers throw around in the office.

Most contracts are full of legal *jargon* that the general public can't understand, so one is forced to pay outrageous attorney fees just to get a contract translated.

jaundice (JON diss) *n.* prejudiced view; yellow discoloration of the skin and eyes

Her yellow, discolored eyes gave the hint of a disease related to *jaundice*.

Sheila took a *jaundiced* view regarding the dropping of the seventh period. (*adj.*)

jaunt (jawnt) *n.* a short pleasure trip

My parents are always taking *jaunts* in their new motor home.

Mary and Bryan always enjoy their annual *jaunt* to the mountains.

jeopardize (JEP ur dize) *v.* to put into hazard, risk, or imperil

Not having an attorney review a complex real estate contract could *jeopardize* the sale.

Bryan did not want to *jeopardize* his family on a boating trip, so he made sure all the required safety equipment was aboard his vessel.

jetsam (JET sem) *n.* cargo or equipment thrown overboard to lighten an imperiled vessel; discarded odds and ends

The castaways used *jetsam* from their wrecked ship to build a shelter on the deserted island.

The rescue helicopter followed a trail of *jetsam* which led them to the survivors of the sinking vessel.

jettison (JET uh sun) *v.* to throw overboard in order to lighten a ship or airplane, usually in an emergency

The crew had to *jettison* the dangerous cargo.

The smugglers *jettisoned* all illegal materials before the Coast Guard cutter caught up to them.

jilt (jilt) *v.* to reject (a lover)

After Jane was *jilted* she found another man to soothe her fettered feelings. (*adj.*)

Milt *jilted* Charlotte at the altar because marriage was not the answer for him.

jingoism (JING goh iz um) *n.* aggressive nationalism and patriotism, especially as directed against foreign countries; belligerent bigoted patriotism; warmongering

Patriotism can be misdirected into *jingoism* and intolerance of other nations very quickly.

Skinheads' practice of *jingoism* is apparent in the overt statements and actions against immigrants to this country.

jocular (JAHK yuh lur) *adj.* inclined to joke; jovial; merry; amusing or intended to cause amusement

Candice had a *jocular* personality and spread laughter wherever she went.

Every time I went into his store, the *jocular* old man would greet me with a hearty laugh and a new joke.

jostle (JOS uhl) *v.* to bump, push, or shove roughly

Try not to *jostle* that bag; it contains five dozen eggs.

We loved the concert, but we didn't like being *jostled* by the unruly crowd.

joust (jowst) *n.* a combat with lances between two knights, a tilting match; any combat suggestive of a joust

Running and enjoying the competition, Bill and Harry *jousted* with each other playfully. (*v.*)

It was a *joust* to the death between Sir Lancelot and the Black Knight.

jovial (JOE vee ul) *adj.* joyfully exuberant, with a spirit of good fellowship

Pearl's *jovial* attitude carried everyone through the Christmas party.

A *jovial* crowd met the team at the airport.

jubilation (JOO buh LAY shun) *n.* a feeling of great happiness; exultation

The winner of the lottery showed her *jubilation* by jumping up and down and screaming, "Hooray!"

The crowd expressed its *jubilation* by throwing streamers and confetti as their winning team paraded by them.

judicious (joo DISH us) *adj.* exhibiting sound judgement

Linda's mother explained the importance of being *judicious* with her allowance.

Joanne was far from *judicious* when she spent all of her vacation money on lottery tickets.

juggernaut (JUG ur not) *n.* large overpowering destructive force or object

The first atom bomb proved to be a *juggernaut* that destroyed entire cities.

Uncontrollable winds are *juggernauts* causing various types of destruction.

junction (JUNGK shun) *n.* a place where things meet or join; the act of joining or state of being joined; connection

The shopping mall is near the *junction* of the New Jersey Turnpike and Garden State Parkway.

The water leak was at the *junction* of the two pipes.

juncture (JUNK chur) *n.* a decisive or crucial point

What is the *juncture* in time for the new millennium? Is it 2000 or 2001?

At this *juncture* in college, a decision must be made whether to stay or leave.

junket (JUNK et) *n.* a dessert, an excursion by officials to gather facts

She ordered vanilla *junket* for dessert.

A congressionalial junket took them to the smaller countries in Asia.

junta (HOON tuh) *n.* a small group that rules a country after taking power by force; a small legislative body or deliberative council

The country appointed a *junta* to govern its new province, temporarily, after they overthrew the old ruler.

The self-appointed *junta* rules the neighborhood, but they are only a gang of delinquents who are about to have their powers erased by the local police.

jurisdiction (joor is DIK shun) *n.* the extent of authority or legal power

The judge could not make a ruling because the crime occured out of his *jurisdiction*.

Every classroom is under the *jurisdiction* of the teachers.

juxtapose (JUK stuh pohz) *v.* to place side by side

It is interesting to *juxtapose* the writings of Mark Twain and Bret Harte.

Although the play is a tragedy, several moments of comedy are *juxtaposed* with the tearful scenes.

karma (KAHR muh) *n.* fate, destiny; good or bad vibrations from something or someone

All his life he possessed a protective *karma* that kept him out of harm's way.

Louise often told her friends it was her *karma* to die young and beautiful.

kilter (KIL tur) *n.* good working condition; a sound of readiness

I used two hooks to insure the proper *kilter* of the oil painting.

The engine was out of *kilter*.

kin (kin) *n.* family relationship; relative

Through genetic research, we are searching for other *kin* somewhere in the world.

After the automobile accident the police could not release the victim's name to the press until the next of *kin* was notified.

kindle (KIN dl) *v.* to cause to burn or ignite; to arouse or inspire

Because Christine once had feelings for him, Joe thought sending flowers might again *kindle* her affections.

The fire *kindled* when he squirted on some lighter fluid.

kinetic (ki NET ik) *adj.* lively; active; having to do with motion

Lisa was pleased when she learned that the sorority president said she has a *kinetic* personality.

I learned the power of *kinetic* energy the first time I flew on an airplane.

kinship (KIN ship) *n.* natural connection or family relationship

We experienced a sense of *kinship* during our very first meeting in Europe.

It was only their *kinship* that made her agree to lend money to her cousin.

kiosk (KEE osk) *n.* a small structure with one or more sides open

The international fair had many *kiosks* containing food, drink, cake, and lottery tickets.

Trade shows lease *kiosks* to vendors so they may display their goods.

kismet (KIZ met) *n.* fate

The happy couple attributed the success of their relationship to *kismet*.

It was *kismet* that they both returned to their old high school on the same day twenty years after graduation.

knell (nell) *n.* a clear resonant sound; a bell, esp. at a funeral

The *knell* tolled loudly to notify the town of a funeral for the mayor.

The bells in the center of town *knelled* a warning the bank was being robbed. (*v.*)

labyrinth (LAB uh rinth) *n.* a maze

The high school seems like a *labyrinth* to freshmen on the first day of classes.

For our science project, we trained a rat to find its way through a *labyrinth.*

lacerated (LASS uh ray tud) *adj./v.* mangled, jagged, torn

Playing with a knife, Charlie *lacerated* his right hand by catching the blade first.

The doctor removed the patient's shirt and found a large *laceration.* (n.)

lackadaisical (lack uh DAZE ih kul) *adj.* lacking energy and vitality; languid

A *lackadaisical* attitude on the football field invites physical injury.

Her *lackadaisical* attitude created the illusion she was not a responsible person.

lackluster (LAK lus tur) *adj.* lacking energy and effort; lacking brilliance; dull

The group gave a *lackluster* portrayal of Shakespeare's play.

My hair is so limp and *lackluster* I can't do a thing with it.

laconic (luh KAHN ik) *adj.* brief, using few words

Benjamin's *laconic* speech habits gave him a reputation for thoughtfulness and intelligence.

The fictional heroes of the old west were usually cowboys who spoke *laconically*, if at all. (*adv.*)

lambaste (lam BAST) *v.* to give a thrashing; scold

The drill sergeant *lambasted* his troops for their poor performance on the obstacle course.

The fierce storm *lambasted* the ship and its crew.

lament (la MINT) *v.* to express sorrow or regret; to mourn

John *lamented* his decision about not going to college after high school when all his friends came home for spring break.

The song *Cowboy's Lament* is a ballad about the lonely life of those who drive cattle for a living. (*n.*)

It is *lamentable* that Roscoe quit college in his sophomore year; his professors considered him the brightest engineering student in his class. (*adj.*)

lampoon (lam POON) *v.* to attack or ridicule someone in a satirical way

In a humorous skit, the comedian *lampooned* the President.

When the boss leaves the office, Sylvester always *lampoons* the poor man's lisp.

landmark (LAND mark) *n./adj.* any prominent feature of a landscape; an event; of critical importance

Indians learned to read the *landmarks* and to mark trails.

The underdog winning the Super Bowl is always a *landmark* event.

languid (LANG gwid) *adj.* lacking energy; weak; showing little interest in anything

Jill finished the triathlon, but at the finish line she *languidly* sank to the ground. (*adv.*)

The teacher's *languid* approach to American history did not motivate the class.

languish (LANG gwish) *v.* to become weak or feeble; sag with loss of strength

An outdoorsman all his life, Mr. Franklin quickly *languished* in his job as a night watchman.

(To *languish* is to be *languid*.)

The fish in the aquarium hardly stirred, moving *languidly* when they moved at all. (*adv.*)

larceny (LAHR suh nee) *n.* the crime of taking something that does not belong to you; theft

The pickpocket was charged with *larceny*.

Billy committed *larceny* when he stole the pumpkins from Mr. Green's garden.

largess (lahr JES) *n.* generosity

The church was successful largely because of the *largess* of its older members.

The Johnsons' *largess* was evident in their large donation to the school library.

lascivious (luh SIV ee us) *adj.* feeling, expressing, or causing sexual desire; exciting or expressing lust; obscene; lewd

She thought his comments were lewd and *lascivious* because they embarrassed her.

Her boss's constant *lascivious* attention toward her prompted her to charge him with sexual harassment.

lassitude (LAS uh tood) *adj.* listlessness; torpor, weariness

After eating three servings of Thanksgiving dinner, George succumbed to a feeling of *lassitude* and fell asleep on the couch.

Having worked for the cannery for twenty years without a raise, Charles became discouraged with his employers and approached his daily work with unenthusiastic *lassitude*.

latent (LAYT nt) *adj.* lying hidden or undeveloped; potential

Because the disease was in a *latent* state, no one knew she was ill.

Jeri's parents were unaware of her *latent* desire to study law and to become an attorney.

latitude (LAT i tood) *n.* scope, freedom, range, leeway; the distance north or south of the equator

Carl allowed his children a fair amount of *latitude*.

The new school system allows great *latitude* in selecting classes.

lattice (LAT us) *n.* crossed wooden or metal strips arranged in a diagonal pattern

The *lattice* formed an attractive fence around the garden.

George built many attractive *lattice* designs to encourage the growth of his roses.

laud (lawd) *v.* to praise

The entire country *lauded* the Olympic champions.

The former smoker *lauded* the merits of living a smoke-free life.

laudable (LAWD uh bul) *adj.* worthy of being praised

Hector's teacher told him she thought it most *laudable* that he wanted to become a doctor, but an "F" in biology was not going to help him achieve his goal.

During the rainy season it appeared *laudable* of Tim to bring an umbrella and escort the girls to their bus after school, until they found out he was running for student president.

lavish (LAV ish) *v.* to give a lot or too much to; to expend or give abundantly or limitlessly; to squander

She *lavishes* more attention on that dog than she does on her children.

I *lavished* her with so much praise that she began to feel uncomfortable and self-conscious.

lax (laks) *adj.* irresponsible, not diligent, relaxed

The coach was too *lax* about training, and his team finished with a losing record.

John's *lax* habit of paying his bills on time was reflected on his credit report.

layman (LAY mun) *n.* a person who is not trained in or does not have a detailed knowledge of a particular subject; a man who is not a member of the clergy

The book is supposed to be the *layman's* guide to auto repair, but I don't understand many of the technical terms it uses.

The physician tried to explain the illness to Mom in *layman's* terms, but he found it impossible not to revert to medical terminology that she did not understand.

leery (LEER ee) *adj.* refusing or reluctant to believe

Doctor Jones was *leery* about the new medication for arthritis.

The child was *leery* upon seeing the strange man and refused to go with him.

legacy (LEG uh see) *n.* something handed down from one who has gone before or from the past; a bequest

The *legacy* of the copper mining industry is the creation of mountain wastelands where beautiful, unspoiled forests once stood.

The Johnson family's ancestral *legacy* was to have blonde hair and green eyes.

legerdemain (lej ur duh MANE) *n.* sleight of hand, trickery, deception, illusion

Most magicians use *legerdemain* instead of actual magic.

They showed on TV the actual *legerdemain* used to create many illusions.

legion (LEE jun) *n.* a large number; multitude

Amanda has a *legion* of admirers.

Legions of students take the SAT every year.

lesion (LEE zhun) *n.* wound, injury, especially one created by a disease

The nurses told Crystal to keep the bandage on her knee until the *lesion* healed; otherwise the open sore would be prone to infection by air-borne bacteria.

Ebola is an infectious disease characterized by open *lesions* of the skin.

lessor (LESS or) *n.* one who grants a lease

Charlotte signed as the *lessor* at the car agency since she was the manager.

The real estate agent advised the *lessor* that the future tenants had questions.

lethal (LEE thul) *adj.* capable of causing death; fatal or deadly

Capital punishment in the United States relies heavily upon *lethal* injection.

Prescription drugs and alcohol can be a *lethal* combination.

lethargic (lu THAWR jik) *adj.* lacking in energy; feeling unwilling or unable to do anything

When I first got home from the hospital, I was too *lethargic* to clean house.

Flu symptoms include feeling listless and *lethargic.*

lethargy (LETH ur gee) *n.* a lack of energy; laziness; sluggishness; torpor

Lethargy is common in cats because they have smaller hearts and lungs than other animals.

At the nursing home *lethargy* is common amongst the residents.

levee (LEV ee) *n.* an embankment designed to prevent flooding of a river

They built a *levee* to protect the city; however, the water rose to thirty feet and destroyed everything.

The boats landed at the *levee,* which is called a "quay."

leverage (LEV er ij) *n.* positional advantage, power, clout, influence

The wingman took a *leverage* position and scored a hockey goal. (*adj.*)

The foreman has *leverage* over his workers because he decides the work assignments.

levitate (LEV ih tayt) *v.* to rise or float in the air

The young girl *levitated* high over the stage without any apparent support beneath her.

The magician caused the young boy to *levitate* high over the audience.

levity (LEV uh tee) *n.* frivolity; lightness

Our strict history teacher allowed no *levity* until the last day of school.

Levity is not often apparent in a courtroom.

lexicography (lex ih KOG ruh fee) *n.* writing, editing, or compiling of dictionaries

John listed *lexicography* as his profession while working for Random House.

The hours doing research for *lexicography* are tedious.

lexicon (LEX a kon) *n.* a dictionary; vocabulary terms used in or of a particular profession, subject, or style

The *lexicon* used by air traffic controllers is incomprehensible to non-pilots: "down wind to twenty seven, hold three twenty at two thousand, traffic at eleven o'clock, two miles."

Sailors have a nautical *lexicon*; "port" means left, "starboard" means right, "bow" means front, and "stern" means rear.

liaison (LEE ay zahn) *n.* a communication link between groups or persons; connection; alliance; unpermitted secret love affair

There is an unfortunate lack of *liaison* between the departments, so effective communication is severely lacking.

The union representative in our department is the *liaison* between the employees and the union.

libel (LYE bul) *n.* written falsehood that injures another's reputation

Mark's attorney accused the newspaper of *libel* for printing that his client had been arrested for drunken driving when he actually had been visiting his sick grandmother.

The things the candidate's brochure said about his opponent bordered on *libel*.

liberal (LIB uh rul) *adj.* favoring civil liberties and social programs, unbiased, generous

Mama's in Englewood is famous for *liberal* servings of veal parmigiana.

Shirley's *liberal* donation of a million dollars will be used for research.

libertine (LIB ur teen) *adj.* an immoral or licentious man

Don Juan could be considered a *libertine* as the story is told.

Jerry went to college only to become a *libertine*.

licentious (lye SEN shus) *adj.* acting in a promiscuous, uncontrolled and socially unacceptable manner; not within the bounds of morality or propriety; immoral

Because of her *licentious* behavior and reputation, Amanda is no longer considered a good girl.

College students these days are said to be so *licentious* that a mere "dorm mother" is not enough; they almost need a chaperone for every room.

lieu (loo) *adv.* instead of; in place of

In *lieu* of entering the university in September, Roger decided to work and save some money to start in January.

Mike thought it was prudent to buy a family van in *lieu* of a sports car.

ligneous (LIG nee is) *adj.* woodlike

The *ligneous* material made the furniture very heavy and dark.

They polished the *ligneous* material, resulting in a beautifully finished product.

limpid (LIM pid) *adj.* perfectly clear; transparent; lucid

The park is laced with numerous small rivers and crystal blue, *limpid* streams.

Her report is *limpid*, to the point, easy to read, and leaving no question unanswered.

lineage (LIN ee uj) *n.* descendants of a particular ancestor or family

Charlotte's *lineage* reverts to the Mayflower passenger list.

Henry was checking his lineage through genealogy sources when he discovered he was of royal blood.

lionize (LIE uh nize) *v.* to treat a person as a celebrity, to idolize

McGwire was *lionized* by many fans when he set the new home run record.

Elvis has been *lionized* and imitated by many singers since his demise.

liquidation (lik wi DAY shun) *n.* a closing of one's business by collecting assets and settling all debts

I've heard rumors that the corporation is going into *liquidation*.

We can usually pick up some good bargains at a *liquidation* sale.

listless (LIST lis) *adj.* tired and weak, lacking energy or interest; lethargic

As the golf game continued in the 96 degree heat, Jack's stroke became *listless*.

Deborah wasn't being lazy, but her recent illness has made her feel limp and *listless*.

litany (LIT un ee) *n*. a long list; recital that involves repetition or incantation; tedious recounting

Once again she had to hear his *litany* of complaints about how badly he was treated.

If you ask Mrs. Peabody about her husband, you will get a *litany* of all of Mr. Peabody's faults and bad habits he has acquired over their forty years of marriage.

literal (LIT uh rul) *adj*. true to fact, not exaggerated, actual or factual

Jeff complained his statement was taken out of context and not quoted *literally*. (*adv*.)

The congressman said his report on crime was the *literal* truth.

lithe (lythe) *adj*. bending easily and gracefully

The gymnast was so *lithe* that she dismounted without a sound.

The dancer was as *lithe* as a cat as he leapt across the stage.

litigant (LIT i gant) *n*. a person involved in a lawsuit

Hank was the *litigant* in the lawsuit against Allstate Insurance.

Joan, as the *litigant* in the case, was offered a settlement which she accepted.

litigate (LIT uh gayt) *v*. to try in court

Because our case could not be settled out of court, our attorney suggested that we *litigate*.

Adam wrote a letter to the public relations office stating that their company's facial cleanser caused his acne and threatening to *litigate* if they did not find a way to clear up his zits before prom.

livid (LIV id) *adj*. of a purple or dark blue color, usually caused by an injury; black and blue, as from a bruise; extremely angry; full of rage; furious

There was a large, *livid* bruise on her upper arm from her fall.

The rude letter from his mother-in-law had him so *livid* he couldn't see straight!

loath (lohth) *adj*. unwilling; reluctant

She'd be *loath* to admit it to her ladies group, but she doesn't really like opera.

I am *loath* to go out the door without my morning cup of coffee lest I fall asleep at a stop sign!

loathe (lohth) *v.* to feel intense dislike, to hate or detest

Stan *loathes* cream and sugar in his coffee.

In Dr Suess's book *How the Grinch Stole Christmas,* the Grinch loathed Christmas.

lobby (LAHB ee) *v.* to try to prompt legislative action; to exert influence

Many groups have been *lobbying* Congress to change the gun laws.

The group of college students went to the White House to *lobby* against another war.

logistics (loh JIS tiks) *n.* the management of the details of an operation

The Normandy invasion is a great example of military *logistics.*

The *logistics* involved in building the Golden Gate Bridge required an immense amount of time and resources.

loiter (LOY ter) *v.* hang around; linger

A sign outside the players' entrance to the stadium said, "No *Loitering,*" but autograph hounds *loitered* there before and after games anyway.

The supporting actor was on stage during most of the play, but he was so ineffective it was almost as if he were a *loiterer.* (*n.*)

loll (LOL) *v.* to recline in a relaxed manner, to hang loose, droop, dangle

The dog stood in the heat with his tongue *lolling.*

George has been *lolling* around the house all day causing great concern to his parents.

longevity (lawn JEV uh tee) *n.* great span of life or time

The ninety-year-old owes his *longevity* to riding his bike ten miles every day.

Certain cultures seem to hold secrets of *longevity.*

lope (lope) *n./v.* a steady, easy gait faster than walking; to move with such a gait

They complained his *loping* strides made many run after him to keep up.

The pony was *loping* until the rabbit ran under her causing the pony to break stride.

loquacious (lo KWAY shus) *adj.* overly talkative

Marsha's teacher told her she would have to curtail her *loquacious* behavior, but Marsha was talking so much she didn't hear what he had said.

I never call Jeanne because she is so *loquacious* that I know I'll be on the phone for hours.

lout (lowt) *n.* a rude, stupid, or awkward person; someone who is clumsy or unmannered; oaf

Joe is such a big, lazy *lout*, but Peggy married him anyway.

I have never in my life danced with such a *lout*. He ruined my brand new shoes by stepping all over them!

lucid (LOO sid) *adj.* clear; easy to understand

My math teacher gives such *lucid* explanations that I do well on every test.

After the accident, Joe was not quite *lucid* for several minutes.

lucre (LOO kur) *n.* monetary reward or gain, money

I was offered ten percent *lucre* after the business audit for increased sales.

The signing bonus was a fraction of the *lucre* made from all the book sales.

ludicrous (LOO di krus) *adj.* ridiculous or foolish; laughable because unreasonable or unsuitable

The charges seemed *ludicrous* at first, but damning evidence kept piling up against him.

The idea of having babies at age 70 is *ludicrous*, but she was determined to try.

lugubrious (loo GOO bree us) *adj.* exaggeratedly mournful

Edgar Allan Poe is one of the most *lugubrious* American authors.

When Theresa found another boyfriend, Jimmy was *lugubrious* for several days until he started seeing someone else.

luminary (LOO mih nahr ee) *n.* a celestial body; a person attaining eminence

John was a *luminary* among professional bowlers.

FDR was a *luminary* as president and the founder of Social Security.

luminous (LOO muh nus) *adj.* glowing; giving off light

The harvest moon is usually the most *luminous* of the year.

My travel alarm clock is so *luminous* that it lights up my tent.

lummox (LUM ox) *n.* a large, ungainly, and dull witted person

The *lummox* scared many on the football field but moved like he had two left feet.

George was a lovable *lummox* who wasn't very bright but had many friends.

lure (loor) *n.* a decoy, snare, an attraction, enticement, allure

The truth of the matter is that cheese is not a good *lure* for mice.

Junior was *lured* home from the playground by the promise of apple pie. (*v.*)

lurid (LOOR id) *adj.* deathly pale or glowing through a haze.

The clouds hung low with a *lurid* gleam just before the thunderstorm.

After the accident, Nancy's skin was *lurid*, but she eventually came around.

lush (lush) *adj.* luxuriant; characterized by richness or abundance

Their backyard is like a paradise with *lush* foliage everywhere.

Cindy brushed back her *lush* dark hair.

lyrical (LIR i kul) *adj.* expressive of emotions, and often having the quality of a song; showing sincere emotion and strong feeling; songlike; poetic

The *lyrical* noise of city traffic is music to my ears, since I was born and raised in Manhattan.

The *lyrical* poetry made me feel the same anguish the author was feeling, and it brought tears to my eyes.

macerate (MAS uh rayt) *v.* dissolve; to soften by soaking; to emaciate; to wither

The tablet will *macerate* in water and can be swallowed thereafter.

Toilet paper is designed to *macerate* in water.

machination (mak uh NAY shun) *n.* scheming activity for an evil purpose

The overthrown dictator never really understood the *machinations* that led to the coup.

In the big city, every gang performs its own ruthless *machinations*.

magnanimous (mag NAN uh mus) *adj.* generous; noble in spirit

The mayoral candidate was *magnanimous* in defeat, telling his constituents to support his opponent.

Lucy *magnanimously* gave the taxi driver a tip even though she knew he had taken her on a circuitous route to the theater.

magnate (MAG nayt) *n.* powerful business-person

Our neighbor made a fortune as a pest control *magnate*.

It seems that the *magnates* have taken control of professional baseball.

magnitude (MAG nih tood) *n.* great extent, amount or dimension, enormity

The *magnitude* of the Empire State Building impresses tourists from all over the world.

The *magnitude* of the census has great impact on the future expenditures.

maharajah (mah huh RAH zhuh) *n.* ruling Indian Prince, esp. one of the major states

The visiting *maharajah* wanted to see how our bus system operates.

The *maharajah* was part of the legislature from the Gandhi State of India.

maim (maim) *v.* to disable or disfigure; to cripple

Joshua saw action in the invasion of France, where he was *maimed* when he stepped on a land mine and lost his leg.

Every year people are *maimed* in automobile accidents by drunk drivers.

maladjusted (mal uh JUS tid) *adj.* poorly adjusted; unable to adjust properly to the stresses of daily life

Justin was *maladjusted* when he first came to our school, but he has learned to fit in.

Many young teenagers are *maladjusted*, but by the age sixteen, they become more at ease with themselves.

maladroit (mal uh DROYT) *adj.* clumsy; inept

Actor Chevy Chase was famous for his *maladroit* roles.

Bob was upset with the mechanic's *maladroit* attempt to repair his car.

malady (MAL uh dee) *n.* illness; sickness; disease

In Edgar Allan Poe's writings, most of his main characters have some sort of *malady*.

I was most unhappy to hear of her *malady*; I hope she recovers soon.

malaise (ma LAYZ) *n.* a vague feeling of bodily discomfort, as at the beginning of an illness

Beth's *malaise* began when she awoke with a sore throat.

A sudden *malaise* overcame Jonathan when the postman delivered a certified letter from the IRS.

malapropism (MAL uh PRAHP iz um) *n.* the wrong use of one word instead of another because they sound similar to each other, and which is amusing as a result; the humorous or ridiculous misuse of a word

In the sentence "The price of food in Japan is gastronomical," the word "gastronomical," which refers to the stomach, is a *malapropism*, because it should be "astronomical," which relates to high cost.

We laughed at our five year old son's *malapropism* when he said there was entirely too much "violins" on TV instead of "violence," which is what he meant.

malcontent (MAL kon tent) *n.* one who is dissatisfied with existing conditions

The labor strikers were *malcontents* who did not even work at the company.

We seem to always have one *malcontent* who can negatively impact team spirit.

malevolent (ma LEVO lunt) *adj.* wishing or showing evil or harm to others

Although she may look sweet and innocent, that young lady is one of the most *malevolent* people I have ever met.

The witches were put in the story to serve as a *malevolent* force.

malfeasance (mal FEE zunce) *n.* an illegal act by a public official

No one would testify that the president was guilty of *malfeasance* even though they openly discussed his crime in private.

The mayor was guilty of *malfeasance* for giving a contract to his brother's company.

malice (MAL is) *n.* a desire or intention to harm others or see them suffer

Our government is based on justice, with *malice* toward none.

We could not believe that such a young girl could harbor such *malice* toward her neighbors.

malicious (muh LISH us) *adj.* intending to cause harm; spiteful

The actress denied the *malicious* rumors, saying that certain people were trying to ruin her career.

The vandals left a trail of *malicious* destruction behind them.

malign (muh LINE) *v.* to slander, to speak harmful and evil untruths

The candidate was preparing a brochure carefully not to *malign* his opponent.

The National Enquirer is notorious for *maligning* celebrities.

malignant (ma LIG nunt) *adj.* harmful; evil; dangerous

She had to begin treatment immediately because the tumor was *malignant*.

We wished the neighbors would leave; they were a *malignant* presence in our neighborhood.

malinger (muh LING ger) *v.* to pretend to be ill to avoid doing work

Whenever Tom had chores to do on the farm, he would *malinger*, claiming to have a headache.

Many students fail to do their homework, but few will admit it is because they *malinger*.

malleable (MAL ee uh bull) *adj.* capable of being shaped, easily altered or influenced, flexible

The poll for the election became *malleable* when one party overloaded the results.

The class decided to choose a *malleable* metal for the sculpture.

malnutrition (mal noo TRISH un) *n.* inadequate nourishment

If she stays on that marshmallow diet much longer, she will die of *malnutrition*.

Many prisoners of war suffered from *malnutrition*.

malodor (mal OH dor) *n.* a bad odor

After the storm, the *malodor* made it clear that the sewers were not working.

A *malodorous* stench filled the car after we ran over the skunk. (*adj.*)

mammoth (MAM uth) *adj.* huge; gigantic

Herman Melville's title character, Moby Dick, is a *mammoth* whale.

When Jane returned from vacation, she found a *mammoth* amount of work piled on her desk.

mandate (MAN dayt) *n.* a command or authorization to do something

Our new boss felt he had a *mandate* to fire anyone he didn't like.

The university's *mandate* said Jack had to take English I before he could take the creative writing course that he really wanted.

mandatory (MAN dah tor ee) *adj.* authoritatively ordered or commanded; necessary

Attendance at Sunday Chapel is no longer *mandatory* for the students.

When you go to vote, it is *mandatory* to show photo identification.

mania (MAY nee uh) *n.* an unusually strong and continuing interest in an activity or subject; extreme desire or enthusiasm; a psychological disorder characterized by excitability

He worried about his wife's sudden *mania* for exercise after she had led a sedentary life at home for many years.

Belinda was in such a state of uncontrolled *mania* that she had to be hospitalized for psychiatric treatment.

manifest (MAN ih fest) *adj.* clearly apparent to the sight or understanding; obvious

There is *manifest* danger in lighting a match near a gas pump.

The teacher's anger was *manifest*; you could hear it in her voice.

manifesto (man ih FES toh) *n.* public declaration of beliefs

Zach wrote his *manifesto* before he announced that he would run for class president.

The Communist Manifesto was Karl Marx's statement about government.

manifold (MAN uh fowld) *adj.* having many forms, features, or parts

When we visited the newspaper office, we realized it is made up of *manifold* elements.

A great poem is comprised of *manifold* aspects.

mar (mar) *v.* render less perfect, impair, spoil

Beth arrived scantily dressed to *mar* her ex-husband's wedding ceremony.

The antique furniture was *marred* by scratches during delivery.

marauder (muh RAWD er) *n.* raider, intruder

Among the legendary pirate *marauders* of the eighteenth century were Captain Kidd, Calico Jack Rackham, Charles Vane, Blackbeard, and Sir Henry Morgan.

A band of *marauders* looted the town.

marginal (MAHR jih nul) *adj.* small in amount or effect; barely above a minimum standard of quality; insignificant; in the margin

The difference between the two bids was only *marginal*.

The *marginal* notes that the previous student had written in the textbook were quite helpful to me.

maritime (MAYR ih time) *adj.* near the sea; concerned with shipping or navigation

While in our nation's capital, we visited the *Maritime* War Museum.

Rick's desire is to become a *maritime* lawyer.

mar (mahr) *v.* to make imperfect, less attractive; spoil; disfigure

The water stains *marred* the finish of our rosewood coffee table.

The model's face was *marred* for life after her auto accident.

marrow (MARE oh) *n.* soft, fatty vascular tissue in the bones

Bone *marrow* is an organ for blood cell production in humans.

Doctor Smith wanted to test her bone *marrow*, taking a small sample from the hip.

marshal (MAHR shul) *v.* to assemble for the purpose of doing something; also an officer in the police or military (*n.*)

Marshaling their forces, the British defeated Rommel at El Alamein.

Wyatt Earp was the *marshal* of Dodge City.

martial (MAHR shul) *adj.* warlike; having to do with combat

Walter has a black belt in the *martial* arts, so don't mess with him.

After the uprising, the government was in a state of *martial* law.

martinet (mart in ET) *n.* a very strict disciplinarian

The English professor was a *martinet*; if the paper contained one grammatical error, he refused to accept it.

Some people believe it is easier to be a *martinet* than it is to make decisions.

martyr (MAHR tur) *n.* someone willing to sacrifice and even give his/her life for a cause; also, one who pretends suffering to gain sympathy

She was a professional *martyr*, all-suffering for her children, or so she would tell them ten times a day.

Joan of Arc was undoubtedly the most famous *martyr* in modern history, burned at the stake because she refused to go against her beliefs.

matron (MAY trun) *n.* a mature looking married woman or widow; mature woman in charge

The *matron* met us at the door and escorted us to the dinning room.

The woman prisoner was met by the *matron* and taken to her cell.

mean (meen) *n.* average, midpoint between extremes

The students were given a math problem to determine the *mean* of a series of numbers.

A land surveyor must determine the *mean* high water line when calculating the area of oceanfront property.

meander (mee AN dur) *v.* to wind in broad curves; to wander aimlessly in speech or movement; to ramble

Hikers can *meander* along the path next to the river for several miles.

Must I listen to Uncle Waldo *meander* drunkenly about a lot of meaningless nonsense?

median (MEE dee un) *n.* average, midpoint

The vertical line that divides a histogram into equal parts is the *median.*

The *median* strip divides a highway into two roads going in opposite directions.

mediate (MEE dee ayt) *v.* negotiate

John attempted to *mediate* between the union and General Motors for a contract.

The judge ruled the case had to be *mediated* before it would be heard.

mendicant (MEN di kunt) *n.* street beggar, alms seeker

You just about trip over *mendicants* on the streets of Istanbul.

Some *mendicants* are people who cannot face everyday normal life.

mediocre (mee dee OH kur) *adj.* unimpressive, ordinary, average, passable

Harvey's school work is *mediocre* even though he tries twice as hard as other students.

The new drug for arthritis is *mediocre* and less effective than aspirin.

medium (MEE dee um) *n.* an instrument, means, or agency; a method or way of expressing or accomplishing something; material used by an artist

The work of art was done in mixed *media,* and included wood shavings, pieces of metal, glue, and oil paint. (*plural*)

I think television is the best *medium* to advertise your product because your ad will reach millions of people.

medley (MED lee) *n.* a collection of various things

The performer sang a *medley* of western songs.

The latest fad is a *medley* of vegetables in frozen packets.

megalomania (mehglow MAY nee uh) *n.* personality trait characterized by delusions of grandeur, power, and wealth

Hitler's *megalomania* was apparent in most of his speeches.

When Bill told me he wanted to be king of the world, I knew it was his *megalomania* talking.

melancholy (MEL un kahl ee) *adj.* sad, gloomy, weary

It was a *melancholy* day, gloomy and dark.

The best word to describe Jim is *melancholy*; no matter what the situation, he always walks around looking like he has lost his best friend.

melee (MAY lay) *n.* a situation that is confused and not under control; a confused mingling or turmoil; free-for-all

Sometime during the *melee* three shots were fired, but in all the confusion, I was not sure from which direction they came.

As the crowd rushed the store in a general *melee*, everyone trying to get to the bargain table first, I was separated from my friends.

mellifluous (muh LIF loo us) *adj.* sweet sounding, musical, harmonious, sweet flowing

The ringing of the church's bells gave off a *mellifluous* sound.

From across the lake the *mellifluous* voices of the choir could be heard.

memento (muh MEN toe) *n.* a remembrance; keepsake; souvenir

Leaving the museum, the parents purchased a *memento* for their daughter.

After their date, he gave her a fraternity pin as a *memento*.

memoir (MEM wahr) *n.* a narrative of experience happening to the writer

Many *memoirs* are written by ghost writers for publishing houses.

Many novels are really the *memoirs* of the writer telling of his or her own life experiences.

menagerie (muh NAJ uh ree) *n.* a collection of animals on exhibit

Busch Gardens has a wonderful *menagerie* of lions, tigers, elephants, and other wild animals roaming free and on display in a park-like setting.

To have a house pet is one thing, but Susan keeps so many parrots and cats in her house, it is a virtual *menagerie*.

mendacious (men DAY shus) *adj.* deceitful, dishonest, lying

Bert's *mendacious* profit report forced stockholders to sell at once.

Charlie's *mendacious* testimony at the trial was refuted by the prosecution.

menial (MEE nee uhl) *adj.* servile, low; fit for servants

The nurse had to perform many *menial* tasks before she was able to prove her ability.

Many college students are forced to do *menial* work in order to pay the bills.

mentor (MEN tur) *n.* a teacher, tutor, counselor, esp. in business, an experienced person

Harry wrote his thesis on stem cell functions with his *mentor's* guidance.

Rita spent years *mentoring* junior employees at the computer factory. (*v.*)

mercenary (MUR suh ner ee) *n.* a hired soldier; someone who will do anything for money

England hired Hessians as *mercenaries* during the American Revolution.

Some of the people involved in Watergate were considered *mercenaries*.

mercurial (mur KYOOR ee ul) *adj.* following no predictable pattern

Jeff's *mercurial* attitude leaves one to wonder if he's responsible.

The research for a cancer cure is quite *mercurial* due to the many side effects.

merger (MUR jer) *n.* alliance, fusion, consolidation, unification

The proposed AOL and Warner *merger* is on hold until further notice.

Before a *merger* is approved today, the SEC must give its blessings.

meritocracy (mare ih TOK ruh see) *n.* a system of rule in which lead
ers are chosen based on ability and talent instead of wealth and position

Professor Tom believes that the education system should be a *meritocracy.*

Athletics is one system where *meritocracy* prevails.

meritorious (mare uh TORE ee us) *adj.* deserving praise, reward,
esteem

Chuck's hard work produced *meritorious* results and a pending scholarship.

Her hard work at the library provided her a *meritorious* award for
student service.

metamorphosis (met uh MOR fuh sis) *n.* transformation, change of
form, mutation

The *metamorphosis* of human cells is happening every second.

A complete cycle of *metamorphosis* is from the caterpillar to the butterfly.

metaphysics (met uh FIZ iks) *n.* the study of what exists, the study of
ultimate reality

The *metaphysical* answer to dimensions is in 24 areas, not just 3.

Stan devoted his life to *metaphysics.*

mete (MEET) *v.* to distribute by or as if by measure; allot

Allison stood in the doorway in a witch costume and *meted* out Halloween candy to all the kids.

The sergeant *meted* out ammunition to all soldiers in the platoon.

meteor (MEE tee or) *n.* a shooting star, transient fiery streak in the sky

A *meteor* that strikes the Earth is called a meteorite.

The shooting stars provided a *meteor* show of exploding light and
color.

meticulous (meh TIK yuh lus) *adj.* carefully attentive to every small
detail; painstaking; precise and careful; fussy

Aunt Brenda was so *meticulous* about her house that she used to check
everything for dust with a white glove after the maid left.

It is *meticulous* work to build models for a living.

microcosm (MYE kroh kahz um) *n.* a little world, could be in miniature

A *microcosm* hung around the cat's neck in the movie *Men in Black*.

The planet Earth is just a *microcosm* in the giant Milky Way.

midriff (MID riff) *n.* the middle area of the torso, the diaphragm, in the human body

On her *midriff*, she wore a tattoo that everyone could see.

The belly dancers' costume bares their *midriff*, which is culturally acceptable.

mien (meen) *n.* air, bearing, character, demeanor

She's preceded by her reputation as a lady of noble *mien*.

Annie had a beautiful *mien* and was the ideal person to model.

migraine (MIE grane) *n.* an excruciating headache

A drug that could not be used to treat *migraines* finally was used in cancer treatment.

Her *migraine* started on the left and settled in the middle of the head.

migratory (MIE gra tory) *adj.* roving, wandering, nomadic

Most American Indian tribes in the Old West were *migratory* and followed the movements of the buffalo.

Wild geese *migrate* to Canada in the summer and to Mexico in the winter. (*v.*)

milieu (mill yoo) *n.* environment or surroundings

After a long sea journey, a sailor on land for the first few days feels out of his *milieu*.

The New York Stock Exchange is a *milieu* of frenzied activity during trading hours.

millennium (mi LEN ee um) *n.* a period of one thosaund years

How did you celebrate the end of the *millennium* on New Year's Eve 1999?

The year 2000 signifies that two *millennia* have passed. (*pl.*)

mimic (MIM ik) *v.* to imitate or copy

Rich Little *mimics* many famous personalities when performing on stage.

The teacher accused Harry of *mimicking* her voice when she was out of the room.

mince (mince) *v.* to cut into small pieces; speak directly and frankly, affected elegance

She *minced* onion, celery, and bell peppers for her stir-fry recipe.

The officer *minced* few words with the driver of the stolen car.

minuscule (MIN us kyool) *adj.* tiny, extremely small

The map of Romania was *minuscule* and almost blinding at times.

The insides of an ameoba are *minuscule* and difficult to see with a microscope.

mirage (muh RAJGE) *n.* unreal reflection; an optical illusion

Her beauty was mostly a *mirage* created by the art of cosmetics.

Desert caravans often see *mirages* on days when heat waves reflect off the burning sands.

mire (myre) *n.* an area of deep, wet, sticky earth; a swampy area filled with such soil; bog; marsh

The wagon's wheels sank deeply into the wet, red *mire*.

If you keep moving at a steady pace, you will avoid getting stuck in the *mire*.

misanthrope (MISS an thrope) *n.* a person expecting the worst from people, hater of mankind

Hitler was a *misanthrope* and treated people poorly to secure his own ends.

The terrorist was a *misanthrope,* causing death to many he hated.

miscellany (MISS uh lay nee) *n.* collection of various things

Seth's home was a collection of *miscellaneous* paintings, writings, and books. (*adj.*)

Anthology 2000 was an interesting *miscellany* of poems written by amateurs.

misconstrue (mis kun STROO) *v.* to take in the wrong sense, misunderstand, or misinterpret

Bruce *misconstrued* the numbers his wife selected for the lottery, but won anyway.

The builder *misconstrued* the architectural plans and built the dinning room three feet short.

miser (MI zer) *n.* a stingy person; tightwad; hoarder

Marilyn, the *miser*, would not contribute a penny to any charity.

The old *miser* lived a simple life, but when he died we found out he had saved over a million dollars.

misnomer (miss NO mur) *n.* an incorrect or inappropriate name

A nickname like "Speedy" is a *misnomer* when given to one who is slow at what he does.

We usually have dinner at a very small Italian restaurant called *The Spaghetti Factory*, obviously a *misnomer* of major proportions.

mitigate (MIT uh gayt) *v.* moderate in severity, alleviate, soften

Alzheimer's disease will be *mitigated* by experimental drugs in about one year.

In order to *mitigate* the traffic problem, the city has proposed adding four more lanes.

mode (mohd) *n.* a way or method of doing something; type, manner, fashion

Once he became a lawyer, Hal put aside his jeans and dressed in the *mode* of his contemporaries: conservative dark suits, white shirts, and ties.

Our vacation was spent in a laid-back *mode*, sleeping-in late and then catching rays on the beach.

modest (MAHD ist) *adj.* shy, reserved, unassuming, unshowy, demure

Helen served a *modest* but tasty lunch for the club, which everyone enjoyed.

Anthony made only a *modest* donation to the kids collecting money for school.

modify (MAWD ih fye) *v.* to change or alter

Nancy's nose job will certainly *modify* her appearance.

The editor sent the manuscript back for me to *modify*.

modulate (MAHJ uh layt) *v.* to vary the loudness, pitch, intensity, or tone of; to adjust a particular measure or proportion

Teachers *modulate* their approach in response to their students' needs.

Modulate your tone of voice when speaking in court.

modus operandi (MO duss op uh RAN deye) *n.* manner in which something is done

The corporation's *modus operandi* produced profits and proved to be top notch.

The Yankees base their *modus operandi* on the team's magnitude and abundance of money.

modus vivendi (MO dus vih VEN dee) *n.* manner of living, way of life; lifestyle

Wealthy people enjoy their *modus vivendi* without care of expense.

Elvis's *modus vivendi* included the acquisition of many expensive cars.

mogul (MOH guhl) *n.* a very rich or powerful person; a magnate

Howard Hughes was a famous *mogul* who was rarely seen in public.

After forming Microsoft, Bill Gates became the most recognized computer *mogul*.

mollify (MAHL ih fye) *v.* appease, calm, placate, to pacify

Red roses would not *mollify* her hurt feelings.

Gloria could not be *mollified* because she was denied the promotion promised her.

mollycoddle (MOL ee kod ul) *n.* to pamper, to spoil someone with kind treatment, overindulge

The way they *mollycoddle* Ian, he'll always be a spoiled brat.

Phil was *mollycoddled* to the point that he was not able to cope with the world.

molt (molt) *v.* to shed periodically an outer covering of skin or feathers

Snakes *molt* periodically, leaving the outer skin behind as waste material.

The male peacock *molts* before appearing in his colorful plumage.

momentum (moh MEN tum) *n.* the force or speed of an object in motion; strength or speed of movement; impetus

The *momentum* of the truck caused it to go through the brick wall.

Technology seems to create its own *momentum*; if something can be done, it will be done.

monarchy (MON ark ee) *n.* supreme power or sovereignty held by a single person, kingdom

Monaco is a *monarchy*, one of the last remaining such kingdoms.

Kings, queens, and *monarchies* are disappearing from the earth.

moniker (MON ih kur) *n.* word or words by which one is addressed, nickname

"Babe" is the *moniker* for Herman Ruth, the former baseball homerun king.

World War II hero General Patton's *moniker* was "Blood in Guts."

monolithic (mah noh LITH ik) *adj.* characterized by massiveness, rigid, uniform, usually formed from a single thing

Jaime placed a *monolithic* stone in his back yard.

Philip Morris is a *monolithic* corporation with powerful holdings worldwide.

monosyllabic (mah no sih LAB ik) *adj.* very brief or blunt, having only one syllable

The coach used *monosyllabic* signals during the game to send in plays.

The teacher refused to use last names, calling everyone by *monosyllabic* grunts.

monotonous (muh NOT uh nus) *adj.* arousing no interest or curiosity

Helen spoke in *monotonous* phrases, putting everyone to sleep.

The night work at the newspaper was *monotonous*, but the pay was excellent.

morass (meh RAS) *n.* anything that hinders, traps or overwhelms; low-lying, soggy ground

The jeep sank deep into the *morass* and could go no further.

A *morass* of feelings overcame Harold when he learned his mother had cancer.

moratorium (mawr uh TAWR ee um) *n.* a stopping of an activity for an agreed period of time; a temporary ban on, or suspension of, some activity; a period of delay

A *moratorium* was declared on new construction until the sewer system could be extended to accommodate the growth.

Dad was so upset after paying the bills that he declared a *moratorium* on spending and took away all of our credit cards.

mordant (MOR duhnt) *adj.* sharply caustic, as wit; sarcastic

Mary had a *mordant* tongue, causing ill-will among her co-workers.

His *mordant* attitude held up the commissioner's meeting.

mores (MAWR ayz) *n.* customary cultural standards; moral attitudes, manners, habits

According to Chinese *mores*, it is polite for dinner guests to belch at the table as a gesture of appreciation and enjoyment.

The problem with some community *mores* is that the older generation clings to outdated moral attitudes no longer appropriate for the times.

moribund (MOR ih bund) *adj.* fading out, waning, dying

Many of the early customs were *moribund* by the year 2000.

Typewriters have become *moribund* with the growth of computers.

morose (muh ROHS) *adj.* melancholy, depressed, sulky, sullen

Clara felt *morose* after reading *The Shining* and turned to the comics for help.

Danny's *morose* attitude was infectious and no fun for his family.

mortify (MOR tih fye) *v.* disconcert, shame, to embarrass, to humiliate

Jeff was *mortified* when the dean asked what happened at the fraternity party the previous night.

Billy *mortified* his sister with by showing her boyfriend pictures of her ex-boyfriend.

mosaic (moh ZAY ik) *n.* a detailed pattern made from many different tiles or pieces

At the Caracas Race Track, a *mosaic* mural depicting a horse race is displayed.

The wall surrounding the house was covered with *mosaic* art work.

motif (moh TEEF) *n.* a pattern or design; a similar dominant or recurring element or theme

We chose the curtains with a blue flower *motif.*

My new house will be decorated throughout in a Mexican *motif.*

motive (MO tiv) *n.* a reason or justification to do something, incentive, enticement

Joe, what was Carl's *motive* for prevarication?

The basketball player's *motive* for changing teams was a salary increase.

motivate (MOH tih vayt) *v.* to incite or impel

A good teacher always knows how to *motivate* her class.

The coach *motivated* his team with an inspiring speech.

motley (MAHT lee) *adj.* consisting of many different types, parts, or colors that do not seem to belong together; variegated; extremely varied or diverse

The ship's *motley* crew was made up of different nationalities, ages, and backgrounds.

Our dog had a *motley* litter. All six puppies were different colors, some were tiny, some huge, but all adorable.

mottle (MOT el) *v.* to mark with spots or blotches of different shades or colors

The dog shook himself off in the living room and *mottled* the furniture with mud.

After the rain Sally's car windows were *mottled* with water spots.

mountebank (MOUNT uh bank) *n.* charlatan, one who claims to be who he is not

Carson was the best *mountebank* known for years until arrested by the IRS.

The old medicine men were *mountebanks* selling snake oil to unassuming patients.

mundane (mun DAYN) *adj.* commonplace, earthly, everyday, banal

Artists often have difficulty with the *mundane* affairs of normal life.

Wealthy people are not familiar with the *mundane* problems of the working class.

municipal (myoo NIS ih pul) *adj.* of or belonging to a town or city; of or relating to a local government or governmental unit

Seattle's *municipal* sanitation department has sent out leaflets explaining the change in collection days and times.

There is an underground parking lot for all of the *municipal* employees, including the police officers and judges.

munificent (myoo NIF uh sunt) *adj.* benevolent, very generous, lavish

Chelsea Park is one of the *munificent* gifts to the city for the children.

Dr. Mote, in his will, left a *munificent* amount of money to the Mote Marine Lab.

munitions (myoo NISH unz) *n.* material used in war, ammunition

Munition sales constitute large illegal profits for many arms dealers.

The army's quartermaster handles all *munitions* purchases and inventory.

murmur (MUR mer) *n.* undertone, mumble, a low, unclear sound.

The rescue crew heard a *murmur* from underneath the wreckage and therefore knew that there was a survivor.

The underwater screen saver on the computer gives off various *murmurs* all day.

muse (myooz) *v.* to ponder; meditate; think about at length

Chess is a game of skill whereupon each player *muses* over all the possible plays before deciding which piece to move.

Though the odds of winning the lottery are very low, it is fun to *muse* about what you would do if you actually won.

muster (MUS tur) *v./n.* to collect or gather; the act of inspection or critical examination

In 1836, the Texans at the Alamo *mustered* all the troops available to defend against the invading Mexican Army.

The restaurant owner inspected the kitchen and said the eating utensils did not pass *muster* and that the dishwasher must wash them over again.

myopia (mye OH pee uh) *n.* nearsightedness, narrow mindedness, intolerance, lack of foresight

Dr. Cline ordered a prescription to correct Carl's condition of *myopia.*

Jason's *myopia* about foreign lotteries proved correct; they are mainly illegal.

myriad (MIR ee ud) *n.* an extremely large number

Jane said she had a *myriad* of things to do to get ready for the party.

On a clear night the sky is filled with *myriad* stars. (*adj.*)

mystic (MIS tik) *adj.* having hidden or spiritually symbolic meaning; arousing a sense of mystery; enigmatic

Meditation and yoga supposedly can give you a *mystic* feeling, as though you are one with the universe.

The thick fog hanging over the sea and the distant sound of fog horns emitted a *mystic* aura, and we half expected to see the Loch Ness Monster emerge from the deep.

nadir (NAY dur) *n.* point of greatest adversity or despair

In sales you must understand that *nadirs* and peaks equal the bad and good times.

The Great Depression was the *nadir* of despair of the 1930s.

narcissism (NAHR si siz um) *n.* inordinate fascination with oneself

Total concern for yourself, or *narcissism*, will jeopardize interpersonal relationships.

Steve's *narcissistic* attitude creates difficulty at his place of employment since all decisions revolve around his wishes. (*adj.*)

nascent (NAS unt) *adj.* beginning to form, grow, develop

His ideas were *nascent* when he outlined the novel, but as he thought about them, they came to fruition.

The *nascent* country had a long way to go before it would be completely self-governing.

nautical (NAW tih kul) *adj.* relating to sea navigation

The captain and his crew handled the *nautical* trip through the Panama Canal.

The admiral entertained us with his stories of *nautical* adventures.

nebulous (NEB yuh lus) *adj.* unclear and lacking form; vague; hazy, confused, or indistinct; cloud-like or indefinite in outline

It was almost dark, and in the distance and fog, I could make out only the *nebulous* silhouette of the soldiers marching toward the house.

My roommate seems to have a *nebulous* concept of "sharing responsibilities" since he does nothing in the house and has paid very little toward expenses for the month.

nefarious (nih FARE ee uss) *adj.* extremely wicked, villainous, openly evil

During wartime, *nefarious* schemes are often contemplated by both sides.

Hinkley's *nefarious* plot to kill the president was unsuccessful.

negate (nih GATE) *v.* to deny, refuse to admit the truth, to end formally and with authority

When counting the votes for the election, the secretary of state's action to stop the hand-counts was *negated* by the Supreme Court of the State of Florida.

Progress on the study has been *negated* due to the lack of funds.

negligence (nay glih gens) *n.* carelessness, inconsideration, indifference

Hasson's *negligence* caused her to crash into a parked car on campus.

Negligence can be avoided by being conscientious.

nemesis (NEM eh sis) *n.* an opponent that cannot be beaten or overcome

Cancer was the *nemesis* that finally killed the ailing man.

Potato chips are Paul's *nemesis*; if he takes one bite he can't stop eating them.

neophyte (NEE uh fyte) *n.* someone who has recently become involved in an activity and is still learning about it; a beginner or novice at any activity

This computer course is for *neophytes*, so I should have no trouble understanding the material.

Neophytes in medicine are also referred to as interns.

nepotism (NEP uh tiz um) *n.* favors shown by those in high positions to relatives and friends

Totally inept, Howard was a real estate agent for the company only because his uncle, the president, was not above a little *nepotism*.

The president was accused of *nepotism* when he chose his cousin for a top advisory position.

nest (nest) *v.* to fit snugly together

To save space, we purchased three small tables that *nested* into each other.

Holly berries were *nested* colorfully within the wreath.

nettle (NET l) *v.* to irritate; vex

Little brothers always *nettle* their older brothers by tagging along and being bothersome.

Rashes and insect bites can annoy and *nettle* their victims.

neutral (NOO truhl) *adj.* unbiased, not taking sides, objective

Sweden was a *neutral* country during World War II.

Referees in a sporting events are supposed to be neutral, so no team has an advantage.

neurotic (noo rawt ik) *adj.* characteristic of or having mental disorders

We hadn't realized how *neurotic* Michael was until we realized that he kept leaving the dinner table to wash his hands.

Every family seems to have one *neurotic* member.

newfangled (NOO FANG guhld) *adj.* new, untested, fond or given to novelty

When introduced the horseless carriage was a *newfangled* contraption.

The Industrial Revolution produced many *newfangled* inventions.

niggling (NIG ling) *adj.* petty, trivial, inconsequential, annoying

The *niggling* details were handled by the secretary, while the boss handled the more important business.

During long car rides, constant battles between children can be *niggling.*

nihilism (NIE uh liz im) *n.* total rejection of established laws and institutions

Hitler's rise to power was a result of his *nihilistic* beliefs about the present government. (*adj.*)

Stalin's *nihilism* marked the continuous reign of terror after the revolution.

nimbus (NIM bus) *n.* halo, a cloud, aura, atmosphere surrounding a person

The *nimbus* over the angel's head on the top of the tree glowed in the dark.

The rock star was surrounded by a *nimbus* of fame.

nirvana (nur VAH nuh) *n.* a state of blissful peace and harmony; a state of freedom from all suffering; a state of perfection

In her speech the candidate promised a *nirvana* of better jobs, less crime, and more education.

While soaking in the hot, scented water, the harried mother had a feeling of *nirvana*, as though she hadn't a care in the world.

nocturnal (NAUK tur nawl) *adj.* of or occurring at night

Nocturnal animals sleep during the day and are active at night.

A *nocturnal* person is one who stays up late at night.

noisome (NOY sum) *adj.* having an unpleasant odor; harmful, or injurious to health

Tobacco smoke is now considered so *noisome* that smoking has be come prohibited in a majority of public places.

When I opened the garbage can, the odor was so *noisome* I thought I might suffocate before I could get the lid back on.

nom de plume (nom duh PLOOM) *n.* pen or fictitious name

The man used a *nom de plume* and became a successful "female" columnist.

The writer's *nom de plume* insured privacy for her and her family.

nomad (NOH mad) *n.* one without a permanent domicile, one who moves from place to place

289

The vagabonds lived like *nomads,* traveling from state to state.

The Native Americans of the Plains region were *nomads* who traveled following bison.

nomenclature (NOH mun klay chur) *n.* a specialized system or set of names and terms used in a particular science, art, or other field of study or training; a system for naming things; terminology

The most difficult part of becoming an x-ray technician is learning all the medical *nomenclature.*

The *nomenclature* of nuclear physics is another language entirely.

nominal (NAWM uh nul) *adj.* so-called; minimal; insignificant

The decision to marry is not a *nominal* one to be taken lightly.

Charlotte posted a sign about the *nominal* charge for lunch so that no one would forget his or her money.

nonchalance (NAWN chuh lawns) *n.* cool confidence and unconcern; casual indifference

The actress's *nonchalance* while she waited to audition gave her a cool, calm appearance.

Doug pretended *nonchalance* during the argument, but underneath he was seething.

nonchalant (nawn shuh LAHNT) *adj.* behaving in a calm manner, showing that you are not worried or frightened; not showing excitement or anxiety; coolly confident, unflustered, or unworried; casually indifferent

She waited her turn to perform, trying to look *nonchalant,* but her stomach was tied in knots.

The well-prepared trainer appeared *nonchalant* when he stepped into the circus ring with the Bengal tiger.

nondescript (non dih SKRIPT) *adj.* of no recognized, definite type; ordinary

Dawn's personality was *nondescript*; she never stood out in a crowd.

The famous actor wore *nondescript* clothing so that he wouldn't stand out in public.

nonentity (nawn EN tuh tee) *n.* something that exists only in the imagination

The boyfriend whom she speaks so highly about is really a *nonentity;* that's why no one has ever met him.

Unfortunately for the family, the family fortune was a *nonentity.*

nonpartisan (non PAR tih zun) *n./adj.* not supporting or controlled by any group, unbiased

Nonpartisans have no affiliation with any political party.

Being an independent thinker, he preferred to remain *nonpartisan* rather than attach himself to a specific group.

nonplus (non PLUS) *v.* to baffle, to confuse, disconcert, bewilder

The older couple was *nonplussed* by the new Direct TV settings.

Joe was *nonplussed* by the game of hearts and therefore lost badly.

nostalgia (nahs TAL juh) *n.* remembrance, longing for the past, homesickness

Toni's old records create the feeling of *nostalgia* when she listens to Sinatra or other old artists.

When the couple celebrated their thirtieth wedding anniversary by visiting Niagra Falls, feelings of *nostalgia* embraced them.

nostrum (NOS trum) *n.* elixir, potion, remedy, patent medicine, panacea

The native witchdoctor prescribed an old *nostrum* to clear up the rash.

Old wives' tales contain such *nostrums* as "Starve a fever, feed a cold."

notoriety (noe tuh RIE uh tee) *n.* unfavorable, usually unsavory renown, widely recognized infamy

News tabloids create *notoriety* about famous people which may or may not be true.

John Dillinger's *notoriety* as a bank robber earned him a place in history.

notorious (noh TOR ee us) *adj.* known for something bad; infamous; blatant

Cleveland's guest at the party was a *notorious* jewel thief from London.

Although innocent, Keith's *notorious* reputation made job-hunting difficult.

novel (NAHV ul) *adj.* innovative, unusual, original, new

My advice to you is to take a *novel* approach when you attempt to solve the problem.

Thomas Edison's *novel* idea to replace the gas lantern was the light bulb.

novice (NOV iss) *n.* one who is starting to learn a profession, trade or sport

Although our new employee is a *novice* in terms of sales, he has helped boost profits in our store this week.

Tom could be considered a *novice* in the trades, yet his craftsmanship is superior.

noxious (KNOCKS ee us) *adj.* physically or mentally destructive, harmful to human beings

The *noxious* pollutants discharged into the bay by the paper mill killed all the marine life.

The *noxious* ideas espoused by the cult really messed up the boy's mind.

nuance (NOO ahns) *n.* subtle change, variation, finesse

The poem admirably expresses different *nuances* of emotions and love.

Ginny's best artistic works portray the *nuances* between light and shadow.

nullify (NUL ih fy) *v.* to make useless; cancel; undo

The purchase contract was *nullified* because it was never signed by the buyer.

Jane wanted her marriage annulled because her husband was trying to *nullify* their prenuptial agreement.

numismatist (noo MIZ muh tist) *n.* a coin collector or specialist

The *numismatist* was selling rare two cent coins to the public.

Art sold his coin collection to a *numismatist* who was collecting Spanish Colonial coinage.

nurture (nur chur) *v.* to nourish, to feed; to educate; to train; to foster

Mother birds *nurture* their young.

Kenneth *nurtured* the abandoned puppy and kept him as his own.

nutritive (NOO truh tiv) *adj.* having to do with promoting nutrition

Older adults like to eat figs for their *nutritive* benefits.

Many foods are considered more *nutritive* than hot dogs.

oasis (oh AY sis) *n.* a fertile spot in a desert or barren place, an enjoyable place, haven, sanctum

Las Vegas is an *oasis* of entertainment and fun in the Nevada desert.

The library was an *oasis* of quiet; perfect for study.

obdurate (AHB dyoo rit) *adj.* callous, headstrong, stubborn, insensitive

Anita's spoiled child was *obdurate* in her refusal to eat vegetables.

The teacher's *obdurate* refusal to change the grade made the athlete ineligible to play in the championship game.

obeisance (oh BAY suns) *n.* a gesture of the body, such as a bow, made to indicate respect or submission; obedience and respect; reverence

The delegate attacked the newspapers for their uncritical *obeisance* to the rich and the powerful in order to serve their own purposes.

The commoner knelt in *obeisance* to the Queen.

obese (oh BEES) *adj.* extremely fat; grossly overweight

People may become *obese* if diet and exercise routines are not carefully followed.

Obesity is a problem caused by lack of exercise, poor diet control, and slow metabolism. (*n.*)

obfuscate (AHB fuh skayt) *v.* to obscure, blur, complicate, confuse

Abe's confusing questions merely *obfuscated* the clear issue of better housing for the poor.

The old man's memories were *obfuscated* as the years past seemed to blend together.

objective (ahb JEK tiv) *adj.* not influenced by personal prejudice or feelings; unbiased; fair or real; impartial

Guidance counselors are *objective*, listening to both sides of students' stories.

Jurors must come to a fair and *objective* verdict regardless of personal feelings and opinions.

oblique (oh BLEEK) *adj.* at an angle; indirect or evasive

The lattice trim formed *oblique* angles at the base of the front porch.

The restaurant owner made *oblique* references to the impatience of his customers without stating specific names.

obliterate (uh BLIT ur ayt) *v.* to destroy entirely; to remove all signs of

The hurricane virtually *obliterated* the small coastal town.

Over time, the statue's features were *obliterated* by the wind and rain, leaving it unrecognizable.

oblivion (uh BLIV ee un) *n.* nothingness, total forgetfulness

James Dalton, once a well-known writer, is now relegated to *oblivion*.

Usually quite thoughtful, Beth was in a state of *oblivion* at the mall and forgot to purchase a gift for the bride.

obloquy (AWB luh kwee) *n.* verbal widespread abuse of a person or thing

He never ran for public office after the *obloquy* concerning his father's campaign.

The slanderers hoped to ruin his reputation, and their *obloquy* did just that.

obscure (ub SKYOOR) *adj.* unclear; confusing; unknown; hard to understand

The point of John's speech was *obscure* because he talked in circles.

Their ancient Greek-Hebrew language renders the Dead Sea Scrolls *obscure* to all but the most learned scholars.

obsequious (ub SEE kwee us) *adj.* ingratiating, fawning, subservient

Hemingway, the chief executive, prefers *obsequious* underlings as they bolster his ego.

The *obsequious* royal household servants follow demanding rules.

obsess (uhb SES) *v.* to haunt the mind to an abnormal degree

Captain Ahab is *obsessed* by the thought of killing Moby Dick.

Jerry is seeing a psychiatrist because she tends to *obsess* over the smallest incidents.

obsolete (AWB suh leet) *adj.* no longer in style; no longer useful or needed; outmoded

Typewriters have been rendered *obsolete* by computers.

Clothing styles become *obsolete* quickly, necessitating the purchase of a new wardrobe several times a year.

obstinate (AWB stuh nit) *adj.* stubborn, unyielding, inflexible, unbending, self-willed

The family was too *obstinate* to evacuate the house when the flood began.

Frank's *obstinate* attitude made dealing with his brother a continuous argument.

obstreperous (ob STREP er us) *adj.* not submitting to discipline or control; boisterous; vociferous

The *obstreperous* opponents made so much noise their team was charged with a misconduct foul.

The striking mob was *obstreperous*, knocking down the barrier to the company.

obtrude (aub TROOD) *v.* to impose oneself or one's ideas on others; to stick out

Tim hoped his parents wouldn't *obtrude* upon his plans for camping over the weekend.

The fallen tree *obtruded* into the road and was causing a traffic jam.

obtrusive (ub TROO siv) *adj.* noticeable in a way that is unpleasant or unwanted; aggressive and self-assertive; having a tendency to butt in where not welcome; meddlesome

The undercover police wore cut-off jeans and t-shirts to make their presence less *obtrusive*.

The next door neighbor is so *obtrusive* that he is always coming over to snoop and gossip.

obtuse (ob tuse) *adj.* insensitive; block-headed, slow in comprehension

Hazel was so *obtuse* in math that she never did pass a single test.

Some people are *obtuse* and unwilling to accept new ideas.

obviate (AHB vee ayt) *v.* to prevent or eliminate in advance; render unnecessary or irrelevant; to avert

A peaceful solution would *obviate* the need to send a UN military force.

This new medication will *obviate* the need for a lengthy recovery period.

occult (uh KULT) *adj.* relating to mysterious or supernatural powers and activities; mysterious; known or available only to the initiated; secret; mystical

Witchcraft and black magic deal with the *occult.* (*n.*)

The group claims such *occult* powers as raising unknown spirits and casting spells on enemies.

ocher (OAK ur) *n.* any of a class of natural earths, ranging in color from pale yellow to reddish yellow

The dandelions on the pottery were painted *ocher.*

The child used a crayon marked *"ocher"* to color the sun.

octave (OK tuv) *n.* a series of group of eight, a series of musical tones

The singer surprised everyone with the number of *octaves* she could sing.

A tenor's voice is many *octaves* above bass.

octogenarian (AWK tuh ji NER ee un) *adj.* between the ages of 80 and 90 years old

When my grandfather became an *octogenarian*, the president sent him a birthday card.

These days it is not unusual to see many *octogenarians* driving on the interstate.

odious (OH dee us) *adj.* extremely unpleasant; causing and deserving hate; loathsome or repellent; vile; evil

As the *odious* monster approached, the crowd immediately dispersed.

The candidate used such *odious* tactics to win the election that he was later ousted from office.

odyssey (AHD uh see) *n.* a long trip or period involving many different and exciting activities and changes; an extended, wandering journey of adventure or quest

The movie follows one man's *odyssey* to find the mother he was separated from at birth.

My quick jog around the block turned into an afternoon *odyssey* when I kept running into friends who needed my help with one thing or another.

offal (AW fal) *n.* waste parts, especially of a butchered animal; rubbish

Near the butcher shop, the dog rooted through the *offal* for scraps of food.

The young cheetah left the *offal* of his prey to the buzzards.

officious (uh FISH us) *adj.* ready to serve; eager in offering unwanted services or advice

Uncle Dan was so *officious* that he wanted to help me work on my antique cars even though he knew nothing about engines.

Employees are usually very *officious* when they first start a job.

ogle (OH gul) *v.* to gaze with an amorous, flirtatious, or impertinent look

The gorgeous lady tourist in Italy was *ogled* by all the men.

The teenagers drove by slowly, *ogling* the cute guys on the curb.

ogre (OH gur) *n.* a perversely bad, wicked person; a monster in fairy tales

The giant *ogre* fell when Jack chopped down the beanstalk.

The old man acted like an *ogre,* guarding his cabin with wild dogs and a shotgun.

olfactory (ahl FAK tur ee) *adj.* of, concerning, or stimulating the perception of smells; connected with the ability to smell

Damage to the *olfactory* nerves can result in the loss of the sense of smell.

Mother's dinner appealed to my *olfactory* senses, but it tasted like yesterday's wet sneakers.

oligarchy (AHL uh gahr kee) *n.* a government or state in which a few people or a family rule; a small group of powerful people

An *oligarchy* controls the region with very little representation by the common people.

I am living under an *oligarchy* because, basically, my two children rule my life.

ominous (AHM uh nus) *adj.* suggesting something unpleasant will happen; indicating or threatening future evil or unpleasantness; of or serving as an omen

Those black, *ominous* clouds mean a powerful, nasty storm is coming.

The *ominous* silence in the room foreshadowed the unpleasant events to follow.

omnibus (OHM nih bus) *n.* volumes of a single author or works; a bus

PBS had a program called *Omnibus* concerning various works by famous British authors.

Charlie drove many of his classmates to the outing in his English *omnibus*.

omnidirectional (om nee duh REK shun ul) *adj.* sending or receiving signals in all directions

Triangulation with *omnidirectional* instruments was used to locate the spy's radio.

The outdoor concert used *omnidirectional* speakers so everyone could hear clearly.

omnipotent (awm NIP uh tunt) *adj.* having unlimited power or authority

The ancient Persian shah was *omnipotent*.

Many in today's society believe that doctors are *omnipotent*.

omniscient (ahm NISH unt) *adj.* having or seeming to have unlimited knowledge; all-knowing

The magazine claims to be *omniscient* about everything needed to be successful.

The story was told by an *omniscient* narrator who revealed the thoughts of all the characters.

omnivorous (awm NIV uh rus) *adj.* eating any food

We were afraid that the dinner guests might be vegetarian; however, they were quite *omnivorous*.

A number of the larger species of dinosaurs was *omnivorous*.

oncology (on KOL uh jee) *n.* the medicinal study of tumors and cancer

Physicians practicing *oncology* found that doses of chemotherapy will often shrink a cancerous tumor.

The tissue was sent to the *oncology* department to check for cancerous cells.

onerous (AHN ur us) *adj.* hard to endure; burdensome; oppressive

Bob's *onerous* duties included clearing the south forty acres and planting it with tomatoes and carrots before nightfall.

After our truck ran out of gas, we had the *onerous* task of pushing it two miles to the nearest gas station.

opacity (oh PASS ih tee) *n.* state of quality of being opaque, degree of light transmission to nonpenetration

The dense *opacity* of the car windows violated the law and produced accidents.

His glasses had been changed to decrease the *opacity* for use as sunglasses.

opaque (oh PAYK) *adj.* unable to transmit light, impossible to understand

An *opaque* curtain covered the entrance to the shower.

The complicated explanation was so *opaque* that even the professor couldn't understand it.

operatic (op uh RAT ik) *adj.* relating to opera; melodramatic

On Verdi night, the opera house performed famous *operatic* selections.

The soprano sang in a warbling, *operatic* voice.

operetta (op uh RET uh) *n.* a light, opera-like theater work

H.M.S. Pinafore is a famous *operetta* written by Gilbert and Sullivan.

The drama club decided to perform an *operetta* instead of a full length opera.

opportune (AHP ur tune) *adj.* occurring or coming at a good time

Ed *opportunely* dropped by Janet's house just as dinner was being served. (*adv.*)

Mrs. Childs, our teacher, said the weekend before our final exam was an *opportune* time for last minute studying.

opportunist (awp ohr TOON ist) *n.*. one who takes advantage of every opportunity without regard for moral values

Thoughtless *opportunists* sold t-shirts and bumper stickers mocking the tragic event.

Our quarterback was an *opportunist* who took advantage of the other team's mistakes.

opposition (op uh ZISH un) *n.* action of opposing, resisting, disagreement, hostility, those who oppose

I don't understand his *opposition* to the release of oil.

The *opposition* was quick to reply to the charge of subliminal advertising.

opprobrious (uh PROH bree us) *adj.* expressing condemnation or scorn; accusing of shameful behavior; worthy of scorn or shame; disgraceful

The bully's *opprobrious* behavior on the school bus got him kicked off for the rest of the year.

Her parents think skin tight micro mini-skirts, short shirts, high heels, and ruby red lipstick is *opprobrious* attire for a 14 year old girl.

optimism (OP tu miz um) *n.* encouragement, happy expectancy, hope, a positive outlook

Nothing can daunt Ralph's cheery *optimism* that influences every one around him.

Optimism about the new product caused the company's stock to rise.

optimum (OP tuh mum) *adj.* the most advantageous; the best in condition, degree, or amount

Fran said she had the *optimum* job, working at home on the word processor while watching soap operas.

As the conditions were *optimum*, with no wind at the track, the U.S. Olympic team had hopes of breaking the world record in the 440-yard relay.

opulent (AHP yuh lunt) *adj.* affluent, wealthy, luxurious

The *opulent* family lives in a big mansion in the nicest section of town.

The millionaire lived in *opulent* style, surrounding himself with luxuries.

orator (ORE uh tur) *n.* public speaker, esp. one of great eloquence

The contestants practiced their speeches for weeks prior to the *oratorical* contest. (*adj.*)

Abraham Lincoln's ability and quality as an *orator* are evident yet today in "The Gettysburg Address."

ordinance (AWR duh nuns) *n.* a law or rule made by a government or authority; a regulation, law, decree, or rule, especially one issued by a city or town

A city *ordinance* forbids the parking of cars in this area.

According to an old *ordinance* in a small Georgia town, it is against the law to sing out of tune.

ordnance (ORD nunce) *n.* cannon, artillery, military supplies

The battleship's *ordnance* pounded the beach head prior to the amphibious landing.

The general asked the *ordnance* division to upgrade all military supplies going to the front.

orifice (ORE ih fiss) *n.* an opening or aperture, mouth

The divers discovered an underwater *orifice* in the rocky ledge.

It is polite to keep the *orifice* closed while chewing food.

originate (uh RIJ ih nayt) *v.* to create or bring into being

Edgar Allan Poe is believed to be the one to *originate* the modern short story.

Let's check the postage to see where the package *originated.*

ornery (ORE nuh ree) *adj.* ugly and unpleasant in disposition or temper; stubborn

The *ornery* child picked fights with all his classmates.

The hillbillies were *ornery* when revenue agents searched for illegal moonshine.

ornithology (or nih THAHL uh jee) *n.* branch of zoology dealing with birds

When studying *ornithology*, one will find that the bones of all birds are hollow.

Bird watching is a division of *ornithology*.

orotund (or uh tund) *adj.* having strength, richness, fullness and clarity of sound

The speaker's *orotund* voice projected throughout the auditorium without any microphone.

The singer's *orotund* voice filled the church.

orthodox (OR thuh dahks) *adj.* conventional, going by the book, sticking to established principles

An *orthodox* religion is one that holds fast to unchanging, historical views.

The views of those who still believe the world is flat, as many did in the thirteenth century, are *unorthodox*.

oscillate (AHS uh layt) *v.* to move repeatedly from side to side or up and down between two points; to vary between two feelings or opinions; to waver; vacillate

Laura *oscillates* between cooperation and hostility.

As the subject watched the pendulum *oscillate*, back and forth repeatedly, his eyes became very heavy.

osmosis (ahs MOH sis) *n.* the process by which something passes gradually from one part to another through a membrane; a gradual, subtle, and usually unconscious absorption, as of ideals or mannerisms

I am hoping that my son learns spelling by *osmosis*, since his teacher's conscious efforts to teach it don't seem to be working.

In a liquid, the higher concentration will pass through to the lower concentration by *osmosis*, until there is an equal concentration on each side of a membrane.

ossify (AHS uh fi) *v.* fossilize, to convert into bone, to become rigid

Does cartilage *ossify* or remain soft and pliable?

Fred's opinions *ossified* right after college, and his views are still unchanging.

ostensible (o STEN seh bul) *adj.* appearing as such; offered as genuine or real

The *ostensible* reason that Mr. Jones became a substitute teacher was that he needed the money.

The *ostensible* purpose of this book is to improve the reader's vocabulary.

ostentatious (ahs ten TAY shus) *adj.* flaunting wealth, pretentious, showing off

The grandfather warned his heirs not to be *ostentatious* with their considerable inheritance.

Jane's mother told her the gown was too *ostentatious* to wear to the party.

osteoporosis (oss tee oh puh ROE sis) *n.* a disorder caused by calcium loss, brittle bones, fracture, mainly in women

The older woman's bones kept breaking because of her *osteoporosis*.

Osteoporosis can be prevented with sufficient calcium in the diet.

ostracize (AHS truh syze) *v.* to exclude from a group; to shun

Andre felt *ostracized* by the members of the club, but the truth was they couldn't understand his accent.

After gaining a reputation as a cheap-shot player with the Pittsburgh Steelers, he joined the Dallas Cowboys only to find he was *ostracized* by the Dallas players as well.

oust (owst) *v.* to eject; to force out; to banish

The fans wanted Roger *ousted* for making too much noise during the tennis match.

The student was *ousted* from school after he attacked the principal.

outgrowth (OWT groth) *n.* a result, a part growing out of something; a consequence; conclusion

The police investigation is an *outgrowth* of numerous complaints.

The tree had an *outgrowth* of fungus and mushrooms.

override (OH vur ryde) *v.* to ignore or refuse to accept that which already exists or operates; to prevail over; to overrule

The legislature voted to *override* the presidential veto, making it null

303

and void.

Their panic will *override* all other considerations as they rush to get out of the building.

overt (oh VURT) *adj.* not hidden or secret; openly apparent

There are no *overt* signs of tampering with the painting, but the damage may be well hidden.

It was obvious by his *overt* flirtations that Jim liked Suzanne.

overture (OH vur chur) *n.* an approach made to someone in order to discuss or establish something; an opening gesture, as for initiating a relationship or other interaction; an intro to a musical work

The country's leaders rejected all *overtures* from the enemy for a peace settlement.

The company's initial *overture* to the union was flatly rejected because the wages offered were too low.

overwrought (OH vur rot) *adj.* overexcited, agitated, riled, greatly disturbed, nervous

Sam was *overwrought* about the increase in college tuition, since his scholarship had not increased.

The Western European people are *overwrought* about the extremely high price of gasoline.

oxymoron (ahk see MAWR ahn) *n.* a figure of speech in which two contradictory words are used together in a phrase; two words used together which have, or seem to have, opposite meanings

Unhappily married couples think the term "marital bliss" is an *oxymoron*.

"Fresh squeezed juice from concentrate" is an *oxymoron* some companies use to sell their juices.

pacifist(PAS ih fist) *n.* one who is in opposition to war or violence

The *pacifists* protested the boxing match by lying on the mat and refusing to move.

Because of Brad's *pacifistic* personality, he refused to fight. (*adj.*)

pacify (PAS uh fye) *v.* to calm, appease, soothe, placate

King Rex *pacified* the huge mob with promises to repeal the unpopular tax.

Herb *pacified* his baby son with a pacifier.

pact (pakt) *n.* covenant, compact, formal written agreement; promise

The Yalta meeting formed a *pact* between the Allies in 1943.

The graduates made a *pact* to meet every year beginning in five years.

painstaking (PAYN stay king) *adj.* extremely careful, thorough, meticulous

After many years of *painstaking* research, Dr. Snow created a drug to prevent strokes.

The *painstaking* editing of a manuscript is a tedious task that takes many hours.

palatable (PAL ih tah bul) *adj.* delicious, appetizing, tasty, easily accepted

A great chef can cook a *palatable* meal without much effort.

Although many ideas for a revolving scholarship were rejected, the alumni meeting produced a few *palatable* ones.

palatial (puh LAY shul) *adj.* ostentatiously magnificent, extravagant, opulent

The thirty-one room estate falls into the *palatial* category.

The completely glass building was the center of the *palatial* mountain retreat in the Alps.

palisade (pal ih SAYD) *n.* a fortification of timbers set in the ground; an extended cliff

The king built a *palisade* of logs to fortify his castle.

The stone *palisade* followed the course of the river, winding its way through the canyon.

pall (pawl) *n.* cloth covering

The *pall* was placed on the body before the coffin was closed.

The priest placed the *pall* over the chalice until the next service.

palliate (PAL ee ayt) *v.* to make less serious or severe; to mitigate

The accident situation was *palliated* by the arrival of emergency vehicles.

The nurse *palliated* the patient's burns by applying cold, wet bandages to the sensitive area.

pallid (PAL id) *adj.* pale, faint or deficient in color

Her *pallid* countenance gave her the appearance of a walking ghost.

The dress was a *pallid* shade of yellow that almost looked white.

palpable (PAL pah bul) *adj.* capable of being touched or felt

The answer is as *palpable* as the nose on your face.

Fear ran *palpably* through the crowd as the man wielded a pistol. (*adv.*)

palpitate (PAL pih) *v.* to pulsate with unusual rapidity from stress, disease, or emotion

Because of John's infection, his heart *palpitates* like a beating drum.

The contestants' hearts *palpitated* as they awaited the final results.

paltry (PAWL tree) *adj.* of little value, trivial, inconsequential

Irma, the waitress, was angry with the *paltry* tip of one dollar.

Dutch worked his way up from a *paltry* mail clerk to president of the company.

pan (pan) *v.* put down, censure, to criticize harshly

Peter *panned* the book in his newspaper review, causing its sales to drop drastically.

Even though movie critics *panned* the film, it became number one on sales charts.

panacea (pan ih SEE uh) *n.* cure-all, solution for all problems

The new diet pill was supposed to be a *panacea* for all overweight people.

The couple thought a baby would be the *panacea* for their faltering marriage.

panache (pa NASH) *n.* dashing elegance of manner or style

Eric entered the room with *panache*, wearing his new tux, Rolex watch, and $500 shoes.

It was evident by the woman's *panache* that she was a member of the royal family.

pandemic (pan DEM ik) *adj.* widespread; general

AIDS has spread in *pandemic* proportions around the world.

Boating is a *pandemic* form of outdoor recreation in Florida.

pandemonium (pan duh MOH nee um) *n.* place or scene of wild disorder, chaos

When the team scored the winning run at the bottom of the last inning, *pandemonium* broke out.

When the president was shot, the country was instantly in a state of *pandemonium*.

panegyric (pan uh JIE rik) *n.* a tribute, made orally or in writing

A *panegyric* by the President was expressed to the returning veterans.

A *panegyric* was delivered by phone to the winning Olympic athletes.

panjandrum (pan JAN drum) *n.* a self-important or pretentious person, a bigwig

Many companies hire *panjandrums* to advertise their products.

A list of *panjandrums* was used to obtain donations for the campaign.

panorama (pan ah RAM ah) *n.* an unbroken view of a wide area

We enjoyed the scenic *panorama* while taking a hot air balloon ride.

The Grand Canyon offers *panoramic* views of great splendor. (*adj.*)

pantomime (PAN tuh mime) *n.* art of conveying emotions by gesture, without speech

Mime performer Marcel Marceau was one of the first *pantomime* actors.

Without containing one word, Red Skelton's *pantomime* produced many laughs from the audience.

parable (PAR ah bul) *n.* a simple story illustrating a moral or religious lesson

The story of the boy who cried wolf is a *parable* about the consequences of telling lies.

The point of the *parable* told by the pastor during the sermon was that one should build a foundation on solid ground.

paradigm (PAR ah dime) *n.* a pattern that serves as a model or example

When designing the Luxor Hotel in Las Vegas the architects used the Great Pyramids of Egypt as their *paradigm*.

The Model-T was used as a *paradigm* by many other automobile manufacturers in the early 1900s.

paradox (PAIR uh dahks) *n.* two apparently contradictory statements that nevertheless are true

Dr. Jekyll was a *paradox*; he was kind and gentle until he became the vicious Mr. Hyde.

The statement, "You have to be cruel to be kind" is a paradox.

paragon (PAR ah gon) *n.* a model or pattern of excellence

Although Joyce was a *paragon* of virtue, she was also good fun to be with.

William named his shoe company *Paragon* Shoes, with expectations that customers would think his shoes the best.

parallel (PAR uh lel) *n./adj.* a comparison between two things; extending in the same direction and at the same distance apart at every point

The two witnesses told *parallel* stories with only minor differences.

Parallel lines never meet.

paramount (PARE uh mount) *adj.* most important, influential, significant, superior

Helping the injured workers was *paramount* to their survival.

The *paramount* task of any national political convention is to nominate a candidate.

paranoia (par uh NOY uh) *n.* a mental illness of unreasonable anxiety, especially believing someone is out to get you, or that you are an important person

Julie's *paranoia* was so advanced she thought everyone who came to her door was an assassin who had come to kill her.

Joshua was absolutely *paranoid* about walking under a ladder. (*adj.*)

paraphernalia (para uh fur NALE ee uh) *n.* equipment, apparatus or furnishing needed for a task

Paraphernalia carried by some travelers makes their luggage weigh a ton.

Sports *paraphernalia* is sold at nearly all sporting events.

paraphrase (PARE uh frase) *v.* to restate a text or passage which make it more clear

Paraphrase, or write the notes in your own words, instead of just copying them.

The reporters *paraphrased* the president's speech during the evening news.

pariah (puh RIE uh) *n.* outcast, socially, despised or avoided, member of the low cast

Years ago people living on the other side of the tracks were *pariahs*, unacceptable to their wealthier neighbors.

In old days, suspected witches were treated as *pariahs* of society and were sometimes even burned at the stake.

parley (PAHR lee) *n.* a conference, especially between enemies

The National Football League owners and players held a series of *parleys* to reach a settlement on salary caps.

After a brief *parley*, the defense attorney and the prosecuting attorney agreed to settle the dispute out of court.

parochial (puh ROH kee ul) *adj.* narrow or confined in point of view; restricted

St. Thomas *Parochial* School was having a holiday honoring their patron saint.

The local candidate's views were too *parochial* for him to become a national figure.

parody (PARE uh dee) *n.* humorous or satirical imitation of serious writing

The students laughed as they read the *parody* of a typical holiday scene.

Spaceballs is a *parody* of the movie *Star Wars*.

paroxysm (PAR uk siz um) *n.* a sudden outburst or attack

Although it was not a time for levity, a *paroxysm* of laughter filled the auditorium.

The *paroxysm* of cramps in his hand left him unable to paint.

parquet (par KAY) *n.* wooden floor forming a pattern, part of an area in a theater

Since he prefers wood to carpet, Kevin installed *parquet* floors in his oceanfront condo. (*adj.*)

Concert tickets in the *parquet* sold for the highest prices of all the seats in the hall.

parry (pary) *v.* to ward off a blow; to turn aside; to avoid skillfully, to evade

The boxers *parried* blows as each waited for an opening to strike a knockout punch.

Parrying with respective verbal arguments, the politicians blamed each other for the increase in statewide crime.

parsimonious (pahr suh MOH nee us) *adj.* sparing, miserly, frugal, stingy

The old couple was *parsimonious*, and they never needed financial help.

The *parsimonious* millionaire never donated a cent of his money to charity.

partisan (PART ah zun) *n./adj.* supporter of a person, group or cause; showing bias

The victim's *partisans* rallied to support his cause.

Advertising agents should be *partisan* to the products they sell.

partition (PAR tish un) *v./n.* dividing of something into parts; an interior structure dividing a larger area

Korea was originally one country before being *partitioned* into North and South Korea.

In most tennis clubs, fence *partitions* separate the courts from each other.

passe (pas SAY) *n.* out of date, no longer chic

Many photographs of *passe* fashions from the 1940s exist.

Self-repair of autos is *passe* with the advent of computerization of cars.

patent (PAT unt) *n./adj.* copyrighted; obvious; apparent

Edison held the *patent* on the early phonograph.

The answers on the test were so *patent* that everyone in the class earned an "A."

paternal (puh TUR nul) *adj.* patriarchal, father-like

The young man's boss was a *paternal* figure in his life, replacing the father he had never known.

Even though he has no children of his own, Jack's *paternal* behavior causes all his nieces and nephews to adore him.

pathology (puh THAHL uh jee) *n.* the science or study of the origin, cause, and nature of disease

Jay took classes in *pathology* and histology, required courses for a biology major.

Body tissue was sent to the *pathology* department to determine the cause of death.

pathetic (puh THET ik) *adj.* pitifully unsuccessful; ineffective; expressing or arousing pity

The score of 47-0 showed what a *pathetic* football game it had been.

The *pathetic* old man came to our window to ask for money while we were at the stoplight.

patriarch (PAY tree ahrk) *n.* the leader of a family or tribe

As the *patriarch* of the family, Grandfather made all the big decisions.

The tribe turns to the *patriarch* for leadership and guidance.

patrician (puh TRISH un) *n.* blue blood, one of noble birth, an aristocrat

Sir James, as a *patrician*, was permitted a seat in the House of Lords.

In Roman times, *patricians* wore special togas of royal purple, while the peasants wore dull brown tunics.

patrimony (PA trih moh nee) *n.* an inheritance from a father or an ancestor; anything inherited

Ill-will in the family was a result of arguments over *patrimony* after the death of the father.

When his mother died, Jonathan used his *patrimony* to set up a business.

patronize (PAY truh nyze) *v.* to do business with; to be client of, to treat as an inferior

Don't *patronize* me; I am not a child, I'm your wife!

Phil *patronized* the restaurant on Sundays for its "all you can eat" special.

paucity (PAW suh tee) *n.* scarcity; shortage; poverty; deficiency

Due to lack of information, the newspaper provided a *paucity* of articles about the invasion.

The senior citizen tax rebate was defeated by a *paucity* of support from retirees.

peccadillo (pek ah DIL oh) *n.* a slight or trifling sin; a minor offense

The reporters were more interested in the president's personal *peccadilloes* than in the state of the economy.

Being ticketed for running a red light is a mere *peccadillo* compared to driving while intoxicated.

pecuniary (pi KYOO nee er ee) *adj.* consisting of or relating to money

Alex's concerns about college were specifically *pecuniary* since his father was out of work.

Ryan wanted to take Jessie to the prom but couldn't afford to because of his *pecuniary* problems.

pedagogue (PED uh gawg) *n.* a teacher; one devoted to study

The old man had once been a *pedagogue* in a one-room school house.

Ichabod Crane was the first *pedagogue* to move to Tarrytown, New York.

pedant (PED unt) *n.* person making excessive or inappropriate display of learning

The *pedant* in the class was always asking questions to showoff his knowledge.

The *pedant's* lecture was so scholarly that no one understood it.

pedestrian (peh DES tree ahn) *adj.* ordinary; moving on foot

Most of the villages in the Andes Mountains have only *pedestrian* traffic on the very steep roads.

The right frame can make a *pedestrian* painting look like a million bucks.

peerless (PEER lus) *adj.* better than all others; unmatched in excellence

The pageant winner had *peerless* beauty.

His *peerless* abilities were rewarded when he was named employee of the year.

pejorative (pi JOR uh tiv) *adj.* belittling, uncomplimentary, ridiculing, disparaging

The star sued over the *pejorative* comments made by the broadcaster.

The teacher's *pejorative* remarks about Bobby's paper discouraged the student writer.

penance (PEN uhns) *n.* act done in repentance for a wrongdoing

As *penance* for having a party while my parents were away, I have to clean the house every Saturday for the next year.

Frank felt that for robbing the old shopkeeper, he must pay *penance* to God.

penchant (PEN chunt) *n.* strong inclination, taste, or liking for something

Pregnant women often have a *penchant* for pickles and ice cream.

Charley had a *penchant* for card counting and was prohibited from casinos.

penitent (PEN uh tunt) *adj.* sorrowful and remorseful for past misdeeds

Clark became *penitent* when he learned his careless driving put two people in the hospital.

The pickpocket pretended *penitence* but continued to rob when he was released from jail. (*n.*)

pensive (PEN siv) *adj.* expressing or revealing thoughtfulness, or sometimes sadness, dreamy

Being in a *pensive* mood, Mary sat staring out the window.

With a *pensive* look on his face, the old man began to reminisce about his past.

penury (PEN yoo ree) *n.* destitution; indigence; insufficiency

313

Homeless people endure *penury* for many reasons.

The stock market crash of 1929 found many investors in *penury*.

perceive (pur SEEV) *v.* to understand; grasp mentally

Some concepts are easier to *perceive* than others.

The child was able to *perceive* the gravity of the situation by the way his father was reacting.

perceptive (pur SEP tiv) *adj.* having keen insight, or intuitive understanding

Her reports are full of *perceptive* insights.

My best friend was always *perceptive* of my feelings, no matter how I tried to hide them.

percolate (PUR kuh layt) *v.* to cause a liquid to pass through a porous body, to filter

As the coffee *percolated* and the rolls baked, a tempting aroma filled the room.

Carl's ideas *percolated* through the political gathering and gained support.

peregrination (PUR ih gruh nay shun) *n.* travels, wanderings

Ninth graders love to study the *peregrinations* of Odysseus.

The man was an interesting story teller who told us of all his *peregrinations* throughout the south.

peremptory (puh REMP tuh ree) *adj.* irrevocable, decisive, final, dictatorial

The general issued a *peremptory* order that overrode the major's earlier directions.

My parents' *peremptory* refusal ended my thoughts of attending college in Europe.

perennial (puh REN ee ul) *adj.* perpetual, everlasting, enduring, continual

Marion is a *perennial* visitor to St. Michael's Church.

The landscape gardener suggested planting *perennials* instead of annual plants.

perfidy (PUR fuh dee) *n*. treachery, treason, disloyalty, faithlessness

Jill could not abide Jack's *perfidy* in selling government documents to a foreign country.

Carl's *perfidy* made him the object of an investigation into the missing treasury plates.

perforated (PUR fur aye tud) *v*. to make a hole by boring, punching, or piercing

The page of coupons is *perforated* so consumers can easily tear them apart.

The iceberg *perforated* the hull of the ship.

perfunctory (pur FUNGK tuh ree) *adj*. indifferent, apathetic, unenthusiastic, careless

The boss expected no answer to his *perfunctory* question about the state of my health.

The *perfunctory* audience was relieved when the speaker finally concluded.

peripatetic (per ih pah TIT ik) *adj*. wandering, traveling continually, roving

The wanderer is a *peripatetic* individual traveling the entire country.

Ancient *peripatetic* groups crossing Romania were called gypsies.

peripheral (pur IF ur ul) *adj*. not central or of main importance; not essential; external

First, we have to catch the thief; getting the money back is a *peripheral* issue.

Use your *peripheral* vision to see if any cars are beside you before returning to the slow lane.

periphery (puh RIF uh ree) *n*. the outermost part within a boundary, the outside edge

Colonel Mason posted guards at the *periphery* of the camp for night security.

The outlaw lurked on the outermost *periphery* of the ranch, waiting until nightfall to approach the house.

perjury (PUR juh ree) *n*. false testimony under oath

Charlie's story was obviously *perjury*, false and in conflict with the evidence.

Telling the truth prevents *perjury* in a court room.

permeate (PUR mee ayt) *v.* to flow or spread through; penetrate

The smell of baking cookies *permeated* Grandma's house.

Before the explosion, witnesses said the smell of gasoline *permeated* the flight cabin.

pernicious (pur NISH us) *adj.* extremely destructive or harmful, deadly; fatal

Nuclear waste materials are *pernicious* vehicles of death.

Too much chlorine in the water can be *pernicious* and dangerous to health.

perorate (PUR uh rayt) *v.* to lecture, give a sermon, to speak formally

At the medical conference, Dr. Clara *perorated* about the possible conclusions of future research.

The preacher *perorated* for over an hour until the church service was finally concluded.

perpendicular (pur pen DIK yu ler) *adj.* upright or vertical; being at right angles to the plane of the horizon

The tall mast of the sailing ship was built *perpendicular* to the deck.

Because the wall was not *perpendicular*, it gradually succumbed to gravity and fell over.

perpetrate (PURP uh trate) *v.* to be responsible for or guilty of a misdeed

The election fraud was *perpetrated* by the Democratic Party.

The thief *perpetrated* the robbery at the First National Bank.

perpetuate (pur PETCH oo ayt) *v.* to cause to continue or to be remembered

We place flowers on Grandmother's grave to *perpetuate* her memory.

The City will help *perpetuate* the memory of Dr. Martin Luther King, Jr. by naming a street after him

perplex (pur PLEKS) *v.* to bewilder; to confuse, mystify

Calculus *perplexed* Stan, and he regretted taking the course for credit.

The functioning of the entire brain has *perplexed* medical science for years.

perquisite (PURK wuh zit) *n.* a material favor or gift, usually money for service

The winning coach's *perquisites* included a free car and a bonus from the alumni committee.

The president's *perquisites* were membership in a country club and a vacation in Greece.

persevere (pur suh VEER) *v.* to continue in spite of difficulty

Even though writing the research paper was difficult, Joe *persevered* until he had it completed.

Because he forced himself to *persevere*, Hemingway was taken from the airplane wreck alive.

personify (per SON ih fye) *v.* to think of or represent as having human qualities; to typify

In her poem she *personifies* death as a man crawling toward a gate.

Benjamin Franklin *personifies* all the finest attributes of the Revolutionary period.

pertinent (PUR tuh nunt) *adj.* relevant, of concern, to the point

Manny's remarks on patriotism were *pertinent* to the July 4th celebration.

The private eye had *pertinent* information that helped the police solve the case.

perturb (pur TURB) *v.* to disturb greatly, disquiet, upset

The teacher was *perturbed* by the student's lack of interest.

The child was *perturbed* when asked to clean up a mess he did not make.

peruse (puh ROOZ) *v.* scrutinize, read carefully, review

For a day the lawyer *perused* the baseball contract checking its validity.

He *perused* the newspaper ads looking for a new car to purchase.

pervade (pur VAYD) *v.* saturate, penetrate, to spread throughout

The aroma of the fresh baked bread *pervaded* the entire house.

The final day of Tex's vacation was *pervaded* with sadness.

perverse (pur VERS) *adj.* stubborn; contrary; intractable

The mean principal takes *perverse* pleasure in suspending students.

The *perverse* hunting guide had apparently returned to camp without us, and we were lost in the woods within the hour.

pesky (PES kee) *adj.* annoying; disagreeable

I have to give my speech even though I have a *pesky* cold.

His little brother is the most *pesky* child I have ever met.

petrified (PET ruh fied) *v.* convert into stone; numb with astonishment and horror

The *petrified* forest in the Southwest is a beautiful, famous landmark. (*adj.*)

The doctor's suggestion *petrified* the patient.

petulant (PET yoo lant) *adj.* ill-humored, irritable, cranky

My mother told me not to play in the house the day my father lost his job, saying he was in a bad mood and very *petulant*.

A *petulant* little creature, spoiled rotten by her parents, she has everything imaginable, yet seldom ever smiles.

phantasmagoria (fan taz muh GORE ee uh) *n.* an illusion of perceiving something that does not exist

Plain-looking Jenny had a *phantasmagoria* about being in the Miss America pageant.

Mike's *phantasmagoria* had him scoring a touchdown in the big game.

phenomenon (fuh NAWM uh nun) *n.* extremely unusual or extraordinary thing or occurrence

One *phenomenon* in *The Scarlet Letter* is the giant "A" that appears in the sky.

At the circus we saw a two headed turtle; a true *phenomenon*.

philanthropic (fi lan THRUHP ik) *adj.* of or showing love of mankind,

philanthropist

especially through charitable gifts and deeds

Will Rogers was a famous *philanthropic* humorist who always said he never met a man he didn't like.

The gentleman was too *philanthropic*, giving to anyone in need and keeping so little for his own family that his wife left him.

philippic (fe LIP ik) *n.* a verbal denunciation characterized by harsh, insulting language; a tirade

The coach, in seeking to rouse the team, shouted bitter *philippics* against the opposing team.

Dad always directed *philippics* at me whenever I got a bad grade.

philistine (FIL ih steen) *n.* a person lacking in or smugly indifferent to cultural, intellectual pursuits

William was too much of a *philistine* to patronize the arts.

The *philistine* lacked intellectual and cultural interests and sat around watching sports all day.

phlegmatic (fleg MAT ik) *adj.* not easily excited to display emotion, apathetic, sluggish

The nurse's *phlegmatic* attitude toward death helped her cope with it on a daily basis.

The student's *phlegmatic* spirit was obvious as he sat slumped disinterestedly in his chair.

phobia (FOE bee ah) *n.* a persistent, illogical fear

Those who have a *phobia* about heights should avoid climbing towers.

Claustrophobia is the *phobia* of a person who fears small, confined spaces.

phonics (FON iks) *n.* method of teaching based on the sound of each word

The school uses the *phonic* method to teach reading. (*adj.*)

The child had problems spelling after learning to read by *phonics*.

photogenic (phoh toe GIN ik) *adj.* suitable, especially attractive for photography

Some movie actors and actresses are not very attractive in person, but they have become successful because they are very *photogenic* on screen.

Very *photogenic*, the Statue of Liberty is probably the most photographed public monument in the world.

phraseology (fray zee AHL oh jee) *n.* choice of words, the way words are used

We studied the author's *phraseology* in order to better understand his poetry.

Jerry's gift for *phraseology* resulted in a stirring speech and his subsequent election to the student council.

pictorial (pick TOR ee ul) *adj.* graphic, represented by drawings or picture

After the film was developed, the group met to share *pictorial* memories of the vacation.

Travelogues are *pictorial* presentations with a narrated background.

pied (pyed) *adj.* multi-colored, especially of more than one color in patches

For safety purposes, hot-air balloons are most always *pied* so they can be seen by powered aircraft flying nearby.

The court jester wore a *pied* hat that matched his multicolored outfit.

piety (PYE uh tee) *n.* worshipful devotion to God or family; reverence

The new minister exhibited such *piety* that he was much admired by the community.

My grandmother showed *piety* by reading from her Bible every day.

pigment (PIG munt) *n.* a coloring matter or substance

George mixed the *pigment* to obtain a new color.

The use of thick and thin *pigments* on the painting produced different dimensions and style.

pilfer (PIL fer) *v.* to take another's property without permission

The two ladies *pilfered* small items but were caught before leaving the store.

The man wore a coat in order to *pilfer* silverware from the restaurant.

pillage (PIL luhge) *v.* to rob of goods by violent seizure, plunder; to take as spoils

The enemy invaders *pillaged* the village, taking everything not tied down and killing the cows and chickens.

After the kids and their school friends *pillaged* the refrigerator, there was nothing left but a little catsup and mustard.

pinion (PIN yun) *v.* bind the wings so as not to fly; confine

The handcuffs were used to *pinion* his hands.

The falcon was *pinioned* so it wouldn't fly away.

pinnacle (PIN uh kul) *n.* highest point; culmination

Stephen King was very young when he reached the *pinnacle* of success as a writer.

We tried to make it to the *pinnacle* before nightfall, but we were forced to make camp one more night before reaching the top.

pious (PI us) *adj.* devout or virtuous; holy

Elizabeth *piously* said her prayers every night before bed. (*adv.*)

The nuns lived a *pious* life in the convent.

piquant (pi KONT) *adj.* pungent or sharp in taste or flavor, tart

Piquant seasonings were added to the bland casserole.

Mexican foods are known for their *piquant* flavorings.

pique (peek) *v.* irritate; also to arouse curiosity

Their cousin *piqued* her three cousins by not inviting them to her wedding.

The introduction of the mystery movie *piqued* my interest, so I kept reading.

pithy (PITH ee) *adj.* brief, forceful and meaningful in expression; concise

In just a few minutes, John gave a *pithy* evaluation of the president's lengthy health-care agenda.

The consumer limited her statements to *pithy* complaints about the store's service.

pittance (PIT unce) *n.* small amount or share; scanty income or remuneration

The company paid only a *pittance* of the actual cost of the survey.

Charlie's allowance in 1950 was a *pittance* compared to today's standards.

pivotal (PIV uh tul) *adj.* decisive, critical, vital

Carlos was offered a new job at a *pivotal* time in his life, just as he had made the decision to move back to Venezuela.

The *pivotal* votes were cast in the largest states.

placard (PLACK urd) *n.* paperboard sign or notice posted in a public place

The *placard* announced a town meeting at which we could vote on the candidates.

Kelly won $50 in a *placard* contest to announce the town's centennial celebration.

placate (PLAY kayt) *v. to* win over, conciliate, mollify, appease, soothe

Kay apologized, hoping to *placate* the angry man.

The teacher erred in marking the test and *placated* the wronged student with a higher grade.

placid (PLA sid) *adj.* calm and peaceful; smooth or tranquil

The *placid* lake was perfect for canoeing.

Her child had a *placid* temperament, unlike my little wild one!

plagiarize (PLAY jur ize) *v.* to use another's idea or work and claim it as your own

A musician can be sued for *plagiarizing* another artist's music and profiting from it.

Some students try to *plagiarize* their reports by copying the words from another source.

plaintiff (PLAYN tif) *n. a* person who brings a complaint into a court of law

Because she is the *plaintiff*, she is trying to sue the defendant.

The *plaintiff* was called to the stand to explain his part of the story.

plaintive (PLAIN tive) *adj.* full of an expression of sorrow

The *plaintive* feelings in the song expressed the writer's despair.

Judy's *plaintive* reaction to the loss of her pet was expected.

plaited (PLAY tud) *v.* braided, esp. of hair or straw

The lady *plaited* the straw into a beautiful dolly.

She *plaited* her hair into two braids to suggest the look of someone from Switzerland.

platitude (PLAT uh tood) *n.* stereotyped expression, commonplace, a cliche, a dull or trite remark

The professor spouted *platitudes* of encouragement at the freshman class during the orientation speech.

The valedictorian's speech was full of *platitudes* and overgeneralizations about life.

plausible (PLAW suh bul) *adj.* convincing, feasible, believable, credible

Jane's clothes were soaked, so her story of falling into the creek was *plausible*.

The jurors found the evidence *plausible* and returned a verdict of not guilty.

playa (PLY uh) *n.* lowest point of any desert like territory, an area that is flat, salty, and retaining water

The *playa* of the southwestern desert is six miles below sea level.

He found water in the *playa* but discovered it was salty and undrinkable.

plebeian (pluh BEE un) *n.* one of the common people

Tyler, being a *plebeian*, was not born into a wealthy family.

The princess blew kisses to the crowd of *plebeians*.

plebiscite (PLEB uh site) *n.* direct vote regarding important questions

A *plebiscite* was called for the new amendment to the federal constitution.

The community called for a *plebiscite* of the citizens before declaring it a city.

plethora (PLETH or ah) *n.* a state of excessive fullness; superabundance

The Christmas tree was surrounded by a *plethora* of gifts for the seven children in the family.

Jake opened the back door and a *plethora* of mosquitoes flew in.

pliable (PLYE ah bul) *adj.* receptive to change; easily persuaded or controlled; easily bent or twisted

Students demonstrate their *pliability* when they remain open to new ideas. (*n.*)

Putty is a *pliable* material that can be easily shaped.

plight (plyte) *n.* a condition or situation, especially a distressing one

In most stories the *plight* of the good guys appears at its worst just before the climax.

Determined to rescue the fifty hostages from their *plight*, the police rushed the aircraft before the terrorists could cause further harm.

plucky (PLU kee) *adj.* brave and spirited; courageous

Because Roger has such a *plucky* attitude, we asked him to be the captain of our skydiving team.

Her *pluckiness* made her a perfect candidate for the police force. (*n.*)

plumb (plum) *n.* a device used to measure the depth of something

The fisherman used a *plumb* to find the depth of the river.

The construction workers needed a *plumb* so they would know how high to build the dock.

pneumatic (noo MAT ik) *adj.* filled with or containing compressed gas

Billy used a *pneumatic* pump to fill his bicycle tires.

The team carried a portable *pneumatic* device so they could keep the basketballs inflated.

poignant (POYN yunt) *adj.* moving, affecting, lamentable, distressing

Jesse's hard luck story was full of *poignant* expressions, bringing tears to many.

The stabbing of Carmen was a *poignant* scene causing great emotion.

polarize (POH luh ryz) *v.* to break up into opposing factions or groups

Once the tour bus arrived in the city the group *polarized* and half spent the day at the beach and the remaining went shopping.

The football stadium was *polarized,* with home fans occupying the south bleachers and visiting fans occupying the north bleachers.

polemic (puh LEM ik) *n.* controversial argument against a controversial issue

The editorial page contained a convincing *polemic* against the adoption of the new building code.

The preacher delivered a *polemic* about the sins of abortion.

poltroon (pol TROON) *n.* a coward

Only a *poltroon* would desert his squad while they were under attack.

Many considered him a *poltroon* because he was in his 30s yet still afraid of the dark.

polygraph (POL ee graff) *n.* a test to determine if a person is telling the truth

Polygraphs are not always accepted in court since their validity is questionable.

The defendant refused to submit to a *polygraph*, making the prosecutor doubt his innocence.

pompadour (POMP uh dore) *n.* hairstyle for a man or a woman

In former times, men wore powdered wigs and big *pompadour* hairstyles.

The *pompadour* was named after the unusual hair styles of the famous Madame Pompadour.

pompous (PAWM pus) *adj.* showing an exaggerated air of importance

The *pompous* and opinionated talk show host quickly lost his following, and his show dropped in the ratings.

Daniel always acts so *pompous* and uppity when he wins a game.

ponder (PAWN dur) *v.* *t*o think deeply about

Some people go to church to *ponder* the meaning of life.

Issac Newton was one of the first to *ponder* the idea of gravity.

ponderous (PAHN dur us) *adj.* burdensome, awkward, cumbersome

Bart struggled with the *ponderous* package.

The killer's guilt is a *ponderous* burden he will have to bear.

pontiff (PON tiff) *n.* a high or chief priest; the Pope; the Bishop of Rome

The white smoke indicated a new *pontiff* had been elected.

The *pontiff* stood before the tribes announcing the decision of the gathered council.

pontificate (pahn TIF uh kayt) *v.* to act or speak arrogantly; to be conceited, overconfident, egotistical

The conceited quarterback continually *pontificates* about his position on the football team.

Don't *pontificate* about your good luck; it could change at any moment.

porcine (PORE sein) *adj.* reminiscent of or pertaining to a pig; resembling a pig

After an around-the-world cruise, during which each meal was a grand feast, Bob and Helen returned home with *porcine* figures.

She had a *porcine* attitude about food; she would eat anything and everything.

porous (POOR us) *adj.* allowing air, gas or liquid to pass through; having or full of holes

The *porous* paper was used to filter out the solid materials.

The *porous* barrier let the salt water through, but kept the sharks enclosed.

portal (POR tul) *n.* an entrance, door, or gate

As we stepped through the *portal* of the Sistine Chapel, we all were awestruck.

Beyond the porch steps stood a huge wooden *portal* that led to a reception area.

portend (por TEND) *v.* to warn of as an omen; forecast

The black clouds *portended* a terrible storm.

The king believed that his dreams *portended* some great event, so he approached his sages for an interpretation.

portent (POR tent) *n.* forewarning, foreboding, sign, warning, omen

The high winds were a *portent* of a rough flight ahead.

The kidnapper's threatening note was just a *portent* of the cruelty he was capable of committing.

postern (POSS turn) *adj.* entrance in the rear, a gate, a door, private entrance, castle

The new king slipped unnoticed out of the castle by the *postern* to meet a commoner.

The guard was left orders to permit the important visitor to enter by the *postern* to avoid the crowds at the public entrance.

posthumous (PAHS chuh mus) *adj.* happening or continuing after one's death; published after the death of an author

Painters often struggle through life penniless, since their fame and value is often *posthumous*.

The war veteran's wife received his *posthumous* Purple Heart.

postulate (PAHS chuh lut) *v./n.* to assume without proof; a selfevident axiom

Carole *postulated* that Ryan would go to his locker after class, so she headed in that direction.

The unprepared student's *postulate* is that he will study tomorrow.

posture (PAHS chur) *v./n.* to act or speak in an artificial or unnatural way; a position of the body; stance

Mrs. McDuffy is wearing her mink coat while she *postures* about cruelty to animals.

A model practices her *posture* by balancing books on her head.

potent (PO tunt) *adj.* having great power or influence; mightily cogent

A *potent* fighting force finally conquered the raiding troops.

Several *potent* arguments were heard before the amendment was defeated.

potentate (POE tun tate) *n.* a powerful ruler; an important person

Potentates are usually not elected officials, but instead are the descendants of a line of rajahs, sheiks, emperors, kings, and queens.

The Shah of Iran was an Iranian *potentate* who lived in the twentieth century.

potpourri (POH poo ree) *n.* a mixture or medley

Sometimes when my mother doesn't know what to make for dinner, she puts all the leftovers into the pot and calls it *potpourri*.

In scouts we collected the petals of all kinds of wildflowers and made a *potpourri.*

pragmatic (prag MAT ik) *adj.* practical, matter of fact, down to earth

Esther's problems necessitate *pragmatic* solutions, not fancy, expensive theories.

Jerry's *pragmatic* on-the-job experience was beneficial to the new company.

pratfall (PRAT fawl) *n.* a fall on the buttocks: a humiliating defeat or failure

After his *pratfall*, the clown's hat was askew.

Hugh considered his campaign for school president a *pratfall* when he only received one vote, which was his own.

prattle (PRAT l) *v.* to babble; to talk meaninglessly

Mary and Leslie *prattle* about everyone in the neighborhood.

The three-year-old *prattled* for hours although no one understood what she was saying.

precarious (pruh KA REE us) *adj.* unsafe, unsteady, unstable

The car hung in a *precarious* position, dangling over the edge of a cliff.

The *precariousness* of their situation did not fully strike the fishermen until their small boat arrived at the dock only moments before the storm struck. (*n.*)

precedence (PRESS uh dunce) *n.* the act, condition or right of preceding, priority of way

Her family takes *precedence* over her career, so she resigned when her son became seriously ill.

Since he has been away at college, her older brother's wishes have *precedence*, so he gets to choose the first vacation stop.

precedent (PRES uh dunt) *n.* example, pattern

The winning time was a *precedent* that all other runners tried to break.

Helen set a *precedent* as the first woman president in the corporation.

precept (PREE sept) *n.* command or directions given as a rule of conduct

328

The boss set the *precepts* all company employees must follow.

The *precepts* set down by the chairman stated the policy of the club.

preceptor (pri SEP tur) *n.* teacher, principal of a school, instructor

In college extra *preceptors* are available to help with the difficult courses.

Preceptors are ordering books to use for the new class.

precipitate (pri SIP uh tayt) *v.* hasten, expedite, accelerate

World War II *precipitated* John's induction in the military services.

The underground explosion *precipitated* an avalanche of snow which trapped the campers.

precipitous (pruh SIP uh tuss) *adj.* characterized by unthinkable boldness and haste

Henry's *precipitous* plan was to join the Navy with a fake I.D.

Joan asked Gary to marry her in a *precipitous* manner, writing her request on a billboard along the heavily traveled Route 7.

preclude (pri KLOOD) *v.* thwart, hamper, hinder, to prevent something from happening

Janice's full schedule will *preclude* her visit to the countryside.

Attendance at the meeting was *precluded* by the bad weather.

precocious (pri KOH shus) *adj.* showing unusually early mental development or achievement; unusually mature

Lucy was a verbally *precocious* child who spoke almost like an adult.

The very *precocious* young lady finished high school by the age of twelve.

precursor (pri KUR sur) *n.* forerunner, something that goes before and indicates

Bernard's polite letters were only *precursors* to blackmail.

Sweating, pain in the left arm, and difficult breathing are *precursors* to a heart attack.

predatory (PRED ah tor ee) *adj.* victimizing or destroying others for one's own gain; pillaging

The tiger shark is a *predatory* fish.

During the Middle Ages, many *predatory* bands of men roamed England, robbing and pillaging small villages.

predecessor (PRED uh ses ur) *n.* a person who had a job or position before someone else; a thing that comes before another in time or in a series

My *predecessor* worked in this job for twelve years before I was hired.

The latest model is faster and sleeker than its *predecessors*.

predestine (pre DESS tin) *v.* to govern and decide by, or as if by, fate

According to her horoscope, she was *predestined* to make a big mistake today.

According to the fortune teller, Dayne was *predestined* to marry his enemy's daughter.

predicament (pri DIK uh munt) *n..* an unpleasant or dangerous situation that is difficult to get out of or solve; a dilemma

With no money and no job, he found himself in a real *predicament*.

My dog got in a *predicament* yesterday while chasing a rabbit, he got stuck in a storm drain.

predilection (pred uh LEK shun) *n.* tendency to think favorably of something, partiality, penchant

Shirley's *predilection* for fatty foods only increases her cholesterol problems.

Don's *predilection* for reading books led to his career as an author.

predispose (pree dis POHZ) *v.* to set up or influence a behavior or condition; to lay the groundwork for

A medical test to determine if a woman is *predisposed* to breast cancer can help her take precautions.

His good manners *predispose* people to like him.

predominant (pri DAHM uh nunt) *adj.* having greater importance or influence; most common

Seven girls have the *predominant* role as cheerleaders, with only two boys on the squad.

The *predominant* feature of the hammerhead shark is the shape of its head.

preeminent (pre EM ih nunt) *adj.* most important, influential, superior

The famous young doctor was *preeminent* in the field of DNA research.

Dr. Martin Luther King, Jr., became *preeminent* in the battle for civil rights legislation.

preempt (pree EMPT) *v.* to take the place of due to priorities, usurp

The homecoming court presentation *preempted* the normal half-time show.

An emergency announcement *preempted* the regularly scheduled TV show.

preen (preen) *v.* dress smartly; to pride or congratulate oneself for achievement

The queen *preened* herself in the elaborate ceremonial robes of the past royalty.

Joseph *preened* himself for having graduated at the top of his class.

pregnant (PREG nunt) *adj.* filled with meaning that has not been expressed; significant; having young developing in the uterus

There was a *pregnant* pause in which each knew what the other was thinking.

Celine was six months *pregnant* when she had her baby shower.

prehensile (pri HEN sil) *adj.* adapted for grasping or holding

The elephant uses its trunk in a *prehensile* manner to grab its food.

It is amazing the way a *prehensile* eagle carries large fish in his claws.

prelude (PREL yood) *n.* an introductory event occurring before a more important one; opening for something bigger to follow

John's act is going to be the *prelude* for the headliners.

Stretching should always be a *prelude* to a strenuous work-out.

premeditated (pree MED ih tayt id) *adj.* thought of or planned before being done; prearranged or plotted

The police believe the killing was *premeditated* since they found evidence of the murderer's plans in his apartment. (*v.*)

The *premeditated* murders by the serial killer were solved by the police detective.

premise (PREM iss) *n.* something to be taken as truth without proof

A creative writing course is based on the *premise* that the students have some writing ability.

She charged her purchases on the *premise* that she would be able to pay for them after payday.

premonition (PREE muh NISH un) *n.* a warning or feeling that something will happen

Theresa had a *premonition* that something would happen to her sister.

Justin had such a strong *premonition* that he canceled his flight and stayed home with his family.

prenatal (pre NAY tull) *adj.* previous to birth

Prenatal care starting as early as possible is paramount to the birth of a healthy child.

Prenatal ultrasounds help to determine the gender of the unborn infant.

preponderance (pri PAHN dur uns) *n.* the largest part or greatest amount; majority; superiority in weight, quantity, size, etc.

The *preponderance* of evidence made the police declare the crash an accident.

The *preponderance* of women in the teaching field is apparent at any elementary school.

prepossess (pre puh ZES) *v.* to possess or dominate beforehand as a prejudice

Eileen *prepossessed* the idea that her written article was the best, so she refused to listen to any criticism.

Charlotte was *prepossessed* with the White Witches and the good they do before she truly understood their purpose.

preposterous (prih POSS tur uss) *adj.* senseless, absurd, ridiculous

The *preposterous* suggestion was promptly ignored by the group.

The *preposterous* weather in the area varies from snow to sunshine in one day.

prerogative (pri RAHG uh tiv) *n.* a right, privilege, exercise, by virtue of rank

332

The wealthy man thought society owed him such *prerogatives* as BMWs, estates, and plenty of money.

Jamie's *prerogative* was to inherit her grandfather's position and become the president of the company.

presage (PRES ij) *v.* to portend, forecast or predict; prophesy

Karen's tears *presage* a sad story about to be unfolded.

They say people experience an "aura" that *presages* the oncoming seizure or migraine headache.

presentiment (pre ZEN tih ment) *n.* a sense that something is about to occur; a premonition

Ray had a *presentiment* that he would hear from Tony before the end of the day, and sure enough he did.

The sage had a *presentiment* of an impending disaster that would befall the village, so he tried to warn the people.

prestigious (pres TEE jus) *adj.* highly esteemed; having an illustrious name or reputation

The rich girl was sent to a very *prestigious* private school.

Dad was just promoted to a rather *prestigious* position in the company and now has a fancy title.

presumably (pri ZOO muh blee) *adv.* probably; supposedly

Presumably they can afford to buy a car or they wouldn't be looking.

Presumably there will be an afternoon thunderstorm tomorrow, since this is the rainy season.

presumptuous (pri ZUMP choo us) *adj.* overconfident; arrogant

Pete's *presumptuous* attitude made everyone uncomfortable.

Tom told Daisy that her *presumptuous* little affair was over.

presuppose (pree suh POHZ) *v.* to think that something is true in advance; to assume beforehand

Theresa *presupposes* that Ethan will give her an engagement ring for Christmas, but Ethan is still thinking about the big step.

Just because he earns a lot of money, people shouldn't *presuppose* he had a formal education.

pretentious (pree TEN chus) *adj.* giving the appearance of great importance in an obvious way; showy; self-important

The movie star lives in a huge, *pretentious* house.

Melissa was very *pretentious* when explaining her new position, bragging about the big salary and tremendous benefits.

pretext (PREE tekst) *n.* a false reason put forth to hide the real one

Her *pretext* that she was staying over with a friend was a weak one, and her mother saw through it immediately.

His *pretext* was that he had a dental appointment, but we all knew he was sneaking off to see Sally.

prevalent (PREV uh lunt) *adj.* widespread, in general use or acceptance

Blue jeans seem to be the *prevalent* attire among school children.

Tiger Woods has become a *prevalent* name in golf.

prevaricate (prih VAYR uh kayt) *v.* to lie, perjure, fib, deceive, falsify

Mary's poor grade indicates she may have *prevaricated* a bit about how long she studied for the test.

Joe *prevaricated* because he did not want to explain his whereabouts on the night of the murder.

primal (PRYE mul) *adj.* being first in time; original; of importance

The need for love is a *primal* instinct.

Having a date for the prom seems a *primal* concern to many girls.

principal (PRIN sih pul) *n.* the main performer in any production, first or highest in rank

The two *principal* characters fought over top billing and salaries. (*adj.*)

The *principal* of the school decided which teacher to hire.

principle (PRIN sih pul) *n.* a broad or basic rule or truth

Because of her high *principles*, she refused to go along with the illegal plan.

Alcoholics Anonymous is based on a few *principles* that members must follow.

pristine (PRIS teen) *adj.* extremely pure; untouched

The coin discovered under layers of ash was still in *pristine* condition.

Those who know about the island keep it a secret because they want to continue to enjoy its *pristine* beaches.

privation (prye VAY shun) *n*. lack of the basic necessities or comforts of life; destitution; poverty

My state of *privation* is only temporary until I find a job and a place to live.

Nuns give away their worldly possessions to live a life of *privation*.

probity (PRO bi tee) *n*. morality, integrity, uprightness, honesty

Bankers must display *probity* since they work with large sums of money and could be tempted to help themselves.

The jurors doubted the *probity* of the witness since he was related to the suspect.

problematic (prob leh MAT ik) *adj*. unsettled, doubtful or questionable

Drawing conclusions about life on Mars is *problematic* due to inconclusive evidence.

The lack of a babysitter on the night of the party caused a *problematic* situation for the young couple.

proclaim (proh KLAYM) *v*. to announce publicly or officially; to declare

She confidently *proclaimed* victory even as the first few votes came in.

The king *proclaimed* his daughter's birthday would be a royal holiday in the kingdom.

procrastinate (PRO cras tuh nate) *v*. to put off until a later time

Not doing today what you can *procrastinate* until tomorrow is not very wise.

He was always late with the payment since he *procrastinated* instead of just writing the check when the bill arrived.

procure (pruh KYOOR) *v*. to obtain or acquire something by special means; secure something with an effort

We *procured* maps and directions from the tourist office.

Our museum employs a person to *procure* items of special interest for display.

prodigal (PROD ih gul) *adj.* recklessly extravagant; unrestrained

Grandville, the *prodigal* son, returned home because he was penniless.

Louise's *prodigal* habit of giving money to people with sob stories left her penniless.

prodigious (pra dij us) *adj.* enormous in size, quantity, degree; marvelous; amazing

The construction of the Panama Canal was a *prodigious* undertaking.

Prodigious marathon runners run twenty-six miles in a few hours.

prodigy (PRAHD uh jee) *n.* gifted child, great talent, expert, wonder, phenomenon

Mozart was a *prodigy* who could read, play, and improvise music at age five.

Max was a child *prodigy* who finished high school by eleven years of age.

profane (pro FAYN) *adj.* irreligious, agnostic, atheistic, sacrilegious, secular

Karl used more proper language in place of *profane* terms to avoid criticism.

Both sacred and *profane* music was played at the memorial service.

profess (pruh FES) *v.* to lay claim to, often insincerely, pass oneself off

Pierre *professed* to be royalty only to admit later he had lied.

Henry *professed* to be a doctor but was picked up for having a phony license.

proffer (PROF fur) *v.* to put before a person for acceptance, offer

The company's leased car was *proffered* to Mary Ann as a perk of the job.

Carole's parents *proffered* a vacation if her grades improved to a "B" average.

proficient (pruh FISH unt) *adj.* skillful; very good at something

Wally was the most competent, *proficient* ice skater in our league, but he wasn't good enough to make the Olympic team.

June was so *proficient* as executive secretary, she was promoted and became president of sales.

profligate (PRAHF luh git) *adj.* recklessly prodigal and extravagant

Frank's *profligate* way of living is reducing his bank account.

The *profligate* sports hero threw money around wastefully.

profound (pro FOWND) *adj.* intellectually deep or penetrating; reaching to, rising from, or affecting the depths of one's nature; far-reaching

Many psychologists believe violence on television and in film has a *profound* effect on our behavior toward others.

Advertising has a *profound* effect on the failure or success of many products.

profusion (proh FYOO zhun) *n.* extravagant expense; an abundant supply or display

Jill so impressed her date that when she arrived home, she found a *profusion* of roses from him.

The painter's many creations are a testament to his *profusion* of creativity.

progeny (PRAHJ uh nee) *n.* offspring or descendant; a product of creative effort

The young mothers chased their *progeny* outdoors so they could enjoy a cup of coffee and a moment's peace.

The musician's young *progeny* will be a star one day.

prognosticate (prog NOS ti kayt) *v.* to foretell or predict

It is the weatherman's job to *prognosticate* the weather so we will know what to wear in the morning.

One could *prognosticate* the outcome of the game after watching only the first four downs.

progressive (pruh GRES iv) *adj.* moving forward, dynamic, advancing, ongoing

Claude was an up-and-coming *progressive* politician.

Lou Gehrig's disease is a *progressive* infection which intensifies with time.

prohibition (PROH uh bish un) *n.* the act of prohibiting; a law that forbids

The most famous *prohibition* in this country was the ban on alcohol.

The dress code makes clear the *prohibition* of body piercings.

proletariat (proh luh TER ee ut) *n.* class of wage earners, those who do manual labor

The members of the British *proletariat* now in office in England are known as the Labor Party.

Industrial *proletariat* wages are about $15 per hour in the big cities.

proliferate (pro LIF uh rayt) *v.* to increase in number and spread rapidly, regenerate

Germs *proliferate* when sick people come to work.

Sue's rabbits *proliferated* until she was forced to buy two more cages for the offspring.

prolific (pro LIF ik) *adj.* producing offspring, producing abundantly, yielding propagating

Sonja's pet hamsters were so *prolific* she was constantly trying to give away babies.

Hayden was a *prolific* composer who wrote one hundred and four symphonies.

prolong (proh LAWNG) *v.* elongate, perpetuate, to lengthen in extent or duration

Because of the airline strike, we have to *prolong* our visit until next Thursday.

The football game was *prolonged* because the game ended in a tie.

prompt (PRAHMPT) *v.* to inspire, strongly encourage, incite

The student was *prompted* to major in music by his choral instructor.

Thank you for *prompting* the actors during rehearsal of the play.

promulgate (PRAHM ul gayt) *v.* to proclaim; to publicly or formally declare something; set forth

Professor Tomlinson *promulgated* to the freshman that only 50 percent would remain for their sophomore year.

T.H. Huxley *promulgated* Darwin's Theory of Evolution in numerous texts.

propagate (PRAHP uh gayt) *v.* to reproduce, breed, multiply; to spread or circulate

The new diet was *propagated* in a pamphlet describing its benefits.

Some scientists *propagate* the theory that cancer is inherited.

propensity (pruh PEN suh tee) *n.* a natural inclination or tendency; a predilection, preference

Most children have a *propensity* for candy.

Zack had a *propensity* for making money and became a millionaire.

propinquity (proh PING kwi tee) *n.*. proximity, nearness; kinship

Because of the *propinquity* of our neighbor's yard, we sometimes hear things we shouldn't.

The *propinquity* of Leonardo di Vinci and Michelangelo was remarkable; the two great artists lived within the same time, at the same place.

propitious (pruh PISH us) *adj.* marked by favorable signs or conditions, opportune, well-timed

We have gathered together on this *propitious* occasion to report a profit.

They phoned at 3:00 am which was not a *propitious* time since I was asleep.

proponent (pruh POH nunt) *n.* enthusiast, supporter, advocate

The coach was a *proponent* of the old famous double-wing backfield, so his team used it repeatedly.

The *proponents* of the candidate gathered to support her.

propound (pruh POWND) *v.* to offer for consideration; to propose or suggest

My children *propound* outlandish reasons they have to be taken to the toy store.

Since the group was still hungry, I *propounded* that they return to our house for dessert.

proprietary (pruh PRYE uh ter ee) *adj.* belonging to a proprietor; characteristic of an owner of property

The father treated the rental car in a *proprietary* way, taking care as if it were his own.

The *proprietors* of the stores in the mall met to discuss ways to increase their business. (*n.*)

propriety (pruh PRYE uh tee) *n.* correctness, decorum, dignity, good manners

Young man, always conduct yourself with *propriety* in front of your grandmother and her friends.

When being presented to royalty, *propriety* demands a curtsy or a bow.

propulsive (proh PUL siv) *adj.* propelling; having a propelling force

The *propulsive* punch sent the other boxer flying across the ring.

Nuclear energy is the *propulsive* force in modern submarines.

prosaic (proh ZAY ik) *adj.* unimaginative, dull, common, ordinary

The housekeeper purchased *prosaic* items of cheese and wine instead of champagne and caviar.

The history professor's *prosaic* lecture put about ten students to sleep.

proscribe (proh SKRYBE) *v.* condemn, outlaw, banish, exile, prohibit

Rules *proscribe* the use of drugs by athletes in the Olympics.

In the new restaurant, smoking was *proscribed* everywhere except outdoors.

prose (PROZ) *n.* ordinary speech or writing, (as opposed to poetry),

The words were written in *prose*, but they sounded very poetic.

Jason's delivery of his *prose* put people to sleep.

prosperous (PROS pur us) *adj.* thriving, opulent, affluent, wealthy, well-off

In his fancy new car, Craig presented the appearance of a *prosperous* businessman.

The auction got off to a *prosperous* start with a bid of one hundred thousand dollars.

prosthesis (pross THEE sis) *n.* a device external or implanted, supplement for a missing part

After Jeff's leg was amputated, he was fitted for a *prosthesis*.

Doctors replaced the injured man's missing ear with a *prosthesis*.

protagonist (proh TAG uh nist) *n.* the leading character in a novel, play, or other work; hero

The *protagonist* in the story was able to save the injured captain.

The *protagonists* of the war effort were honored at the end of the fighting.

protean (PRO tean) *adj.* having many aspects, uses or abilities; very changeable

Carlson's *protean* talent to be three different characters in a play was a magnificent gift.

Harry's *protean* abilities made him a valuable asset to the group.

protégé (PROH tuh zhay) *n.* someone whose welfare, training or career is promoted by an influential person; a person under the care or guidance of another interested in his welfare

The high-powered attorney adopted the law student as his *protégé*.

Some famous actors began as the *protégés* of older, more experienced actors.

protocol (PROH tuh kawl) *n.* the rules of etiquette and ceremony observed by heads of state, diplomats; an original or preliminary draft or copy of an agreement

The President of the United States must be aware of the *protocol* of many foreign delegates.

Mr. Jones has written the *protocol* for the new contract to be in effect next year.

protrude (pro TROOD) *v.* to push outward, swell, project, jut out

Nails *protruded* from the board, and were removed for safety reasons.

A third eye *protruded* from the forehead of the giant monster.

provident (PROHV ih dunt) *adj.* having foresight, prudent, parsimonious, frugal

Frank was a *provident* man who prepared for his future.

We must be *provident* with food supplies during the hurricane season.

provincial (pruh VIN shul) *adj.* parochial, limited to one's small outlook of the world, narrow

His *provincial* outlook was due to his extreme narrowmindedness.

Harriet, a farmer's daughter who had never traveled far from her village, had simple, *provincial* manners.

provisional (pruh VIZH uh nul) *adj.* tentative, stopgap, transitional, conditional

The *provisional* treaty was ratified by the U.S. Congress and later made permanent.

The *provisional* plan is to appoint a new officer until elections can be held.

provocation (prahv uh KAY shun) *n.* something that causes anger or irritation; incitement or cause

The speaker's *provocation* caused the crowd to riot.

The attack on Pear Harbor was the *provocation* that caused the United State to declare war on Japan.

provocative (prah VAWK uh tiv) *adj.* exciting, attracting attention, provoking, irritating

Jack's *provocative* remark started a heated argument.

Betty wore a very *provocative* red satin gown, which had all the males staring at her.

prowess (PROW is) *n.* exceptional skill and bravery

The *prowess* of the Sioux chief, Crazy Horse, in leading his warriors into battle, is legendary.

Although Jody brags of his golf *prowess*, his friends say he is a hacker.

proximity (prox SIM uh tee) *n.* nearness in place or time, order

Phil's overbearing voice was in *proximity* to my private desk, and my customers could hear every word he uttered.

All the shot-put marks were in the *proximity* of the school's record.

proxy (PROK see) *n.* written authority allowing another to act

Blue Cross is now checking the *proxy* votes before the yearly meeting at which delegates vote in person.

The injured man signed a *proxy* giving his son the right to handle his banking accounts.

prudent (PROOD unt) *adj.* sensible, discerning, level-headed

A *prudent* investor always diversifies his stock portfolio by purchasing many different stocks.

It was a *prudent* decision to finish school before starting the new job with extended hours.

prudish (PROO dish) *adj.* overly concerned with being modest or proper

Catherine was so *prudish* that she brought two forks in her packed lunch, one for her salad and one for her meal.

The *prudish* woman avoided the noisy cowboy as if he were the devil himself.

prurient (PROOR ee unt) *adj.* having lewd or indecent thoughts; characterized by an extreme interest in sex

Most teenage boys have a *prurient* fascination with young fashion models.

The *prurient* content of that movie makes it unsuitable for the younger crowds.

pseudonym (SOO duh nim) *n.* an alias or false name; an assumed name

Samuel Clemens used the *pseudonym* Mark Twain.

Most people have several *pseudonyms* for internet chat rooms.

psyche (SYE kee) *n.* the human soul; the mind

The study of poetry often helps students to examine their own *psyches*.

A true appreciation for classical literature encompasses one's entire *psyche*.

pucker (PUK er) *v.* contract, crease, shrink, to gather into wrinkles

Lemon makes your mouth *pucker* because of the sour effect.

The hem was *puckered* because there was extra material when she shortened the skirt.

pugnacious (pug NAY shus) *adj.* ready or eager to fight; overly aggressive or quarrelsome

Larry's *pugnacious* attitude kept getting him into fights.

The *pugnacious* generals would not even attend the peace treaty talks.

puissant (PWIS ahnt) *adj.* potent, powerful, mighty

General Patton and his men were a *puissant* force during World War II.

A *puissant* antibiotic was needed to fight his double pneumonia.

pummel (PUM ul) *v.* to hit or pound repeatedly with the fists

The prize fighter *pummeled* the face of his opponent until the referee finally pulled him away.

Chefs need to *pummel* dough to prepare it for baking.

punctilious (pungk TIL ee us) *adj.* conscientious and precise; extremely attentive to detail

My teenage daughter is *punctilious* about applying her makeup, taking over an hour to make sure she looks perfect.

Mom, with her *punctilious* house cleaning, is always following me with a broom and dust cloth.

pundit (PUN dit) *n.* a person who knows a great deal about a particular subject; an expert

Since he studied social studies at the university, Grandfather is a *pundit* on American history.

Young children are usually *pundits* on the Saturday morning cartoons; they can tell you all about every character.

pungent (PUN jent) *adj.* forceful, sharp or biting to taste or smell

Sonny's beef ribs were served with a hot, *pungent* sauce.

Bennett's *pungent* satires made him quite a few enemies on the newspaper staff.

pumice (PUM es) *n.* porous form of volcanic glass used as an abrasive

The foot doctor suggested using a *pumice* stone for the heavy, rough, calloused skin.

The old lady scrubbed the filthy European tile floors with *pumice* and vinegar.

punitive (PYOO nuh tiv) *adj.* intended as a punishment

The *punitive* action called by the referee was a ten minute penalty for the player.

The gang had to collectively pay $10,000 in *punitive* damages for spray painting the building front.

purblind (per blind) *adj.* having poor vision; nearly or partly blind

A childhood disease left Helen Keller *purblind.*

The *purblind* man was undergoing surgery to restore his sight.

purge (purj) *v.* to free from guilt, to clean out

The faculty *purged* the fraternity house after the drinking incident.

The doctor injected the new antibiotic to *purge* the body of pneumonia.

purist (PYOOR ist) *n.* someone who strictly observes traditions or conventions

The family are *purists* who celebrate every holiday exactly as they did in the "old country."

Al's *puristic* religious beliefs alienated him from his old friends. (*adj.*)

puritanical (pyoor uh TAN ih kul) *adj.* having very strict standards of moral behavior; rigid; prudish

Some very strict religions are *puritanical* in their teachings.

Mary's co-workers thought she was *puritanical* until they observed her wild behavior at the company picnic.

purport (pur PORT) *v.* to claim or profess, to declare, to give the appearance, often falsely

John *purported* to have run a mile under four minutes.

Dave *purported* to the police that he was attacked, but no one really believed his story.

purvey (pur VAY) *v.* to provide, furnish, supply items as a business or service

Income tax forms are *purveyed* through the mail or are available at all post offices.

The uniform company *purveyed* the outfits for the waiters and waitresses.

pushover (POOSH oh vur) *n.* a person easily influenced or exploited

When the young boy begged for candy, his father, a *pushover*, quickly gave in.

Betty was a *pushover* when it came to door-to-door salesman, she bought everything.

pusillanimous (pyoo sih LAN ih muss) *adj.* lacking courage, or resolution, cowardly

The lion was the *pusillanimous* character in the *Wizard of OZ*.

His first night on the job, the *pusillanimous* cop turned and ran away during the holdup.

putative (PYOO tuh tiv) *adj.* commonly accepted

Punting on the fourth down is a *putative* act in football.

The *putative* method of shopping these days is paying by credit card.

putrefy (PYOO treh fy) *v.* taint, deteriorate, to rot, decompose

Vince left the venison on the counter overnight causing it to *putrefy*.

The *putrefied* remains of a body were found in the woods. (*adj.*)

pyromaniac (pye roe MAY nee ak) *n.* a person with a compulsion to set things on fire

The North Port brush fires were set by a *pyromaniac*.

Many arsonists are deemed *pyromaniacs* because they set fires without monetary gain.

quaff (kwaf) *v.* to drink heartily

After football practice, I *quaffed* a whole gallon of water.

Fraternity parties often involve the *quaffing* of large quantities of beverages.

quail (kwayl) *v.* to shrink with fear; to cower; to lose heart and courage

A leader is one who does not *quail* in the face of adversity.

The previously beaten dog *quailed* each time his new owner raised his hand.

quaint (kwaynt) *adj.* agreeably old-fashioned or curious; picturesque

Visiting the many *quaint* little cafes in Paris is like taking a step back in time.

The Amish people, with their horses and buggies, have *quaint* customs.

qualify (KWAHL uh fye) *v.* to make eligible, adapt, make competent, or capable

In order to *qualify* to play in the U.S. Open one must accumulate enough points by playing in many other tournaments.

In order to *qualify* for food stamps, one's income must be below a certain level.

qualitative (KWAHL uh tay tiv) *adj.* concerned with quality or qualities

The last inspectors are responsible for the *qualitative* aspects of the final product.

The *qualitative* analysis of the product showed illegal mercury deposits.

qualm (kwam) *n.* feeling of uneasiness, doubt, or sickness

When she stood up to give the graduation address, she looked as though she didn't have the slightest *qualm*.

The criminal pulled the trigger without a *qualm*.

quandary (KWON duh ree) *n.* perplexity or uncertainty, predicament

The problem of financing schools is a *quandary* becoming more difficult each year.

The police were in a *quandary*; the butler's fingerprints were all over the murder weapon, but he was two thousand miles away during the time the murder was committed.

quarantine (KWOR un teen) *n.* a strict isolation imposed to prevent spread of disease

Before the age of antibiotics, sick people were placed in *quarantine* to prevent the spread of infectious diseases.

The young mother tried to keep her four-year-old in *quarantine* so he would not catch the measles.

quarry (KWOR ee) *n.* an animal that is being hunted down, especially with dogs

The dogs staked out their *quarry* until the hunters caught up to them.

The *quarry* was surrounded, but instinct told it to keep fighting.

quasi (KWAY zye) *adj.* to a degree but not completely; resembling but not being

Her party was a *quasi* disaster.

Some companies manufacture *quasi* designer clothes. They look like them, but they are cheaper!

quaver (KWAY vur) *v.* shake tremulously, quiver or tremble

The frightened child *quavered* as he waited for the clerk to find his mommy.

San Francisco *quavers* now and then as an earthquake threatens the area.

quay (kee) *n.* a structure beside the water to which boats can be tied; wharf, pier, landing

Many boats are tied up along the *quay* of the Ohio River.

We like to fish from the *quay*.

quell (kwel) *v.* to extinguish; to put down or suppress by force

The mother attempted to *quell* the infant's cries by singing a lullaby.

The National Guard was sent in to try to *quell* the rioting crowd.

querulous (KWER uh lus) *adj.* complaining, grumbling, whining, disagreeable

The tired and haggard mother was exhausted by her *querulous* children's constant demands.

The *querulous* old woman was never satisfied with her treatment no matter how hard the nurses tried.

query (KWEER ee) *n.* a question or inquiry; a request for information

Because I didn't understand, I offered a *query* to the speaker after his speech.

Forms are one type of *query* about a person's financial status.

queue (kyoo) *v.* to form or to wait in line

During the Wimbledon Tennis Championships, fans *queued* outside the gates the day before and spent the night waiting for the gates to open the following morning.

The sisters decided not to attend the movie because a line was *queuing* up as they arrived, and they didn't want to stand in a *queue* in the cold, night air. (*n.*)

quid pro quo (kwid pro KWO) *n.* one thing in return for another

The theory of "*quid pro quo*" is used by advertisers when they offer a free gift for buying a product.

The kidnapper wanted *quid pro quo*; he would surrender the kidnapped child for one million dollars with no strings attached.

quiescent (kwye ES unt) *adj.* at rest, inactive; dormant

The stadium remains *quiescent* until football season starts.

You have to make your mind *quiescent* so a hypnotist can do his job.

quietude (kwi i TUDE) *n.* a condition of tranquility

Gene and Chris chose their property for the air of *quietude* and peace that pervaded the area.

The war zone's *quietude* took the reporters by surprise.

quintessential (kwin tuh SEN chul) *adj.* being the most perfect or typical example of something

Michael Jordan is a *quintessential* basketball player.

Miss America is promoted as the *quintessential* American woman.

quip (kwip) *n.* a witty remark or reply

Our English teacher is especially known for his good-natured *quips*.

Aaron's *quip* was lost on the five-year-olds.

quirk (kwurk) *n.* a peculiarity of behavior; an unaccountable act or event

Bryan has the strangest quirk; he chews on his tongue whenever he concentrates on something.

It was a *quirk* of fate that Elizabeth was sick at home the day her bus was involved in an accident.

quisling (KWIZ ling) *n.* person betraying one's own country, helping an invading enemy

Hitler declared some Germans *quislings* and imprisoned them as spies.

Benedict Arnold, an American siding with England, was a *quisling* during the Revolutionary War.

quixotic (kwik SAHT ik) *adj.* idealistic and totally impractical

Professor Callan said it is *quixotic* for society to ignore the world's environmental problems.

Sue had the most *quixotic* ideas about what her life would be like if she ever won the lottery.

quizzical (KWIS ih kul) *adj.* questioning; teasing, mocking; expressing puzzlement

The teacher gave Johnny a *quizzical* look upon hearing his ridiculous excuse for being late.

Kelly is a very *quizzical* child, always wanting to know why everything happens as it does.

quotidian (kwoh TID ee un) *adj.* commonplace; ordinary; everyday

Brushing one's teeth is a *quotidian* event.

Winning the lottery certainly isn't a *quotidian* event.

rabble (RAB ul) *n.* disorderly crowd or mob, lower class

The *rabble* hung out at the junk yard.

The police were accused by the *rabble* of violating their first amendment rights.

rabid (RAB id) *adj.* violent; raging

The *rabid* dog was coming down the street, straight at us.

My father was *rabid* when he learned my teenage sister was pregnant.

raconteur (rayk un TYOOR) *n.* one who is talented in storytelling

He knew many jokes and was a witty and entertaining *raconteur*.

Jeff was an excellent *raconteur* who held his audience spellbound for hours.

raffish (RAF ish) *adj.* cheaply vulgar in appearance or nature; tawdry; disreputable

The *raffish* character had been seen at the murder and was taken in for questioning.

His *raffish* appearance made people think he was a low-life.

rail (rayl) *v.* to speak bitterly; to complain violently

The sergeant *railed* his recruits about how poorly they completed the obstacle course.

It really bothers me when other students *rail* about how hard their classes are instead of just doing their work.

rakish (RAY kish) *adj.* appearing fast, neat appearance; dashing, casual look

The *rakish* speedboat flew across the lake.

When the *rakish* young man entered the room everyone staired.

raiment (RAY munt) *n.* clothing; wearing apparel

The wardrobe director did a wonderful job using only *raiment* of the time period.

The Persian military officer wore the *raiment* of his office.

rambunctious (ram BUNK shuss) *adj.* difficult to control, handle, turbulent

King John became *rambunctious* and greedy while Richard was on the crusades.

The party room became *rambunctious,* and the police were summoned to restore control.

ramification (ram ih fuh KAY shun) *n.* a branching out; a development growing out of and often complicating a problem or pain

Courtney did not realize being late for work three mornings in a row would have *ramifications* until her boss fired her.

The *ramification* of failing the state test is not graduating.

rampage (RAM page) *n.* uncontrolled self-indulgence, furious or violent act

The demented man went on a *rampage,* wounding several passers-by.

The Mississippi River has gone on a *rampage* and flooded the country-side.

rampant (RAM punt) *adj.* happening often or becoming worse, usually in an uncontrolled way; widespread

Disease is *rampant* in the dirty, overcrowded refugee camps.

Crime is *rampant* in some major cities.

rampart (RAM part) *n.* a fortification, a bulwark or defense

The Americans attacked the outer *ramparts* of the German fort in the mountains.

The hill served as a *rampart* protecting the town from floods.

rancor (RAN kur) *n.* bitter resentment or ill-will, hatred, malice

The *rancor* of his ex-wife exploded into physical violence as she ran him down with his new car.

The *rancor* between company and union was so intense it was difficult to bargain.

ransack (RAN sak) *v.* to search thoroughly; pillage

April had to *ransack* her room in order to find the overdue library book.

The king and his men were busy *ransacking* the village and did not know a truce had been called.

rapacious (ruh PAY shus) *adj.* covetous, mercenary, insatiable, greedy, plundering, avaricious

Blackbeard and his crew were a *rapacious* lot of pirates.

Jeremy, in his *rapacious* way, became wealthy but friendless.

rapport (rah PORE) *n.* harmonious mutual understanding, fellowship, camaraderie

The new people developed a *rapport* with the other neighbors in the area.

The teacher's close *rapport* with her students was obvious as they listened spellbound to her stories.

rapture (RAP chur) *n.* extreme pleasure and happiness; bliss; ecstasy

A banana split is *rapture* for a dieter.

The young newlyweds were in a state of constant *rapture*.

rarefied (RAR uh fyde) *adj.* not ordinary; interesting to a select group only

The Malaysian restaurant down the street went out of business because it catered to a *rarefied* clientele.

His last book was too *rarefied* to become a best seller.

rash (rash) *adj.* characterized by speaking or acting too quickly; reckless

He knew his behavior was *rash*, but once he started he was unable to stop himself.

I couldn't believe Vanessa could be so *rash* as to criticize our principal to his face.

ratify (RAT uh fye) *v.* to officially approve; endorse; agree to

Four countries have now *ratified* the agreement.

The majority must *ratify* the amendment before it is enacted.

ratiocination (rash ee oh suh NAY shun) *n.* logical reasoning

Ratiocination got him through his science exam, as he figured out most questions.

Most folks lose all *ratiocination* when they fall in love.

rationale (rash uh NAL) *n.* the reasons or intentions for something; basis

I don't understand your *rationale* for choosing Paris as a vacation site.

Being on call for the hospital was my *rationale* for owning a beeper.

rationalize (RASH uh nuh lyz) *v.* to explain in a reasonable way

The group of little boys were attempting to *rationalize* their behavior before they were forced to explain to their parents.

Criminals always try to *rationalize* their reasons for committing a crime.

raucous (RAW kus) *adj.* loud, excited, and not controlled; rowdy and wild

The audience broke out in *raucous* laughter after the off-color joke.

Linda had such a *raucous* sixteenth birthday party that her parents grounded her until she is eighteen!

raze (rayz) *v.* to destroy completely; to knock down completely; to level

Developers *razed* the old buildings on the site to make way for new construction.

The city was completely *razed* by the tornado.

reactionary (ree AK shuh ner ee) *adj.* opposing political or social change; opposing liberalism; ultraconservative

The administrator's *reactionary* beliefs about women's equality kept Joan from getting the promotion, even though she was far more qualified than Thomas.

Reactionary groups stand in the way of progress and change.

realm (relm) *n.* kingdom; region; area

After Charlie won the competition, he felt he was lord of his *realm*.

Carrie knew that her *realm* was the classroom, so she became a college professor.

rebuff (re BUF) *v.* to refuse to accept; to snub or reject

Our request for assistance has been *rebuffed*, so we'll have to do the job ourselves.

Rob *rebuffs* all of Julie's advances, continuing to ignore her.

rebuke (ri BYOOK) *v.* take to task, scold, reprimand

The boss *rebuked* Jan for throwing out important files by mistake.

Jamie's sharp *rebuke* will hopefully cause the dog to obey next time. (*n.*)

rebut (ri but) *v.* refute evidence or argument, to contradict, to prove to be false

In his argument, West *rebutted* his opponents' charges and won the case.

He *rebutted* the paper's criticism by explaining the true circumstances.

recalcitrant (ri KAL suh trunt) *adj.* showing strong objection, obstinate, unwilling, stubbornly defiant

The *recalcitrant* student refused to bring his book to class.

Carl's *recalcitrant* attitude about accepting monetary help from his parents explained his frugal lifestyle.

recant (ri KANT) *v.* to take back, retract, repudiate, disavow

Charlotte *recanted* her original charge that her car was stolen and instead said her brother had borrowed it.

The newspaper *recanted* the story because some details were misinterpreted by the writer.

recede (rih SEED) *v.* to move back or away from a point, limit or ebb

The tidal waters *receded* after the heavy rainstorm, so people returned home.

Our beaches are *receding,* causing great concern to the environmentalists.

receptive (ri SEP tiv) *adj.* favorable, open minded, willing to accept

The inventor hoped to find the examiner at the patent office in a *receptive* mood.

The class was *receptive* to the traveling show of European art and enjoyed the cultural lesson.

recidivism (ri SID uh viz um) *n.* repeated relapse into past condition or behavior; a tendency to return to criminal ways

The rate of *recidivism* shows our prisons don't usually reform or rehabilitate the inmates.

That child's *recidivism* is unbelievable; he just doesn't change after punishment.

reciprocal (rih SIP ri kul) *adj.* showing mutual respect; characterized by mutual give and take

Reciprocal trade agreements cause economic growth for both countries.

The *reciprocal* exchange in research has produced many valuable products for each company.

reclaim (ri KLAYM) *v.* to take back; to claim again

The tribe set out to *reclaim* its lost lands.

Residents want to *reclaim* their streets from drug dealers.

recluse (reh KLOOS) *n.* a person who lives in voluntary isolation from others

The other students thought Chloe was a *recluse* because she chose to stay home and study.

The old man lived like a *recluse,* miles from his nearest neighbor.

recoil (ree KOIL) *v.* to retreat; shrink back

A grisly car wreck always makes us *recoil*.

Pamela *recoiled* in fear when she saw the snake slithering toward her.

reconcile (REK un syl) *v.* to reunite, conciliate, to settle a dispute; to make up

Father was able to *reconcile* with his brothers concerning the disagreement fifty years earlier.

Megan and Scott *reconciled* after breaking up two weeks ago.

recondite (REK un dyte) *adj.* profound, hard to understand; over one's head

Jennie submitted a *recondite* thesis, and the committee could not comprehend it.

Modern Physics Journal is a *recondite* magazine, absolutely incomprehensible to the average reader.

recrimination (rih krim ih NAY shun) *n.* a countercharge against an accuser

The undercover agent's *recrimination* against the FBI was revealed in his book.

The attorney's *recrimination* against the insurance company for nonpayment of claims resulted in his client's retrieval of funds for medical expenses.

rectify (REK tuh fy) *v.* to correct, to straighten, amend, revise, set right

The accountant rectified the errors before the ledgers were audited.

The official *rectified* his call after viewing the instant replay.

redeem (ri DEEM) *v.* to buy back; exchange something for money or for goods; to make up for

You can *redeem* the coupon for cash.

The gardener can *redeem* himself by replacing my rare plants.

redolent (RED uh lunt) *adj.* fragrant, aromatic, savory

On Labor Day, neighborhoods are *redolent* with the aroma of barbecued foods.

European stores in the Caribbean are *redolent* with French perfumes.

redoubtable (rih DOUT uh bull) *adj.* widely known and esteemed, eminent

The company wanted a *redoubtable* celebrity to be the spokeswoman for their new product line.

The *redoubtable* President Carter is working for Habitat for Humanity.

redress (ri DRES) *v.* to correct a wrong; to make amends for

Affirmative action to help minorities is intended to *redress* wrongs done in the past.

There is no adequate *redress* for the accidental loss of a limb, but monetary compensation can replace the loss of wages. (*n.*)

redundant (rih DUN dunt) *adj.* excessively wordy, repetition

Jimmy's multiple stories of his success became *redundant* causing people in the audience to doze.

Bob's *redundant* report was fifteen pages long, it could have been shortened to eight pages.

referendum (ref uh REN dum) *n.* a vote in which all the people in a country or an area decide on an important question

The employees demanded a *referendum* on the appointment of the new department head.

There will be a *referendum* before the legislature passes the bill.

reform (ri FORM) *v.* to improve, to change for the better, rehabilitate, restore

The alcoholic joined a support group and *reformed* his drinking habits.

The athlete *reformed* his method of training and became a star.

refractory (ri FRAK tuh ree) *adj.* disobedient; hard to manage; headstrong

The *refractory* mule went exactly where it wanted.

Storm is such a *refractory* child that he spends much of his day in time-out.

refulgent (rih FUL junt) *adj.* shining brightly, gleaming, radiant

His *refulgent* eyes showed his pleasure over the lucrative deal.

Crystal chandeliers at the house made a *refulgent* setting for the party.

refurbish (ree FUR bish) *v.* to make clean, fresh, and attractive again; to make like new

Karen *refurbished* her kitchen and it now looks brand new.

I am going to *refurbish* my mom's antique table for her.

refute (ri FYOOT) *v.* rebut, invalidate, challenge, prove to be false

Columbus *refuted* the idea that the world was flat.

By actually cloning them the scientist *refuted* earlier claims that stem cells couldn't be used for cloning.

regale (rih GAYL) *v.* to entertain lavishly, feast, make merry

The gracious hosts *regaled* their visitors with delicious food and fabulous entertainers.

Opening night parties *regale* the critics and stars in opulent splendor.

regime (ri ZHEEM) *n.* a particular government; a system or method of government

Castro's *regime* is communistic.

The new dance teacher's *regime* was so strict that half the students dropped out.

regimen (REJ uh mun) *n.* a set of rules; a regulated course

His doctor put him on a strict *regimen* of exercise and low-fat food.

Students will find that the *regimen* for membership in the honor society is very rigid.

regurgitate (rih GURJ ih tate) *v.* to cause to surge or rush back, vomit

Some mother birds feed their young by *regurgitating* food.

The stomach flu causes victims to *regurgitate*.

reign (rayn) *n.* the exercise or possession of supreme power

Many believe the king's *reign* was a time of great progress.

Queen Elizabeth has *reigned* over England since the 1950s.

reiterate (re ITR uh rate) *v.* to state again

The teacher *reiterated* that the test would be easy.

In court, the woman *reiterated* the divorce demands she had presented to her husband.

rejuvenate (ree JOO vun ayt) *v.* to restore the vigor, health, or appearance of youth; to make young again

Helen's vacation *rejuvenated* her.

Remodeling can do much to *rejuvenate* old neighborhoods and keep the city from declining further.

relapse (RE laps) *n.* a return to a former state, regression, reversion

The student's grades improved drastically but suffered a *relapse* when he became overconfident and quit studying.

The patient appeared to be improving, but he suffered a *relapse* and went into a coma.

relegate (REL uh gate) *v.* assign to an inferior position, place, exile

Because of the discipline code, Joe was *relegated* to detention.

He *relegates* the less pleasant tasks to his assistant.

relentless (ri LENT lis) *adj.* unyielding, severe, strict, harsh, uncompromising

Unafraid to trample his former friends, Carl was *relentless* in his pursuit of fame and fortune.

The general was *relentless* in his attempt to take the territory from the enemy.

relevant (REL uh vunt) *adj.* applicable; pertinent

The DNA tests were *relevant* to the defense's proof of their not guilty plea.

The details of the incident are *relevant* to the penalty.

relic (RELL ik) *n.* something that has survived from an earlier time; something kept sacred because it was associated with a saint

The old ship was a *relic* of the Spanish-American War.

The stone tablets are supposedly *relics* of biblical times.

relinquish (ri LING kwish) *v.* to give up doing, professing, or intending; to surrender, give in

He never *relinquished* his ambition to become a circus clown and finally performed with a well-known circus.

The retiring executive merrily *relinquished* his control of the company with a wave from his yacht.

relish (REL ish) *v./n.* to take pleasure in; pleasurable appreciation; an appetizer

The kicker *relished* the moment as the football split the uprights for three points.

That type of pickle *relish* makes a hamburger tasty.

remand (rih MAND) *v.* to remit, send back or consign again

The Supreme Court *remanded* the case to a lower court.

The Book of the Month Club permits members to *remand* unauthorized books.

reminisce (rem uh NISS) *v.* to recall the past, usually pleasantly

Sometimes when we are feeling nostalgic, my wife and I lie back, listen to the music of the 1960s, and *reminisce* about when we were dating.

The *reminiscent* qualities of his art brought back fond memories of Paris in the 19th century. (*adj.*)

remiss (rih MISS) *adj.* guilty of neglect, lacking due care, lax

He is terribly *remiss* with his family since his professional life occupies about twenty hours a day.

Sharon was *remiss* in not calling 911 and failing to take her mother to the hospital.

remission (ri MISH un) *n.* a period of time when an illness is less severe; release from an obligation

Her leukemia is in *remission*, and doctors are optimistic that it will not recur.

The judge granted Tim a *remission* of his jail sentence in exchange for community service.

remonstrate (rih MON strate) *v.* to say or plead in protest, object, or disapprove

Patrick Henry *remonstrated*, "Give me liberty or give me death."

The dissatisfied tax payers *remonstrated* years later about the school debt of 1997.

remorse (re MORSE) *n.* a strong feeling of sadness or guilt for having done something wrong

John refused to feel any *remorse* for doing what he considered the right thing to do.

Feeling *remorse* for hurting loved ones is the first step to an apology.

remote (ri MOT) *adj.* distant, out-of-the-way, far away, unfriendly

Sharon dreamed of traveling to *remote* South Sea islands.

To our parents, space travel seemed only a *remote* concept and possibility.

remuneration (ri myoo nuh RAY shun) *n.* pay for work or services

The level of that physician's *remuneration* is outrageous, almost double that of his peers.

Sometimes the gratitude one gets for helping others is all the *remuneration* that is needed.

renaissance (REN uh sonce) *n.* period from the 14th to 17th century in Europe, rebirth or revival, reawakening

The *Renaissance* was the new beginning of art, literature, and learning in Europe.

The school underwent a total *renaissance*, using state funds to remodel and revitalize the curriculum.

rend (rend) *v.* to tear or rip

Don't *rend* her photos just because you are mad at her today!

Trying to climb over that fence, I managed to *rend* my pants beyond repair.

render (REN dur) *v.* to cause to be; to give or provide; to represent something

New technology *renders* a computer obsolete in a year.

Sister Beatrice *renders* service unto God.

rendezvous (RON day voo) *n.* a pre-arranged meeting at a certain time and place

James scheduled a *rendezvous* with Jill at Hernando's Hideaway for 9:00 that night.

The two spies *rendezvoused* at the cross-roads after they successfully completed their missions. (*v.*)

renounce (ri NOWNCE) *v.* to give up voluntarily by formal declaration, cast aside

To marry an American woman, King Edward *renounced* all rights to the English throne.

The candidate *renounced* his candidacy, but his name was still on the ballot.

renowned (rih NOWND) *adj.* celebrated; famous; notable; eminent, distinguished

Sukeyaka, the young Japanese poet, is *renowned* for Haiku poetry.

Renowned entertainers and movie producers attend Nice's film festival.

reparation (rep uh RAY shun) *n.* amends, restitution, compensation

Swiss banks made *reparations* by paying the Holocaust victims for their losses.

He was ordered to pay *reparations* for the damage he caused to the school.

repartee (rep ur TEE) *n.* a quick, witty reply; witty and spirited conversation

Dad keeps me in stitches with his never-ending *repartee*.

The comedian's *repartee* kept the audience laughing throughout his entire performance.

repent (ree PENT) *v.* to feel sorrow for having done wrong

Ryan went to confession so he could *repent* for his sins.

Many people *repent* before they die.

repercussion (ree per KUSH un) *n.* effect or result of some event or action, often negative

Sam did not realize the *repercussions* of writing nasty letters until he received the threats.

Laura realized the *repercussion* of eating too much of her Halloween candy; she got a belly-ache.

repertoire (REP ur twar) *n.* the stock of special skills a person is able to perform

The band liked Sergio's song so much that they added it to their *repertoire*.

A good teacher has many tricks in her *repertoire* to make learning fun.

replenish (ri PLEN ish) *v.* replace, renew, restock, fill again

The soda salesman *replenished* the cans in the soda machine.

Charlie's restaurant *replenished* all its food and supplies after the hurricane.

replete (ri PLEET) *adj.* full or supplied to the utmost

We ordered our pizza with "the works"; it was *replete* with sausage, ham, pepperoni, olives, onions, and anchovies.

Bob's *replete* backpack had everything you needed for camping.

replica (REP lih kah) *n.* a copy, exact copy of a reproduction, facsimile

From her trip to Italy, Joan brought *replicas* of the statue of David for gifts.

Today they are making expensive *replicas* of antique furniture.

replicate (REP lih kayt) *v.* to copy or repeat something; to duplicate

Researchers tried to *replicate* the original experiment.

For my parents' wedding anniversary, Dad tried to *replicate* their first date.

repose (ri POHZ) *n.* rest; tranquillity; relaxation

Exhausted after completing the marathon, Linda enjoyed a long *repose*.

Nora returned to her dorm room for a brief *repose* between classes.

reprehensible (rep ri HEN suh bul) *adj.* deserving of reproof, rebuke, or censure

Georgia's manners were *reprehensible*; she should know better than to eat with her hands.

Dog fighting is a *reprehensible* act, as well as an illegal one.

repress (ri PRES) *v.* to prevent from being expressed; to hold back

The government *repressed* all aid until the victims showed proof of their need.

It was getting harder for Bill to *repress* his feelings for Jayne since the two were constantly thrown together.

reprimand (REP ruh mand) *n.* a formal admonishment or censure; official rebuke

His boss gave him a severe *reprimand* for being late.

Susan received a stern *reprimand* for coming home past curfew.

reprisal (ri PRYZE ul) *n.* revenge; retaliation; vendetta; vengeance

Any military action could cause a *reprisal* against the United Nations troops in the area.

Sam went out with Joe's girlfriend, and in *reprisal*, Sam's girlfriend went out with Joe.

reproach (ri PROHCH) *v.* to express disapproval of

Although he realized his behavior was not beyond *reproach*, he didn't think it was bad enough for him to be suspended from school. (*n.*)

While at trial, the defending lawyer *reproached* the tactics of the prosecutor and appealed to the judge to have the prosecutor's remarks stricken from the records.

reprobate (REP ruh bayt) *n.* a morally unprincipled person; a degenerate

The *reprobate* calmly put his hand into the offering plate, helping himself to a handful of change.

Mom thinks that Jimmy is a *reprobate* just because he drives a motorcycle.

reprove (ri ROOV) *v.* to criticize or correct gently; reproach; chide, scold

Arlene *reproved* Bill for leaving the master bathroom in disorder after he used it.

When Margie giggled in the middle of church, her mother Irene *reproved* her with a stern look.

repudiate (ri PYOO dee ayt) *v.* disavow, revoke, annul, nullify

The government of Ethiopia *repudiated* the treaty signed by the former ruler and promptly broke its terms.

Jim *repudiated* the claim by the IRS that he had received illegal payments, and he was determined to prove his innocence.

repugnant (ri PUG nunt) *adj.* causing a feeling of strong dislike or disgust; offensive; distasteful

His language was so *repugnant* that nobody wanted to be around him.

I am so full that the thought of eating anything is totally *repugnant* to me.

repulse (ri PULS) *v.* to send back, to reject, rebuff, ignore, avoid

The U.S. Army *repulsed* the attacking German forces, sending them back into the Black Forest.

Charlie's unfriendly neighbors *repulsed* his offers of friendship.

reputed (ri PYOO tid) *adj.* generally supposed to be such

The *reputed* gunman was hiding out in a rundown house at the edge of town.

Although Mrs. Smith is *reputed* to be a fine teacher, the kids in her class do not agree.

requisite (REK wuh zit) *adj./n.* compulsory, essential, mandatory; requirement

The "help wanted" ad stated that prior experience in computer auto repairs was a *requisite* skill.

One *requisite* for admission to college is high SAT scores.

rescind (ruh SIND) *v.* to take back or make invalid; revoke

The vote *rescinds* zoning decisions made earlier in the decade and returns the property to its original use.

The payment was *rescinded* when the work was found to be faulty.

reserved (ri ZURVD) *adj.* self-restrained, modest, not showy

The English are supposed to be *reserved*, but we found them warm and friendly.

The *reserved* young lady sat quietly in the corner.

reside (re ZID) *v.* dwell, occupy, inhabit, to live in a place

Gail *resides* in the outskirts of Salt Lake City.

Jim and Meg *reside* at the hotel during the Olympic games.

residual (ree ZID joo ul) *adj.* remaining behind as a residue; left over

Although the worst of it has been removed, the *residual* oil from the spill still has to be cleaned up.

There was a *residual* bitterness between the remaining clans in the aftermath of the war.

resignation (rez ig NAY shun) *n.* withdrawal from job or position; passive submission or surrender

Lorna accepted her parents' divorce with quiet *resignation*.

My boss has no choice but to accept my *resignation*.

resilient (ree ZILL yunt) *adj.* able to resume shape after being pressed or stretched; elastic; able to recover quickly from illness

He proved to be a *resilient* opponent and eventually won the match after being behind by two sets.

Grandpa is so *resilient* he was back at work just two weeks after his surgery.

resolute (REZ uh loot) *adj.* set in purpose, steadfast, earnest, determined, unwavering

Dennis made a *resolute* decision to master a foreign language and kept at it until he finally did.

Her *resolute* decision to diet resulted in a loss of 35 pounds.

resonant (REZ uh nunt) *adj.* having or producing a full deep or rich sound, vibrant

As a result of the twenty-one gun salute, the *resonant* thunder could be heard miles away.

The *resonant* voice of the speaker could be heard without a microphone.

resound (ri ZOUND) *v.* reverberate, echo, vibrate, to ring

The sound of church bells *resounded* throughout the Alpine Valley.

The Kennedy name *resounded* throughout American history.

resourceful (ri ZORS ful) *adj.* able to deal effectively with different situations, innovative, proficient

Boris was a clever, *resourceful* young man, able to solve many of the problems in the chemistry department.

Marianne's *resourceful* ideas resulted in a successful new pre-school program.

respite (RES pit) *n.* delay; postponement; a brief interval of rest

The condemned man was given a *respite* to enjoy his favorite meal before his execution.

The class had worked so hard throughout the semester that the teacher gave them a *respite* before their exam.

resplendent (ri SPLEN dunt) *adj.* brilliant; filled with splendor; radiant; shining

Chloe wore a formal gown *resplendent* with red and gold sequins.

The gulf is absolutely *resplendent* under the full moon.

responsiveness (ri SPONS siv nis) *n.* ready ability to respond, friendliness

George's *responsiveness* at the interview was mediocre, so he was not offered the job.

Her friendly *responsiveness* makes Andrea one of the most popular girls in the class.

restaurateur (reh stuh ruh TUR) *n.* owner or manger of a restaurant

The *restaurateur* from Chicago opened a new restaurant in Florida.

Dave, the *restaurateur*, named the fast-food chain after his daughter.

restrictive (ri STRIK tiv) *adj.* limiting

Restrictive clothing is not the best choice when exercising.

Jeremy did not like private school because he thought the rules were too *restrictive*.

resurgent (re sur jent) *adj.* able to rise after defeat

After losing the first two sets, the *resurgent* Pete Sampras won the next three sets to win the match.

Resurgent and strong determination help dedicated climbers finally conquer Mount Everest.

resurrection (rez uh REK shun) *n.* rising from the dead; revival

According to some beliefs, Easter is about the *resurrection* of Jesus.

If the entire community helps, the *resurrection* of the burned down church is possible.

retaliation (ri TAL ee ay shun) *n.* revenge, retribution

The soldiers swore *retaliation* for the unnecessary killing of one of their own.

Hannibal declared his attack on Rome was in *retaliation* for earlier attempts made against him.

retard (ri TARD) *v.* hinder, impede, to slow down, to hold back

Lack of sunlight *retards* growth in many botanical organisms.

The antibiotic *retarded* the bacterial growth and assisted recovery.

reticent (RET ih sunt) *adj.* characteristically silent or quiet

Although he is not unfriendly, Ray is a *reticent* person.

Edgar Allan Poe was a *reticent* man who put his thoughts on paper.

reticulate (rih TIK yoo lit) *v.* cover with a network

The farmer *reticulates* his strawberry plants with netting to keep the birds away from the fruit.

The new face of the building was *reticulated* with a display of geometric figures.

retiring (ri TYR ing) *adj.* shy, modest, quiet, self-effacing

Bill's *retiring* manner made him shy and uncomfortable around the women employees.

The *retiring* writer never mentioned his best-seller in his remarks to the composition class.

retort (ri TOHRT) *v./n.* to reply in a sharp fashion; a biting remark

When Gerald's father told him to turn the game off, he *retorted* with, "Make me!"

Sasha's biting *retort* quieted the crowd, so the speaker could continue.

retract (ree TRAKT) *v.* to pull back in; to take back, cancel or revoke

After Barbara uncovered the new facts she had to *retract* statements she had made in published articles.

The pilot *retracted* the landing gear soon after takeoff.

retraction (rih TRAK shun) *n.* formal statement renouncing an inaccurate or unjustified comment, abjuration

The newspaper printed a *retraction* about Jerry and Betty getting married when they learned they were really being divorced.

His *retraction* of his comment came too late to prevent a civil suit for libel.

retrospect (RE truh spekt) *n.* hindsight; looking backward

In *retrospect*, I realize I should have gone to law school, but I can't change my past.

In *retrospect*, the situation was funny, but it was embarrassing at the time.

revamp (ree VAMP) *v.* to renovate; to revise or reconstruct

This curriculum needs to be *revamped* since it hasn't been changed in ten years.

I can *revamp* that old sofa and make it look brand new.

revel (REV ul) *v.* to take great pleasure or delight; to celebrate; to take part in uproarious activities

If I hit the lottery, I am going to *revel* in all the luxuries I can't afford now!

After the homecoming victory, the football team came here to *revel* all night.

revelation (rev eh LAY shun) *n.* something revealed, insight, exposure, prophecy

The star's autobiography contains many shocking *revelations*.

The gypsy's *revelations* came true when the young prince was found hidden in an abandoned cave.

revelry (REV ul ree) *n.* uninhibited celebration; joyful, exuberant activity

The *revelry* on the Fourth of July could be heard for miles.

The loud gaiety and *revelry* from the New Year's Eve party attracted the police.

reverberate (ree VUR buh rayt) *v.* to cause a sound to re-echo

In the cave, our voices *reverberated* off the walls, causing an eerie effect.

While we stood on the rim of the Grand Canyon, we could hear the *reverberations* of pebbles that had broken loose and fallen to the depths. (*n.*)

revere (ri VEER) *v.* to regard with great devotion or respect, to honor

Mother Teresa was greatly *revered* by all who knew of her humanitarian work in India.

The author was *revered* with a Pulitzer Prize for fiction.

reverence (REV ur uns) *n.* a feeling of deep awe, respect and love

The class chose the teacher for whom they had the most *reverence* to be their graduation speaker.

Every religion has a document which the followers hold in *reverence*.

revert (ri VURT) *v.* to go back in thought, action, or speech

When the whole class started to fail, the teacher *reverted* to his old way of teaching so they could start learning again.

When he realized that I did not speak Italian, he *reverted* to French so we could converse.

revile (ri VYLE) *v.* to criticize strongly; to berate

President Clinton was *reviled* for his apparent lies.

The group was *reviled* for taking action without contacting all members.

revive (ri VYV) *v.* to reawaken, to bring back to life, recovery

The injured man was *revived* after he received medical attention.

The repertory company *revived* musicals from the 1950s for summer stock.

revulsion (ruh VUL shun) *n.* a strong, often sudden feeling of dislike or disgust; a feeling of loathing

Most of us feel *revulsion* at the thought of the many gruesome murders committed by Charles Manson.

I stepped back in *revulsion* when I saw the dead body in the road.

rhapsodize (RAP suh dyze) *v.* to express oneself in an enthusiastic manner; to gush

I can't help but *rhapsodize* when I talk about my boyfriend and how perfect he is.

The fairy tales *rhapsodize* about the princess meeting Prince Charming.

rhetoric (RET or ik) *n.* the art or study of using language effectively and persuasively; over-elaborate language

The study of *rhetoric* is a necessary part of any literature class.

William Cullen Bryant was a master of *rhetoric* and one of our country's most famous editors.

ribald (RIB uld) *adj.* rude; vulgar, lewd, off-color

I was embarrassed by the *ribald* conversation at the next table.

The *ribald* language coming from the locker room was unbelievable.

rife (ryfe) *adj.* abundant; great in number or amount

Disease is *rife* throughout the poorer sections of India.

A new, tough administrator was sent to restructure the hospital, which was *rife* with errors.

rift (rift) *n.* fracture, a narrow crack, a split, a break in friendship

The blast from the homemade bomb created a *rift* in the rock face.

There should be no *rifts* between good friends.

rigidity (ri JID ih tee) *n.* stiffness, unwillingness to change, lack of pliancy

The coach's *rigidity* resulted in the team's trying the same play over and over.

The ice-cold air behind him caused *rigidity* in the hockey player's back muscles.

rigorous (RIG ur us) *adj.* strict, harsh, severe, exacting, austere

Summer football training involves *rigorous*, effective exercise twice a day.

Many of the college students dropped out of the class, unable to meet its *rigorous* requirements.

rind (RYND) *n.* a tough outer covering, esp. of a fruit, bark of a tree

A *rind* of lemon is placed into espresso coffee to eliminate the bitter taste.

The *rind* of the oak tree is used in making cork and stoppers for bottles.

riposte (rih POAST) *n.* quick sharp return in speech or action, counterstroke

His explosive *riposte* caught the other boxer's jaw and won the match.

Her brilliant *riposte* to the insult brought laughter, and the outraged speaker was deflated.

rivet (RIV it) *n./v.* something that fastens two parts together; also to hold the attention of

Most naval ships, army tanks and fighter aircraft have metal plates for their outer bodies that are held together by *rivets*.

Most kids are *riveted* to the television on Saturday mornings.

robust (roh BUST) *adj.* hale, hardy, energetic, able-bodied, vigorous

Such strenuous exercises could only be endured by a *robust* individual.

The *robust*, healthy man easily carried the frail child to safety.

rogue (rogh) *n.* mountebank, scoundrel, dishonest person

Florida is rounding up all *rogues* practicing medicine illegally.

Beware of *rogue* investment companies promising high yields of interest on your money. (*adj.*)

roster (raw ster) *n.* a list of names; especially of personnel available for duty

The football program has a *roster* for both teams.

Tom saw his name on the duty *roster*.

rote (roht) *n.* a memorizing process using routine or repetition, often without comprehension

Although Allison had not been in a church for years, she knew how to do everything correctly by *rote*.

The teacher taught as if by *rote*; a computer would have had more personality.

rotund (roh TUND) *adj.* round, corpulent, globular

Joey's *rotund* shape forced his mother to buy chubby-sized clothes.

Sheryl sold beanbags, which were generally *rotund* in shape, at the store.

roue (roo AY) *n.* an immoral man, libertine, wanton, profligate

The *roue* was prosecuted for his attempts to molest innocent children.

A *roue* tried to scam the old lady out of her life's savings.

rout (rowt) *v.* to defeat completely; to root, search, poke around; to drive or force out

Sue *routed* Mary in the race for class president, winning by 90 percent of the vote.

Pigs are so dirty because they *rout* in the mud all day, searching for food.

routine (roo TEEN) *n./adj.* customary procedures; habitual, regular, ordinary, expected

Getting up early is part of Gary's *routine* for summer football practice.

At least once a year, a *routine* medical check up is advisable.

rudimentary (roo duh MEN tuh ree) *adj.* basic, crude, undeveloped; related to fundamental principles or skills

Before we studied it in history class, we had only a *rudimentary* understanding of that time period.

The eating utensils and tools of early cave dwellers during the Ice Age were very *rudimentary* .

rue (roo) *v.* to feel sorry about something; to regret; mourn

He'll *rue* the day his teenage daughter received her driver's license when he starts paying the high insurance costs.

I *rue* the day I met him because he has caused nothing but trouble!

ruffle (RUF uhl) *v.* to disturb the smoothness of, to upset mildly

The wind *ruffled* Sally's hair during the open air game.

The blindside tackle *ruffled* the quarterback's composure.

ruminate (ROO mih nate) *v.* to ponder; to reflect upon

Because she had made up her mind, Nancy did not need time to *ruminate* when Pete asked her to marry him.

Michael often *ruminated* about a better way to train his horse.

rustic (RUS tik) *adj.* countrified, unsophisticated, unpolished, rural

The *rustic* cabin in the mountains caused many hardships for urban people.

Every fall we enjoy the *rustic* scenery of the rural countryside.

ruthless (ROOTH lus) *adj.* without mercy or compassion; pitiless or cruel

Terrorists are *ruthless*, not caring how many people get hurt.

In order to vacation abroad, we had to do some *ruthless* cost-cutting at home.

sacrosanct (SAK roh sangt) *adj.* blindly accepted, unquestioned, sacred

The Aztec tribe considered its burial grounds *sacrosanct* to the outside world.

General Eisenhower's orders to those in his command were *sacrosanct* during World War II.

saga (SAH gah) *n.* a long story, often telling the history of a family

The *saga* of Odysseus is an ancient adventure story retold throughout history.

Moby Dick is a *saga* written by Herman Melville about a huge whale and the man who would kill him at any cost.

sagacious (suh GAY shus) *adj.* discerning, shrewd, keen in judgment, wise; perceptive

Among those who knew him in the world of academics, the professor was thought to be a *sagacious* man.

Caron hopes that the court will reach a *sagacious* decision in her case.

sage (sayj) *n.* a person of wisdom and prudence

Native American tribes regarded their medicine man as a *sage* with special healing powers.

In Chinese culture, the grandparents are regarded as the *sages* of the family.

salient (SAY lee unt) *adj.* readily attracting notice, noticeable, important

At the meeting, Henry listed the *salient* points to be discussed.

Jane's *salient* feature was her ears; they stuck out like the wings on a bat.

sallow (SAL low) *adj.* lacking color; pale; sickly-looking

Myra returned the flowers to the florist because they arrived *sallow* and droopy, instead of fresh and colorful.

A person with jaundice appears to have a *sallow* complexion.

sally (SAL ee) *n.* a sudden onslaught; an excursion or expedition; a clever rejoinder

A *sally* of troops stormed the castle wall.

John was fast on his feet and could make quick-witted *sallies* that amused his friends.

salubrious (suh LOOB ree uss) *adj.* favorable to promoting or contributing to good health

A regimen of daily exercise is *salubrious* to a person's well-being.

Green tea is said to be *salubrious* because it is believed to rid the body of toxins.

salutary (SAL yuh ter ee) *adj.* wholesome, healthful, remedial

A low sodium diet has a *salutary* effect on a person's blood pressure.

A two week vacation in the Bahamas was *salutary* for Abraham; he looked tanned and well rested when he returned to work.

salutation (sal yoo TAY shun) *n.* a greeting or welcome; words used at the beginning of a letter or speech

Start your letter with the *salutation* "Dear Friends."

Princess Di stood in the receiving line, graciously accepting *salutations* from all the guests in attendance.

salvation (sal VAY shun) *n.* a person or thing that causes one to be saved from danger

In many ways my father was my mother's *salvation*, standing by her and helping her in any way he could.

America is the *salvation* of many less fortunate countries.

sanctimonious (sank tih MONE ee uss) *adj.* practicing hypocrisy; pretending to be sincere

They resented the Senator's *sanctimonious* remarks on immorality in America since everyone knew he was a lecher and a womanizer in private life.

Grandpa is a *sanctimonious* old coot, but we still love him.

sanctuary (SANGK choo ayr ee) *n.* a holy place or place of protection

Many German farmers offered *sanctuary* to Jews fleeing the Nazi's.

The wedding was held in the *sanctuary* at 4:00 on Saturday.

sanguine (SANG gwin) *adj.* cheerful, confident, optimistic

Jessie's *sanguine* personality was exactly what Ben needed to get him out of the doldrums.

Jim is the most *sanguine* person I know, he always seems to make everyone laugh.

satiety (suh TY i tee) *n.* the state of being overly satisfied

When the king reached *satiety*, he dismissed all of his servants and the food that they bore.

Thanksgiving is the day of *satiety*.

savoir faire (SAV whah FAIRE) *n.* ability to say and do the right thing at the right time

When it rained on the garden party, Ben handled the situation with *savoir faire*, getting the guests inside and making a bad situation into an amusing one.

Charlie's diplomacy in awkward social situations proved he has the *savoir faire* to be a diplomat.

savory (SAY ver ee) *adj.* pleasing to the taste or smell

A *savory* smell came from the kitchen, and John realized his mother was baking a cake.

Josh ate the cake slowly and *savored* the flavor of nutmeg and cinnamon. (*v.*)

scale (SKAYL) *n./v.* something calibrated; a device used to measure; series; to climb up

Any measuring instrument with graduated markings is called a *scale*.

The fireman *scaled* the ladder and was on the roof of the burning building in a matter of seconds.

scant (skant) *adj.* very little or not much; barely sufficient; meager

Shana's *scanty* bikini drew much attention when she appeared on the beach.

The water supply is *scant* during the summer months because there is hardly any rain.

scapegoat (SCAPE goat) *n.* one who is made an object of blame for others

Mary said she was not one of the sorority sisters who stayed out late, and she wouldn't be the *scapegoat* for those who did.

Henry was always the *scapegoat*, taking the blame for whatever happened, whether he was to blame or not.

schism (SKIZ um) *n.* a division; discord or disharmony; separation

There is a *schism* in the church congregation; some want traditional organ music while the others prefer a jazz band.

Coach Waldrop said the *schism* between the offensive and the defensive teams needs to be resolved if we are to win the championship.

scintilla (sin TILL uh) *n.* a minute amount, spark, trace

Joan's husband did not show a *scintilla* of remorse after his mother-in-law moved out.

The detectives could not find a *scintilla* of evidence at the crime scene.

scintillate (SIN tuh layt) *v.* to sparkle; dazzle; stimulate

The conversation at the annual comedian's ball *scintillated* with witty remarks.

Gloria wore a diamond necklace and earrings that *scintillated* like stars.

scion (SIE on) *n.* a descendant directly from the same parents or ancestors

Charlie and Jim are *scions* of the same great-grandmother.

The genealogical records confirmed that Louise was a direct *scion* of King Charles IV.

scoff (skawf) *v.* to make fun of; to mock in disapproval

The coach *scoffed* at the notion that he was about to resign.

Ralph's father *scoffed* at his fear of the dark, saying maybe he had heard too many ghost stories.

scorn (skohrn) *v.* to treat with a great lack of respect

Roger was *scorned* by friends because he refused to play any sports.

Harry *scorns* his brother when he drinks and drives.

scotch (SKAHCH) *v.* suppress, thwart, to put an end to

John did his best to *scotch* rumors that he was going to marry Ruth.

The sheriff *scotched* the prison riot by calling in the National Guard.

scrupulous (SKROO pyu les) *adj.* careful of small details; honest; conscientious

377

Because his parents were such *scrupulous* people, even as a boy Jim learned early the difference between right and wrong.

President Abraham Lincoln is known for his *scrupulousness* in the conduct of his affairs. (*n.*)

scrutinize (SKROOT uh nyze) *v.* to look very carefully; to examine

Each day newspaper proof readers *scrutinize* an entire newspaper line by line for errors.

Each inch of a commercial airplane must be carefully *scrutinized* for safety hazards before it is put into service.

scurrilous (SKUR ih luss) *adj.* offensive to accepted standards; grossly abusive

The council's *scurrilous* attack on the mayor caused his resignation.

John Rover's *scurrilous* drunken behavior at his ex-wife's wedding caused him to be tossed out onto the street.

seamless (SEEM lus) *adj.* without noticeable change from one part to the next; smooth; without a seam

The school enjoyed a *seamless* transition from one computer system to another.

Seamless tube socks are much more comfortable than those with seams.

sear (SEER) *v.* to scorch or burn; to brand

The cattleman *seared* his brand on all his cattle.

Cooking the steaks on a grill lift *sear* marks on the meat. (*n.*)

seasonal (SEE zun ul) *adj.* pertaining to or dependent on the seasons of the year, or a specific season

Construction work in the north is *seasonal,* so people go south for jobs in the winter.

From July to November, hurricanes are a *seasonal* weather problem in Florida.

secede (si SEED) *v.* to withdraw from a group or an alliance

The American Civil War began when the South *seceded* from the Union.

As a publicity stunt in the 1980s, the Florida Keys tried to *secede* from the United States to create their own country "The Conch Republic."

seclude (sih KLOOD) *v.* to place in or withdraw into solitude, sequester; cloister

The monk was *secluded* in a monastery high on a mountain top.

The judge sequestered the jury, and they were *secluded* in a hotel.

seclusion (sih KLOO zhun) *n.* a place away from people and busy activities; solitude; privacy

After the death of her husband, Agnes spent her days in the *seclusion* of her room.

The prisoner was so violent the warden placed him in *seclusion* for thirty days.

sect (sekt) *n.* a group with a uniting theme; a small religious group

John Boswell formed a *sect* he called, "The Winter Nude Bathing Association."

The Hindu religion is divided into many small *sects* that are similar yet different from each other.

sectarian (SEK tayr ee un) *adj.* bigoted or narrow-minded

Graham was *sectarian* when it came to his educational views; his way was the only way.

John has no racial or religious prejudices; in this respect he absolutely was not *sectarian*.

secular (SEK yuh lur) *adj.* having nothing to do with religion, pertaining to worldly things

Secular humanism believes in promoting human values outside of religion.

Our minister's *secular* hobbies are tennis and water-skiing.

sedate (sih DAYT) *adj.* calm, quiet, or composed

Everyone at the funeral was uncharacteristically *sedate*.

The puppy was *sedate* enough that we could let him out of his crate for an hour or two each day.

sedentary (SED en ter ee) *adj.* not prone to exercise; of or marked by much sitting about

A *sedentary* lifestyle makes a person susceptible to heart problems.

Sedentary jobs are those that require little activity.

sedition (sih DISH un) *n.* willful violation of allegiance to one's country; treason

Mutiny on the Bounty is a story of *sedition* on the high seas.

The Confederates were *seditionists* from the United States during the Civil War of 1861 to 1865.

sedulous (SED yuh luss) *adj.* characterized by steady attention and effort; diligent

The worker's *sedulous* attention to detail made it possible for the company to manufacture a quality product.

The football team's *sedulous* practice sessions produced a strong, winning team.

seethe (seeth) *v.* to be agitated, as by rage; to churn and foam as if boiling

Billy's father began to *seethe* as he reviewed the children's phone bill.

When he learned that his kingdom had been conquered, the king *seethed* with anger.

segregate (SEG rug gate) *v.* to separate or keep apart from others

To *segregate* truth from fiction is the duty and obligation of every trial jury.

The fishermen *segregated* the marketable fish from the junk fish which they returned to the sea.

self-deprecating (self DEP rih kay ting) *adj.* belittling or undervaluing oneself; excessively modest

Although a world famous artist, Terry was *self-deprecating* about his accomplishments.

Margaret's *self-deprecating* account of her career as a violinist amused the audience.

self-made (self MAYD) *adj.* succeeding without help from others

Bill Gates is a *self-made* billionaire.

My aunt Grace is a *self-made* gourmet chef who never went to cooking school.

semantic (SEE man tic) *adj.* pertaining to the meaning of words

The judge ruled both parties were really in agreement, the problem was *semantic* confusion.

Defeated or cheated, that's a *semantic* argument; either way the bottom line is we lost the game, right?

seminary (SEM ih nar ee) *n.* a school for religious training

Scott decided not to become a minister and left the *seminary* to attend college and become an attorney.

Bill attended a Baptist *seminary* in Georgia.

senile (SEE nile) *adj.* mentally confused usually associated with old age

We wanted to hear stories about our family's past, but Grandma was too *senile* to clearly tell them.

Some elderly people become *senile* long before their bodies wear out.

sensory (sen SOHR ee) *adj.* related to sensations; neurological

The buffet was a *sensory* delight; everything looked good, smelled good, and tasted good.

Our eyes, ears, nose, and skin are all *sensory* organs; it is through them that we make contact with the world around us.

sententious (sen TEN shus) *adj.* self-righteous; given to arrogant moralizing; preachy

President Clinton gave a *sententious* lecture on the importance of honesty in politics.

The salty old sailor gave a *sententious* speech about how to sail a boat.

sentient (SEN shunt) *adj.* able to perceive by the sense; conscious; cognizant

Michael's father was *sentient* to the fact his son had stayed out all night.

Humans and animals are *sentient*, while rocks are not.

sequential (si KWEN shuhl) *adj.* following one after another, in an orderly pattern

The teacher asked us to put all the playing cards in *sequential* order.

The players roster was listed in *sequential* order according to their jersey number.

sequester (si KWES tur) *v.* to set or keep apart; seclude; isolate; put aside

John's jury was *sequestered* for the weekend in a hotel where they could not meet with anyone.

Restaurants *sequester* smokers in an area apart from the non-smokers.

serendipity (ser un DIP uh tee) *n.* accidental good fortune; finding something good accidentally

It was *serendipity* the way Phil first met Hilda; she slipped and fell on a banana peel, and he helped her up.

Our arrival at the department store *serendipitously* coincided with the beginning of a sale. (*adv.*)

serene (se REEN) *adj.* clear; calm; tranquil

George likes to go to the lake on weekends because it is so *serene* and peaceful away from the city.

(The state of being *serene* is *serenity*.)

Marsha was the picture of *serenity* as she calmly marched down the aisle in her wedding dress. (*n.*)

serpentine (sur pun TEEN) *adj.* snakelike in shape or movement; winding as a snake

Really good mystery stories have *serpentine* plots that lead the reader first one way, then another, always keeping him guessing to the very end.

Jack dashed through the line with *serpentine* moves, dodging defenders all they way down the field until he scored the winning touchdown.

serrated (ser AY tud) *adj.* saw-toothed

The bricks were laid around the flower bed in a *serrated* pattern.

The *serrated* knife cut the tomato like melted butter.

servile (SUR vil) *adj.* slavishly submissive or obsequious; fawning

Dave's attention to Mary was *servile*; he was at her beck and call all hours of the day.

Unlike dogs, cats are independent pets and are rarely *servile* to their owners.

sever (SEV ur) *v.* to cut off; separate; divide

After the saw *severed* the man's hand, doctors were unable to reattach it.

The guillotine was an execution device invented to *sever* the head.

severance (SEV uh runce) *n.* a breaking off; a division into parts

Bob's new company offered him a generous *severance* package even before he signed a contract to work.

When Joan's job was terminated, she received two months' *severance* pay.

severity (suh VARE uh tee) *n.* sternness; intensity; austerity

The *severity* of the winter snow storms made the roads impassable.

The attorney protested to the judge that the *severity* of the punishment exceeded that of the crime.

shackle (SHAK ul) *n./v.* a restraint; handcuffs, chains, irons; a manacle; the act of restraining with such a device

The prisoner was led away in *shackles*.

The prisoner was *shackled* and placed into the squad car.

shear (sheer) *v.* to strip or deprive; to clip or cut

Sheep are *sheared* of their wool once or twice a year, depending on how fast it grows.

Napoleon was *sheared* of his power before he was sent into exile.

sheer (sheer) *adj.* transparently thin; unmixed with something else

The miners drilled a mile through *sheer* rock.

The comedian uttered some *sheer* comic nonsense, and the laughter reached the ceiling.

shibboleth (SHIB uh luth) *n.* a slogan, motto, catchword; any usage that distinguishes one group from another

The secret handshake is a *shibboleth* of Dad's men's club.

"We bring good things to life" is the *shibboleth* for General Electric Company.

shrewd (shrood) *adj.* sly; able to turn a situation to one's advantage

Buying low and selling high is the mark of a *shrewd* businessman.

The owner of the Jets made some *shrewd* player trades, getting two good defensive tackles for one quarterback he had been ready to cut from the team.

shrine (SHRINE) *n.* a holy site; sacred tomb; monument

Every day women from the village come to pray at the *shrine* of the Virgin Mary.

In the state of Pennsylvania, Gettysburg is a national *shrine* of the American Civil War.

shun (shun) *v.* to slight deliberately; take pains to avoid

Nancy didn't invite Ira to her daughter's wedding, so Ira now *shuns* Nancy whenever he sees her.

The miners who belonged to the union *shunned* the non-union workers at the factory.

shunt (shunt) *v.* to move or turn aside; to evade by putting aside or ignoring

The crash was caused by failure of the trainman to *shunt* the train onto the proper rails.

The running back dashed down the field *shunting* right and left to avoid the tacklers.

simper (SIM per) *v.* smirk; giggle; snicker; smile foolishly

The teacher didn't know she had a run in her hose until she figured out why the children were *simpering* and pointing at her.

Jeff and Ruth *simpered* when Beth entered the room dressed in her outlandish Easter Bunny outfit.

sinecure (SY ni kyoor) *n.* any office or position providing an income but requiring little or no work

When a company gets too large, sometimes positions become *sinecure* and the laziest hope to secure them.

Until Al Gore was elected, the country tended to look at the position of Vice President as a *sinecure*.

singular (SING gyuh lur) *adj.* unusual and easily noticed; remarkable; unique

His *singular* performance on the violin surpassed anything he had done before.

The interior decorator is noted for his *singular* style of mixing old and new, traditional and art deco.

sinister (SIN ih ster) *adj.* frightening; evil; malign; threatening

After years of silence, *sinister* rumblings were heard from the volcano above the village.

The height of the movie's action came when the *sinister* villain abducted the young girl and tied her to the railroad tracks.

sinuous (SIN you uss) *adj.* having many curves, bends or turns; winding

Climbing the *sinuous* road, Jeb saw that the maximum speed was fifteen miles per hour.

The police were suspicious of arson and asked witnesses *sinuous* questions about how the forest fire started.

skeptical (SKEP tih kul) *adj.* having or showing doubt; questioning; not easily persuaded

Randy said he was *skeptical* of the company's ability to deliver its quota of tractors in the time allowed on the sales contract.

Philip was *skeptical* when George said he could get four seats on the fifty yard line at the Super Bowl.

skiff (SKIF) *n.* a small boat for sailing or rowing

Large boats usually carry a *skiff* so they can anchor and row ashore if the need arises.

Skiffs are too small and therefore not practical to take out in the open ocean.

skirmish (SKUR mish) *n.* a short fight that is usually not planned; a brief conflict

There was a slight *skirmish* between two spectators on the sidelines of the field.

The newspaper reported there was a *skirmish* between government troops and rebels outside the city last night.

skittish (SKIT ish) *adj.* nervous and easily frightened; jumpy

Whenever she heard a loud noise, the kitten would become *skittish* and hide under the nearest chair.

The horses became more *skittish* as the thunderstorm drew nearer.

skulk (skulk) *v.* to lie or keep in hiding; move silently and furtively

The thief *skulked* in the shadows as he planned how he would break into the house.

The lion *skulked* in the tall reeds waiting for the antelopes to graze closer.

skullduggery (skul DUG uh ree) *n.* trickery; underhandedness

Pirates in the eighteenth century practiced all types of *skullduggery* to gain an advantage over their victims.

After Howard's arrest, he admitted to numerous counts of *skullduggery* that had gone unsolved in the town in past years.

slake (slayk) *v.* to quench; to satisfy a craving

Ben read everything he could in an attempt to *slake* his desire for knowledge.

Jeannie *slaked* her nicotine craving by going outdoors to have a cigarette.

slander (SLAN dur) *v.* to speak badly about someone in public; to defame, spread rumors

The movie star sued the magazine for *slandering* her good name by printing an article that defamed her character.

Desperate political candidates sometimes use underhanded tactics by planting *slanderous* stories about their opponents. (*adj.*)

slight (SLYT) *adj.* an insult; something negligible; smallish in size

Jeff had only a *slight* temperature when he thought he was burning up.

The coach assumed Jim was too *slight* to play football and suggested he try tennis.

sloth (slawth) *n.* laziness; sluggishness; lethargy; idleness; a lazy person

Sloth is not a desirable character trait in the nursing profession; consequently Jane had difficulty getting good jobs.

Harper was so tired after working in the steel mill all week, his weekends were devoted to nothing more than being a TV *sloth*.

slovenly (SLUV un lee) *adj.* untidy; careless in appearance, habits, or work

Although Matt had a great deal to offer the group, his *slovenly* appearance tended to repel others.

Many wealthy people are among the most *slovenly* ones I know.

sluggish (SLUG gish) *adj.* lacking mental and physical alertness and activity

The cortisone shot made Josh *sluggish*, so he sat on the beach rather than surf with his friends.

The mechanic said the engine was *sluggish* because it needed a tune-up.

smarmy (SMAR mee) *adj.* excessively flattering; ingratiating; servile

The MC gave a *smarmy* "hello" and called the audience the best ever.

Gerald said that being *smarmy* is just a fancy word for "sucking up" to someone.

snafu (sna FOO) *n.* a complete foul-up

Snafu is originally a military expression meaning "Situation Normal All Fouled Up."

The wedding party was a complete *snafu* because none of the guests showed up since they had not received invitations.

snit (snit) *n.* agitated or irritated state; excited distress

Geraldine was in a *snit* all week after she failed to get the leading role in the senior play.

Grandmother was in a *snit* because she hadn't received any thank-you notes.

sobriety (suh BRYE uh tee) *n.* the state of being sober; seriousness

Jame's *sobriety* frightened some; he was always so serious.

Drivers of cars that weave on the highway are subject to *sobriety* tests by the highway patrol.

sociopathic (SO see uh path ik) *adj.* characterized by antisocial behavior lacking sense of moral responsibility

Her anger at everyone who disagreed with her, and other *sociopathic* behavior, made Joan a poor candidate for graduate school.

The boxer's *sociopathic* tendencies made him a dangerous fighter who showed no mercy to his weaker opponents.

sojourn (SOH jurn) *n.* a temporary stay or visit

Huck Finn went on a *sojourn* through the South with his friend Jim.

Our European *sojourn* is always the highlight of our summer.

solace (SAHL is) *n.* help and comfort when one is feeling sad or worried; consolation; cheer

When Karen's grandmother died, she found *solace* in her memories of their time together.

When Mark is troubled, he finds *solace* in a good book and hot bath.

solicit (sa LIS it) *v.* to ask for; to seek

Campaign workers were going door to door *soliciting* votes for their candidate.

The Moore's neighbors *solicited* their help in finding their missing dog.

solicitous (suh LIS uh tis) *adj.* zealous; thoughtful; anxiously caring or attentive

Willie was always very *solicitous* toward his friends in the hospital.

At the viewing, the undertaker was extremely *solicitous* to the family members.

solidarity (sahl uh DAR uh tee) *n.* agreement between and support for the members of a group; sense of unity

All the members wore a ribbon to show their *solidarity* with AIDS victims.

To help create *solidarity* among the students, we let them design and vote on the school uniforms.

soloist (SO lo ist) *n.* a person who performs alone

Helen was the *soloist* for the musical performance at Carnegie Hall.

The lead singer from Zulus became a *soloist*.

solstice (SOL stiss) *n.* the longest and shortest days in any year; the sun's greatest distance from the equator

The *solstice* occurs twice a year on the longest and the shortest day.

The *solstice* occurs in June and December, marking the beginning of summer and winter.

solvent (SAHL vunt) *adj.* financially sound; able to pay all debts

After many years of investing and saving his money, Frank finally became *solvent.*

To become *solvent* three years after college graduation is Robert's main goal.

somatic (suh MAT ik) *adj.* of the body; physical

Doris' pain was *somatic,* and the doctor determined she had broken some ribs.

June's *somatic* infection was serious enough to require hospitalization.

somber (SOM bur) *adj.* depressing; gloomy; dark

Most everyone who attends a funeral wears *somber* clothing, generally black or gray.

The music was gloomy, and it soon cast a *somber* spirit over the entire audience.

somnambulist (som NAM byoo list) *n.* a sleepwalker

Richard said he was a *somnambulist,* but he always ended up in the kitchen eating.

Joey was a *somnambulist* who was sleepwalking when he stumbled and broke his leg falling down the stairs.

somnolent (SOM nuh lunt) *adj.* sleepy; drowsy; tending to cause sleep

Hector was not suited to work the night shift and constantly was in a semi-*somnolent* state.

The movie was boring, and Jenny became *somnolent* in her seat.

sonorous (SON uh russ) *adj.* producing sound, especially deep and rich, resonant

John Barrymore's *sonorous* voice enraptured audiences across the land for decades.

The *sonority* of the school choir singing Christmas carols was uplifting and delightfully spiritual. (*n.*)

soothe (sooth) *v.* comfort; to calm, to ease pain

Bruce attempted to *soothe* the hard feelings between the antagonists.

The doctor prescribed medication which *soothed* Cheryl's back pain.

sophistry (SOF i stree) *n.* unsound or misleading but clever argument

The used car salesman was an expert at *sophistry,* which is why he had such a great sales record.

Adam's *sophistry* helped get him through college.

sophomoric (sahf uh MAWR ik) *adj.* childish and silly; juvenile; immature

Mr. Truman's behavior of dancing on the table top was *sophomoric* for a sixty-year-old man.

Robert's *sophomoric* remarks at the business meeting embarrassed the whole department.

soporific (sop uh RIF ik) *adj.* tending to cause sleep, inducing sleep

Dan took Benedryl for his rash, but the *soporific* effects had himdozing for hours.

Rip Van Winkle did not need anything *soporific* to help him sleep for twenty years.

sordid (SAWR did) *adj.* morally vile; amoral; shameful; dirty and in bad condition

In 1995, Americans were glued to their TV sets to hear every *sordid* detail of the O.J. Simpson trial.

The *sordid* condition of the workers' bathrooms was shocking.

sovereign (SAHV run) *n.* a king, queen; supreme ruler; monarch

Prince William will be the next *sovereign* of England.

Perhaps the *sovereign* in America is a huge computer in the middle of the Pentagon!

spacious (SPAY shus) *adj.* roomy; affording sizeable space; commodious

Our yard is *spacious* enough for a swimming pool and deck.

Frank liked *spacious* cars, so he bought a Lincoln.

spasmodic (spaz MOD ik) *adj.* pertaining to the nature of a spasm; intermittent; fleeting

The pain in her hip was *spasmodic,* coming and going periodically.

Gina's *spasmodic* training as a gymnast was not sufficient for her to become Olympic quality.

spate (spayt) *n.* a sudden outpouring

We have had a *spate* of burglaries in town recently.

A *spate* of department store sales occurs after every Christmas holiday season.

spatial (SPAY shull) *adj.* existing or occurring in space

The International Space station is the first step to a *spatial* community.

The NASA shuttle program is a step in universal *spatial* relations.

spawn (spahn) *v.* to give rise to; to produce in large numbers; to give birth

The flu outbreak *spawned* major attendance problems at the school.

Salmon always return to their native streams to *spawn*.

specious (SPEE shus) *adj.* seeming to be right or true but really wrong or false; deceptive; misleading

Jeff's argument is not *specious*; it's true that chickens do cross the road to get on the other side.

Medical doctors always viewed acupuncture as *specious* until recent years when they no longer are so sure.

specter (SPEK ter) *n.* a ghost or phantom

After the kids yelled "trick or treat," a *specter* appeared in the door and scared them away.

The *specter* of Christmas Past is terrifying to Ebenezer Scrooge in Dickens' *A Christmas Carol*.

spectrum (SPEK trum) *n.* a range of objects; ideas or opinions

A wide *spectrum* of ideas for the senior prom was represented at the meeting.

A rainbow reveals a wide *spectrum* of colors.

spendthrift (SPEND thrift) *n.* a person who is extravagant or wasteful, esp. in money

Marta is a wonderful person but she is a *spendthrift* when it comes to buying clothes.

Carla was a *spendthrift* who always maxed out her Visa card.

spew (spyoo) *v.* to cause to flow or to throw up; vomit

The old car *spewed* oil all over my driveway.

The great fish *spewed* Jonah onto the shore.

spiel (shpeel) *n.* high-flown speech or talk; esp. for the purpose of persuasion

The car salesman's *spiel* was that the car had been owned by a little old lady who only drove it to town.

Television advertising is the mother of all *spiels* for every product imaginable.

splinter (SPLIN tur) *n./v.* a sharp piece broken or split off from something; sliver; fragment; to break into splinters

The Green Party is a small *splinter* group of the Democratic Party.

The woodsman *splintered* the log into small pieces.

spontaneous (spahn TAY nee us) *adj.* happening without apparent cause; impromptu; voluntary; impetuous

The forest fire was caused by the *spontaneous* combustion of volatile materials.

Judith's remarks were *spontaneous* and completely unplanned.

sporadic (spuh RAD ik) *adj.* now and then; few and far between; stopping and starting

The gunfire was *sporadic*, starting and stopping all through the night.

The snowfall has been *sporadic* in New England ever since Christmas.

spur (spur) *v.* to move to action

The general *spurred* his troops to make one last effort to take the hill.

The principal's talk on good citizenship *spurred* the students into not littering the school grounds.

spurious (SPY UUR ee us) *adj.* not genuine; false

The Senator made *spurious* claims about his opponent's views of labor reform.

A *spurious* story is one that is absolutely false, no doubt about it.

spurn (spurn) *v.* to reject with disdain

Rose *spurned* Jeff's advances; she could see he was insincere and showing off for his friends.

John thought he had made a fair offer for the house, but the seller *spurned* it.

squalid (SKWOL id) *adj.* dirty and wretched, as from poverty or lack of care

It was a wretched house, dirty inside and full of junk; it is amazing how people could live in such *squalid* conditions.

Haiti is the poorest Caribbean country where the people live in terribly *squalid* run-down towns.

squall (skwall) *n./v.* sudden disturbance; violent gust of wind followed by rain, snow or sleet; to make a sudden, loud noise

The *squall* swept over the fishing fleet, drenching the sailors with driving rain.

The baby *squalled,* so her mother knew she was wet and wanted her bottle.

squander (SKWAHN dur) *v.* to waste; misspend; fritter away

Helen, decided not to *squander* her money on such an expensive dress.

The visiting team *squandered* their chance for a touchdown at the one yard line.

squeamish (SKWEE mish) *adj.* easily shocked, offended, upset, or nauseated

Nancy does not like to go to any movies rated higher than PG-13 because she is *squeamish.*

Many children are so *squeamish* that they are afraid to go to the doctor's office.

staccato (stuh KAH toe) *adj.* having abrupt disconnected elements; rapid fire

The Mexican's speech came in *staccato* bursts of Spanish that the tourists could not understand.

Playing the guitar in a *staccato* style is typical of flamenco music.

stagnate (STAG nayt) *v.* to be or become motionless; to fail to grow or develop

The local economy *stagnated* when the factories closed.

High costs have caused the building industries to *stagnate*.

staid (stayed) *adj.* settled or sedated; marked by dignity and seriousness

Jerry's *staid* personality was evident in the dull, colorless clothing he wore.

Marilyn asked for a divorce from her husband because she said he was too *staid* and never had any fun.

stalemate (STALE mate) *n.* any position or situation where no action can be taken

Talks between union and management came to a *stalemate*, so both parties ceased negotiations.

Construction on Ken and Jill's house reached a *stalemate* when the sub-contractors went on strike.

stalwart (STAWL wort) *adj.* very loyal to someone or something; sturdily built; having physical strength

Never weakening in her resolve, Nancy has always been a *stalwart* supporter of medical research.

A *stalwart* friend will stand by you unconditionally.

stanch (stanch) *v.* to stop the flow of liquid, esp. blood

The doctor put pressure on the cut, and that *stanched* the flow of blood.

The children dug a trench to *stanch* the incoming tide.

stark (stahrk) *adj.* empty or bare; blunt; complete or utter; extreme

The walls of the house were *stark* from floor to ceiling; not a photo or picture was to be seen anywhere.

In the 70s, running through public places *stark* naked was a fad called streaking.

static (STAT ik) *adj.* showing little or any change; still; suspended

Sales became *static* when the economy slowed country-wide.

The Broadway opening was a failure; the new play had a good first act then became *static,* and nothing interesting seemed to happen.

stationary (STAY shun air ee) *adj.* standing still; not moving

The market price for flat monitors has remained *stationary* all summer.

The prosthesis stayed *stationary* in the hip bone after surgery.

status quo (STAH tus KWO) *n.* the existing state or condition

The *status quo* of the corporation's profit margin, neither going up or down, was displeasing to the stockholders.

The president proposed a tax cut in order boost the *status quo* of the economy.

staunch (stonch) *adj.* firm or steadfast in principle; loyal

The Green Bay Packers have *staunch* fans who are behind them win or lose.

To be a *staunch* believer in something means your support of something is ironclad.

steadfast (STED fast) *adj.* unfaltering; tenacious; unwavering

It is said that a *steadfast* romance is a love that never wavers.

Zeke planted ivy along the wall, forming a *steadfast* network of green.

steep (steep) *v.* to immerse, saturate, absorb, or imbue

The women picked herbs to *steep* in water, making a fine tea.

The Jewish religion is *steeped* in tradition.

stentorian (sten TOR ee un) *adj.* very loud

In a most *stentorian* voice, the representative explained why his product was the most useful.

Mr. Maxwell is known for his *stentorian* voice, which can be heard throughout the halls of the school.

stereotype (STER ee oh type) *v./n.* to fix a conventional notion or concept; a fixed conventional notion, an oversimplified conception, opinion, or image of a person or group usually critical in judgement

Everyone at our school tends to *stereotype* cheerleaders.

Calling all blondes dumb is a *stereotype* that is obviously ludicrous.

sterile (STAYR ul) *adj.* uncontaminated; pure; infertile

The premature infant was kept in a *sterile* incubator for months.

The nurse tore open a *sterile* syringe package in order to draw blood from the donor.

stickler (STIK lar) *n.* a person insisting on something; purist

Horace was a *stickler* for details, and he drove the car salesman crazy.

The track coach was a *stickler* for fitness and preparation.

stigmatize (STIG muh tize) *v.* to mark with disgrace or infamy

The father's crime *stigmatized* the entire family.

People with a mental disorder are *stigmatized* by society.

stilted (STILL tud) *adj.* rigidly constrained; awkward, as lacking in grace and spontaneity

The pompous speaker made *stilted* remarks about the farm which irritated the farmer and his family.

It was a *stilted* affair with little conversation and less friendship.

stint (stint) *n./v.* a period of time spent doing a particular job or activity; to restrict or hold back

He took up boxing during his ten year *stint* in the army.

That restaurant does not *stint* on portions; it is almost impossible to eat all they serve.

stipend (STYE pund) *n.* income; salary; allowance

As a student advisor, she receives a small monthly *stipend* from the college.

Retirees receive a monthly *stipend* from the government.

stipulate (STIP yuh layt) *v.* to make an express demand as part of an agreement

Ludwig *stipulated* the exact amount he could pay the contractor.

The condo rules *stipulate* that no pets are to be kept by the residents.

stopgap (STOP gap) *n.* a temporary measure

Candles are a *stopgap* for light when electricity fails.

As a *stopgap*, Congress passed appropriations to keep the government operating.

stoic (STOH ik) *adj.* detached; impassive; unruffled

Ann appeared *stoic* in defeat, but she cried like a baby in private.

Harry impressed everyone with his *stoic* behavior during the crisis.

stoke (stoke) *v.* to poke; stir up; to feed (as a fire)

Gerry *stoked* the furnace by shoveling in more coal.

The coach's halftime speech *stoked* his players into a fighting frenzy.

stolid (STAHL id) *adj.* showing little or no emotion; apathetic; impassive

Stolid and unaffected, the police officer listened to her explanation.

Not a ripple of emotion passed over the face of the *stolid* deserter when informed he would be shot at dawn.

stout (stowt) *adj.* plump; stocky; thick and strong

The man was short, a bit *stout* around the middle, but with a radiant smile.

It is wise to have a sturdy, *stout* fence to protect your vegetable garden from the wild deer.

stratagem (STRAT uh jum) *n.* a plan or trick to achieve something; a scheme; a ruse

Barry devised a clever *stratagem* for escape from prison; he would pretend to be dead.

The doctor asked his associates what their *stratagem* was for healing the patient.

stratify (STRAT uh fye) *v.* to form into layers

The construction crew *stratified* the underbed of the road for more support.

The geological rock formation showed *stratified* areas with gem like quality. (*adj.*)

stricture (STRIK chur) *n.* a restriction, a limitation, a negative criticism

The *strictures* given by the movie critics were a severe blow to the box office revenues of the picture.

New condo owners often find *strictures* in the bylaws.

strident (STRYD nt) *adj.* harsh-sounding; shrill

The *strident* sounds of battle were all around us, and we feared for our lives.

The band needed more practice to sound less *strident*.

strife (stryfe) *n.* a bitter conflict, quarrel, fight

He was thin and gaunt and had led a life full of *strife*.

It was a time of great *strife* in the kingdom because of three seasons of failed crops.

stringent (STRIN junt) *adj.* rigorously binding or exacting; strict; severe

Hurricanes require the use of *stringent* safety precautions to protect the public.

Military colleges have *stringent* rules of conduct which students are required to follow.

stupefy (STOO puh fie) *v.* to make numb with amazement; to stun into helplessness

The magician's trick *stupefied* his audience.

Billy *stupefied* his parents by bring home a report card with all As.

stupendous (stoo PEN dus) *adj.* very great in amount or size; extraordinary; remarkable

John ran up such *stupendous* debts he will never be able to pay them.

When the department of sanitation went on strike, *stupendous* piles of garbage lined the streets.

stupor (STOO pur) *n.* a state in which a person is almost unconscious; a stunned condition

The man who drove the car had been in a drunken *stupor*.

The movie was so riveting we stared at the screen in a wide-eyed *stupor*.

stymie (STIE mee) *v.* prevent from accomplishing a purpose

We were *stymied* from reaching our destination when the mechanic refused to fix our car on a holiday.

Ric's chess move was so unorthodox it *stymied* his opponent into utter confusion.

subdue (sub DOO) *v.* to conquer; overcome; get the better of

The paramedics *subdued* the injured man for his own protection.

Alexis' soothing words *subdued* the child's fear and screams.

subjugate (SUB juh gayt) *v.* vanquish; make subservient; suppress

In Mexico, the Spanish Conquistadors *subjugated* the Aztecs to do their bidding.

An aggressive woman, Hilda *subjugated* her mild-mannered husband and made him do all the housework.

sublime (suh BLYME) *adj.* impressive; inspiring awe; majestic

The *sublime* melody worked itself throughout the entire musical.

The priest's *sublime* voice made him the object of admiration in his parish.

subliminal (sub LIM ih nul) *adj.* operating below the level of conscious perception

Advertisers sometimes place *subliminal* messages on TV; they appear too rapidly to be seen by the naked eye but are believed to make impressions on the subconscious mind.

Nicole *subliminally* attempted to make Dennis ask her out on a date. (*adv.*)

submissive (sub MIS iv) *adj.* obedient; yielding, compliant; giving in easily

Joan was *submissive* to her husband and always gave in to his wishes over her own.

A good time to be *submissive* rather than aggressive is when an officer pulls you over for speeding.

subordinate (suh BOR duh nit) *adj.* lower in position, importance, or rank; inferior

A private is *subordinate* to every other military rank, the bottom of the totem pole.

Nina was disliked at work because she acted as if her co-workers were her *subordinates*. (*n.*)

subsequent (SUB suh kwunt) *adj.* recurring or coming later or after

The first ticket costs five dollars, and *subsequent* ones will be three dollars.

Charlie started off poorly in his job, and *subsequent* events proved he was unqualified to be a brain surgeon.

subservient (sub SIR vee unt) *adj.* submissive

Many high school boys are far too *subservient* to their girlfriends.

The king chose only the most *subservient* to be among his retinue.

subside (sub SYDE) *v.* to weaken; to diminish or lessen; sink or settle

When his mother's pain didn't *subside*, Matt drove her to the hospital.

Forecasters predict the high winds will *subside* today, and the afternoon weather will be calm.

subsidiary (sub SID ee ayr ee) *adj.* being in a secondary or subordinate relationship

All college sports are *subsidiary* to football, which earns more money for colleges than all other collegiate sports together.

AT&T is a company owned by a larger company, Bell Communications. Therefore, AT&T is a *subsidiary* of Bell.

subsidize (SUB suh dyze) *v.* to pay part of the cost; to provide financial assistance

The government *subsidizes* the rent of some qualified low-income families.

Jeffery works as a waiter to pay part of his college tuition, but his father *subsidizes* him for the balance.

subsistence (sub SIST unce) *n.* means needed to support life; or a livelihood

The oxygen we breathe is a necessary *subsistence* for every human being.

Unemployment compensation is not intended to provide the *subsistence* for luxurious living.

substantiate (sub STAN shee ayt) *v.* to show something to be true; to support with facts; to prove

The police have enough evidence to *substantiate* complaints of vandalism.

As yet there has been no way to *substantiate* claims of aliens visiting

Earth that is acceptable to the general public.

subterfuge (SUB tur fyooj) *n.* an action taken to hide something from someone; a trick; a ruse

His excuse that he missed his own wedding because he was lost in the woods sounded more like *subterfuge* than truth.

The customs official discovered the diamond smuggler's *subterfuge* of concealing diamonds in a candy bar.

subterranean (sub tuh RAY nee un) *adj.* secret, hidden; lying beneath the earth's surface

While we were scuba diving, we were delighted to explore some *subterranean* caves.

Our house is infested with *subterranean* termites.

subtle (SUT ul) *adj.* elusive; discerning; not obvious

Burt's *subtle* understanding of labor problems made him a natural for the job as a labor negotiator.

Jenny's way of flirting with her eyes was very *subtle* yet effective on boys she wanted to encourage.

subversive (sub VUR siv) *adj.* traitorous, treasonous, corrupting, overthrowing, undermining; insurgent

The McCarthy hearings are a black spot on the U.S. Senate during which Senator McCarthy accused innocent people of being Communist *subversives.* (*n.*)

Subversive activities against a government are attempts to bring about change in a treasonous way.

successive (suk SES iv) *adj.* consecutive; following immediately one after another

Pat underwent seven *successive* operations in seven months.

The tennis semi-finals and finals were held on *successive* nights.

succinct (sek SINGKT) *adj.* brief and to the point; concise and terse

During halftime the coach inspired his players with a *succinct* plan on how they could win the game.

The attorneys had a *succinct* meeting in the parking lot before entering the courthouse.

succor (SUCK ur) *n.* help, relief, aid; assistance

The volunteers gave *succor* to the wounded victims after the hurricane.

The local vicar was always quick to *succor* those who were suffering from one problem or another. (*v.*)

succulent (SUK yuh lunt) *adj.* full of juice

The strawberries were so *succulent* that we ate as we picked them.

She placed a bowl of *succulent* grapes in front of us and told us to help ourselves.

succumb (suh KUM) *v.* comply with; accede; to yield; die

The lady *succumbed* to her illness, and her body was sent to the funeral home.

The parents finally *succumbed* to the children's pleading and gave them ice cream.

suffice (suh FYSE) *v.* to be enough; to be adequate

Three pies should *suffice* for a dinner party of six.

Our old car will have to *suffice* until we can afford to buy a new one.

suffrage (SUF rij) *n.* the right to vote

In our history class, Kathryn learned about the women's *suffrage* movement, which gave women the right to vote.

Suffrage in the United States is given to all adult citizens who have never been convicted of a felony.

suffuse (suh FYOOZ) *v.* to spread through or over; to cover; to saturate

The garden was *suffused* in the orange glow of morning sunlight.

If unattended, weeds will *suffuse* your lawn, leaving no grass at all.

sullen (SUH lun) *adj.* silent and unpleasant; dark, gloomy, or dispiriting; sulky

Bill's roommate become quite *sullen* when Rick reminded him he hadn't paid his share of the rent.

The soldiers stared at the revolutionary leader with expressions of *sullen* dislike.

sultry (SUL try) *adj.* marked by much heat; damp and warm

The belly dancer swirled past the audience with numerous *sultry* hip-swinging moves.

The weather had been unbearably *sultry* all week in Miami.

summons (SUM unz) *n.* an order to appear in court; an authoritative command or message

Clem received a *summons* to appear in the president's office at ten o'clock.

The Knights of The Round Table received a *summons* to meet with King Arthur.

sumptuous (SUMP choo us) *adj.* luxurious and expensive; lavish; splendid

I could never afford to live in such a *sumptuous* apartment.

Grandma prepares a *sumptuous* Christmas dinner every year.

sundry (SUN dree) *adj.* various; several; miscellaneous

A *sundry* store is usually like a five and dime; a store carrying a variety of miscellaneous items for the household and personal use.

Last week there were *sundry* articles in the newspaper about the need for prison reforms.

supercilious (soo por SIL ee us) *adj.* arrogant; self-important; pompous

Albert's *supercilious* behavior, such as telling the media the team couldn't win a game without him, made him unpopular among the other players.

Don't you just hate *supercilious* salesmen who act as if they are doing you a favor to let you buy from them.

superficial (soo pur FISH ul) *adj.* narrow-minded; short-sighted; on the surface only

Fortunately, Nancy's injuries were *superficial*, minor scrapes and a few bruises.

Sue is a businessperson, not a housewife, as she has only a *superficial* understanding of cooking and home economics.

superfluous (soo PUR floo us) *adj.* extra; unnecessary; redundant

Giving Billy a toy car for his birthday was *superfluous*; he already has more cars than are at the Daytona 500.

Joy told her mother it was *superfluous* for her to remind her to put on sunscreen every time she went to the beach.

superlative (soo PUR lu tiv) *adj.* of the highest quality; foremost; praiseworthy; superb

No amount of literary *superlatives* can do justice to the superb novels written by Ernest Hemingway. (*n.*)

Joe is recommended as a carpenter who does *superlative* cabinet work.

supersede (soo pur SEED) *v.* to take the place of; to make obsolete; to replace

There are many new environmental laws *superseding* each other, so it is impossible to know which one is in effect.

Every month it seems some new medical study on the best care for the heart *supersedes* the last study.

supine (soo PYNE) *adj.* lying on the back with the face turned upward; inclined

When the investigators arrived, the body was still *supine* in the middle of the living room floor.

The chiropractor had Jill lie in a *supine* position so he could adjust her neck.

supplant (suh PLANT) *v.* to take the place of

After the school superintendent retired, she was *supplanted* by the deputy superintendent.

The scheduled boxing match was postponed and *supplanted* by a Hawaiian dance contest.

supplicate (SUP lih kate) *v.* to pray humbly; make humble; an earnest entry or petition

Mr. Crosland is a county commissioner who sets aside two days a week to hear the *supplications* of the voters in his district. (*n.*)

The bishop *supplicated* his parish to succor the victims of the earthquake.

supposition (sup uh ZISH un) *n.* presumption; an assumption; theory; opinion

Herman acted on the *supposition* that his wife wouldn't object to his owning a motorcycle.

The *supposition* of the 15th century that the earth was flat was proven false.

suppress (suh PRES) *v.* to end by force; to prevent from being expressed or known; to subdue

The governor called in the National Guard to help *suppress* prison riots.

The pretty woman could barely *suppress* a smile when the seven year old said he wanted to marry her.

surfeit (SUR fit) *n.* an overabundant amount; especially related to eating and drinking

Thanksgiving is a day when there is a *surfeit* of food at the dining room table.

The beach store had a *surfeit* of bathing suits, so they held a bathing suit sale.

surly (SUR lee) *adj.* broodingly and sullenly unhappy; bad tempered; testy

The neighborhood teens disliked the *surly* owner of the supermarket who always checked their IDs.

The *surly* sky spelled danger as black clouds drifted over the horizon.

surmise (sur MIZE) *v.* to guess; to infer (something) without sufficient evidence

Detective Culleton quickly *surmised* the identity of the murderer by the obvious clues present at the crime scene.

When everyone began to laugh, Jonathon *surmised* he was the butt of a practical joke.

surreal (suh REE ul) *adj.* having an unreal quality; dreamlike

There is a *surreal* quality to Jane's paintings; her flowers look real and unreal at the same time.

There is a *surreal* calm in the eye of a hurricane; the winds abate and a strange stillness invades the air.

surreptitious (sur ep TISH us) *adj.* done or acting in a secret, sly manner

Suture

Helen *surreptitiously* crept around the car, hoping to get the cat out from under it. (*adv.*)

The magician was so *surreptitious* during his magic trick that the audience was completely fooled.

surrogate (SUR uh git) *adj./n.* substitute; replacement; stand-in; relief

Surrogates for actors in movies are called "stand-ins."

A *surrogate* mother is a woman who agrees to bear a child for someone else.

surveillance (sur VAY lunce) *n.* act of carefully watching; esp. when unknown to the person being watched

The F.B.I. had Smithy under constant *surveillance* for two months.

The C.I.A. secretly had the Russian Embassy in Mexico City under *surveillance*, filming everyone who entered or left.

susceptible (suh SEP tuh bul) *adj.* easily influenced or likely to be hurt by something; vulnerable; receptive to

Some people are more *susceptible* to peer pressure than others.

Omar is very *susceptible* to colds.

sustenance (SUS tuh nunce) *n.* means of sustaining life; nourishment; livelihood

The shipwreck survivors had enough *sustenance* to last for one week.

The army survival team learned in the forests there is *sustenance* in wild berries and edible plants.

svelte (sfelt) *adj.* slim; slender

The ballerina appeared as *svelte* as an angel as she floated effortlessly across the stage.

The *svelte* waitress was able to move easily between the crowded tables.

swagger (SWAG ur) *v.* to strut; saunter; stride insolently

Greg *swaggered* into the room grinning like a Cheshire cat.

General Patton *swaggered* along the battle lines wearing his traditional pearl-handled pistols.

sweeping (SWEE ping) *v.* to influence or extend over a great area;

Hip-hop is a new music *sweeping* the nation.

The F.B.I. agents were visually *sweeping* the crowd for early signs of trouble.

swelter (SWEL tur) *v.* to suffer from oppressive heat

We were afraid that we would *swelter* in the desert heat without water and shade.

The children *sweltered* in their classroom because the air conditioner was broken.

swindler (SWIN dlur) *n.* a cheat; a con man; fraud; deceiver

Carson was a distinguished-looking man who was known as a real estate *swindler*.

The *swindler* got away with over $500 by cheating the other poker players.

sybarite (SIB er ite) *n.* a person devoted to luxury and pleasure

Being a billionaire, John lived the life of a *sybarite,* buying pleasure at any price.

Sybarites were citizens of Sybaris, an ancient Greek city in southern Italy.

sycophant (SIK uh funt) *n.* one who flatters another excessively; fawner

Royalty are often surrounded by *sycophants* who cater to their every whim.

The CEO's assistant was a "yes" man, a *sycophant*.

symbolism (SIM bu liz um) *n.* the practice of representing things by symbols

The ancient Egyptians practiced *symbolism* to the extreme; many animals represented various gods in their religion.

Writers like Nathanial Hawthorne include *symbolism* in all their works.

symmetry (SIM ih tree) *n.* beauty based on excellence of proportion

The Tower Bridge has a *symmetry* unequaled in London's architecture.

The *symmetry* of a rose is so perfect and so simple, yet man cannot duplicate it.

symposium (sim POE zee um) *n.* a meeting or conference for discussion of a topic

The *symposium* on health-care was scheduled at the university during the first week in March.

A *symposium* of baseball coaches was held in January.

symptomatic (sim tuh MAT ik) *adj.* of or having to do with symptoms

The doctor explained that her reaction was *symptomatic* of an allergy.

We had to keep in mind that her behavior is *symptomatic* of how she feels about herself.

synchronize (SING kra nyz) *v.* to cause to occur at the same time; to make simultaneous

The captain had his troops *synchronize* their watches in order to begin the attack at the same time.

One of the jobs of a film editor is to *synchronize* the stunts so the audience cannot detect where the stunt man took over from the actor.

synonym (SIN uh nim) *n.* a word having the same or nearly the same meaning

"Buddy" and "pal" are *synonyms.*

"Cash" and "capital" are *synonyms* for the word "money."

synopsis (si NOP sis) *n.* outline; summary; brief

Gerald's three page *synopsis* of the six-hundred-page novel outlined the plot of the story quite well.

Tell me a *synopsis* of the movie, so I'll know if I've seen it.

syntax (SIN taks) *n.* the grammatical arrangement of words in a sentence

Pay attention to the *syntax* of each sentence when writing an essay.

Students have the opportunity to learn proper *syntax* in English class.

synthesis (SIN thuh sus) *n.* the combining of elements to form a unified entity

Synthesis of ideas was the idea behind the symposium for environmental sciences.

Nylon is a *synthetic* material created by a *synthesis* of chemicals mixed together.

systemic (sis TEM ik) *adj.* affecting an entire system, as the body

The computer virus was *systemic* to the Hewlett-Packard Corporation.

Septicemia is a serious *systemic* bacterial infection that can affect all internal organs.

table (TAY bul) *v.* to remove from consideration

The officers of the company voted to *table* the matter of higher wages until some future time.

The president decided we should *table* the discussion for the time being.

taboo (tuh BOO) *adj.* improper or unacceptable

The cow is a sacred animal in India, so eating beef is a religious *taboo*. (*n.*)

Witchcraft was *taboo* in early America, sometimes leading to the punishment of death.

tacit (TASS it) *adj.* conveyed indirectly without words or speech; implicit

The neighbors had a *tacit* agreement not to walk their dogs on each-other's lawns.

The Morrison children seem to have a *tacit* agreement never to speak ill of each other.

taciturn (TAS ih turn) *adj.* reserved in speech; sparing of words; quiet

Joseph was so *taciturn* we couldn't tell if he had enjoyed the party or not.

The advantage of being *taciturn* is that when you speak rarely, you seldom say anything stupid.

tactical (TAK ti kul) *adj.* showing skill in tactics; characterized by skillful maneuvering

He made a *tactical* error in agreeing to argue with an opponent who was a professional debater.

Tactical military operations are designed to outsmart the enemy.

tactile (TACK tul) *adj.* pertaining to the sense of touch

The dentist's injection caused the temporary loss of *tactile* sensation in

409

the patient's gum.

It is believed a blind person has a *tactile* ability more sensitive than the norm.

tactless (TAKT lus) *adj.* having no skill in dealing with people; rude; insensitive

A tactful person smoothes rough going while a *tactless* person only makes the problem worse.

Brad makes *tactless* remarks about his wife's weight in front of her.

tailor (TAY lor) *v./n.* to shape or alter; garment maker; designer

It is the job of an architect to *tailor* the house to the owner's needs.

A Savile Row *tailor* in London makes all of William's suits.

taint (taynt) *n.* a small amount of something, esp. something harmful or unhealthy

The *taint* of scandal followed him for years, no matter what good deeds he did.

The wine had a slight *taint* of vinegar, which meant the wine was turning bad.

talisman (TAL iss mun) *n.* an object with supposed magical powers

She wore a small *talisman* around her neck to ward off evil spirits.

It is strange that people think a rabbit's foot is a good *talisman*, since the rabbit is dead.

tangential (tan JEN chul) *adj.* not especially relevant: only slightly related to a matter at hand

When someone goes off on a *tangent*, he has strayed from the subject or matter at hand. (*n.*)

John's report on butterflies was *tangential* to the fate of forest insects.

tangible (TAN juh bul) *adj.* definite; not vague; touchable

The *tangible* evidence that Billy was home was that the fridge had been raided.

Jeff had no *tangible* reason to believe Jane had a crush on him; he just felt that way.

tantalize (TAN tal ize) *v.* to tease by arousing expectations

410

Jessica *tantalized* many with her dancing, but she refused all offers of a date.

The aroma of fresh-baked bread *tantalized* us.

tantamount (TAN tuh mount) *adj.* synonymous; parallel; equivalent

Being invited to a charity ball is *tantamount* to being asked for a donation.

General Cornwallis' retreat in South Carolina was *tantamount* to defeat.

tardy (TAR dee) *adj.* late; not on time

Gerald, you'll be *tardy* for class if you don't hurry.

The *tardy* progress of the work on the dam put the construction behind schedule.

taut (tawt) *adj.* stretched tightly; tidy

The sailor pulled the lines *taut*, so he could sail against the wind.

The commander was proud that he ran such a *taut* ship.

tawdry (TAW dree) *adj.* gaudy and cheap in appearance or nature

Shirley's *tawdry* dress was the talk of all the gossips at the Governor's Ball.

The children innocently believed the *tawdry* jewels in their mother's bureau were valuable.

tedious (TEE dee us) *adj.* long and boring; dull; wearisome

Learning a new computer program can be a *tedious* process.

Jeb doesn't like tennis and says watching a tennis ball go back and forth over the net is extremely *tedious*.

tedium (TEE dee um) *n.* the condition of being dull or wearisome; monotony; boredom

The *tedium* of a dull lecture puts me to sleep.

The *tedium* of watching summer soap opera reruns is boring.

teem (teem) *v.* to have in abundance; to overrun; swarm

The lake is *teeming* with trout, so you will most likely catch one.

There is a *teem* of thousands of killer bees coming from South America. (*n.*)

411

telegenic (tell uh JEN ic) *adj.* having qualities that televise well

When it was discovered that Phil was *telegenic*, he was awarded his first TV weatherman job.

Judy was so *telegenic* that she started doing commercials when she was only four years old.

temerity (tuh MER uh tee) *n.* boldness; recklessness; audacity

Jack wanted to know where Mrs. Rodsman got the *temerity* to ask him about his personal life.

Ray had the *temerity* to go over Niagra Falls in a barrel.

temperament (TEM per uh ment) *n.* disposition or character

Young Laura has an easy-going *temperament* that makes her a delight to be around.

John Barrymore was a famous actor with a true artist's *temperament*.

temperance (TEM puh runce) *n.* moderation or self-restraint; self-control

A person who totally abstains from alcohol is someone who practices *temperance*.

Use *temperance* when giving advice since your opinion could be taken in the wrong way.

temperate (TEM pur it) *adj.* levelheaded, self-controlled, moderate

We vacationed in Mexico City because of its *temperate* climate; it rarely gets too cold or too hot but is mild all year long.

A leader of people should have a *temperate* attitude and calm disposition.

tempestuous (tem PESS choo uss) *adj.* marked by unrest, disturbance or stormy turbulence

The two candidates for office had a long, *tempestuous* debate, arguing bitterly about the issues.

The ship was endangered by the *tempestuous* roaring winds and high waves.

tempo (TEM po) *n.* rate of motion or performance

The marine band played a number of Sousa Marches with a fast *tempo*.

The *tempo* of urban life is faster than the slower-paced farm life.

temporal (TEM pur ul) *adj.* of or related to time; concerned with worldly affairs; short-lived

Temporal pleasures, such as movies and sports games, last only a short time.

Considering the age of our planet, our time on Earth is *temporal* and insignificant in terms of eternity.

temporize (TEM puh ryze) *v.* to stall; cause delay

Because his star witness was late to court, the lawyer *temporized* by giving a long opening argument.

TV news reporters must be skilled at ad libbing when there are schedule delays and there is a need to *temporize*.

tenable (TEN uh bul) *adj.* justifiable; rational; viable; defensible

"Ignorance is bliss," is no longer a *tenable* excuse for poor performance.

Since *tenable* means refers to something able to be defended, *untenable* means unable to be defended.

tenacious (teh NAY shus) *adj.* tough; stubborn; not letting go

Bulldogs are *tenacious*; once they bite a person, they refuse to let go.

The weeds in our lawn are so *tenacious* we imported a goat to deal with them.

tenet (TEN it) *n.* position; doctrine; a shared principle

The *tenets* of Abraham's religion forbid divorce.

The *tenets* of the defensive line are to prevent anyone from gaining a yard on them.

tentative (TEN tuh tiv) *adj.* unsure; hesitant; depending on a condition

Joey was hired on a *tentative* basis until the regular worker returned to work.

The doctor's *tentative* examination of the patient was rushed and not as complete as it should have been.

tenuous (TEN yoo us) *adj.* unsupported; shaky; frail; flimsy

The acrobat's grip on the bar was *tenuous*, and he soon fell to the ground.

Jose's financial situation was *tenuous,* so the bank declined to make him a loan on his house.

tepid (TEP id) *adj.* somewhat warm; not very strong; halfhearted

A bath in *tepid* water helps to gradually bring down a child's fever.

Sharon took on the house design project with *tepid* interest as she was about to leave on vacation.

termagant (TUR muh gunt) *n.* quarrelsome, loud, scolding woman

That his wife was a *termagant* by nature was apparent in his downtrodden appearance.

Any man who marries a *termagant* deserves what he gets.

terminal (TUR muh nul) *adj.* having a fatal disease in its final stages

My grandfather was diagnosed with *terminal* brain cancer.

Mary is a volunteer at the hospital and works with *terminal* patients.

terminate (TUR muh nayt) *v.* to bring to an end

The boss said he was sorry to do it but the position had been *terminated.*

My father said I must *terminate* the relationship I had with our neighbor.

terrestrial (tuh RESS ul) *adj.* pertaining to Earth or of human life on Earth

Although they can swim, polar bears are *terrestrial* animals and prefer land travel.

Lunar gravity is weaker than the *terrestrial* gravity of the Earth.

terse (turs) *adj.* brief and to the point; concise

Hemingway is best known for his *terse* style of writing.

When Sally becomes annoyed, she speaks in *terse,* short sentences.

tether (teh thur) *v.* to fasten or confine with a rope, chain or something similar

Norman's wife has him *tethered* to a short leash and won't let him play poker with the guys.

We *tethered* the boat to the dock with lines both fore and aft.

theology (thee AHL uh jee) *n.* science of divine things, doctrine

After majoring in *theology*, he taught Eastern religions in college.

Shaw was an agnostic but read many books on *theology*.

theoretical (thee uh RET ih kul) *adj.* not based on experience; in theory only; unproven

The once *theoretical* concept of an expanding universe is now a known fact.

Theoretically speaking, robots may someday be programmed to run governments. (*adv.*)

thesis (THEE sis) *n.* a theory to be proven

Robert's *thesis* was written on the subject of hog snakes and their ability to control the rabbit population in Australia.

To earn his PhD. in biology, Charles did his *thesis* on cloning.

thorny (THOWR nee) *adj.* tough or painful to deal with; full of thorns

Roses are *thorny* shrubs.

Religion and politics are *thorny* topics and are best avoided at a casual gathering of friends.

threadbare (THRED bayr) *adj.* worn and thin from much use; shabby

The beggar's clothing was faded and *threadbare*.

Sue's *threadbare* coat belied the claim that she was affluent.

threshold (THRESH hold) *n.* point at which something starts; entrance

We are on the *threshold* of a new millennium.

Libby has a low *threshold* for pain, especially once the dentist starts drilling!

thrive (THRYV) *v.* to grow strong; flourish; prosper; succeed

Paul's garden seems to *thrive* on the new fertilizer.

Now that the new expressway has opened, the shopping center should *thrive* .

throng (throng) *n./v.* a large group of people gathered closely together, to gather in a throng

Throngs of revelers gather at Times Square in New York City on New

Year's Eve.

The assassins *thronged* around Caesar before they murdered him.

throttle (THRAH tul) *v.* to choke or strangle; to enlarge or reduce the flow of fuel in an engine

I'm so mad at Henry for standing me up; I could *throttle* him.

Roger *throttled* his engine and shot ahead of the pack.

thunderstruck (THUN der struk) *adj.* struck with amazement, terror

The family was *thunderstruck* after hearing about grandma's death.

The *thunderstruck* crowd clapped in amazement when the magician made the elephant disappear.

thwart (thwawrt) *v.* to stop something from happening; to hinder, oppose, or frustrate

Bad weather *thwarted* our plans for a cookout on the beach.

Nothing *thwarts* Justin from practicing ballet four hours each day.

tier (teer) *n.* a row or rank

Our seats at the opera house were in the third *tier* of the balcony.

The Black Forest chocolate cake was made in five *tiers* for the party.

tightfisted (tyt FIS tid) *adj.* greedy; stingy; tight; penny-pinching

Bart's so *tightfisted* he never donates to a charity, not even to buy Girl Scout cookies.

We all thought grandfather was *tightfisted* until we learned of his wonderful generosity.

timorous (TIM ur us) *adj.* full of fear

The *timorous* dog cowered in the corner.

The *timorous* child would not let go of his mother's hand all evening.

tinge (tinj) *n.* a slight trace or coloring

I detect a *tinge* of almond flavoring in the icing.

The slightest *tinge* rose to her cheek when his name was mentioned.

tint (tint) *n./v.* a shade of a color; hue; to color slightly

The blouse was striped in several *tints* of red and blue.

George's speech was *tinted* with sarcasm about his fellow salesmen.

tirade (TYE rayd) *n.* long angry speech; reprimand

The shopkeeper delivered a *tirade* against shoplifters.

The political candidate let loose a *tirade* against his opponent at the debate.

titanic (tie TAN ic) *adj.* of extraordinary size and power; of great influence

The explorers discovered *titanic* water falls at the mouth of the lake.

It will take a *titanic* effort to finish the construction job by Monday.

titillate (TIT uh layt) *v.* to cause to feel pleasantly excited; to stimulate; to tease

The public was *titillated* by the gossip about the president's alleged affair.

The puppy *titillated* the baby.

titular (TICH uh lur) *adj.* existing in name only; nominal; bearing a title

Today's kings and queens have little power and are the *titular* heads of their government, while the real power rests with elected officials.

Uncle John is the *titular* head of the family, so he sits at the head of the table.

toil (TOY ul) *n.* hard and tiring work; labor; exhausting effort

The farmer rested from the backbreaking *toil* of putting in fences.

Tired of the endless *toil* of washing dishes, Joan quit her job as a housewife.

tolerate (TOL uh rayt) *v.* to not interfere with; to respect

Father will *tolerate* no phone calls to our house after 10:00 pm.

Although I *tolerate* my younger sister, sometimes she can drive me crazy.

tonic (TON ik) *n.* something that refreshes; a refreshing or invigorating drink

Vodka and *tonic* is a popular drink in the summer.

Sunshine is the best *tonic* for the dreary winter blues.

417

torpid (TOR pid) *adj.* dormant; inactive; lethargic

During winter, bears sleep *torpidly* in caves. (*adv.*)

Volcanoes may be *torpid* for centuries yet one day suddenly erupt.

torpor (TOR pur) *n.* sluggishness, inactivity, apathy

Her physical *torpor* was caused by a condition the doctors have yet to diagnose.

After the buzzards feasted on the carrion, they fell into a *torpor* and slept on a nearby tree limb.

torque (tork) *n.* a turning or twisting force

Try as Walter might, he still couldn't apply enough *torque* to open the jar of strawberry jam.

When one propeller blade broke, the *torque* tore the engine right out of its mount.

torrid (TOR id) *adj.* intensely hot; burning; passionate; rapid

Many romance novels contain *torrid* love affairs.

A *torrid* zone is a region that is hot all year long.

tortuous (TOR choo wus) *adj.* changing direction frequently; twisting; winding; or crooked

His shortcut through the forest turned out to be *tortuous* and slow.

During the *tortuous* trail to the top of Mt. Everest, many climbers succumb to the extreme heights and cannot continue to the top.

totalitarian (toe tahl ih TARE ee un) *adj.* with an absolute ruler; not tolerating opposing opinions

Hitler, Mussolin, and Stalin were rulers of *totalitarian* states during the early twentieth century.

The *totalitarian* leader was finally overthrown in a violent coup.

totem (TOTE um) *n.* a natural object with animals or birds assumed as an emblem

The "low man on the *totem* pole" is an expression which means the bottom or lowest of a hierarchy.

The natives sold small *totem* poles as souvenirs in Colombia, South America.

totter (TOT tur) *v.* walk with faltering steps; to sway or rock

The old man *tottered* unsteadily down the street.

As the earth trembled in a strong earthquake, the buildings *tottered* from side to side.

touchstone (TUCH stohn) *n.* a test or criterion for quality; gauge

Her voice is marvelous and will be the *touchstone* for all future sopranos.

The Supreme Court of the United States makes *touchstone* decisions that are also known as benchmarks.

tousle (TAU zul) *v.* to cause disorder or dishevel

Burlien *tousled* the file cabinet while frantically looking for the missing file.

The room had been *tousled*, clothing and furniture scattered about in complete disarray.

tout (tout) *v.* to praise highly; publicize; vaunt

You can see him on TV *touting* his hair products.

Jimmy Branch was *touted* as the next Tiger Woods.

toxic (TAHK sik) *adj.* poisonous; injurious or deadly

The industrial plant disposes of *toxic* waste in the appropriate manner.

Toxic levels of some medications can lead to more serious illnesses.

tractable (TRAK tuh bul) *adj.* easily managed or controlled; obedient; tame

A dude ranch needs *tractable* horses for the city dudes to ride.

Boris's dog was easy to train because he was friendly and *tractable*.

traditional (truh DISH uh vul) *adj.* as was done in the past; customary; habitual; established

Birthday cakes are a *traditional* part of birthday celebrations.

Fireworks are a *traditional* event on July 4th of each year.

traduce (truh DOOCE) *v.* to speak maliciously and false of; slander; defame; vilify

That gossip will *traduce* anyone who is not present.

Jennie's *traducements* about Barbara's untrustworthy character were known to everyone present. (*n.*)

tragic (TRAJ ik) *adj.* disasterous; unfortunate; woeful; catastrophic

The *tragic* accident took eight lives needlessly and opened up a congressional investigation.

Some movie stars are known for their ability to play *tragic* roles.

trait (TRAYT) *n.* a feature that characterizes someone; an attribute; quality

The fortune teller was able to describe some *traits* of the lost child.

Confidence and resolution are two *traits* of a good leader.

traitorous (TRAY tur uss) *adj.* having the character of a traitor; treacherous; perfidious

In time of war, any *traitorous* act may result in a firing squad.

Traitorous acts are sometimes considered acts of patriotism by the traitor.

trajectory (truh JEK tuh ree) *n.* the curve described by a projectile in flight

The *trajectory* of the rocket was off course, and it missed the target.

The *trajectory* of a bullet depends upon the speed, weight, and angle at which it is fired.

tranquil (TRANK wul) *adj.* quiet; calm; serene

Twilight in the forest is a *tranquil* time to take a walk.

Marvin took tranquilizers to become *tranquil* after he attended the funeral of his mother.

transcend (tran SEND) *v.* to rise above or go beyond; to surpass

Michael Jordan *transcended* the game of basketball, that many other players have tried to emulate him.

John's research *transcends* the limits of what is currently known about artificial organs.

transcribe (tran SCRYB) *v.* to write down; record; reproduce

The court reporter *transcribed* the testimony of the civil court trial.

The class *transcribed* notes from the professor's lecture on pharmacology.

transfix (tranz FIKS) *v.* to fix in place or hold motionless; to rivet

The mouse was *transfixed* by the snake's stare.

You can *transfix* deer, making them stand still as statues, by shining a light in their eyes.

transgress (trans GRESS) *v.* failing to fulfill or conform; violate a moral law

Sherry *transgressed* many traffic laws, so the judge took away her driver's license.

The enemy *transgressed* so many treaty violations, we no longer could trust them.

transient (TRAN zee unt) *n.* a seasonal traveler who doesn't stay long in a given location

In the winter months, Florida is flooded with northern *transients* who come south to escape the cold weather.

Transient fruit pickers travel from state and state following the crops. (*adj.*)

transition (tran ZISH un) *n.* the process of passing from one form or stage to another

The *transition* from adolescence to adulthood is a given for every human being.

The *transition* from defeat to victory is the goal of every athlete.

transparent (trans PAR unt) *adj.* clear; easily seen or understood

The water off of St. John's Island was so *transparent* you could see the fish.

The *transparent* curtains will never keep the light out.

trauma (TRAW muh) *n.* severe physical or emotional shock; a terrible experience; violent wound

She never recovered from the *trauma* of her mother's death.

The Battle of the Bulge in World War II *traumatized* many soldiers trapped in the Black Forest. (*v.*)

travail (tre VAYL) *n.* strenuous physical or mental labor or effort

Modern medicine has helped lessen the *travail* of childbirth.

When his crop of corn began to flourish, he realized all his *travail* had been worth it.

travesty (TRAV is tee) *n.* a complete failure; mockery; a shameful imitation

The jury's "not guilty" verdict was a *travesty* of justice; it was clearly obvious the defendant did it.

The community theater's production of *Hamlet 2001* was a *travesty* of Shakespeare's work.

treachery (TRECH uh ree) *n.* unworthiness; trickery; a betrayal of trust

Spies who deal in *treachery* against their own countries are guilty of treason.

Mata Hari is a famous German spy who was *treacherous* against her native France during World War I.

treacle (TREE kul) *n.* contrived or unrestrained sentiment

Linda's *treacle* is obvious when speaking about her biological parents.

Louisa May Alcott was a celebrated author despite the *treacle* which fills her plots.

tremulous (TREM yuh lus) *adj.* trembling; fearful; timid

The child was *tremulous* when he learned that his father would hear about what he had done.

The *tremulous* servants awaited the wrath of their master.

trenchant (TREN chunt) *adj.* cutting; incisive; having a sharp point; sarcastic

Roger's *trenchant* remarks at the budget meeting were motivated by his being passed over for a promotion.

Julia had a *trenchant* tongue when discussing her ex-husband.

trepidation (trep uh DAY shun) *n.* fear; apprehension; nervous trembling; anxiety

Trepidation is what people have while anticipating a dangerous occurrence.

Before her operation, Darlene had extreme *trepidation* about the outcome.

trespass (TRES pas) *v.* to invade another's property; to overstep; infringe

The farmer threatened to shoot anyone who *trespassed* on his property.

The fishing boat was seized for *trespassing* into restricted waters.

tripartite (try PAR tyt) *adj.* divided into or consisting of three parts

United States, France, and England formed a *tripartite* agreement that governed West Germany after World War II.

The property owner entered into a *tripartite* agreement with the real estate broker which covered obtaining governments permits, developing the property, and then selling the developed lots.

trite (TRYT) *adj.* stale; humdrum; banal; unoriginal; overused

Nancy, the critic from the *New York Post*, panned the new play because of its *trite* plot.

Doris's speech was energetic but *trite*; she said the same old thing the audience had heard many times before.

triumvirate (trye UM vuh rit) *n.* a group of three persons, esp. in a joint ruling capacity

The judges were a *triumvirate*, and the attorney had to appeal before all three of them.

There was a brief period in early Rome in which a *triumvirate* of rulers governed the Roman Empire.

trivial (TRIV ee ul) *adj.* unimportant; insignificant; inconsequential

Zeke let parking tickets and minor, *trivial* things upset him.

The cost of a yacht is often a *trivial* amount compared to the operating expenses.

trouper (TROOP er) *n.* actor, esp. in a touring company; someone who toughs it out

Mark is known to be a real *trouper* when the going is rough.

George Burns, a *trouper* of stage and screen, performed until he was almost one hundred years old.

truckle (TRUCK le) *v.* to slavishly support every opinion or suggestion of a superior

Sarah is a would-be actresses who *truckles* to every producer, director, or agent she meets.

Brent *truckled* to the teacher, hoping he would get an "A."

truculent (TRUK yu lunt) *adj.* inclined toward conflict; eager to fight

A *truculent* attitude seldom wins friends or influences people in a positive way.

Just because your birthday cake was full of bugs, you don't have to be so *truculent* about it.

trumpery (TRUMP uh ree) *n.* something without use or value; rubbish, trash

Ned's usual conversation about how hard he works is boring *trumpery*.

Nick sold his garage *trumpery* to a flea market for next to nothing.

truncate (TRUNK kate) *v.* to shorten by cutting off

The president *truncated* his speech so everyone could go home.

Because of unforeseen circumstances, our vacation was *truncated* after the first week.

trunk (TRUNGK) *n.* the main body of something; torso; column; chest

George is a heavyweight lifter and has a massive *trunk*.

Amelia shipped the *trunk* by FedEx so it would arrive by the weekend.

tryst (trist) *n.* a secret meeting, esp. of lovers; a rendezvous

Mary and Bryan arranged a *tryst* after school, behind the library.

The three bank robbers arranged a secret *tryst* where they would not be seen by neighbors.

tumescent (too MESS unt) *adj* swollen; teeming; containing many ideas or emotions

Manny was alarmed at his *tumescent* infected ankles and knew the swelling was from red ant bites.

Zelda's *tumescent* concept of an adult theme park fell on deaf ears.

tumor (TOO mur) *n.* a local growth of abnormal tissue; protuberance

The *tumor* on Sam's elbow was analyzed as a non-cancerous growth.

Hitler was a malignant *tumor* on the history of mankind.

tumult (TYOO mult) *n.* noise and excitement; uproar; violent uprising

The garden sits amid the *tumult* of downtown Manhattan.

The doctor performed surgery undeterred by the *tumult* surrounding the accident.

tundra (TUN druh) *n.* the vast treeless plains of the arctic regions

In the frozen *tundra* of Alaska, frozen animals of centuries past have been discovered well preserved.

The climate is severe on the *tundra* of the North Pole.

turbid (TUR bid) *adj.* cloudy or murky; unclear; muddy

It is no fun snorkeling in *turbid* waters because of the low visibility.

The air in Los Angeles is *turbid* because of the industrial city smog.

turbulence (TUR byoo luns) *n.* strong, uneven currents in air or water; confusion; violence; unrest

The plane ran into extreme *turbulence* over the Atlantic.

His songs reflect the *turbulence* of his childhood.

turmoil (TUR moyl) *n.* a state of great agitation, disturbance, or confusion

She grew up in the *turmoil* of the 1960s, amid race riots, war protests, cultism, and drugs.

Ever since John was transferred to Pittsburgh, his family life has been in *turmoil*.

turncoat (TURN kote) *n.* one who changes to the opposite party or fraction; traitor; one who reverses his or her principles

Buchanan is a Republican *turncoat* who is now a Democrat.

No one could believe that Harris would be such a *turncoat* as to play on the rival school's team.

turpitude (TUR puh tood) *n.* immorality; shameful character

The sergeant who had taken government equipment for personal use was dismissed from the military service for moral *turpitude*.

Pete's *turpitude* was evident in the way he spoke to his mother.

tussle (TUS ul) *n. a* vigorous struggle or contest; scuffle

The players were so involved in the game that a *tussle* broke out before half-time.

The mothers broke up the *tussle,* and each apologized for her child's behavior.

tutorial (too TORE ee ul) *adj.* pertaining to or exercised by a tutor

Compaq has new educational *tutorial* software called Presario University.

Harold has a *tutorial* position teaching math to young boys.

tyranny (TEER uh nee) *n.* absolute power, esp. exercised unjustly and cruelly

The Russians revolted against the *tyranny* of the royal family and the Czar.

Coach Waldrop's team considered him *tyrannical* because he was a strict disciplinarian. (*adj.*)

tyro (TY row) *n.* a beginner; a novice

Henry was no *tyro* at running marathon races; he had run fifteen and won three.

I could tell that Roger was a *tyro* at chess when he could not remember how to set up the pieces on the board.

ubiquitous (yoo BIK woh tus) *adj.* being or seeming to be everywhere at the same time

Computers were once rare but today are more *ubiquitous* than typewriters.

McDonald's restaurants are *ubiquitous* around the world.

ulterior (ul TEER ee ur) *adj.* beyond what is seen or avowed; intentionally kept concealed

Sue's *ulterior* motive as a volunteer nurse was to meet some eligible bachelors.

When Ralph volunteered to wash the dishes and take out the garbage, his mother suspected he had an *ulterior* motive, like borrowing the family car.

ultimate (UL tuh mit) *adj.* of the greatest possible size or degree; maximun

Steve is never satisfied when it comes to surfing, he's in search for the *ultimate* wave.

Donald's *ultimate* dream was to retire at the age of 35 and live in Hawaii.

umbrage (UM bridge) *n.* sense of injury or insult; offense; displeasure

Polly took *umbrage* when her husband told her she was wearing too much makeup and looked older by trying to look younger.

America took *umbrage* when Japan bombed Pearl Harbor.

unanimity (yoo nun NIM ih tee) *n.* the quality of being in complete, mutual agreement

The *unanimity* of the convention delegates was obvious on the first ballot.

Jennie's parents were in complete *unanimity* in their decision not to allow her to date at the age of thirteen.

unassailable (uhn uh SAYL uh bul) *adj.* not open to attack, doubt, or denial

The king built an *unassailable* fortress with walls a hundred feet high.

The defendant had an *unassailable* alibi, and nobody could prove it untrue.

unassuming (un uh SOOM ing) *adj.* unpretentious; modest; humble

Despite his wealth and position, Jacob has an *unassuming* mouse-like personality.

Dan's *unassuming* smile made him a favorite with the ladies.

unbecoming (un bee KUM ing) *adj.* detracting from one's appearance, character or reputation

Officer Kelly was demoted for *unbecoming* conduct at the girls school.

Hank's full beard was *unbecoming* in combination with his bald head and pot belly.

unbridled (un BRIDE duld) *adj.* violent; unbounded; unrestrained

The children in that family are *unbridled* and do whatever they please.

Andrea's *unbridled* passion for dancing was evident in every performance she gave.

uncanny (UN kan EE) *adj.* difficult to explain; weird; seemingly beyond the ordinary

John's wife has an *uncanny* ability to anticipate his words.

Barb's *uncanny* resemblance to Tia is scary.

unceremonious (un sare uh MONE ee uss) *adj.* discourteous; abrupt; hasty; rude

August is so rude, he made an *unceremonious* exit right in the middle of Jim Day's speech.

Unceremonious behavior is not acceptable at graduation.

unconscionable (un KONSH un uh bul) *adj.* not guided by conscience; unscrupulous; beyond all reason

Steve's sale of worthless stocks to his own family was *unconscionable*.

It is *unconscionable* to cheat on an exam.

uncouth (un KOOTH) *adj.* awkward; clumsy; unmannerly; lacking refinement

Uncouth behavior is especially inappropriate in church.

Albert's guests were offended by the *uncouth* manners of his young daughter who picked her nose at the dinner table.

unctuous (UNK choo us) *adj.* affected; excessively smooth; suave; mug; oily

Joseph's personality was *unctuous,* and we always felt like he was selling snake oil.

Carlson's *unctuous* tongue had the old ladies at the nursing home in the palm of his hand.

underhanded (UN dur hand) *adj.* marked by treachery or deceit

Kyle knew what the other bids were beforehand, using *underhanded* tactics to win the bidding.

My uncle's *underhanded* behavior landed him in jail.

underlying (un dur LYE ing) *adj.* fundamental; basic; real but not immediately obvious

The investigation focused on the *underlying* causes of the fire.

Joe pretends to be a tough guy, but he has the *underlying* tenderness of a kitten.

undermine (UN dur myne) *v.* to gradually, secretly weaken and destroy;

to impair

Jenny's hints and innuendos *undermined* my plans for her sister's surprise birthday party.

The building's foundation is being *undermined* by the eroding beach.

underpinning (UN dur pin ing) n. a structural support or foundation; a support from below, as with girders or props

The *underpinning* of the huge wall was made of steel beams.

The *underpinning* of any lasting friendship is trust.

underscore (un dur SKAWR) *v.* to emphasize by drawing a line beneath; underline; emphasize

Remember to *underscore* all of the key points in the report with red ink.

After walking to the mailbox and back, my shortness of breath served to *underscore* my need to quit smoking!

underwrite (un dur RYTE) *v.* to insure; to assume financial responsibility; to subsidize

The museum show was largely *underwritten* by a grant from the government of Egypt.

Uncle Herb agreed to *underwrite* my scuba expedition, feeling certain I would find the sunken treasure.

undisposed (un dis POZED) *adj.* not disposed of; not favorably inclined; not prepared

Pete and Susan are disinclined to work and *undisposed* to starve.

John was disposed to find a job but *undisposed* to do any work.

unequaled (un EE kwuld) *adj.* not equaled or surpassed

Joe DiMaggio's 56 game hitting streak is an *unequalled* record in professional baseball.

Harriet grew roses of *unequalled* beauty and won first prize in the flower show.

unequivocal (uhn ee KWIV uh kul) *adj.* clear and firm; allowing no doubt or uncertainty

The U.S. Surgeon General has taken an *unequivocal* stand against smoking.

Parents must have *unequivocal* rules for their children to follow.

unethical (uhn ETH ih kul) *adj.* not conforming to approved standards of behavior

It is considered *unethical* for a judge to rule on crimes committed by his own family members.

Cheating on an exam is very *unethical*.

unfaltering (un FALL tur ing) *adj.* firm; steady

When Helen became mentally ill, Eve helped her with *unfaltering* kindness.

Gatsby's unfaltering love for Daisy is the basis of the novel *The Great Gatsby*.

ungainly (uhn GAYN lee) *adj.* lacking gracefulness; clumsy; awkward

I was *ungainly* as an adolescent, as graceful as a cow on ice!

Newborn deer are *ungainly* and have difficulty walking at birth.

unguent (UNG gwunt) *n.* ointment; salve, usually applied to wounds or sores

Doctor Carroll ordered silver oxide *unguent* for the burn.

Early Americans made their own *unguent* of herbs and other plants.

unilateral (yoo nuh LAT ur ul) *adj.* one-sided; not mutual; done on behalf of one side only

The trade embargo was a *unilateral* decision made by our country.

Marriage should be a mutual contract, not a *unilateral* one.

unimpeachable (uhn im PEECH uh bul) *adj.* completely honest and moral; above doubt; unquestionable

Lord Fletcher was a man of *unimpeachable* integrity and character, loved by all who knew him.

The informant proved to be an *unimpeachable* source of information.

unkempt (un KEMPT) *adj.* uncared for; neglected; disheveled; messy

Today's *unkempt* look causes confusion in schools as to what is appropriate for the dress code.

The county is now checking all *unkempt* lawns and leaving warning notices.

unlettered (un LET urd) *adj.* unsophisticated; ignorant; unschooled

Although Gus is *unlettered* and a high school dropout, he is still the CEO of his tire company.

Jill is *unlettered* in auto selling technique, but she is a willing learner.

unmitigated (un MIH tih gay tud) *adj.* unqualified; not softened or lessened

July was a month of *unmitigated* hot weather.

Walter showed *unmitigated* stress before taking the bar exam for the third time.

unobtrusive (uhn ub TROOS ihv) *adj.* not noticeable; inconspicuous; seeming to belong

A good waiter is efficient and *unobtrusive*.

Undercover police have to be *unobtrusive* so they don't "blow their cover."

unprecedented (un PRESS uh dent ud) *adj.* showing marked departure from previous practice

Holding the Super Bowl in Tahiti would be *unprecedented*.

President Ford's pardon of President Nixon was *unprecedented*.

unremitting (un reh MITT ing) *adj.* existing or occurring without interruption or exception

Unremitting hurricane rains flooded the area with seventeen inches of water.

The boxer's assault of his opponent was *unremitting*.

unsavory (un SAY vuh ree) *adj.* unpleasant in taste or smell; distasteful

The natives in Borneo eat sheep's eyes and other *unsavory* delicacies.

A group of *unsavory* characters hang out at the local pool hall.

unscathed (uhn SKAYTHD) *adj.* not hurt or harmed; completely uninjured

Her husband was severely injured in the accident but she escaped *unscathed*.

The firemen emerged *unscathed* from the fire.

unseemly (un SEEM ly) *adj.* not in keeping with established standards;

not suited to circumstances

Everyone was shocked by Boris' *unseemly* drunken conduct at the wedding.

Kathy and Bill woke the neighbors at the *unseemly* hour of 3:30 a.m.

unsung (un SUNG) *adj.* unrecognized; uncelebrated; not praised or acclaimed

All members of the U.S. Marine's 1st Division were *unsung* heroes in the Pacific.

Character actors in movies give notable but *unsung* performances.

untenable (uhn TEN uh bul) *adj.* incapable of being defended, occupied or lived in; weak or illogical

The players' demands are *untenable*, so it appears the strike will continue.

The house was neglected for so long that it is now *untenable*.

untoward (un TOH ward) *adj.* unfortunate; inappropriate; unbecoming

Untoward remarks about his boss cost the worker his job in the steel mill.

The *untoward* scars left on Monica's face after the accident were the demise of her modeling career.

unwarranted (un WORE un tud) *adj.* having no basis or foundation in fact; groundless

Such strong criticism of the fire chief was completely *unwarranted* as he had been on vacation when the fires took place.

The police were censored for the *unwarranted* entry into the wrong house.

unwieldy (un WEELD ee) *adj.* difficult to handle or manage

The delivery man had a difficult time carrying the *unwieldy* boxes.

A sledge hammer is *unwieldy* and dangerous.

unwitting (un WIT ting) *adj.* inadvertent; unintentional; accidental

The innocent cab driver became an *unwitting* accomplice in the bank robbery.

Harvey's insult, although *unwitting*, pained Janice no end.

upheaval (up HEE vul) *n.* a momentous or sweeping change or disturbance

On December 7, 1941, the Japanese caused a global *upheaval* when they bombed Pearl Harbor and started a war with the United States.

The stock market crash created an economic *upheaval*.

uphold (up HOLD) *v.* to maintain in good condition; support or defend

Pierre offered to fight a duel to *uphold* his family's honor.

The congress *upholds* the U.S. Constitution from all factions that would change it.

upright (UP ryt) *adj.* honest; moral; virtuous ; standing erect

Herb pretended to play the *upright* piano at the party.

Chester was an *upright* citizen noted for his integrity in business dealings.

uproar (UP ror) *n.* noisy excitement or confusion; agitation; ado, commotion

The prime minister's resignation caused an *uproar* and an early election.

The new schedule for school buses caused an *uproar* among parents.

urbane (ur BANE) *adj.* having polish; suave; elegant; characteristic of major cities

The museum director of the Smithsonian is a consummately *urbane* person.

Ronald's *urbane* behavior stuck out like a sore thumb in the mountain village.

usurp (yoo SURP) *v.* to seize by force without legal right

The army revolted and *usurped* control from the rightful government.

The magazine *usurped* copyrighted poems without the authors' permission.

usury (YOO zhur ee) *n.* lending money at excessive or illegal interest rates

Banks do not practice *usury*, but sometimes loan companies do.

Credit card interest rates are *usury*!

utilitarian (yoo til uh TAR ee un) *adj.* stressing usefulness or utility above other features; serviceable

Not all fertilizers have a *utilitarian* purpose in farming.

Ian was *utilitarian;* when he cooked chicken, he saved the bones for chicken soup.

utilize (YOO tuh lyz) *v.* to use, employ; put into service; avail oneself

To prevent reliance on oil for power, more machines must *utilize* solar energy.

Television marketing *utilizes* viewer statistics to reach the most people at any given time.

utopian (yoo TOHP ee un) *adj.* perfect; but only in theory or fancy; idealistic

She was not expecting to find *utopian* communities in Cuba.

In a way, if you like solitude and tranquility, the monastery provides a *utopian* life.

utter (UT er) *v.* to articulate; enunciate; to say

Josh *uttered* a plea for help in a whispery voice that could barely be heard.

Roger was commanded by the F.B.I. not to *utter* a word to anyone about what he had heard.

vacillate (VAS uh layt) *v.* not know one's own mind; fluctuate; to waver

Manny appeared to be certain yesterday, but today he is *vacillating*.

It is not good for a teacher or parent to *vacillate* after making a decision.

vacuous (VAK yoo wus) *adj.* not showing purpose, meaning, or intelligence; empty; devoid of ideas or emotion

Sally's daughter had a *vacuous* expression on her face as if she couldn't believe I was asking her to work!

Juliet doesn't like "blonde" jokes because all blondes are not *vacuous*!

vagabond (VAG uh bond) *n.* a person without a permanent domicile

Joan lived like a *vagabond*, moving from place to place and never settling down.

As a result of the Great Depression which began in 1929, many men were jobless and became *vagabonds*.

vagary (vuh GAR ee) *n*. an erratic, unpredictable action; idea; whim; wild notion

Wilson is confused by the *vagaries* of his girlfriend; one day she loves him, the next day she doesn't.

My daughter's wardrobe is a total *vagary* of her imagination; it contains a little of everything.

vague (VAYG) *adj*. unclear; lacking definite shape or substance; confused

A reformed convict, Dwight was *vague* about his past when applying for a job.

George's paintings always contain a *vague* feeling of sadness.

valedictory (val uh DIK tuh ree) *adj./n*. bidding goodbye; farewell address

Reilly was chosen to deliver the *valedictory* address for the graduation class.

George Washington's *valedictory* to his troops is captured in a famous painting.

valiant (VAL yunt) *adj*. bold; courageous; stouthearted; heroic

In the face of international scandal, Laura was a *valiant* soul who stood by her beliefs.

The soldier received the Silver Star for his *valiant* conduct under fire.

validate (VAL ih dayt) *v*. to declare legally valid; legalize

The couple decided to marry and *validate* their loving relationship.

The parking ticket was *validated* by a merchant in the shopping center.

vanquish (VANG kwish) *v*. to defeat completely; conquer; overcome

Smallpox, a once deadly disease, has now been *vanquished* from existence.

Henrietta *vanquished* her drug problems and returned to work.

vapid (VA pid) *adj*. without liveliness or spirit; dull or tedious; insipid

The teacher has difficulty holding her students' interest because of her dull, *vapid* lectures.

Henry was a great salesman, always enthusiastic about his product and never *vapid.*

variable (VAYR ee uh bul) *adj.* unstable; alterable; changing; shifting

The *variables* in arm wrestling are size, strength, and skill. (*n.*)

The forecaster predicted *variable* winds and rain.

variegated (VAYR ee uh gay tid) *adj.* diversified; varied in appearance

Our travel to New Zealand was *variegated* between mountain climbing, river rafting, and cruising the fjords.

Rudolph painted the room in *variegated* rainbow colors.

veer (ve ur) *v.* change in direction

When you arrive at the castle, *veer* left around the wall to the side gate.

Arthur never *veered* from the path of honor and dignity.

vehement (VEE uh munt) *adj.* zealous; ardent; impassioned, intense

Zelda was *vehement* about not going to the class dance with her brother as her date.

Turk is a *vehement* supporter of private school education.

venal (VEE nul) *adj.* willing to sell one's influence; open to bribery; mercenary; corrupt

The county official was *venal* and accepted many bribes from land developers.

The city had a *venal* administration that was quickly voted out of office.

vendetta (ven DET ah) *n.* any prolonged and bitter feud, rivalry, contention

A *vendetta* between the Hatfields and the McCoys went on for generations and caused many lives to be lost.

Jill carries a *vendetta* against Cindy because she married her fiance'.

veneer (vuh NEER) *n.* a thin layer of material; facade; outward appearance

This is a plain pine table covered by a *veneer* of beautiful teak wood.

Bubba had a *veneer* of sweetness on the outside, but on the inside he was a bully.

venerable (VEN er uh bul) *adj.* commanding respect, impressive; revered because of age

The *venerable* congressman, Sam Rayburn, was honored with a building named after him.

The *venerable* halls of the abbey are lined with paintings of church dignitaries.

venial (VEE nee ul) *adj.* able to be forgiven or pardoned; not seriously wrong; excusable

Lawrence was not perfect, but his mistakes were only *venial*.

The case was not heard because the charges were obviously *venial*.

venom (VEN uhm) *n.* poison

We could feel the *venom* of her words as we listened to the diatribe.

Once the snake's *venom* enters the bloodstream its bite is fatal.

vent (vent) *n.* a means of escape or release; an outlet; a small hole

George felt the need to *vent* his anger in class even if it resulted in suspension. (*v.*)

As the boys searched the coastline, they found a *vent* in which they could hide.

veracious (vuh RAY shuss) *adj.* speaking the truth; honest

The F.B.I.'s *veracious* witness presented a true picture of how the crime actually happened.

It is unfair when *veracious* answers lead to an assumption of guilt.

veracity (vuh RAS uh tee) *n.* truthfulness, honesty, integrity, probity, candor

Shirley sometimes doubts Carl's *veracity*, as he's known to tell stories.

The *veracity* of the Manus Report is unquestionable.

verbatim (ver BAY tym) *adj.* using exactly the same words; word for word

The coach called the team together and said from that moment on, every player had to obey his words *verbatim*.

The witness told the judge he couldn't recite what the accused had said *verbatim*, but the essence of what he said was he thought the police were "on the take."

verbose (vur BOHS) *adj.* wordy; long-winded; not succinct

Senator Munn is so *verbose* it takes hours for him to tell a joke.

No one accuses Jack of *verbosity*; he rarely says over ten words in an entire conversation. (*n.*)

verdant (VUR dunt) *adj.* covered with vegetation; green; leafy; inexperienced

Verdant is a word derived from a French word meaning "green."

The *verdant* hills in the distance look like a picture postcard.

verge (vurj) *n.* the edge; border; brink

He was on the *verge* of saying something but stopped suddenly.

Katie always seems on the *verge* of a breakdown.

verification (veh ruh fih KAY shun) *n.* evidence that establishes or confirms the accuracy of something

The newspaper refused to print the story until it had *verification* of the facts.

The U.S. Government says they have never had *verification* of the existence of aliens and UFOs.

verisimilitude (ver uh si MIL uh tood) *n.* authenticity; plausibility; appearance of the truth

The *verisimilitude* of famous people in wax museums is enough to fool you in a dark room.

The *verisimilitude* of the counterfeit three dollar bill did not fool the sales clerk.

vernacular (vur NAK yuh lur) *n.* everyday language; natural speech; slang

The candidate used a great deal of slang expressions and spoke in the *vernacular* of the steel workers.

Vernacular is street language; proper English should be used in the classroom.

vertical (VUR ti kul) *adj.* upright; standing up; perpendicular to the ground

The cliff rose in a *vertical* wall from the ocean.

The coach measured the players' *vertical* jumping power for rebounding.

vertigo (VUR tuh go) *n.* the sensation of dizziness

The Air Force pilot was tested for *vertigo* before he was permitted to fly.

I was overcome with *vertigo* after riding the ferris wheel at the fair.

verve (vurv) *n.* enthusiasm or vigor, as in artistic works; spirit

The pianist played the concerto with *verve* and enthralled the audience.

Marcia Zeus's latest novel lacks *verve* and reads like her other plots.

vestige (VES tij) *n.* remaining bit of something; a last trace

Brady's diamond rings were the last *vestige* of her ancestors.

The human appendix is a *vestige* of early mankind.

vex (vex) *v.* irritate; annoy; provoke

The neighbor's dog howled throughout the night and *vexed* Darren because it kept him from sleeping.

Jimmy was *vexed* after being stuck in a stalled elevator.

vexatious (vik SAY shus) *adj.* annoying; troublesome

Margaret thinks her little brother is the most *vexatious* person imaginable.

Lou's *vexatious* personality made him a lonely man.

viable (VIE uh bul) *adj.* capable of living; vivid; real; stimulating

Ricardo's plan to raise a sunken ship by filling it with ping pong balls proved not to be *viable*.

The desert is not a *viable* location for planting fruit trees.

vial (VIE ul) *n.* small container for holding liquids, medicines, and dry material

Grandma Rose always carried a *vial* of smelling salts in her purse.

Theresa poured out *vials* of venom and wrath on her detractors.

vicarious (vye KAR ee us) *adj.* second-hand; fantasized; empathic

It gave me a *vicarious* thrill to hear about their vacation in Rome.

People who read fiction have *vicarious* adventures in their minds.

vicissitude (vih SISS ih tude) *n.* upheaval; natural change; change in fortune

Carlos and Neru remained friends through the *vicissitudes* of twenty five years.

Returning from the jungle, he struggled with the *vicissitudes* of city life.

vie (vye) *v.* to compete; to struggle; contest

You don't need to *vie* for my affection because you already have it.

Stan was *vying* for a chance to represent his country in the next Olympics when he tore a muscle on the last lap.

vigil (VIJ ul) *n.* a watch kept during sleeping hours

Most college students keep *vigils* when studying for final exams.

The night watchman's *vigil* lasted till six a.m.

vigilant (VIJ uh lunt) *adj.* watchful; weary; constantly alert

Customs officers are *vigilant* in checking bags and packages in order to find contraband.

The mother alligator is *vigilant* in protecting her young.

vignette (vin YET) *n.* a brief, small decorative design or illustration; a brief written, musical, or film sketch that describes or characterizes an event

Ronda purchased a book of *vignettes* about life in Alaska.

Harry's marriage was barely a *vignette*; he was divorced within three months.

vigor (VIG ur) *n.* energy; vitality; enthusiasm; strength

Sherman presented his ideas with a great deal of *vigor*.

The leader of the Arctic expedition was a man of great *vigor*.

vilify (VIL ih fie) *v.* to speak ill of; defame; slander; libel

Both generals *vilified* their opponents as unpatriotic turncoats.

Carl was wrong to *vilify* his children in front of their friends.

vindicate (VIN duh kayt) *v.* to clear from all blame; exculpate; exonerate

The jury *vindicated* Howard when the butler was proven guilty of the murder.

The U.S. Navy eventually *vindicated* Captain McVay for any blame in the sinking of USS Indianapolis.

vindictive (vin DIK tiv) *adj.* seeking revenge

After being expelled from school, the *vindictive* boy spray-painted the hallways of the school.

After being fired, the *vindictive* filing clerk spread vile rumors about the firm.

virile (VIR yl) *adj.* having manly strength or vigor

In order to be chosen as a professional wrestler, one must be clearly *virile*.

His *virile* qualities are what attracted me to him.

virtuoso (vur choo OH soh) *n.* a person with special knowledge or skills in a field

Itzhak Perlman is a world renowned *virtuoso* on the violin.

Paul Getty was a *virtuoso* collector; his finds are now housed in the Getty museum.

virtuous (VUR choo us) *adj.* righteous; honorable; moral; ethical

Jack said, "Everyone should seek to lead a *virtuous* life."

Samson knew that Delilah was not a *virtuous* woman.

virulent (VIR uh lunt) *adj.* actively poisonous; intensely noxious; lethal

The *virulent* fever claimed many victims during the yellow fever outbreak.

A *virulent* rumor almost ruined Connie's reputation.

viscosity (vis KOSS ih tee) *n.* thickness, stickiness

Molasses has a high *viscosity*.

The *viscosity* of oil determines the way it will flow through an engine.

visionary (VIZH uh neh ree) *n.* a dreamer; one who is idealistic or speculative

Walt Disney was the *visionary* who created Disneyland.

The Wright Brothers were *visionaries* who believed man could fly in machines.

vitality (vye TAL uh tee) *n.* power; vim; liveliness; energy

Good nutrition will increase your vim, vigor and *vitality*.

Jerome felt new *vitality* when he saw the finish line was in sight.

vitiate (VISH ee ayt) *v.* to impair; make faulty; spoil

Dave's nasty temper *vitiates* his good qualities.

The advent of TV *vitiated* the old-fashioned practice of children learning at home with their parents.

vitriolic (vi tree AHL ik) *adj.* acerbic; scathing; caustic;.full of bitterness

To be *vitriolic* is to say or do something so terrible you may never be forgiven.

Joanne's temperament was *vitriolic*; she was full of hate for the world.

vituperation (vy too puh RAY shun) *n.* abusive language

Katie's *vituperation* was surprising in one so innocent looking.

Al's father's *vituperation* is known throughout the neighborhood.

vivacious (vi VAY shus) *adj.* full of energy and enthusiasm; animated

Judy Garland was a bright and *vivacious* actress with a vibrant singing voice.

Joan's *vivacious* personality was infectious; she was always the life of the party.

vivid (VIV id) *adj.* clear; bright; distinct; radiant; stirring

The jockeys wore *vivid* racing shirts as they paraded their horses to the starting post.

The old professor had a *vivid* memory of his college days.

vivify (VIV ih fye) *v.* to give a lift; animate; quicken

The changes in the decor *vivified* the house for the newlyweds.

Music *vivified* the somber atmosphere at the post-graduation ball.

vocation (voh KAY shun) *n.* an occupation, a job

Sherry's *vocation* was working as a night bartender in the Elms.

Henry could not determine what *vocation* he wished to pursue after graduation.

vociferous (voh SIF ur us) *adj.* loud; noisy

A *vociferous* group of girls rushed out of class to start summer vacation.

Randy was very *vociferous* in criticizing Charlotte's plan for fund raising.

vogue (vohg) *n.* style; fashion; general popularity or acceptance

I remember when rock and roll first came into *vogue* back in the 1960s.

Never throw away out-of-style clothing; it may in time come back into *vogue*.

void (VOID) *adj.* empty; blank; vacant; null

I felt a complete *void* in my heart when Charlotte divorced me. (*n.*)

The check was marked *void* and rewritten to avoid a bank fee.

volatile (VAHL uh tul) *adj.* evaporating quickly; unstable; vaporizing; eruptive

Ether is a *volatile* liquid and must be kept in very tightly closed containers

The situation in the Middle East is *volatile* and may erupt into violence at any time.

volition (voh LISH un) *n.* an act of choosing; conscious choice

The general had to decide if the private had deserted of his own *volition* in the face of the enemy.

Peter felt he was joining a fraternity because of peer pressure rather than of his own *volition*.

voluble (VOL yuh bul) *adj.* using a continuous flow of words; fluent; glib; talkative

The five-year-old girl was so *voluble* after the circus that we thought she would never go to sleep.

A few *voluble* students usually do all the talking in our class.

voluminous (vuh LOO muh nus) *adj.* having great volume or fullness;

large; extensive

Her hair is as *voluminous* as a lion's mane.

The novel *War and Peace* takes forever to read because it is so *voluminous*.

voluntary (VOL un tayr ee) *adj.* done of one's free will; unforced; done consciously

The hospital is supported by *voluntary* contributions and volunteer workers.

Winking is a *voluntary* muscular action.

voluptuous (vuh LUP choo wus) *adj.* full and alluring in shape; luxurious

Everyone turned as the *voluptuous* woman entered the restaurant.

A thick, fluffy, *voluptuous* cream puff is one of mankind's greatest inventions.

voracious (vo RAY shus) *adj.* having an insatiable appetite; ravenous

Carl was *voracious* in his pursuit of body building.

Teenage boys tend to be *voracious* eaters.

vortex (VOR tex) *n.* whirling mass; whirlpool

The *vortex* of the tornado whirled its way through the center of town.

The *vortex* of the revolution was to be found in Guadalajara.

vulgar (vul GAR) *adj.* a characteristic by a lack of taste, refinement; crude

Uncle Tom's *vulgar* language at the dinner table embarrassed us all.

The *vulgar* man in the restaurant made us nervous, so we decided to leave.

vulgarian (vul GAR ee un) *n.* a vulgar person, esp. one of wealth

Tony was a *vulgarian* who used curse words to end every sentence.

Money could not buy him membership because of his *vulgarian* mannerisms.

vulnerable (VUL ner ah bul) *adj.* in danger; unprotected; open to attack; susceptible

Children who have not been inoculated are *vulnerable* to chicken pox.

Betsy has always been *vulnerable* to criticism because of her unorthodox lifestyle.

waffle (WOF ul) *v.* to speak or write evasively

The President *waffled* on some of the questions the press asked about the scandal surrounding his administration.

Political speech writers make a living *waffling* on the issues.

waft (wahft) *v.* to move gently on water or air; to blow

The principal could smell cigarette smoke *wafting* down the hallway from the girls' bathroom.

Leaves *wafted* down from the trees, landing softly on the ground like multi-colored feathers.

waive (wayv) *v.* to forget; put aside

He would not *waive* his constitutional right to a fair and speedy trial.

The bank *waived* the returned check fee because the mistake had been the bank's.

wake (wayk) *n.* a gathering held to honor a dead person; waves left by a passing boat; after-effects

The hurricane left thousands of houses destroyed in its *wake*.

Some people feel a *wake* is necessary in order for friends and family to gather and honor the dead person or celebrate his past life.

The water skier jumped the *wake* and did a flip.

wan (wahn) *adj.* with an unnatural or sickly pallor; lacking color

After the dry summer, Jane's flower garden looked *wan*.

After surgery Hillary looked *wan* and very tired.

wanderlust (WAN dur lust) *n.* a strong innate desire to rove

The Rhodes' spirit of *wanderlust* has caused them to move eight times in six years.

Herman's *wanderlust* aroused a question about his reliability.

wane (wayn) *v.* to decrease gradually; to weaken; to fade away

By the late 70s, the band's popularity had begun to *wane*.

The beach is *waning* and in years to come, may disappear entirely.

wanton (WAHN tun) *adj.* uncalled for; malicious; unjustified; unprovoked

Terrorists commit *wanton* destructive acts upon innocent people.

To "eat, drink and be merry" with no thought of tomorrow is a *wanton* way to live.

warrant (WAR unt) *v.* to justify; provide grounds for; to guarantee

Henry's paintings do not *warrant* a second glance; they are very amateurish.

Joe's father *warrants* that his son can broad jump over twenty-five feet.

wary (WAR ee) *adj.* cautious; on watchful guard against; not trustful of

The stranger was *wary* of entering a room full of people he did not know.

Be *wary* of e-mail on the Internet because it is not as private as you might think.

waver (WAY vur) *v.* sway to and fro; tremble, shake; to be undecided

The palm tree *wavered* in the hurricane winds.

The older woman *wavered* on the top step and nearly fell.

wayward (WAY werd) *adj.* unpredictable; disobedient; contrary

Judge Morris sent the boy to a home for *wayward* youth.

The captain complained that it is hard to sail in *wayward* winds.

well-founded (WEL FOWN did) *adj.* based on solid evidence or good reason

The use of stem cells has been *well-founded* in medical literature since 1800.

Mike's attorney proceeded with a civil case on *well-founded* documentation.

welter (WEL ter) *n.* mass; a commotion or turmoil

The huge waves in the Atlantic *weltered* throughout the night. (*v.*)

In New York it is difficult to hear above the *welter* of the street noises.

wheedle (WEED l) *v.* to persuade or influence

446

I tried to *wheedle* five more dollars from my father before I left for the movie.

The class tried to *wheedle* the teacher into not giving any homework over the weekend.

whelp (whelp) *n.* the young of an animal; a youth, esp. one who is impudent or disliked

The female gorilla trampled through the jungle, her three *whelps* following her.

Ziggy, who was given everything in life and who appreciates nothing, is the ungrateful *whelp* of Lord Boone.

whet (wet) *v.* to increase; sharpen; stimulate

I read one of Ernest Hemingway's short stories, and it *whetted* my appetite for more.

The butcher *whets* his blade frequently for a cleaner cut of meat.

whim (wim) *n.* conceit; a sudden idea; a fanciful notion

Elias is spoiled because his mother caters to his every *whim*.

Edith bought the dress on a *whim,* and later returned it.

whittle (WHIT ul) *v.* to cut, trim

Thomas *whittled* while he worked, carving figures of the seven dwarves out of wood.

Jet aircraft are much faster than propeller-driven aircraft and have *whittled* down the time it takes to fly from airport to airport.

wile (wile) *n./v.* a trick to entice; to pass time

Ethel used all her feminine *wiles* to get Josh to go to the ballet.

Leonard *wiled* away many weekends building a boat in the basement.

willful (WIL ful). *adj.* intentional; insistent on having one's way

Petty thievery is a *willful* act that sometimes leads to a life of crime.

Dean *willfully* joined the Army before there was time to draft him. (*adv.*)

wily (WILE ee) *adj.* deceitful; clever; crafty; cunning

Rainbow trout are too *wily* to be caught by amateur fishermen.

The *wily* young boy was able to get into the stadium without paying.

wince (wints) *v.* to flinch; to shrink back

Certain sounds, like the scratching of fingernails on chalk boards, make people *wince*.

The puppy *winced* in fear when the man with a stick tried to pet it.

winnow (WIN oh) *v.* to rid of undesirable parts

The military *winnows* out officer candidates who are not officer material.

The farmer *winnowed* out the weakling cows so the stock would improve in future generations.

winsome (WIN some) *adj.* charming; winning; engaging; attractive

Virginia was a *winsome* young heiress, and her money did not hurt her desirability.

Scott is a *winsome* bachelor who is invited to many parties.

wiseacre (WIZE ake ur) *n.* an obnoxious, self-assertive, and arrogant person

Jim, the stockbroker, is a *wiseacre* who lost most of his clients' money in the market.

The *wiseacre* who claimed to know all about pathology flunked the final exam.

wistful (WIST ful) *adj.* longing; sorrowfully pining; yearning

Judy gave a *wistful* look at the candy store as her mother hurried her past.

Grandmother has a *wistful* look on her face.

withered (WITH urd) *adj.* shriveled; shrunken; dried-up

A few *withered* apples were all that remained on the tree after the storm.

He remembered her as a bouncy cheerleader, not as the *withered* old lady of eighty.

witticism (WIT ih siz um) *n.* a joke

Starting with a few *witticisms* is a good way to break the ice with an audience before making a speech.

Witticisms are not appropriate at a funeral.

wizened (WIZ und) *adj.* shriveled or dried up; withered

Yoda in the *Star Wars* movies was a *wizened* old man.

The ground was strewn with *wizened* oranges, but there were still ripe ones remaining on the tree.

woe (woh) *n.* great suffering or sorrow; distress

She poured out her tale of *woe* as she cried on his shoulder.

Homeless people live a life of *woe* with no home, no money, no place to sleep.

wont (wont) *n./adj.* custom; habit; practice; accustomed

William was *wont* to rise at dawn and jog five miles every morning.

It was Judy's *wont* to be late for everything.

wrath (rath) *n.* extreme or violent rage

The Puritans feared the *wrath* of God for all sins.

After being caught cheating, Judi awaited the *wrath* of the assistant principal.

wrest (rest) *v.* pull away; take by violence

Police say never try to *wrest* a knife away from a person who threatens you.

The driver had too much to drink, so his passengers *wrested* the keys away from him.

writhe (ryth) *v.* to twist or bend; to suffer acutely, as in pain or embarrassment

The fish *writhed* free of the hook and escaped back into the sea.

Tina *writhed* in her seat when the class heard she had failed chemistry for the third time.

yen (yen) *n.* strong longing or desire

The pregnant woman had a *yen* for pickles and ice cream.

Victor has a *yen* to ask Jennifer out, but he is afraid she will say no.

zany (ZAYN ee) *adj.* crazily silly or comical; clownish

Mr. Harris was responsible for the *zany* puppet characters loved by children worldwide.

She keeps me in stitches with her *zany* antics.

zealot (ZELL uht) *n.* someone who is overly enthusiastic about a topic or cause

My sister is a feminist *zealot*, always preaching women's rights

My friend is such a *zealot* about her beliefs that she cannot see another person's point of view.

zealous (ZEL us) *adj.* ardently devoted to a purpose

The *zealous* teenagers cleaned up the house, hoping their parents would let them have a party.

Many newly religious people are quite *zealous* about getting others to convert.

zeitgeist (ZYTE gyst) *n.* the spirit of the age; trend of a particular period

The *zeitgeist* of the '60s was one of freedom, love, and peace.

Christmas season *zeitgeist* is represented by Christmas trees, mistletoe, and carolers.

zenith (ZEE nith) *n.* the peak; the highest point

The sun reached its *zenith* at about noon.

Nick Faldo claimed that winning The Masters Tournament was the *zenith* of his golfing career.

zephyr (ZEFF ur) *n.* a gentle, mild breeze; a fine light quality

A *zephyr* whispered through the palm trees in the summer night.

The manufactured cloth was like a *zephyr;* it was tissue paper thin.

zest (zest) *n.* keen relish; hearty; enjoyment; gusto

Jesse Owens had a great *zest* for winning gold medals.

The special *zest* of this soup was from the chili pepper sauce.

Other books by: New Monic Books, Inc.

Vocabulary Cartoons, Elementary Edition
3rd - 6th Grade

Students learn hundreds of words faster and easier with powerful rhyming and visual mnemonics. Humorous cartoons make learning fun, while mnemonics increase retention. Excellent teaching resource for students of all abilities, particularly visual learners, ESE, ADD & ESL. Contains 210 words every grammar school student should know presented in an easy to read format, also includes 21 review quizzes with matching and fill in the blank problems.
ISBN: 0965242277....................$12.95

Vocabulary Cartoons, SAT Word Power
7th - 12th Grade

Students learn hundreds of SAT level words faster and easier with powerful rhyming and visual mnemonics. Tested in independent school tests, students with Vocabulary Cartoons learned 72% more words than students with traditional study materials. Contains 290 SAT level words with 29 review quizzes with matching and fill in the bank problems.
ISBN: 0965242285....................$12.95

Vocabulary Cartoons,SAT Word Power II
7th - 12th Grade

More Vocabulary Cartoons! Due to the success of *Vocabulary Cartoons, SAT Word Power* our staff went back to work and cranked out another 290 SAT level words with the same zany mnemonic cartoons and rhyming words that made the first edition so popular. If you already have the first edition and are craving more vocabulary mnemonics then this book is for you. Also contains 29 review quizzes with matching and fill in the blank problems.
ISBN: 0965242269....................$12.95

For a free catalog call:
New Monic Books, Inc.
314-C Tamiami Trail, Punta Gorda, FL 33950
(800) 741-1295 phone (941) 575-6463 fax
www.vocabularycartoons.com